Picking Up the Pieces

A Memoir

MARILYN WOUTERS

ISBN: 1536949078
ISBN 13: 9781536949070

This book is dedicated to Marco Peralta, my spiritual son

I want to thank Marco for asking me to write to him about my life in 1995 when times were very difficult for him.

I want to thank my editor Stacey Donovan for her guidance and making the book readable, and my friend Elena for checking up on the legal matters.

To all my friends mentioned and not mentioned, I want to say a big THANK YOU. Without you this publication would not have been possible.

Remember I wrote the story of my life the way I perceived it.

INTRODUCTION

"Get a life!"

That's how a so-called friend, a Zimbabwean living in Dar es Salaam, chastised me one day in the fall of 2007. You see, I had just announced that I was moving. *Again.*

I was leaving Africa for Nueva Andalucía, Spain, to stay with my friend Claudia, whose emotional support gave me the strength to uproot myself yet another time. My cars and antiques, which I had so lovingly collected, no longer mattered to me, and without regrets I sold or gave away most of them to dear and loyal friends. After all, my life and sanity were more important than my possessions.

My departure was coming after an eventful four-year stay in Tanzania and even more eventful fifteen years in the United Arab Emirates. It sounds so nice in the film *Out of Africa* when the character played by Meryl Streep says, "I had a farm in Africa." Well, "I had a school in Africa," and it almost killed me. I was going to Spain to rest. Rest from a lifetime of experiences wonderful and sad, desired and undesired, choices too often spontaneous or thoughtless.

In Spain I meditated and savored the beauty of nature, took long walks with my husky Aztec, my darling puppies Costa and Bella, and Siberian cat Dominic. Spain healed me, and yet...after three years I was ready for a change once more. There were several reasons: winter was coming, and I yearned for warmth; I wanted to live somewhere in the world where I could afford a house girl; and I wanted a home on a beach. I'd been diagnosed with severe osteoporosis, so long walks on rocky mountain trails were no longer advisable. In addition, the beach house should have a high, protective wall because I had three dogs and a cat that liked to roam.

I started googling locations around the globe for a place that would fit these requirements, keeping in mind my retiree's limited budget. Everybody told me I was crazy at the age of sixty-four to even consider moving to another country. Still, I went, not just to another country, but a different continent, as well. In October 2010 I boarded a plane and flew to Sri Lanka, the island nation that remains my home today. I live in a lovely beach house with my two dogs and twenty-three cats. Yes, twenty-three!

In 1995, I started writing my memoirs at the request of friends and acquaintances. I sent the first draft to my editor, Stacey Donovan, who wrote back, *Marilyn, is this about* **you** *or the men in your life?!* Twenty years later, I realize she was right. That initial manuscript had been the work of an angry, frustrated woman who dwelled on the wrongs lovers and husbands had done her. Today, rather than hating those men, I am grateful. I was destined to share a small part of my life with them—sometimes joyfully, sometimes painfully—but always coming away wiser. So join me now as I retrace the unlikely journey of my life. Let's *move*!

THE NETHERLANDS—DORST
(1947-1970)

MY PARENTS

My parents, Ben Wouters and Corrie Musters, grew up in the province of Noord-Brabant, the Netherlands (Holland). In their early teens they became neighbors when my father's family moved to the main street of Dorst, a small village near the Belgian border, where my mother's family had lived for generations.

The story goes that my parents fell in love during World War II. Together their families had built a bomb shelter on my mother's property, which they piled into when air raid sirens wailed. One time my mother brought into the shelter a sack of fruit, which was gratefully received by members of both families, as well as the Jewish refugees who had been hiding in their homes. For my father, my mother saved the choicest pick: a beautiful, shiny red apple. Proud that she had meant it just for him, he took a big bite—and almost broke his front teeth. The apple was wax. Everybody laughed, and he smiled despite his embarrassment. My poor father would endure my mother's retelling of this "romantic" tale countless times in the years ahead.

At war's end, my father took a job in the nearby city of Breda at a beer factory called Drie Hoefijzers (Three Horseshoes). By age twenty-eight he headed the engineering department and felt his salary was sufficient to start a family. He and my mother married April 25, 1946. I think most people would agree they were a good-looking couple. My father always reminded me of Burt Lancaster, the handsome film actor popular in the fifties and sixties. My mother wore her dark hair stylishly, and she dressed after the latest fashions, often in outfits of her own making. A seamstress, she specialized in creating wedding dresses.

CHILDHOOD

I was my parents' first child, born Petronella (Nellie) Maria Cornelia Wouters on April 26, 1947. In 1948 I had a baby sister, Anne-Lies, followed by my sister Marijke in 1949. When another year passed with no sign of a new baby, the village priest came to our home and extolled the benefits of having many children for the Roman Catholic Church. My father told the priest he wasn't going to "experiment" further to meet the church's wishes. He had three daughters, and that was enough.

I was a problem child from the start. Born premature and underweight, I should have been placed in an incubator. However, the summer of 1947 in Holland was so hot that the doctor instructed I be kept in my crib outdoors in the sunshine at all times. A nun from the local convent, Sister Reinilda, a certified nurse and midwife, gave me regular checkups. My mouth was too small for me to suckle properly, so I was bottle-fed. However, Sister did not let my mother's milk go to waste. She arranged for my mother to nurse the newborns of other women in the village.

Dorst was too small to support a doctor's office. A physician from a neighboring village came one day a week, the nuns setting up a room in the convent where he saw patients. Perhaps her "nursing duties" distracted my mother from noticing a problem with my feet, because this doctor had to draw them to her attention. He told her to go to the city hospital and have a specialist examine them further. This was a huge expedition for my mother; the city was a long bus ride away, and she was eight months pregnant with her second child. Tired and irritable when she arrived at the hospital, she was only too glad when her name was called and she could bring me into the consultation room. The specialist checked my feet and told her he saw nothing wrong with them. He wrote down his diagnosis (which was no diagnosis at all, of course!) and handed it to my mother. She returned home, relieved I was all right.

When my next checkup came due, my mother went to the convent clinic, where the doctor asked to see the specialist's note. She handed him the paper. Although the waiting room was full of other patients, the doctor bundled my mother and me into his car and raced us to the city hospital. There he furiously demanded to see the specialist, pulling my mother and me into the consultation room and insisting I be re-examined. X-rays were taken, and I was diagnosed with clubfeet. Within two weeks I was on the operating table to have them corrected. My first steps were in casts, and I wore heavy platform shoes with metal supports until my twelfth birthday.

As a young woman working at that same city hospital, I asked some office personnel to look in the archives for my old file. It revealed that my foot operation had been performed by Dr. de Groot, by that time a well-respected neurosurgeon. I thanked him in person, and he was pleased to see the result of his work.

But back to my childhood... At two years of age, clomping around in those weighted shoes, I was often at the side of my mother's father. Unable or unwilling to say the word *Opa* (grandfather), I called him "Dada." He lived with us and slept in a *bedstee*, an old-fashioned bed space in a cupboard. My opa would constantly chew tobacco, put it in the pocket of his overcoat, take it out and chew on it again. I am told I would often slip my small hand into his pocket, snatch the tobacco and chew it myself.

Sadly, my grandfather left my life before I turned three. I vividly recall the day Sister Reinilda carried me to my parents' bedroom where my grandfather lay dead. Neighbors held a three-day wake for him. For the first and last time I called him Opa.

My father was a typical engineer, often tinkering in his workshop. In his spare time he repaired tractors and other equipment for local farmers, earning extra money. He once bought an old broken-down BMW motorbike, repaired it and added a sidecar. My mother would sit behind my father, while us three little girls squeezed into the sidecar. On summer days our family proudly rode the bike to picnics and motocross competitions.

I have less happy memories of the swing my father made when I was four years old. It was three meters high (a little under ten feet) and constructed with long steel pipes instead of chains. Why he made the thing I never knew. The big boys from the neighborhood would come and do all kinds of acrobatics on it, even executing a complete revolution before jumping off and landing squarely on their feet.

My dad told me I was too young to try the swing, but I was an impressionable child with small brain cells. First chance I got alone, I climbed up on it and pumped it hard, eager to get as high as the boys did. This must have taken a long time, as it was a very heavy thing. I heard my mother calling me inside for lunch, but I didn't listen, so determined was I to perform my circus act. I wasn't scared. Why should I be scared? I'd seen the boys do it many times.

Fed up with waiting, my mother finally went to fetch me. She found me unconscious: I had jumped and fallen onto stones beyond the grassy landing area. I stayed in bed for six weeks with a concussion. Needless to say, the swing was taken down.

In fairness to my father, I should confess that I was accident-prone. That concussion was the first of several. I fell in ditches trying to rescue baby ducks. I slipped on a cow pie while wearing my newly sewn white Sunday dress. I also ruined a suede jacket the first time I wore it by leaning against a freshly painted garden fence.

I could be a hazard to other people, too. One winter day, my sisters and I found a long patch of ice on the sidewalk in front of our home. We slid back and forth across it, making it slicker and slicker. Eventually, we made it so slippery that we could glide at high speed for nearly ten meters (about thirty-three feet). We thought we had made a shining thing of beauty.

The next morning was a Sunday. I awoke early and looked out the window to admire our slide. I was disappointed to see it covered with snow. However, it was definitely still there, as neighbors walking to church discovered. I watched as they slipped and fell left and right, smack on their faces or behinds. Some of them, knowing who was to blame, scowled in my direction. My parents advised my sisters and me not to come out of our rooms that day.

I wasn't much of a student. I am sure nowadays I would be diagnosed with ADD (Attention Deficit Disorder), as I could never focus on my lessons. One day in second grade music class I was chitchatting with my friend Corrie when I was supposed to be singing. Our music teacher, Mr. van der Horst, came up behind us and slapped our heads with the palm of his hand in rhythm to the music, singing,

"Sim sa la bim bom bas sa la do sa la dim!"

We were sent flying from one end of our classroom bench to the other.

Of course, things were different in those days. Students had no rights, and in villages like mine, teachers, principals, doctors, nuns and priests had the same power as GOD. There were few youngsters who would ever question authorities. And anyway, I knew I had done wrong talking in class that day, and couldn't stay mad at Mr. van der Horst, whom we kids nicknamed Bolletje Bink after a popular cartoon character of the time. Blond, round-faced and bespectacled, Bolletje Bink was generally kind and sweet (the "sim sa la bim bom" encounter not representative of him at all). He was actually one of my favorite teachers.

It seemed our family always had white cats as pets. It also seems they were regularly run over on the busy main street in front of our home. My father made a cross to mark the grave of each victim, while the feline cemetery behind the house grew and grew. On the occasion of the first cat being struck and killed, I started crying and kept it up throughout the school day. My teacher (Bolletje Bink again!) asked me what had happened. I could hardly speak, I was so distraught. The only thing Bolletje Bink could make out was that somebody had died and was buried behind the house. Consumed with worry, he asked another teacher to look after his class while he whisked me home. There my mother explained the tragedy. I was permitted to remain home and recover from my loss.

My father shared my love of cats and other animals. He helped me rescue little kittens we found tied up in a box in a forest not far from our home. And once he helped me rescue motherless ducklings we found wandering on the main road. He built a pond for them, and in a few months they grew big and fat. Mother started talking about having duck for dinner, so Dad and I quickly brought them to a pond in the city, where they could fly and be free.

When I was six, my father bought a piece of land in a neglected part of the village. Farmers had told him he was a fool and that nothing would grow there, but he proved them wrong. He built a spacious house, and soon we had large gardens abundant with flowers and vegetables. My father couldn't really take the credit for the gardens, though. They were the work of my mother and Uncle Janus.

Uncle Janus was what in Dutch we call a *suikeroom* or "sugar uncle," an uncle who only gives and does nice things for his nephews or nieces. My mother's oldest brother, Uncle Janus had dark hair, a friendly, square-shaped face and a stocky build. He had never married and had lived with us since I was born. I guess he was asexual, as he never showed a romantic interest in either men or women. Soccer was his world: he founded our village's first soccer club. A typical Sunday for him was going to church, followed by attending a soccer match, then sharing a beer with friends. I liked to watch Uncle Janus smoke his cigars; he'd get a serene expression on his face that made me want to smoke, too. (More on that later.)

The only work my father did in the garden was tending the white asparagus, for which he had a passion. My sisters and I detested this vegetable, so we devised a plan: whoever came home from school first would go to the garden and cover the tips of those long, horrible stems. Of course, it didn't go unnoticed that the bed of white asparagus was failing to thrive, so my father set a trap. He told my mom to spy on us when we got home from school. She dutifully reported our crime, and as punishment we had to consume even more of the nasty vegetable. Today, I still cannot bring myself to eat white asparagus, although I do like the green kind.

The garden offered one thing we all loved: strawberries. Each of us sisters was given two rows of strawberries to pick when they ripened. Naturally, the girl who got home first sneaked to the rows of the other sisters, stole the biggest, reddest berries, and gobbled them before the owner showed up.

I did not take all my thefts so lightly. Once I stole an apple from a neighbor's apple tree. I told no one, and the secret sickened me on my weekly Sunday morning trip to church. I felt too ashamed to take Holy Communion; I left during mass, telling my parents I was ill. I finally found the courage to admit the terrible sin during the next weekly confession and took Holy Communion again.

I mentioned that Uncle Janus enjoyed his cigars. One day I grabbed one from his cigar box and excitedly hid behind some trees in the back of the garden where nobody could see me smoke in secret. A few mere puffs made me wretchedly sick. I stashed the unconsumed portion and stumbled to my mother for help. She thought perhaps I had the flu, baffled why I should look so pale and green and keep throwing up. My uncle just looked at me and smiled. He had seen me sneaking off but didn't rat on me. In many ways, Uncle Janus understood my sisters and me better than my parents did. No wonder we loved him deeply.

TEENAGE YEARS

When I entered my teens, I attended an all-girls school. Lunch break was too short for me to go home and back, so I brought a lunchbox and ate in the schoolyard with friends. Some of the good girls would use this time to study, but I was not one of them. My friends and I would play or chat and do each other's hair. My hair was long then, so my friends took special pleasure in trying out new styles on me.

We had German class after lunch. Mrs. Drent, the teacher, was a short, elderly spinster whose gray curls framed a motherly face. She always wore "healthy," unfashionable shoes on her too-thick legs. One day Mrs. Drent announced that she would immediately start administering an oral exam to us, one student per day. Foreign languages were taught differently then; instead of listening to and repeating lively conversations, we were forced to learn words and sentences by rote. Basically, we were expected to memorize our entire Grammatik textbook and recite it in front of the class. Mrs. Drent called on me first. I hadn't even glanced at the material. I stood in front of everyone with my mouth shut, looking dumber than dumb. Forty-five students started giggling (classes were often large in those days). Not knowing what else to do, I giggled too. Then I looked at Mrs. Drent and told her honestly that I hadn't studied, as I expected her to call on students alphabetically, beginning with those whose surnames started with "A." I had figured it would take her weeks to reach "W" for Wouters.

Mrs. Drent regarded me sternly and lectured that instead of styling my hair during lunch, I would do better studying. She gave me one week's time to prepare for and repeat the test, which I thought was very reasonable. Mrs. Drent also told me to tell what happened that day to my parents and report back what they thought of it.

As you could guess, I put my own spin on the story when I told it to my parents. That's why the next day when Mrs. Drent met me in the hallway and asked how they reacted, I told her that my father had said it was none of her business what I was doing during lunchtime. UH OH. My parents were asked to come to school and meet with the headmaster. From then onwards, every day after school, I had to go straight home and study my Grammatik. When test day came, I stood before the class and recited: "Das Amt, das Band, das Bild, das Brett, das Dach," etc. Today, fifty years later, I still remember most of the Grammatik rules and exceptions. While I lived in Germany and Switzerland, I often thought of Mrs. Drent and how proud she would have been to know that her worst student had become so successful in German and would later even own and run her own school.

I can't say I did well in my other studies. I had difficulty concentrating and increasingly felt my education was a waste of my time. I was restless in our small Catholic village and felt misunderstood by my parents. I longed for adventure and wanted to see the world.

I did find one way to assert my true, exciting self: I changed my name. Out went Nellie ("Nel" was a common nickname for a farm horse) and in came glamorous Marilyn. I was not the only one unhappy with her given name. A group of girls in my class changed their names the same time I did. Everybody soon got used to them, even our parents.

I got my first boyfriend when I was fifteen. His name was Peter de Wit, and he lived in a neighboring village. He was a handsome boy with black curly hair. He passed by our house on his bicycle and asked me to hop on. He pedaled just over the railroad lines, stopped and asked me if I would be his girlfriend ("Wilde gij mijn meiske zijn?"). I said yes, and that was it, never a kiss or hanky-panky. That summer he and I would go swimming with friends in Surae, a natural pond in a nearby forest that was a popular hangout for teens.

Soon after this, my sisters and I became devoted to a community center discotheque called La Cabane. My parents allowed us to go every Saturday, as it was organized and supervised by a friend of my father's. My sisters and I became the wardrobe girls, and when everyone had checked their coats, we joined our friends dancing. The week couldn't pass fast enough for us to hit the floor and let off steam. A forest separated our home from the disco—a dark and dangerous wood, my father believed—so he always drove us directly there at 7 P.M. and collected us at 10 P.M. We found this curfew ridiculous because by ten the fun was just getting started, but he steadfastly adhered to this schedule.

Annually, on the first Sunday in May, Dorst celebrated its patron saint, St. Marcoen, with a special mass and village fair. Year after year on this date, I would be awakened in the early morning by the sound of many people passing our house on foot, by bicycle or bus, on their way to church. The fair or carnival lasted all weekend and featured food stands, games and music until midnight.

I was most impressed with the daring acrobats who performed at the carnival. They claimed to travel all over Europe, so I imagined they were gypsies. I started practicing all kinds of acrobatic acts, determined to be a circus star. I thought, "This explains why I'm so different from my parents. I was adopted…I'm actually a gypsy!" I had almost convinced myself of this before I fell on my head on our stone kitchen floor and had another concussion.

At one carnival when I was about nineteen, I met a young, long-haired musician from the neighboring village of Bavel. He was Cyriel Havermans, later to be bass guitarist of the rock group Focus. Cyriel invited me to sit beside him in the *rups* (worm), a kind of enclosed carousel. It was the perfect place for kissing in secret. All young people rode the worm endlessly.

Cyriel and I enjoyed that ride and other carnival amusements until I told him my parents expected me home by 10 P.M. Like a true gentleman, Cyriel took my hand and escorted me back to my street. We took advantage of our final minutes together by disappearing behind some bushes across the street from my house and exchanging innocent kisses until the church clock "bonged" the hour.

My sisters had already returned home from the fair, and my father was watching for me behind the window curtains. He saw by the streetlight the shadows of two people hugging each other. According to my mother and sisters, he was enjoying the sight, saying, "Yes, kiss her, good, good!"

Then the couple came out from behind the bushes and separated, the boy heading back to the carnival, the girl walking to her house. My father almost had a heart attack. The girl was I.

My sisters ran to their bedrooms, sure there would be big trouble. I stepped into the house. My father lunged from behind the door, trying to hit me. I escaped, running up the stairs. His hand came down, missing me, smacking on the railing. He cursed and shouted with pain, keeping in pursuit. I slammed my bedroom door, but not before his hand slipped inside it. He cried out. I cracked the door open, he pulled back his hand, and I slammed the door shut. He screamed for me to open it again, but I was no fool.

My sisters told me later that they had been crying in their rooms.

The next day my mother advised me to avoid my dad for the next week, so that he could cool down. Eventually he did, and years later we looked back at that night and laughed.

I left high school without graduating. My dearest wish was to go to France, work as an au pair and study French. My old-fashioned father believed that leaving home before marriage was the same as going into prostitution. When I asked permission to apply for an au pair position, his exact reply was, "If you want to drown yourself, you don't need to go to France. You can do that here too. There are enough rivers and canals."

I'm not sure if my father's attitudes were typical of Dutchmen of the time, but they certainly weren't universal. Later, when I lived in Switzerland, I learned that almost every Swiss girl was expected to be an au pair. She would typically live for a year in a different part of the country to learn another one of Switzerland's official languages.

I gave into my father on the au pair matter, but there were many times I opposed his wishes. Consider my trip to Roosendaal.

I had a friend then named Marian, a girl with spiky, chestnut-colored hair and a sprinkle of freckles across her face. One beautiful Sunday afternoon she asked me to go with her to Roosendaal, the town where her new boyfriend lived. Marian thought I could ride on the back of her small motorbike. My family and I had just returned from a three-week seaside camping holiday, so my parents said no to this day trip, thinking perhaps I'd had enough fun for a while. Knowing what you already know about me, you can guess I didn't listen. I snuck out of the house, and away Marian and I went.

We spent only an hour in Roosendaal seeing the guy, and then climbed back on the bike to return to Dorst. I found the back seat extremely small and uncomfortable. The bike's weak motor wouldn't let us go fast, and the speed limit on the bicycle paths of Holland at the time was a considerable 30 kph (about 20 mph). Each of us would steer for about ten minutes, and then switch seats.

As we moved quietly along, I heard a noise behind us. I glanced back and saw an approaching group of faster bikes ridden by *nozems* (boys of bad repute who wore their hair in cowlicks and donned leather jackets). I warned Marian they were catching up to us. Scared, we reduced our speed to let them pass. Sure enough, they pushed us off the path. Marian and I fell off the bike, sprawling onto the tarred road and a grassy field in the middle of nowhere.

I woke up in a strange room with people staring at me. Farmers working in the fields had seen the accident and brought us to their farmhouse. Marian, who was relatively OK, gave them my parents' telephone number. One farmer called my father, who hadn't even known I'd left the house. Later, my sisters told me that my father—my observe-all-traffic-laws father—had sped like a demon to reach me.

When the blood was wiped from my face, I found I had lost three teeth and broken my nose. For weeks afterward it hurt to laugh, smiles tearing open the wounds on my face. Friends who visited me afterward purposely told me countless jokes, especially my first boyfriend Peter. Friends!

LOOKING FOR INDEPENDENCE

After I had recovered, it was time to decide what to do with my life. I knew two things: I wanted to get away from home, and I wanted to help people. The decision wasn't difficult: I would train to be a nurse. My father researched the possibilities and selected St. Fransciscus Ziekenhuis, a nearby hospital in Roosendaal. The hospital had a separate, newly constructed dormitory called Sante Clara for nurse trainees. Nuns ran the hospital and a nurse ran the dormitory, so my parents were confident I'd be well looked after. Lucky me!

Training was not what I'd expected. It had nothing to do with taking care of patients and everything to do with folding gauze bandages, making beds, and delivering and removing food trays. Woe to any trainee caught chatting with a patient! The act could earn a reprimand. I suppose this austere kind of instruction was typical of 1965.

The first year I was stationed in three different wards, including the children's ward, which I liked best. I always told the children stories so they wouldn't notice the needle and be scared when I gave them vaccinations. I was proud of how I kept them smiling.

The neurology ward was a different story. The head nurse was kind, tall and friendly- faced with big brown eyes, an always-smiling nun with a warm heart. The subhead, on the other hand, was downright evil. She was blond with glasses, and I forget her name, but I will never forget how poorly she treated the patients, in particular a Mr. Waterman. A long-time patient, Mr. Waterman had Parkinson's disease and additionally suffered from large bedsores. One particular morning, at the end of my night shift, I was preparing a bowl to wash him, supervised by the subhead. I took my time, trying to be careful and not hurt the gentleman. The subhead impatiently grabbed the washcloth and rubbed roughly over his wounds, indifferent to Mr. Waterman's agony. He cried aloud, big tears rolling down his cheeks. Later he told me that what hurt him most was not the physical pain, but the indignity. He hated the subhead, and I hated her for him.

I often chose the night shift. Working alone and having the extra responsibility suited me. I also appreciated the extra days off I earned. I spent my long weekends in a scenic area called West-Kapelle in the province of Zeeland, driving there and back on my motorbike. I camped with friends who stayed there during their long summer holidays.

Living away from home meant I at last had some freedom. I could choose what I wanted to do with my time, whether studying or relaxing with fellow students. I could also decide how to spend my money. My monthly earnings were exactly a hundred Dutch guilders (what today would be worth about $50 USD), from which my parents took fifty-five to set aside for savings. That left me with forty-five guilders to spend however I liked.

I decided to buy a record player, and spent many happy hours sitting in my room, listening to my favorite albums. At least I did until my parents came to visit one Sunday afternoon. Gazing about with an inspecting air, my father's eyes fell on the record player. He asked where it came from. I proudly told him that I had bought it on an installment plan and was paying a mail-order company only eight guilders a month for the privilege. My father then asked for the original box, took the player, packed it up and sent it back. He told me never ever to do such a foolish thing again, as buying on credit could lead to financial catastrophe. Since that time I have followed his advice and never purchased anything that I could not pay for, cash in full.

My father had built a small fold-up caravan in which we spent several summer vacations camping in West-Kapelle. During the first summer of my nursing training, having worked the night shift for a week and gotten a few days off, I headed for West-Kapelle and joined my family there. During the day we spent time with friends on the beach, and at night we slept in the caravan.

Some boys from Eindhoven had pitched a tent close to my parents' caravan. I decided to join them in their tent to bake some cookies. We chatted, the time flew by, and before you knew it, it was curfew hour. I returned to our caravan.

At sunrise the next morning, my family was startled awake by the sound of loud knocking on our caravan and somebody shouting my name. My father hurriedly opened the door. My current boyfriend Hans, a very handsome dark-haired young man with sharp features, was standing there, and he was in a snit! He commanded me to dress myself and come with him. His friends had told him about my cookie escapade, and he demanded to know what it was all about. What could I say? It was simply cookies and small talk. I hadn't given a single thought to him! Our relationship iced over, and I was happy to return to work in Roosendaal.

A morning soon after the cookie incident, I was called into the office of Sante Clara's housemother, who angrily asked me if I had invited any people for breakfast that day. I looked at her in shock and amazement, no clue what she meant. On their way back home from their holidays in West-Kapelle, my "friends"—six young men dressed like hippies and riding motorbikes—had taken revenge and rung the bell at 5 A.M., telling my housemother they were my guests and were invited for breakfast. That was the end of my good reputation with the nuns. Within a year I decided nursing was not my calling and left Roosendaal.

This meant going home again, as I was only nineteen years old, still a minor according to the laws of that time. In the view of my parents and likely most adults in my village, it was impossible for a woman my age to leave home without a valid reason. And the only valid reason was marriage.

Four difficult years followed. I would ignore my father's rules or rebel against them, frequently resulting in my punishment. Looking back, I realize part of the problem was that I didn't like answering to any kind of authority. My parents were trying to do the best they could with a child they didn't understand.

I clearly remember a day when I came home and found my mother crying in the kitchen. My father had not spoken to her for several days because she had not asked him to play cards. Every week three family friends would come to our house and join my mother in playing *Klaverjassen*, a card game for two pairs of people. While they played, my father would watch TV. During the long commercial breaks, he'd make the guests appetizers, his homemade meat croquettes, which everybody loved. It was never really stated aloud, but it was understood that Dad was forbidden to play cards because he was an extremely sore loser; too often, when an amicable game didn't go his way, things ended in a fight. On a recent evening, one player did not show up, and the group of three started their game, never even thinking to invite my father to be their fourth. Boiling inside, Dad didn't get up to make them their favorite snack, choosing instead to sulk in his recliner. Of course, my mother observed this behavior but didn't dwell on it. Unfortunately for her, my father held a grudge, maintaining "the silent treatment" for many days, even threatening to file for divorce. Being the introverted person my mother was, she suffered quietly and deeply inside without being able to talk for weeks afterward.

On this day when I found her in such pain, I went to her, embraced her and tried to comfort her. She pushed me away, saying *"Doe nie zo gek."* "Don't be so foolish."

Her words hurt me deeply, and I never forgot them.

She was ashamed to let herself go. In her younger days, my mother might have been like me, intelligent but with few outlets for her dreams, ridiculed for expressing her feelings out loud. I swore I would never be that way.

To distract myself from the pressures of living at home, I tried to keep busy. My friends and I liked to shop for antiques, which we found at farms and other places. At a monastery one day I found two prayer chairs and was pleased to get them at a good price. I carried them home on my motorbike. My father examined them, discovered they were full of woodworms, and threw them into our dumpster.

At the time, I was working in a nearby hospital as an operating room assistant. The next morning I swiped from the OR a syringe and a bottle of pure Dettol, an antiseptic liquid similar to Lysol. I brought the things home, planning an act of extermination: Operation Woodworm.

Nobody was home except for Uncle Janus, who was working in the garden. I dragged one of the chairs out of the dumpster. Next, I diluted the Dettol with some water and pulled it into the syringe. Then I stuck the needle into a hole in the wooden chair. I pressed and pressed, but the Dettol was too thick to come out. The needle suddenly jumped from the syringe, spraying the liquid into my eyes.

Shouting for my uncle, I ran to a sink and threw water on my face, eyes afire. I couldn't see and was terrified I'd gone blind. Uncle Janus called my dad, who quickly came home from work and drove me to the hospital where I was treated. Bandages covered my eyes for six anxious weeks. Thank God, when the bandages were removed, I could see again.

Summer returned, and all my friends were spending weekends and vacations in West-Kapelle. Me too, but my two-week break went by too fast. Before I knew it, I had to return to work. I hatched a plan. I would act as if I had a backache for several days on the job, convince the head nurse I couldn't report one morning, and then go back to West-Kapelle. I went into action, "suffering" in the operating room for two days, until the head nurse told me early one morning to please go home and stay in bed. Head hanging, I left the ward, rushed to my motorbike, changed into the blue jeans I had hidden under its seat, and drove three hours to West-Kapelle. At 5 P.M., after a great day with my friends, I left for the three-hour drive back home, telling my parents the reason I was late was I had worked overtime! A satisfying fib… But… God punished me. In the morning I could barely roll out of bed. My back was killing me! In unbearable pain, I forced myself to report for work at the hospital. Walking virtually doubled over, knowing I had no one to blame but myself, I held back tears and started my job. The head nurse, very concerned, took me by the arm and led me to the x-ray department to have a scan done. Naturally, nothing was found. The nurse gave me painkillers and sent me home again to rest, advice I gratefully accepted. I didn't leave my bed for a week.

In April 1967 my mother's health was not good, so I helped her out in the afternoons. Poor Mom could not handle me and my loud music while cleaning, ironing, etc., and begged me after one month of suffering to find a part-time job outside the house. I found a position for the mornings as a secretary to a neurologist, Dr. Flamand, who much later treated Prince Claus for depression. (Claus was the husband of my country's monarch, Queen Beatrix.) Dr. Flamand and his wife were both neurologists and had six children, whom I looked after when the parents went on their much-needed vacations from work and children.

After another few months, Mom told me she felt better and that I should work full time, so I started afternoons as an assistant to a dentist named Dr. Uni. He resided on the Wilhelminastraat, a major street in Breda, and also had his clinic there. For three years I juggled the two jobs until Dr. Uni asked me to join the clinic full time.

After working at the clinic for a year, putting in long hours staring into open mouths, I looked forward to my vacation. It was the custom in the Netherlands then to give an employee an extra month's salary for vacation spending money, which made the break even sweeter. I planned to go camping in Spain with my sister Anne-Lies and her boyfriend, Henny. Anne-Lies had grown into an attractive young woman with long blond hair, and Henny was both nice-looking and charming: he had offered to drive us in his newly purchased secondhand car.

We had agreed to leave at the end of my workday. At quitting time, I fetched my coat and doubled salary (2 x 1,000 guilders, today about $1,000 USD) and ran out the office to my bicycle. It was raining hard, the wind blowing fiercely. Before I straddled my bike I remembered I was supposed to take a package to a local dental lab. I quickly ran back into the building and grabbed the package. I had been gone no more than two minutes, but when I returned to my bike, my bag and the money were gone. I stood in the drenching rain, peering up and down the street, but there was no sign of the thief. I dragged myself back inside the office to tell my boss and his wife, who drove me straight to the police station. Of course, the police could do nothing. I drove home, tears in my eyes. Adios, Spain!

My family sympathized with me. They also faced a dilemma: it was never explicitly stated, but it was understood that I was to be my sister's chaperone. My parents decided that my sister could go alone with her boyfriend, as long as his little brother went, too.

My parents' principles would not permit them to give me money for the trip. If they did so, they felt by rights they'd have to give each of my sisters the same sum, and they didn't have enough set aside for this. However, an angel awaited me in the figure of my Uncle Janus. He knew I had been so looking forward to the trip and felt sorry for me. He went upstairs to his room, came back and took me aside. Handing me an envelope, he said,

"Go and have a nice vacation."

I never loved my uncle more than at that moment. I ran to my room, snatched up my luggage, and off we went to Spain, where we ended up at campgrounds close to Barcelona and its celebrated beaches. Henny's parents had gone on holiday that same day, driving to Poland, where his mother had been born. While driving through France, they decided to alter their plans and also visit Spain. Spain is larger than Holland; it would have been a needle in a haystack to meet up with us, as we all had no clue where we were heading once we left our homes, and there were no cell phones then. At our campsite we set up two tents, a big one for Anne-Lies and Henny and a small one for me and Peter, Henny's twelve-year-old brother. We were relaxing in our camp chairs, sipping drinks and watching the arrival of people, cars loaded, looking for a space for their tents, when Henny and Peter looked at each other in astonishment. They ran to the car that had just passed by and greeted their parents.

FIRST MARRIAGE

I met my future husband Nico in 1967 at the La Cabane discotheque. Three years younger than I, a hairdresser in training, Nico had dark hair and alluring dark eyes. I lost my virginity to him one night after returning from La Cabane in the forest between the two villages, but the experience was not a good one for me. (So my father had been right to warn my sisters and me about the deep, dark woods after all!) I broke off the relationship with Nico, but we soon reconciled and got engaged.

The government expected Nico to fulfill eighteen months of military duty. It was an unpaid obligation, which he didn't like, so he applied for a five-year contract with the NATO air force. NATO promised him an education and a salary, as well as a bonus of 15,000 guilders (a little under $10,000 USD today) at the conclusion of the contract. In December 1969, when I was twenty-three and he was twenty, we wed in a civil ceremony. A week later we scheduled a church wedding. At the reception, Nico suddenly became ill from anxiety, hurrying away to throw up in the bathroom. I looked at him then and I knew: I had made a mistake marrying him.

GERMANY—HESSISCH OLDENDORF
(1970-1973)

HOUSEWIFE

We made a home inside the NATO base compound at Hessisch Oldendorf, a small town close to the river Weser in northwest Germany. Nico had already been at Hessisch Oldendorf for six months when I joined him with my cat, Lummeltje, and hamster, Krummeltje, in April 1970.

After World War II ended, NATO decided that for the protection of Europe, the Allied forces should maintain a presence in Germany. Each year the armies of Great Britain, Belgium, the Netherlands and the United States met there to practice military maneuvers we called "tactical." "Tactical" featured rocket-propelled planes, bombs and radar monitoring. With no consideration for the farms, houses and railways in their path, the four countries played at war, than financially compensated all the people whose property they wrecked.

I had been working and earning money since I was eighteen. For five years I had delivered most of my salary to my parents, who allowed me some pocket money. They put aside the rest, saving it for my marriage. They did the same for my sisters. It was common in those times for the parents of girls to pay for a wedding and help the couple get established, too. I arrived in Hessisch Oldendorf with crates of home goods, and Nico and I soon had one of the best-furnished apartments on the compound. It was also the first time I had ever lived in an apartment, and I realized how lucky I was that my parents could afford to give us good lives. Nothing was bought on credit. My joint parental account paid for our fridge, washing machine, a state-of-the-art REVOX hi-fi, a twelve-piece dining set and everything one needed to live comfortably. Nico and I also bought a new car, the first yellow Fiat 127 in Germany. The purchase was made with my money alone; always a student and not inclined to save money when he had it, Nico didn't contribute a penny.

I was extremely lucky to find a job within a month of arriving in Hessisch Oldendorf. The Dutch school, a mere five-minute walk from our apartment, had advertised an opening for a secretary. I brought my CV and went to see the headmaster, Mr. Hengeveld. Although the interview was brief, I knew immediately I had made a good impression. I thought it unlikely, however, I'd be given this government position. I'd heard that quite a few other women had applied for it, some of who had husbands with good positions in the military and had lived on the Hessisch compound for many years. Other candidates thought they had a sure "in," such as connections with the teachers or children enrolled at the school.

I went on with my life and actually forgot about the job, until one day I received a call from the headmaster. He told me to go to the unit commander and finalize the paperwork so I could start as soon as possible. Many women in the community were jealous of my good fortune.

SECRETARY AT THE NATO SCHOOL

As I look back now, I realize that The Klimopschool (*klimop* is Dutch for "ivy," as in "ivy-covered walls") was the first rung on an educational career ladder that would one day take me to a considerable height. I can't say my first day was all that promising, though. I entered the building and walked through the corridors, looking for the conference room. When I asked one of the teachers where it was, he asked me which class I was in. He thought I was a new student!

I worked with the lovely faculty members of The Klimopschool for three years. My boss, Jo Hengeveld, always serious-looking behind his rimmed glasses, was easy to work for, and when my assignments for him were done I typed (no computers in those days) tests covering all manner of subjects. Some teachers would reliably hand their tests in early, while others could always be counted on to be late (and nag me to type faster). My favorite teachers were Henri Linders (French) and Jitze Vanger (English).

Henri looked like a homeless person just creeping out from under one of the bridges that crossed the Seine in Paris. He favored baggy pants, sported a big black moustache, looked very French and loved teaching. He lived with his second wife, Mattie, a wonderful Belgian countess who belonged to very old nobility, a branch of the Belgian royals. They had two children and a dog. Henri's unorthodox teaching style was ahead of its time; his colleagues criticized him for it until the end-of-year results came in from Holland's Ministry of Education: his students scored at the top of the ranks. Henri's colleagues were also envious of the way his students loved him.

Jitze was charming, intelligent, a good-looking young Robert Redford. He had a wife whom he adored and beautiful children. He asked me to work for him in my free time to type an English course book, which was published shortly afterward.

Henri and Jitze were always the first ones to come with their test papers to be typed, a practice ignored by their colleagues, who gossiped that I was giving those two teachers preference. It was Jitze who started calling me Mereltje (little blackbird), a nickname all the teachers gradually adopted.

You're probably wondering why I'm not writing much about my marriage to Nico. What shall I say? I told you that Nico was the first man with whom I was intimate. My religion and my parents had told me that "IT," sex, was bad and dirty. So he and I had some adjustments to make. Pretty soon, however, we settled down to a life that was pleasant, if a bit boring. Nico's co-workers Hans and Eddy used to come over often, playing cards, watching TV and listening to music, having a good dinner. Once a month, Nico and I drove to Holland for a long weekend to see family and friends. We spent our holidays in different countries in Europe. My job was only five hours a day, and Nico regularly went out of town for military exercises, so I was often alone. I had time for my hobbies, which were knitting, crocheting, horseback riding and cooking.

My cat, Lummeltje, and hamster, Krummeltje, were a constant source of joy. Lummeltje would often walk with me to school. Before long he followed me into the building, jumped up onto the big table in the conference room where I worked, and hunkered down there, content. All the teachers got used to him.

Jo, who didn't care for cats, had never noticed Lummeltje, as he was always busy in his office or walking through the school. The story goes that one morning, while Jo was looking for me and I was off in a classroom talking with a teacher, Jo came into the conference room, saw Lummeltje and angrily asked what the f--- was this cat doing, sleeping on top of the table? Get rid of it! The teachers told him its owner was Mereltje. Jo shook his head and walked out of the room. Lummeltje continued to have daily siestas in his favorite spot until I left Germany years later.

While Jitze's wife was on a break in Holland, I invited Jitze and the kids to have dinner at my house. The next day Jo's wife asked the family for dinner, and the kids mentioned that they had supped at Mereltje's house the night before. Disgusted, the woman cried out,

"What!? You were eating *mereltjes* [blackbirds] yesterday?"

Today, my old colleagues and I still chuckle over the cat and blackbird stories.

Another cat joined our family when the baby of one of the teachers was discovered to be allergic to animal fur. This cat was pregnant, and when her due date drew near, I prepared a box next to the bed. Nico left then for extended duty. Gone for three nights, he never witnessed the ensuing drama.

The cat refused to remain in the box, even when it was clear the kittens were coming. Time and again, she jumped up on the bed onto the pillow next to my head. It really became a struggle, so I gave up and put old towels on my pillow for her to rest upon. With difficulty, the cat started delivering her kittens; she popped out her first baby next to my head around midnight. I took mother and newborn and put them both in the box. Mama cat immediately took her kitten in her mouth, jumped on the bed, stretched herself across the pillow and dropped the wee, wet creature on my chest. I wasn't even able to move my head; if I rolled to the right, mama jumped over my head and placed herself on my right. The same with the left. I decided to just lie there on my back and wait for what was to come.

An hour later the second baby arrived, an hour after that, the third. It wasn't until seven the next morning that mama cat finally delivered her fourth and final kitten. She fell asleep totally exhausted. It was then I saw she had no milk: her breasts were completely dry and hot. I called the vet, who gave her an injection and provided me with medicine to inject her with every three hours. I bought toy baby bottles intended for dolls, poured formula into them, and fed the kittens until their mother recovered from her strenuous delivery. She did eventually get used to the box, but when she needed to use the litter tray, she would take the kittens one by one and bring them to my lap for safekeeping. When she returned she would lie next to me, watching her babies with pride.

So now our home had six cats and some hamsters.

Not long after the kittens came, Nico and I decided to take a vacation, the wife of one of Nico's friends having offered to look after the animals for us. Nico and I headed to Italy, a first-time visit for me. We planned to meet my sister Marijke and her husband at scenic Lake Garda. We had bought a new car, a Renault 16, which carried our tent and boat, a Zephyr, used for my favorite sport, waterskiing, on the river Weser. I know I found Italy very nice, but I don't remember any details of the trip except that while we were passing through Switzerland on our way back, when Nico wanted to stay overnight in Zürich, I told him, "No, I prefer we drive straight home," thinking, *It's not necessary to stop now. I'll come back and see the city another time.* As it turns out, it was very good we didn't stop. What's more, my thought was prophetic. Zürich would later be my home for years.

When we arrived at our front door two weeks after we'd left, I walked in and knelt to welcome the cats. The four kittens had grown and were beautiful. I picked two of them up in my hands, and then glanced down.

My white pants were dotted with strange black spots. I looked closer and a shiver went through me. I was covered with fleas. I dropped the kittens and started scratching, suddenly itching everywhere.

I checked the dining room. On the floor was a bucket of milk; it might have sat there the entire two weeks we were gone. It was mid summer and 35 degrees Celsius (about 95 degrees Fahrenheit), so the milk had soured and stank. Another bucket was filled with stone dry cat food and leftovers of rotten, smelly meat. The cream-colored Berber carpets in all the rooms were black from fleas, the cat bed was disgusting, the doors closed and the odor horrible.

Enraged, I dropped our luggage outside the apartment and ran to the home of the woman who had said she'd look after the animals. Nobody answered. I rang the bell of our neighbor. She opened the door and told me that the pet watcher and her husband had unexpectedly been called to Holland and had hired no one to replace them, leaving this big mess behind.

You won't be surprised to learn that Nico and I couldn't sleep in the house that night.

The next morning I called pest control, which sent out someone who sprayed every nook and cranny. The kittens were taken to the cellar and sprayed separately; I left them there for a week. The two grown cats were more severely affected. They refused to use their litter box anymore, peeing and pooping everywhere in the house. For two months I tried to retrain them, without success. What a horrible time. With tears in my eyes, I brought them to a farmer who lived nearby and agreed to have them. I kept two of the kittens and named them Sampie and Moosje. The two others were adopted after eight weeks.

It had been a hard lesson for me. I never left Sampie and Moosje alone after that experience. Wherever Nico and I went, the cats came with us. They became good travel companions, and didn't even need a carrier. Where we walked they walked, like dogs.

END OF FIRST MARRIAGE
My marriage slowly went downhill. Maybe Nico got a little too comfortable. I was treating him like a mother, looking after him, taking care of

him. I didn't like this role for me, and thought there must be more to life. I tried to communicate this to him, but it fell on deaf ears. Over the three years I had tried to give him signs, but I was definitely not clear enough and gave up. This was a mistake I would often repeat in my relationships. When I'd try to convey my initial worries regarding feelings in the relationship, and saw that there was no understanding or interest from my partner, I would close down and become "my mother," too introverted to express myself further.

Every night before sleeping Nico would ask me, "Do you still love me?"

I had always answered yes. Finally, one night I replied, "I don't know." That's when life became very uncomfortable. We realized we had nothing to talk about, nothing in common. Yet I was afraid to cut our bonds, as I felt the problem was not him but me. What's more, in those times, divorce among small town people was unacceptable. I made myself busy to fill the emptiness in my life. A few evenings a week I worked behind the bar at a local canteen for military personnel. I also organized dances for personnel and their spouses, and movie days for their kids.

Meanwhile, at school we were in need of more teachers. It turned out that our community featured many military volunteers who were fresh out of teachers' college and wanted to earn some extra money before starting their professional lives, so there were plenty of applicants. One Monday during coffee break, I looked out the window and saw a trio of young men approaching the school's front door. "Here come The Three Musketeers," I said. These new teachers introduced themselves as Alex Bultsma, Alex Bounin and Henk Rampen. When the last one said his name, I couldn't stop myself and instantly said, "Disasters. That's just what we need!"

Rampen is Dutch for "disasters."

The men were my age, so we all connected. Lex Bounin was a good-looking, kindhearted Indo (someone of mixed Dutch and Indonesian ancestry). Lex Bultsma was an elderly gentleman in a young man's body. Henk Rampen…well, as I would learn, he was someone who didn't care about anyone or anything.

Henk had a girlfriend, Lilian, twenty years older than he. The two of them lived in a caravan at a campsite in the town of Rinteln on the Weser River. Nico and I got to know them a bit, and when summer came the four of us would take our Zephyr inflatable boat out on the water and go waterskiing or sail in Henk's sailboat. We'd top off the day's fun with a barbecue.

Fall set in. Lilian went back to Holland for a while. Henk was riding back and forth to Rinteln on his bike every day through increasingly bad weather, so Nico and I invited him to stay in our guest room.

Nico always left for duty at 7 A.M. Henk usually went out at 8. My work started at 9, so I would get up after both of them were gone. One morning I was awakened by a kiss on my cheek. I opened my eyes and looked straight into the eyes of Henk, who was kneeling next to the bed. He kissed me on the lips in an extremely intimate way before getting up and leaving.

I was completely flabbergasted. I hadn't seen this coming. However, due to my weak relationship with Nico, it was easy for Henk to sense and take advantage of my vulnerability. I fell in love with him, and we started an intimate relationship right under people's noses. At school Henk and I made a point of not communicating with each other. Still, I believe that some of the teachers realized what was happening, but kept it to themselves.

I was in seventh heaven, not thinking what tomorrow would bring. For me this relationship was serious; I started thinking how to tell Nico that I wanted a divorce. I never realized that whenever I spoke about our future together, Henk didn't respond. I was living in a kind of alternative universe until Lilian came back.

Henk now spent half his time in Rinteln with her. Sometimes the two of them stayed overnight at our place. I couldn't handle that. I was extremely insecure about our love, and so jealous I felt physically ill. Of course, I refused to make love to Nico from the moment I first made love to Henk. Excuses were not always easy to find, and it did not make life easier that I, brought up by old-fashioned Catholic parents, felt I was living in sin. I was delaying the moment to confess to Nico, unable to find the courage or the right moment. Now I know that there is never a right moment. When Nico asked me again if I still loved him, I had to tell him, No, I don't love you anymore. He asked me who it is I love, and I answered, Henk.

It was midnight. Nico got out of bed and got dressed. I heard him start up the car and drive off. I knew he was going to Rinteln. There were no cell phones in those times, so I couldn't warn Henk, who was surprised by Nico, banging on the caravan door. Henk opened the door, and Nico punched him back inside. Nico followed him and kept punching and punching. Henk was too surprised to respond; neither he nor Nico was the fighting kind. Finally, Lilian separated them and asked for an explanation, which Nico happily gave. Henk tried to reason with Nico by suggesting they all come to our house and discuss the matter.

I was scared, sitting in the living room when they arrived. Nobody could get a word out of me. I cried and cried, seeing the mess I was in and not knowing how to get out of it. This was the first time I had ever been confronted with intense feelings, and even today I can't compromise them. Nico wanted me to confess, Henk wanted me to lie and I...I just wanted to be honest and tell the truth.

Henk asked Nico if he could take me to the bedroom to talk, as nobody could get a word out of me. There he calmed me down and asked me to take back my confession to Nico. I told him I could not do that: I'd had enough, and needed to take responsibility for my actions. Henk didn't want that, so he left me crying in the bed and went back to the living room, where he and Lilian stayed for another half hour and then left.

Nico came back to the bedroom and anally raped me. I bled like crazy, but did not dare go to a doctor. That was the moment I lost all feelings and respect for Nico. I told him the next day that I wanted a divorce, with or without Henk in my future.

Nico and I lived in a closed military environment, a compound where gossip quickly spread. Soon everyone knew the state of our marriage, much to my distress. Things got so difficult that in November 1973, after three years in Germany, I decided to return to Holland and stay with my sister Marijke in the town of Nijmegen. I only brought my cats Sampie and Moosje with me from Germany. Although he had promised to do so, Henk did not visit.

During the last weeks of our life together, Nico did some foolish things. I think he would have argued that he was simply bringing color into the colorless life of a soldier without war. Whatever his excuses, acquaintances gossiped about Nico and our separation at a yearly shooting competition that took place in Den Helder, a city in the far north of Holland, about two hours from my hometown. Through the grapevine my parents got wind and summoned me home from my sister's. There a meeting between all parties was arranged, where my parents and Nico's parents suggested we not divorce because of the disgrace, but stay married like brother and sister. I absolutely refused. Fortunately, our military priest from Hessisch Oldendorf came to my rescue. He advised my parents that it was time for me to go my own way.

Word got out that Nico had threatened to kill himself by driving our car from a mountaintop. I went to visit him in the military hospital in Utrecht, where he had ended up after his "suicide attempt." There he told me very clearly that he was advised by his superiors to block our bank accounts. I couldn't believe my ears; he who had had nothing was going to take all our savings! I looked at him and left.

While waiting for the divorce to be finalized, I landed a job as a dental assistant in Zürich, the city I had neglected to visit on my trip back from Italy. My parents were happy to be rid of their ugly duckling. Off I went, twenty-seven years old, boarding a train with only 1,000 guilders (less than $500 USD) in my pocket. Nico had control of our bank account; I never saw a penny from it, and being so fed up with his demands, I left most of my belongings with him. My parents were furious—with me! I had just given away a whole life's worth of savings, including the money I had earned at the school. I didn't care. I wanted to be free and leave the Netherlands. Months later I received a letter from my lawyer stating that Nico and I were divorced as of April 23, 1974. Within a year he was happily re-married. He now has two beautiful children, God bless him.

SWITZERLAND—ZÜRICH (1974-1988)

ASSISTANT TO DR. HUBLER

On January 30, 1974, I arrived by train in the cleanest country I had ever seen. The only thing I had known about Switzerland was that it had three official languages. Turns out I was even wrong about that! It has four: Swiss German, French, Italian and Romansch (an old language with Latin roots). The first big city I had ever lived in, Zürich intimidated me a little, but I promised myself I would "make it" there.

I went directly to the clinic on busy Schaffhauserstrasse in Seebach, a northern district of Zürich. The dentist, Dr. Hubler, was waiting for me. A man in his late fifties with a nervous air, he stood just a little taller than I. His black hair was spread thinly over his skull, and he was dressed in an expensive suit. Dr. Hubler invited me into his car and drove me to my apartment in a boardinghouse on Höhenring, a nice street just a five-minute walk from the clinic. A pretty flower arrangement was waiting for me on the dressing table. Dr. Hubler explained the things I should do the next day, such as finalizing my work permit and learning the best route to work. Soon I was alone and unpacked my suitcase.

Sampie and Moosje were still in Holland, and I already missed them. I wished I could bring them over, but the landlady did not accept pets and regularly inspected the rooms. I would never get used to this practice of inspection, which seemed to be the norm in Switzerland.

Renters at the boardinghouse were mostly single or divorced; some stayed only during the week and left on the weekends to be with their families. Playing music was not allowed after 10 P.M., and the common bathroom and kitchen were not to be used after that hour. The rules were strict and made me uncomfortable, even though I was and still am a quiet person.

Praxis Dr. Hubler (Dr. Hubler's clinic) had a fine reputation. Dr. Hubler only worked part time, three afternoons a week. It was his partner, Dr. Zdravko Antelj, who really made the money. Unfortunately, Dr. Antelj was a foreigner, and what was worse, felt like one. He had a huge inferiority complex, although he would never admit it. Dr. A had earned two degrees in Yugoslavia, one dental, the other medical related, and was much better qualified than most Swiss dentists, but Swiss authorities would not permit him to open a dental clinic of his own. He fiercely resented Dr. H for this, and Dr. H resented him back for his unreasonable feelings. Only money kept the men together.

It takes a long time to build a trusting relationship between a doctor and his or her patients. This is especially the case with dentists. Most patients are anxious; by knowing them better and longer, a dentist can foster an atmosphere of friendship, which makes the patients more relaxed. Dr. H's patients did not like Dr. A, and Dr. A's patients did not like Dr. H. Truth is, however, that if a patient of Dr. H's had an emergency and was forced to go to Dr. A, she or he would not want to return to Dr. H. And if a patient of Dr. A's had to go to Dr. H, she or he would take care to brush his or her teeth diligently for the rest of his or her life. In other words, Hubler was a good human being but a poor dentist, while Dr. A was an a--hole but very good at his job. As Dr. Hubler used to say,

"If the bastard weren't such a good dentist, I would have thrown him out a long time ago!"

I learned a lot from Dr. Antelj, but he drove me nuts. He always had to be right. We would argue over questions as foolish as, what kinds of cars are more popular in Switzerland, hatchbacks or sedans? I remember him standing at the window during breaks, counting the cars on the street below with a crazy intensity.

Antelj and his Dutch wife, Dickie, invited me regularly to their place. They lived just a few minutes from me. Dickie was very nice and enjoyed having someone with whom she could speak Dutch. I admired her for managing to be happy, despite being married to so complicated a person as Zdravko.

At the office I had a seventeen-year-old trainee named Pia. The dentists and I worked hard to get Pia through her exams, as she was already in her third year when I arrived. The poor girl had seen at least six primary assistants come and go. Why? The competition between the two doctors wore down both trainee and primary assistant. How long was I going to last? This was also why Dickie had placed a help-wanted ad in a Dutch newspaper: Drs. H and A were so notorious among the circle of Swiss dental assistants that no one with common sense wanted to work with them.

Soon I no longer had a life. Between processing invoices and all other administrative duties, calling patients to remind them of their yearly consultations, being chair assistant and checking on our trainee, the workload was backbreaking. Then there was the language problem. I had not realized that the Swiss speak not High German, which I had been taught in school, but Swiss German. I didn't understand a word of this "dialect." Dr. A spoke High German anyway, as he was too arrogant to speak Swiss German, and Dr. H spoke Bernese German. This was a dialect that even many Swiss Germans couldn't understand, so how was I expected to? We decided that if Dr. H needed to speak to me, he would do it only in High German. Of course, this was forgotten very soon, and Dr. Hubler, being an anxious and impatient man, often shouted at me in the presence of patients. I became a nervous wreck and decided to leave as soon as my one-year work permit expired.

I was working at the clinic day and night. Occasionally, on a rare day off, I would explore Zürich, strolling through the different quarters of the city. Usually, however, I was too tired to go out. I would read and eat in, saving money so I could sooner buy a car and afford better accommodations.

SWISS HANS

On one of these at-home Saturday evenings, the hall phone rang. Figuring it wasn't for me, I didn't bother to get up and answer it. It seems that everyone else had gone out, as the phone kept on ringing. I finally got up and went into the hallway.

"Höhenring 25, Wouters," I said.

I heard the voice of a young man.

"Would you like to come to the party in Winterthur? It's carnival. Nobody sits home at a time like this!"

I didn't know where Winterthur was, and I didn't know who was speaking to me. I decided it must be a prank. I hung up and returned to my room and my book. Immediately, the phone rang again. I didn't know what to do, get up or let it ring. At last I went into the hall and picked up the phone again.

"Don't hang up, please, I'm your upstairs neighbor," he said. "I'm with some friends in Winterthur, it's carnival, and it would be nice if you'd come have dinner and a drink with us."

I remembered sometimes passing a young Swiss man on the stairs, but I'd never really looked at him. The pleasing tone of his voice and lively music in the background made me think, *Why not?* I asked him how to reach this Winterthur; I didn't know where it was. He said, "Get a taxi and just say Bahnhof Winterthur (railway station). Don't worry about the cost. We'll pay when you get here."

Quickly I called a taxi, and after a thirty-five minute drive I arrived.

Hans and his friends were waiting for me. To be very honest, I didn't even want to know the cab fare; it must have been horrendous for those times. Winterthur was partying. It was a beautiful evening, a festive atmosphere in the streets and restaurants. Hans and his friends were very nice, but when I finally wanted to go home, I thought it best to drive their car, as they had drunk a drop too many.

Almost every evening thereafter, they invited me out for dinner or drinks at one of the many restaurants in the neighborhood. The Swiss like to go to restaurants and prefer to celebrate special occasions, as well as have family dinners and lunches, in restaurants instead of at home. For me, being Dutch, this was a new custom.

I didn't even realize that Hans was after me, as we never met alone, but always in the company of others. However, our friendship deepened, and we decided to rent an apartment together. I went to Holland to fetch Sampie and Moosje.

On my train ride there, I came down with a terrible headache. Ever since I'd come to Switzerland, I'd been sensitive to the *föhn*, a type of dry, warm, down-slope wind that occurs in the lee (downwind side) of a mountain range. *Föhn* winds can rapidly raise air temperatures in a matter of minutes. Central Europe enjoys a warmer climate due to the *föhn*, as moist winds off the Mediterranean Sea blow over the Alps. Like many other Swiss, I suffered from *föhn* headaches, which tend to start after the wind blows and just before it rains.

The train was overloaded. My compartment was full of musician hippies from Ibiza, who had a contract to play in Amsterdam during some festivals. One of them was playing a strange-looking guitar; the sound was beautiful, but it didn't relax me. In fact, it made my headache worse. I got irritated and regularly left the compartment.

Another musician with long black curly hair and a beautiful face saw that I constantly looked out the window, keeping to myself and not engaging in their conversations. He asked if something was wrong. I told him that I had a horrible migraine. He offered to massage my head. I refused, feeling this would be too intimate, and told him I wanted to be left alone. He didn't listen to me, and as I was sitting with my back to him, he took my head between his fingers. The music stopped and nobody made a sound while he told me to relax. I was extremely tense, but slowly after many minutes I almost fell asleep. Gradually, he reduced the pressure, moving his fingers gently over my head. I think he must have massaged every centimeter of my scalp. In thirty minutes the headache was gone.

Telling me to close my eyes, the musician started to play the strange guitar. The music and atmosphere became tranquil and lovely. Unfortunately, the time approached when I had to leave the train to make a transfer. The musicians were continuing to Amsterdam, and I was headed south.

The young man asked me to come with him. I told him that I was going to visit my parents, and then I would go back to Switzerland. He gave me his name, the name of the hotel where he was staying, and the phone number of the manager through whom I could contact him. He asked me for my phone number; I gave it, expecting never to hear from him again. I was wrong. For days afterward, he called and tried to convince me to come to Amsterdam, or barring that, he would visit me at my parents' home. He begged me to come to Ibiza, and gave me his address there. Later I found out that he was quite a famous musician. I only knew that I had responsibilities and could not simply run off.

I worried about Sampie and Moosje being locked in their carriers for the twelve-hour train trip back to Switzerland. Solution? I rented an entire car compartment for the three of us. Amused travelers constantly visited the compartment to watch the cats pad freely about it.

Returning to the boardinghouse, I learned that the apartment Hans and I had arranged to rent would not be available for another week. The landlady did not like this at all, for as I explained earlier, she did not permit pets. Dr. Hubler intervened on my behalf, and succumbing to his charms, she allowed the cats to stay.

Hans and I finally moved into the new apartment, which was only ten minutes by train from Zürich's Seebach district. I could not say that Hans was the big love of my life, but we got along together very well. In the meantime, fed up with the tension between Dr. H and Dr. A, I changed jobs and in spring of 1975 found work as a dental assistant in a small clinic in the Affoltern district of Zürich.

ASSISTANT TO DR. STOCKER

The owner of the clinic, Dr. Stocker, was a kind, gentle soul in his late fifties whose white hair made him look as if he were in his late seventies. He was a wonderful piano player and owned a grand piano, but as a young man he chose to be a rich dentist rather than a poor musician. He trained me as a dental hygienist. Dr. Stocker rested for thirty minutes after seeing every patient, and worked only six hours a day. He never demanded I work overtime and gave me eight weeks of paid vacation a year. There were only ten to twenty invoices for me to process weekly. By now I had overcome my shyness speaking Swiss German, and patients seemed to like my Dutch accent.

In a word, I could finally relax.

I knitted socks for Dr. Stocker; his wife knitted the heels and I knitted the rest. I created beautiful works of macramé and needlepoint, which I sold in the Migros Market behind the clinic. And I indulged a whim by buying my first car—just for me, that is—a red Renault 14 sports car.

Hans and I decided to take a trip to Senegal. I had never flown before, so I was very excited. Our fellow travelers teased me about this and that, as I was the only Dutch among the Swiss. Lucky me, it turns out. Switzerland was not in the EEG (a precursor to the EU) so upon our arrival at the Senegal airport all Swiss passport holders were delayed with lots of paperwork. I, on the other hand, sauntered straight through customs.

We checked in at Club Aldiana in Mbour, the most popular resort in Senegal. It was packed with Germans; it felt as if we had landed in an army camp. The Germans planned and scheduled every minute of their day, leaving nothing to chance—not breakfast, lunch, dinner, water sports, day trips, or relaxation in the evening. Everything was regimented and painfully organized. After two weeks we were happy to leave this noisy crowd of followers and vowed never to go to a vacation spot popular with Germans again.

Back in Zürich, a nasty letter was waiting for me. Dr. Stocker had received notice from immigration that my work permit would not be extended, as there were too many jobless Swiss. I discussed this with Hans, who said not to worry; he would marry me, and that would take care of my immigration status. Dr. Stocker and his wife weren't thrilled with the idea because they weren't thrilled with *him*. Nevertheless, Hans and I married July 29, 1976. Our only witnesses were Jacqueline and Hans Andretto, Hans's closest friends. Their wedding gift was a small ash-gray kitten that we named "Seppie." Soon I received my Swiss passport with my new name: Petronella Müller.

In October 1977 Hans and I vacationed at Beau Vallon Bay in the Seychelles, at that time a relatively unspoiled spot. We had no newspapers, radio or TV, so we did not know that just a few kilometers away the South African air force had foiled a hijacking with a spectacular rescue of hostages by the Israeli Mossad. The world had been holding its breath, and we didn't even know it.

I saw that parasailing was being offered on the beach where we were staying. I said I wanted to try it, but Hans said absolutely not, it was too dangerous. I was terribly disappointed. I had hoped my vacation would have a special moment of freedom, an escape from the ordinary. And... the moment came, after all. Hans got sick, and a doctor told him to stay in bed. Wonderful! Here was my chance!

I quickly bought a ticket from the parasailing guy and put on the parachute outfit. The guy's helpers were snapping the lines into the holes of my parachute when I glanced back. Hans was running towards me, trying to stop the most exciting thing I would do during my whole vacation. I shouted I was ready to the people in the boat, and before I knew what was happening, I saw the line stretching and felt a pull. I ran across the sand and suddenly I was gliding over the water. The faster the boat went, the higher I flew. It lasted about half an hour, and I enjoyed every minute. At last the boat slowed down along the beach so I could land. This was easy for me, as I had seen it done many times before. I was proud of my perfect landing. Hans scolded me, telling me I had been irresponsible, I should have thought about my safety; I shouldn't risk anything that could jeopardize my job, etc. There and then I started thinking that I probably had made a mistake marrying Hans.

When I met him, I thought Hans was an open-minded man who loved adventure. Early in our marriage, he seemed eager to travel everywhere. Hans told me he had lived in South Africa and traveled to many countries, and to me that suggested someone willing to take risks. So when he first showed signs of withdrawing, I figured he was merely changing into the typical, introverted, prone-to-silence Swiss mountain man. People often revert to their earlier selves, after all.

But the transformation was more disturbing than that. After a few visits with me to see my family, he decided he didn't want to go to Holland anymore. Visitors were no longer welcome in our home either, with the exception of my parents and sisters. He even refused to allow the two of us to go out for dinners. We're saving for the future, he'd say.

Because I wasn't allowed to invite people over, we gradually received no more invitations from friends. Besides, whenever Hans would be invited to someone's place for dinner, he would suddenly become ill. I wasn't the kind of person who always wanted to be going out, but not even being allowed to spend time with a girlfriend started to weigh upon me, especially since Hans refused to discuss his problem.

Complaining of backaches, Dr. Stocker started working only three days a week, lying down between treating patients. Because of the pain, he took medicine tablets. Because of the medicine, he got stomachaches. To reduce the stomach pain, he took other tablets. After a time, I realized the man had a prescription drug problem. He didn't want to listen to warnings from his wife, his children or me. He was sure he knew everything about medicine and could treat himself.

All in all I liked the clinic, the patients, Dr. Stocker's family and Dr. Stocker himself, who wouldn't hurt a fly but was the worst dentist I ever met. There were some patients he declared to be well whom I found to have serious, untreated periodontal disease, including cavities. Some of his patients I referred to a specialist, after discussing their cases with Zdravko and Dickie, with whom I was still in contact. Dr. Stocker even allowed me to make some fillings for his own teeth. I should have been flattered—he must have trusted me a lot—but having a dental assistant do the work of a dentist is wrong. Dr. Stocker was simply irresponsible.

SWISS DENTAL ASSISTANT UNION (SZV)
One day Dr. Stocker introduced me to one of his previous assistants, Esther Haab, who kept in touch with several other dental assistants. She told me they were in the process of setting up an organization to protect

us against our employers. Too many Swiss dentists were exploiting us in regards to our pay, insurance fees and pension plans, all things normally paid for by Swiss companies.

Before committing myself to the organization, I discussed the matter with Dr. Stocker. He was totally supportive. He always treated his employees fairly and thought other dentists should do the same.

After a few meetings of the dental assistant group, we formed a committee. Vreni Helbling was voted president, Sylvia Ehrensperger treasurer, and I was secretary to the president. We worked closely together with great enthusiasm. Within one year the Schweizerische Zahnarztgehilfinnen Verein (SZV or Swiss Dental Assistant Union) was recognized by the Swiss government. With a starting membership of 150, we held our first general assembly in May 1979 in Basel.

We waged many battles against the dentists, establishing new contracts and new regulations for them as well as us. Older dentists were especially resistant. They boycotted unionized assistants. Assistants outside the union who had trouble finding work joined us. As a result, our numbers grew and grew, and the bigger we were, the more problems the older bosses had. The younger generation of dentists became our allies, and we started having our own training sessions, held on weekends. Our assemblies were integrated into the dental congress held annually in different cities in Switzerland.

Sylvia Ehrensperger and I became friends. She was on her second marriage and had two daughters, then ages eight and ten. After our first year in the SZV, Sylvia was elected president, and I was voted secretary of the union. We held those positions until 1985, when a fatal incident changed my life.

SARDINIA

But to return to 1979... In October of that year, Hans and I went on holiday to Sardinia, my first visit to the island. We stayed in a resort called Santa Margarita de Pula. It was boring. One week of sunbathing is nice, but we had three weeks in front of us, and except for Cagliari, the capital city, there was not much to visit.

Our resort offered overnight trips to the Gennargentu Mountains, crowned by the soaring peak Monte Spada. As was becoming the norm, Hans had no interest in going, so I went with Regula, a German woman I had met on the beach. She and I were taken to the village of Barumini, a UNESCO World Heritage Site. Barumini is distinguished by its nuraghi—rotund, cone-shaped defensive towers dating to the Bronze Age. Regula and I also explored Nuoro, a village and commune known for its dramatic wall paintings. Birthplace of several renowned artists, Nuoro hosts some of the most important museums in Sardinia. In the village we had freshly made lasagna for lunch—the first and best lasagna I ever ate in my life! From Nuoro we traveled into the mountains. It took us over two hours to reach the top of Monte Spada, with its ski lift and rustic, cabin-like hotel.

We had to quickly shower and change to make our dinner appointment, hosted by the famous shepherds of Sardinia. We were driven by jeep into the high mountains, where we met up with the shepherds. They had rugged faces, and if I had been a sculptor, I definitely would have liked to sculpt some of them. The barbecue featured whole roasted piglets. The shepherds talked about the way they used to live, and we snapped a lot of pictures of them.

After dinner Regula, the other tourists and I went back to the hotel for a drink. We sat by the fireplace with our tour guides, while local people sang and played music of the region. We finally went to bed, tired and stressed, especially us single ladies. It had been exhausting trying to keep the persistent tour guides out of our bedrooms!

The next morning the guides greeted us in a sour mood, resentful that we had not succumbed to their charms the previous night. During our bus ride back to Santa Margarita, a thirty-minute tape of local music was played an excruciating eight to ten times. Following five more days of sunbathing and five days of rain, Hans and I flew back to Zürich, where our duties awaited us.

The SZV took an increasing amount of my time, but since I did my work at the clinic, Hans had no reason to complain. The second general assembly was in July 1980 in Bern. The union invited some lecturers for subjects we thought our members would be interested in. We also prepared a fashion show, and I was one of the runway models. Instead of wearing a bride's dress for the finale, I modeled a dental assistant's maternity uniform! The event was a big success, and we all went home satisfied after a weekend of hard work.

CYPRUS

Hans and I decided to vacation that fall in Cyprus. We ended up in Ayia Napa, today a well-known resort. At that time, the hotel was still under construction, but some bungalows were available, as well as a restaurant and disco. Hans and I would walk along the beach and stop at little huts where local fishermen grilled their catch and sold them to the few passing tourists.

We rented a car and gradually discovered the whole island: the Troodos Mountains; the village of Lefkara, famous for its beautiful embroidery work; Paphos, still a charming fishing village in those times, now a popular tourist destination; and Nicosia, the capital. We traveled to the island's west coast and gazed upon the very waves from which, it was said, the goddess Aphrodite arose at birth. There were good restaurants aplenty, and if we'd known this ahead of time, we wouldn't have stayed at the same hotel for two weeks but moved along constantly, sampling the cuisine everywhere. Chefs were welcoming, inviting us into the kitchen to show us how the food was prepared.

Upon returning to Switzerland, Dickie and Zdravko told me that things were not going well at Dr. H's clinic. Assistants were coming and going in rapid succession. Zdravko asked if I wanted to come back. He kept going on about it but, of course, I refused. Life with Dr. Stocker was great.

One afternoon in the spring of 1981, while working on a patient in Dr. Stocker's clinic, I received a call from Dr. H. He asked if I would come to his clinic after work; he had a proposal for me, he said. I said NO.

A few minutes later, Zdravko called and said he had told Dr. H that he wanted to work with me only. He was sick of all the Swiss assistants, whom he found to be arrogant and didn't know how to treat patients (his words, not mine). He practically begged me to come and see Dr. H. Finally, I gave in. I called Hans and told him about the call and that I would be late coming home that evening.

RETURN TO DR. HUBLER

Dr. H's clinic was situated above a small restaurant, Café Ami. I had made good time leaving Dr. Stocker's clinic, and I guessed that Dr. H was not finished with his patients yet, so I decided to have a coffee before our meeting. Erika Hochreutner, the restaurant owner, was not there. I glanced at the *Stammtisch*, a table where friends of the owner and/ or "the regulars" commonly gathered. Most people seated there I knew. One was unfamiliar—a very young woman who was dominating the conversation, talking about the clinic and its patients in excessive detail. I was drinking my cappuccino and listening without saying a word when Erika came in. She was happily surprised to see me. We sat together for a while, and then I asked her about the girl sitting at the Stammtisch, still chatting.

"Oh, that's Dr. H's trainee, she's really something else," she said. Until that moment, I had not decided what to think about the proposal Dr. H was going to make to me. But now… I asked Erika to bring the young woman to me. Erika told her that I wanted to speak to her, and after taking her time, the girl finally got up and came to my table.

She was a slim brunette with very long legs, and her face should have been pretty, but her eyes were cold and unfeeling. I told her to have a seat. She did. I said, "You're working at Praxis Dr. H, is that right?" She answered yes. "Why are you giving out all this information about patients to people at the Stammtisch?" I asked. "You know Rule Number One: Confidentiality. Never, ever talk about things going on in the clinic, and if you cannot resist retelling some interesting incident, never mention the names of the patients involved. The people at the Stammtisch all know you work with Dr. H; they know the patients you just mentioned by name, and tomorrow the whole of Seebach will know your stories."

Looking at me without shame, not even blinking an eye, she said it was none of my business. I folded my hands under my chin and replied, "Oh, yes, it *is* my business, and if I ever hear or see you giving confidential information to outsiders again, you're through."

She shrugged her shoulders and returned to the Stammtisch.

Presently I saw her talking to Erika, who told her I had once been the primary assistant at Praxis. She gave me a dirty look and continued her conversation. Erika returned to my table, and I asked for the check. She said, "This one's on the house. Are you going to see Dr. Hubler?"

I said yes, and while we were walking toward the restaurant's kitchen, we passed the Stammtisch. I wished everybody good evening, and held out my hand to the girl, saying, "May I introduce myself? My name is Müller, and I am your new boss." She had automatically taken my hand, but snatched it back. I turned around and walked away with an air that said, *I am **not** playing games.*

Now there was no turning back. I went upstairs and sat down with Dr. H. I played "hard to get," and he treated me as if he'd never had a better assistant, as if I were a long-lost daughter. That we had parted with a fight was a fact he seemed to have forgotten. But never mind. I stayed very cool and let him do the talking. When he finished, I told him what I expected from him...*if* I would come back!

In those days it was common for dentists to demand a contract, not to protect the employee, but the employer. I demanded that my conditions be in writing and signed by both dentists; I would be working mainly with Dr. Antelj, since Dr. Hubler had almost totally retired and showed up to the clinic only once a week to do administrative work and treat some patients who were practically old friends. I would also take care of all the administrative duties and training of the *Lehrtochter* (dental trainee). Both men agreed to sign.

Poor Dr. Stocker practically fell over when I told him I was resigning in April after years of undemanding work. He was understandably hurt; he thought we had become good friends. He asked me to speak to his wife, but she couldn't make me change my decision. I phoned Pia, my former trainee at Dr. H's clinic; I knew she was looking for a part-time job. I explained the situation. She liked the hours and didn't mind assisting a bad dentist. She introduced herself to Dr. Stocker, they liked each other, and she worked for him until she got married five years later to... get ready for it...a dentist!

I had forgotten what it meant to work in Dr. H's clinic, but soon I had everything under control. With Monika, the gossipy trainee, I started off very well, acting as if nothing had happened between us. Unfortunately for her, she interpreted this as weakness on my part, and as I will soon show, she was aiming for disaster.

GRACE

We had a very nice American dental hygienist named Grace, who was of German and South American background. To my eyes she was beautiful, but she thought she was too fat and was constantly dieting and exercising. She had a boyfriend named Rudy. Shortly after I returned to Dr. H's clinic, she ended that relationship and gave a month's notice, planning to return to her home on Long Island. She booked her flight and informed her parents she would see them soon.

On a Thursday evening a week after she handed in her resignation, Grace went to a disco opposite the clinic. She had a drink, saw this good-looking guy, had another drink and started to leave. Somehow she remembered seeing the fellow before and glanced back. He was heading in her direction. He asked her to dance, and that was the end of "Back to the USA," as Bruce Springsteen might have sung it.

Like Grace, Chris Jacquemai also had a string of broken relationships behind him and was fed up in general with everything and everybody. They met each other at just the right moment. They danced, laughed, and who knows what they ended up doing that night, but anyhow, they got married a year later. Chris resigned his job as an electrical engineer in a charming but remote part of Switzerland and started up his own company in Zürich, providing spare parts and programming for computers for huge companies and schools.

Grace returned to our practice, making us all very happy.

As Zdravko was the one who had insisted Dr. H rehire me, he now did his best to get me on his side, but I made it clear from the beginning that I was not going to play favorites. Zdravko never believed it; for him it was clear I liked Dr. H better, which made him jealous.

I think I can speak for Grace as well as myself when I say it was simply easier to like Dr. H. He came to the office only once a week; on that day we would have lunch together and discuss problems at the clinic, if any.

Every year, on the last workday before Christmas, Dr. H used to wait until Dr. A left. Then he would neaten his office desk, call us in and give us all little presents he had wrapped himself. When he saw how happy we were with these gifts and our Christmas bonus—an extra month's salary—tears would spring to his eyes. He'd down a few whiskies and grow emotional, telling us that his wife and children were so used to having money that they had forgotten about the meaning of Christmas and the joys one could find in the little things in life.

We could look out the window and see Dr. Antelj hiding on the other side of the street in the freezing cold, waiting until the lights in the clinic went out, torturing himself with the knowledge that he was not wanted there with us. It drove him nuts to see us coming out of the clinic, wishing each other Merry Christmas and a Happy New Year.

Grace got me involved in dieting and exercise. She really did not need either, as she was a beautiful young woman, slim, with long black wavy hair and a perfect figure. We tried every regimen around. For years, Grace had lived on Diet Coke and low-fat yogurt; I think that may be why her body didn't react as quickly as mine did to the different exercise programs we tried. I remember what happened when we signed up at an expensive new fitness club not far from the clinic. Our measurements were taken, and we were promised we'd lose at least 150 cm (about 59 inches) from our bodies. All we had to do was wear a kind of plastic outfit, lie in a futuristic-looking plastic pod, do various movements and then relax. I liked it because it meant sleeping and losing weight. Really! They had to wake me up after every session. (Grace still reminds me of it.) After six weeks my body was in good shape, my unwanted centimeters having melted away. But Grace…? Nothing. She lost only a few centimeters here and there. That's why, when the treatments were finished, we didn't repeat them. Today we still talk about it, and Grace still gets mad!

DR. ANTELJ

Winter came, and with it skiing season. Swiss dentists tended to take off Thursdays rather than Saturdays, so Zdravko proposed that he, his wife, Dickie, Grace and I go skiing on a Thursday afternoon. There would be no crowds or lines at the ski lifts. Grace and I were longtime skiers, but Dickie was a beginner. I asked my first ski instructor, Ueli, to give her a lesson. A former professional, Ueli was seventy-five years old and looked like a real Swiss mountain man, complete with beard and craggy face. He did his best to give Dickie confidence on the slopes.

I hate to admit it, but Zdravko, who was also a beginner, learned incredibly fast. He had watched how-to programs on TV, copied the moves and *z-o-o-m*, off he went, sliding down wonderfully, feet nicely together, knees a little bit bent, body straight but not too rigid. The TV instructors would have found him fascinating. Grace and I would have preferred to see him being human for once and take a few tumbles.

Dickie did her best, but most of the time she was lying in the snow instead of standing on her skis. She was getting fed up when she finally managed her way down a slope without too many problems. Ueli saw that she needed to be shored up, and said, "Dickie, that was very good. You see, you can do it!"

Zdravko, having just arrived and overhearing Ueli, sneered and replied, "What are you talking about? She's terrible! She doesn't know how to place her feet or bend her knees. No wonder all she does is fall!"

We all looked at him, horrified. Dickie burst into tears and took off her skis without a word. She never went skiing again. Zdravko's popularity level had not been high before, but after this incident Grace and I treated him like the shit he was. Following a big argument with him the next day at the clinic, Grace and I started skiing together on Thursdays. Alone.

At the age of seventy-five, Dickie divorced Zdravko. Better late than never!

SKIING AND "SPYING"

I always looked forward to my sister, her husband and daughter coming to visit during the Easter holidays. One time we decided to go sightseeing and skiing at Klewenalp, a major tourist resort in the Swiss Alps. Under a rich blue sky, we made our way up to the open country terrace of the mountains and gazed down upon all the happy skiers. I told my sister and her family that I wanted to take some photos on this brilliant day, and I left them to ski on my own.

I was so focused on one gorgeous shot after another that I was slow to realize I didn't hear people anymore, only the occasional calls of birds. I looked around... I had no idea where I was. I spotted a black flag—in Europe, the symbol for a most difficult steep *piste*, or trail. Before going up in the cable car, I had read that this *piste* was closed. And I could guess why.

I broke out in a sweat, recalling frightening stories of avalanches. What could I do? I didn't dare shout, for fear the sound would start an avalanche, so I whispered, *Help, help!* Who could hear me that way? Nobody. I don't know how many times I whispered this help, help, my cry echoing softly through the mountains.

I spotted an emergency phone beside the trail. Skiing to it carefully, I cranked the handle hard to create power and spoke into the receiver. No reply. I waited five minutes and tried again. Nothing. I now had to take off my skis, as the melted snow had become mixed with soil. I looked down from the steep hill and I slid on my rear end to the next phone and the next, throwing my skis in front of me and following them, gliding and gliding. My ass hurt. Miles and hours seemed to pass. I thought I would collapse with exhaustion.

It was not until the fourth phone, while I was quietly sobbing and turning the handle, that I heard a deep male voice asking me in Swiss German, "What are you doing there? The trail is closed!"

Relieved, I whimpered that I had been taking photographs and lost my way. The voice replied that I should continue on the trail, as the end was not much farther. If I were not down in thirty minutes, they would send a helicopter to look for me. In the meantime, my sister, growing alarmed, had notified security that I was missing.

On the final mile of the trail, the snow had completely gone, and my butt scraped muddied earth. I stood and carried my skis on my shoulders, which were by now red and blistered. Below me I saw a farmer on a tractor working in a field. Slipping, gliding and falling, utterly worn out, I headed for the man, who brought me to the cable car station. Everybody was happy that I was safe and sound, me included.

Once a year I went to Holland with some of my girlfriends. I always took friends who had never been there before. They enjoyed it, and I did too because we always visited places in my home country that were also new to me. I think in time I knew my way around the country as well as any professional tour guide. We usually took one week to cross the country, staying at friends' places along the way before arriving at my parents' home. We were undemanding guests and thanked my folks by taking them out to nice restaurants for dinners.

During one of these trips, just after our third SZV general assembly in Montreux, I had the opportunity to visit one of the four famous U-boats of the Royal Netherlands Navy. A friend of mine, Agnes, lived near the main naval base at Den Helder. She was married to a navy man named Roland. They were both Indos, of mixed Dutch and Indonesian descent; their families had repatriated to the Netherlands after Indonesia, a colony of the Netherlands for 170 years, became independent. It was a long time since I had seen these friends and their children, Jessica and Melissa, so I phoned and said we wanted to visit and perhaps stay overnight. On this trip, Grace was with me, and I knew she and Agnes would like each other.

We spent a nice evening together, and before we retired for the night, Roland promised to arrange for us to see his sub, the Tijgerhaai (tiger shark), anchored nearby. We rose early, and I secretly took along my camera. It was the first and possibly only time Grace and I would ever board a U-boat, so how could I resist?

Roland showed us the engine room, sleeping cabins, kitchen and dining room. In the command room we watched the periscope rise and fall. What I found most interesting were the narrow gangways. Walking through them I'd totally lose my sense of direction.

I was pleased with my photos, and later I proudly showed them to Dr. H. He thought I had captured some top-secret images.

"You would have made a good spy," he said.

HANS AND SCIENTOLOGY

Around this time, Hans and I moved into a larger and more luxurious apartment on the Weiherstrasse. It had a fireplace, airy rooms and a scenic view of Illnau-Effretikon. We now had a guest room, so my family could more comfortably visit me once a year. Also around this time, Hans developed an interest in model trains. He would build a set, sit in his study and run the trains over and over again.

Often after work, Hans went out for a beer with his colleagues. One co-worker, Peter Brunner, was taking evening courses at an "institute." He invited Hans to come with him, although he didn't tell Hans exactly what this place of learning was. It seemed strange to me, but Hans wanted to go. The "institute" was the Church of Scientology, founded in California by L. Ron Hubbard. Apparently, this group worked by demanding lots of money from you and making you take courses until you were "clean," meaning free of troubles. In Switzerland there was already a number of lawsuits brought against Scientology, and the government warned the public to stay away. Hans gave this cult some money, but I don't know how involved he got because he kept quiet about it. I only know that Peter's wife, who became "clean" after "graduating" from her courses in California, did not react as a "clean" person should after she discovered in Peter's car ladies' underwear that was not hers.

MONIKA

Back at the office, the trainee, sixteen-year-old Monika, was becoming a problem. She'd show up to work late, still half asleep and dressed in dirty jeans. One morning, when Dr. Antelj called her to assist him with a patient, she had only just got into the jacket of her uniform when she ran to his side. He saw what she was wearing below the jacket and shouted, "I told you, no jeans in the clinic. Take those off!"

She looked at him, and while I was standing behind him I had trouble keeping a straight face because she started to take off her pants in front of him and the patient. Neither of them could believe their eyes. When she'd almost finished, standing there in her long bare legs, Zdravko recovered from his shock and shouted, "Get out of here, I never want to see you in this room again. Get out!"

Furious, Dr. Antelj refused to work with her from then on. That meant my duties suddenly doubled, and Monika was virtually jobless. She worked only on the day when Dr. Hubler came in. Monika respected Dr. H and feared making mistakes in front of him. It took some weeks before I discovered that every time before she entered his room, she stepped into the bathroom first. When I asked her about it, she said, "I need to smoke a cigarette to calm down."

Inhaling this "cigarette" made her eyes look strange. I don't think I need to tell you what she was smoking.

A lot of men started phoning the office; she would run to be the first on the phone. I became suspicious and started listening in on her conversations. Monika caught on and tried to speak in some kind of code. Learning that she was flunking at school, and trying to talk to her without result, I contacted her mother and asked to see her.

We met on a Thursday afternoon, my day off. The poor woman burst into tears. It seemed there were big problems at home. Monika often stayed out late or vanished from her room after saying goodnight. She claimed to be a babysitter, and had a "special friend" who employed her several times a week. The mother didn't know this friend and suspected she had a bad influence on Monika. I promised the mother that I would speak to her daughter, and she promised to do the same.

Unfortunately, Monika again turned a deaf ear. She became overly friendly with some of our male patients. Thankfully, she made a misstep. She had given her business card to one of our older patients, a man named Töndury who had given her the impression that he liked her. She had forgotten to check his file; if she had, she would have learned that Dr. Töndury was one of Switzerland's most respected attorneys, one of our most faithful patients and a close friend of Dr. Hubler's. Töndury gave Monika's business card to Dr. H, and he and Dr. A hired a private investigator. I was not informed about this, but I had told Dr. H that I suspected Monika had a venereal disease, and I refused to use the main bathroom. I had also told him I thought she was a drug addict and earning money as a call girl. Every day she wore new clothes, expensive leather pants and jackets that were impossible on an income generated from babysitting and being a trainee at our clinic.

Finally, Dr. H told me to call the parents for a meeting with Monika present. It was all very dramatic, especially when the P.I. submitted the evidence, including photographs. There was more than enough justification to meet Swiss legal requirements to fire a *Lehrtochter* (Trainee). Monika, alias Samantha, was the sole owner of a massage parlor in Niederdorf, which was the red light district in Zürich. She had been inviting all Dr. H's male patients to visit her. Dr. Hubler's name and telephone number were actually printed on her business card! Monika was asked to roll up her sleeves. Her father almost had a heart attack when he saw the needle scars on her arms. Monika broke down and cried. The parents took her away, and we never heard from her again.

I told Dr. H that I refused to train any more dental assistants. I preferred to be left in peace, working on my own, rather than constantly checking on and controlling someone else. He agreed to this.

TRIPS TO FRANCE AND FLORENCE
In 1982 I was so busy with the clinic and union meetings (the fourth annual meeting of the SZV was in Chur) that Hans and I didn't have time for any extended trips, although on long weekends we sometimes went to Tessin, the Italian region of Switzerland, where we camped beside Lake Astano. In 1983 we made up for that lack of vacation by taking a long trip through France. I planned the whole thing: we would stay overnight at ten different locales. We bought a tent big enough to sleep eight, the easy blow-up kind the military uses in the Alps of Switzerland.

This was Hans's first time camping, and he figured a roomy tent would be more comfortable.

We went straight to Paris, then north to Normandy, exploring the historic beaches of World War II. From there we headed west along the coast to Brittany, down to Mont Saint-Michel, the storied island featured in the French language textbook of my childhood. Next we ventured into vineyard country, exploring Saint-Émilion. We stopped at beautiful Biarritz, crossing back over the Pyrenees, followed by a visit to Lourdes. Lourdes really shocked me. It was overrun by souvenir shops, just a moneymaking place. I felt no spirituality in it at all. I was reminded of the story in the New Testament when Jesus finds the priests using the temple as a market and throws them all out. Lourdes needed a Jesus.

We stayed a week at a small village near St. Tropez, where we rented a villa ten meters (about thirty feet) from the beach. Hans, saying he felt tired and unwell, stayed behind there while I drove alone to visit Nice and St. Tropez. When I returned I found Hans alone with a woman who had been staying with a group of young people in the villa next to ours. I assumed it had been an innocent encounter until I started hearing rumors that Hans was f---ing other women while I was doing the shopping or cooking in the tent. He denied everything, but I could see he was lying, and I was disgusted. I now remembered Sardinia and our other holiday destinations when he didn't want to accompany me on my excursions.

Our drive back to Switzerland took us through Monaco, snow-covered Grenoble and Geneva, but the chill in our relationship kept me from enjoying the scenery. The trip had not brought Hans and me any closer. In fact, we were now even farther apart. I threw myself into my work, both for the clinic and the union.

Grace and I unexpectedly had a week off, so we decided to travel to Florence by train. We slept in a couchette (a first for me) and the next day we arrived in this beautiful city. Everything in Florence was gigantic, the cathedral, the houses. It was almost impossible to capture an entire building in a single photo. We saw the famous Ponte Vecchio, Michelangelo's *David* and many palazzos adorned with famous paintings.

We took a side trip to Pisa and had our photos taken beside the legendary tower. Time flew, and soon we returned to Zürich to our husbands.

HANS AND DEPRESSION

Hans was very private and didn't really like to discuss what went on in his life before meeting me. From his sisters I learned that he had lived and worked in South Africa for many years. There he met and lived for a time with a black woman. She came with Hans to Switzerland, but in those days apartheid wasn't limited to South Africa. Ostracism took its toll on both of them, and she returned to Africa. It was only many years later that I realized how much he must have loved her, and that I was merely a poor replacement.

We worked full time and lived a comfortable life, but Hans became more and more introverted. Often when I came home from work I would find him in his study, sitting and staring into space. When I would ask what he was thinking about, he would actually reply, "Nothing."

Sometimes I wondered if the Hans I had married was not the real Hans; if that earlier self had been only a performance of some kind, and this withdrawn person was the real him. I had no experience with depression, so I didn't understand his transformation. I wasn't alarmed, just confused.

It took a brush with death to make me see that I meant nothing to him.

I had been working at the clinic five and a half days a week. On a Saturday at noon, I left Praxis and took the highway, headed for home in Effretikon. A woman driving in front of me kept picking up music cassettes from the passenger seat and looking at them instead of keeping her eye on traffic. I thought, *I have to get past that lady, or I'm going to be in trouble*. I passed her quickly, than checked my rearview mirror. I guess she'd found the cassette she'd been looking for because her eyes were on the road again. The woman stepped on the gas and overtook me. We were now driving at 120 kph (about 75 mph). She slowed down again, perhaps deciding she'd put in the wrong tape, and starting flipping through her collection. Her erratic driving unnerved me, so I tried to pass her. Suddenly she pulled to the left where I was, forcing me into the median rail. I tried to break gently, knowing a hard brake could flip the car, but the wheels spun wildly, and I turned full circle twice. *Wham.* A Mercedes rear-ended me at full speed, totaling my car.

Miraculously, I was unharmed, as was the owner of the Mercedes, whose car could still run. Oncoming drivers stopped and offered help. One witness, who had noted the license plate of the erratic driver, called the police. When they arrived I was in such shock I could hardly speak, so we agreed that the police, the owner of the Mercedes, and my husband and I would meet at Mövenpick restaurant on the highway just after the exit to my village.

The Mercedes owner gave me a lift home. I left him waiting in the car while I ran in to get Hans. He was napping. I woke him, breathlessly told him what had happened, and asked him to join me at the restaurant to make a statement. He looked at me with disinterest and said no, I should deal with it myself. I looked at him and my blood went ice cold. I left him and handled the matter alone. Angels had been watching over me…there's no other explanation for how I could have stepped out alive from that crumpled car…but my husband didn't care what happened to me. All my affection for him vanished.

Still, I wasn't ready to file for divorce. It was my second marriage, so I was determined to hang on. Hans and I became more acquaintances than lovers, hardworking Swiss people who lived together, nothing more, nothing less.

During the Easter holidays of 1985, my friend Agnes came to visit us with her two pre-teen girls. As I mentioned earlier, Agnes was of Indonesian background; she and her children were dark-skinned and beautiful. The girls, genuinely liking Hans, would hug him when he came home from work. I saw this irritated him, and I couldn't understand why. He would clean the house obsessively, even vacuuming the balcony. When I pointed out that the house was already clean, he wouldn't speak to me. He started ignoring the children, spending most of his time in his study. I don't believe Agnes and her kids ever realized what was going on, thank goodness. When they returned to Holland, I tried to talk with Hans about his behavior, asking him to please explain himself. He only pulled back from me more. Each night we were strangers lying in bed next to each other.

"DAYS OF GRACE":
LONG ISLAND AND CALIFORNIA

My husband's depression increasingly left me unable to laugh or feel happiness. Grace came to the rescue. When her husband's business kept him too busy to spend the summer holidays with her at her parents' house in Brookhaven, Long Island, she invited me to come with her. I had an especially long vacation ahead of me, as Dr. H had sold the clinic and Dr. A was preparing to enter a new partnership with one of Dr. H's old friends, a dentist/artist named Dr. Jean Hasler who ran a dental clinic with two other partners on Grossmünster Platz in Zürich. Dr. A would not need my services for a few weeks.

I had a great time with Grace. We arrived at Kennedy Airport, where her family collected us in a limousine. We explored Long Island with her sisters, sailed a boat with her father, lolled on the beach, saw *Cats* the musical, had a scrumptious dinner in New York City, and listened to Bruce Springsteen while driving the car all over Long Island. In the warm embrace of Grace's family, I became my old self again, and my decision became clear: I would leave Hans.

At this time, when my emotions were so often running high, something wonderfully funny happened that I've never forgotten. One day Grace and I took an extremely small ferry to Fire Island. On the trip we had a long, loud discussion about intimate stuff. Well, why not? We didn't need to worry about anyone overhearing us, as we were speaking Swiss German. Who on earth speaks Swiss German except the Swiss? Even any eavesdropping German tourists would have difficulty understanding us. So we spoke freely about our likes and dislikes regarding sex. I don't remember how long the trip lasted, but I'll never forget that just as an elderly lady prepared to disembark, she turned around and said in Swiss German, "Wiederluege miteinand" (Goodbye to you both). Grace and I looked at each other and broke into hysterical giggles like a pair of teenage girls.

From Long Island Grace and I flew to the San Diego airport. We had arranged to meet the ninety-six-year-old mother of a dentist in Zürich who was formerly Grace's boss. It was the mother's last wish to see the Native Americans of the Southwest. We had rented a van in which *Oma* (Grandmother) could sit comfortably in the back, using the whole seat as a kind of bed. We collected Oma and her granddaughter Vreni from the airport.

The trip was exceptional. We had not made any reservations, and friends in Switzerland had told us we would have big problems getting hotels in high season. We believed in our luck. From San Diego we drove to Gila Bend, then headed for Phoenix, Grace and I taking turns driving. It was getting late and we wanted to be in Phoenix before dark to find a hotel. The speed limit was 50 mph and I drove for sure 60. Suddenly, Grace said, "Slow down, Mer, there's police on the other side of the road." Of course, I didn't brake, but only gradually reduced my speed.

The police car turned on the two-lane road and came after us, siren wailing, as if we were criminals. I stopped, the police car stopped, and a policeman got out and walked toward our van. Before I could roll down the window, Grace said, "Mer, turn on all your charm." The policeman looked inside the car and then at me. I responded with a sunny but strategically puzzled expression. He asked for my driver's license. He looked at the side that indicated my age, so with a smile I said, "Please look at the other side. That's where my photo is. My age doesn't matter." His expression didn't change. He asked if I knew how fast I was going. I looked at him and, waving my hands like question marks, hazarded a guess of fifty. He again looked at me and asked where we were going that we were in such a hurry. I replied that Oma was tired, and we needed to find a hotel in Phoenix before dark. He gave me back my license and told me to follow him. My heart was hammering; we all thought he was leading us to the police station to book us. Once in Phoenix, he stopped and told us that just around the corner there was a hotel with rooms ready for us. We thanked him as he left us with a smile.

The next day we went to Montezuma Castle National Monument, north of Phoenix. Then we drove through Navajo territory and found a motel at the Grand Canyon. Passing through the Navajo Nation made us sad; we all realized that the people who had lived here first had gotten a raw deal from the newcomers from England and Europe. From the vast lands they had roamed before, the Navajo now had to survive as a tribe confined to a desert. Very sad.

We flew over the Grand Canyon in a helicopter, which offered impressive views. It was a wonderful experience driving though Bryce Canyon and Goosenecks State Park…beholding the mighty Colorado River…finally arriving atop a mountain at midnight to gaze upon Las Vegas in the distance, bright as a star.

As colorful as Las Vegas was at night, during the day it was depressing. We experienced the casino and the wedding chapel. We were lucky with the hotel: it was the cheapest we had during the whole trip, and also one of the nicest. Still, we didn't care to spend more than twenty-four hours in the city.

We decided to head for Death Valley, but not before checking the car. At least, that was our intention, but we could not find the water tank, and what was more disturbing, we couldn't find the engine! We looked around and around until a truck driver came up to us and asked if we needed help. I looked at him and said that we couldn't find the water tank. He grinned and said, "Ladies, are you coming from another planet, or were you just always riding bicycles?" Then he opened the driver's side door, lifted the seat, and there was the engine. Relieved, we filled up, thanked the trucker and drove off.

Death Valley was really death, desert and more desert. We were happy that we didn't get stuck and had checked the car before entering the endless, dry terrain. Arriving in Los Angeles Grace and I dropped Oma and Vreni at the airport, concluding what we all agreed was a beautiful trip.

From there Grace and I went to San Francisco. Mark Twain supposedly said, "The coldest winter I ever saw was the summer I spent in San Francisco." This sure was true for us. We had intended to explore the city for several days, but because we were shivering and "longing" for Long Island, we changed our flight and returned two days early to Brookhaven.

As my visit drew to a close, our conversations became somber. Grace advised me to look after my finances, as I had already lost everything once before in my life. I told her not to worry; my husband was not that kind of man. The last night I spent with Grace and her friends, we made a point of not discussing Hans. However, the mood failed to lighten, for everyone talked about some gruesome news: a man in a neighboring village had suddenly murdered his entire family, and no one could understand the motive...

HANS AND MADNESS

I flew back to Switzerland, and Hans picked me up from the airport. We had only just begun the drive home when he excitedly told me he wanted to buy me my dream car, a Mercedes convertible. I was surprised and told him I didn't need it; we each had a car, and that was enough. I stepped inside our apartment and was greeted by the sweet scent of floral bouquets. Years ago I might have loved coming home to flowers, but on this day they only made me uncomfortable. I also had an odd feeling when I put my dirty clothes in the hamper and didn't see any of Hans's clothes there. However, I was too tired to spend any time thinking about anything Hans had said or done that night. I went to bed, taking Seppie, the cat, with me.

I had a habit of sleeping with my head under the blankets. I'm not sure if it was my subconscious mind or my guardian angel that woke me when Hans came into the room and told Seppie to get out, but I folded back the blankets with both hands to see what was going on, and this action saved my life. Hans had looped a belt from a suitcase around my neck and was pulling with all his might to strangle me. My hands, caught within the belt, thrashed to keep it from pressing my throat. Hans's face and mine were only inches apart. I could see the madness in his eyes—he had no clue what he was doing. All I could think about was the story I had heard before leaving Long Island: a man kills his entire family. *Why?* Fighting my own crazy thoughts, knowing I had to get him off me, I started to talk, talk, talk, telling him how much I loved him, how we had to get through this horrible crisis together, we had to go to a marriage counselor, and on and on.

I don't remember all I said or for how long, but slowly the madness disappeared from his eyes, and he started crying. He was afraid I was going to go to the police. I told him, no, we have to solve this problem, and we will do this together. In the meantime my thoughts were running amok. How could I escape without him catching me? I didn't want to let on that I was frightened as hell.

Hans left the bedroom, sobbing. I got up and pretended that everything was normal. I prepared something for us to eat and we ate it, my thoughts awhirl the whole time. I finished emptying my suitcase and readied the laundry. This is when I reconfirmed that Hans had no laundry at all; since he was planning to kill us both, he had thrown all his dirty clothes in the garbage.

Hans wouldn't allow me to go to the laundry room, which was in the basement of the apartment building. My mind raced in circles as I tried to think how to get out of the apartment. Jumping off the balcony was not a good idea, as we lived on the top floor.

Suddenly, I got an idea.

It was my custom to phone the people I had visited when I returned home from a trip to Holland or elsewhere out of the country. That's why Hans wasn't suspicious when I told him I wanted to call Grace. I tried Grace several times but couldn't reach her. Assuming she was at the beach, I called her brother's friend Mark, who owned a real estate firm in Bellport. When he answered the phone, I said,

"Hi, Grace! This is Marilyn."

"Marilyn? But…this is Mark. You're not talking to Grace."

"I know, Grace! I just wanted you to know I arrived home, and I loved my time at your parents' house. And say, do you remember the story you told last night about that man and his family? It's the same here… Thanks again so much to you and your family for having me. Bye!"

Mark called around to find Grace. When he finally reached her at the beach house, he conveyed the strange conversation he had with me. She called my boss, Dr. A. It was late at night, but Dr. A understood the seriousness of the matter and phoned my home. Hans answered. Zdravko asked if I had arrived back from the US, and if so he needed my help at once with the setup of the new clinic. Hans gave me the phone. Zdravko asked me if I could remain safely with Hans through the night, and without giving myself away, I answered only with "yes" or "no" so that Hans would not be suspicious.

Of course, I never closed an eye that night. I kept a thousand percent alert, telling Hans I was unable to sleep because of jetlag. I counted the hours until it was finally seven in the morning, dressed myself, went to my car, and as I prepared to drive off, Hans came downstairs to say goodbye to me.

It was the last time I would see him alive.

I went straight to the home of Zdravko and Dickie. We phoned a psychologist who handles emergencies. He told us that people who say they will kill themselves never do, and therefore he wouldn't help us. I spoke to my husband's doctor, who agreed that Hans was depressed, but that he would never kill himself. I spoke to the parish priest, who told me that he didn't know Hans. I didn't know whom else I could reach out to, but I did know one thing: I would not go back to that apartment.

For a great part of her life, Dickie had been a nurse specializing in psychiatric medicine. After I had recovered a bit from the shock and stopped crying, she told me to call Hans and tell him I wasn't coming back. I put the phone on speaker, so Zdravko and Dickie could hear every word. Hans asked me where I was; I told him I was in a hotel and wasn't coming back because I was too scared. He begged me to come home, promising me the moon and the stars if I would. All the time Dickie looked into my eyes and shook her head, *No, no, no.* Dickie saved my life that day. If she hadn't been there, I would have returned to Hans.

He asked which hotel I was at; I told him I was too frightened to tell him. He went quiet a while and then said OK, all right; he would take some time off and go to Tessin, our favorite camping spot. He'd call me when he got back.

We said goodbye.

The next morning I went to work at the new clinic at Grossmünster Platz. There was a lot to do, as we were opening the following week. Questions assaulted my mind. I remembered at the airport Hans telling me he wanted to buy a Mercedes. Why? That was so unlike him. He had become very stingy over the years, refusing even to take some inexpensive trips with me, always saving, saving for the future. We both made good money, so I wasn't really happy with all this saving. I remembered Grace's warnings about finances. Could she know Hans better than I did?

A couple of days passed. I called the bank and asked a teller and another bank employee how much was in our account. They refused to tell me, and said I had to ask in person. I reminded them that I was working in Zürich. (The bank was near our home in Effretikon, a considerable distance away.) I asked them, if they wouldn't discuss exact figures with me, could they at least tell me if half the original amount was still there.

This they were willing to tell me. The answer was *No.*

I looked at Zdravko and said,

"I have to go home. Hans has killed himself."

Zdravko wouldn't believe it. He advised me to call Hans's former co-worker and best friend Hans Andretto (he'd been one of our wedding witnesses, you may remember) and ask him to go with me to the apartment and check it out. Hans's friend was surprised to hear such a story from me, but he immediately agreed to come. I picked him up, and when we arrived at my apartment building, I gave him the key to our apartment, as Zdravko had advised me not to go myself but to ask Hans Andretto to go and check the door.

My neighbor had just come home from shopping. She looked at me and said, "Hey, Hans told me last week that you would arrive this week. I remember you telling me you would return last week, and I came with flowers to welcome you back, but Hans told me, no, I was mistaken. Something strange, though. He has left the radio on, it's really loud. Also, I took Seppie. He was meowing in front of your door and seemed very hungry, so I fed him."

At that moment Hans Andretto came back down the stairs from our apartment. He told me the door was locked from the inside, and he couldn't open it. I looked at him. Then I looked at the neighbor and asked her if I could use her phone to call the police and tell them my husband had killed himself. Both Hans Andretto and the woman looked at me in disbelief.

Even today I don't know how I stayed so calm; I managed everything as if it were happening to somebody else. I am always at my best in a crisis, but this was MY crisis. (Inevitably, I did at last react, experiencing an emotional collapse three years later.)

We entered the woman's apartment. I called the police and told them what was running through my mind. It seemed ages, but in reality it was only five or ten minutes before two policemen arrived with tools to break open the door. I waited in my neighbor's place until they came back. Again, it seemed ages. When they finally returned, my heart was in my throat. They looked at me, and although they said nothing, I knew I'd been right. I wasn't allowed into the apartment; the police asked the neighbor if she were willing to identify my husband, as they needed a witness. The poor woman was unable to work for three months afterward, the sight was so shocking to her.

A few days later at the police station, I was told that Hans had first taken sleeping pills. Then he had slit his wrists. Finally, he had hung himself on the hinges of the bedroom door with a wire so thin it had sliced his throat. They also told me that he had prepared everything very carefully: the flowers, his throwing away all his clothes, telling the neighbor I would not be back until next week. They found the package of sleeping pills, the razors and additional wire all in the same place. The night that he tried to kill me should have been our last night alive: August 30, 1985.

Thank God, Dickie was there to protect me. Without Dickie and Zdravko, I don't know how I would have managed to get through this period. I returned to the apartment just once, to empty it. I gave most of our things away, as I could not live with the memories they evoked. Once again I was broke, my bank account empty. Today, I still have no clue where the money went.

The church service was quiet with only family and close friends. I asked that a recording be played of Hans's favorite song, *Mother*, performed by Barbra Streisand. It seems odd now that he would like that song so much, because Hans had a strange relationship with his parents. He told me he hated them for bringing him into this world; he had never asked to be born. He also said that poor people shouldn't be allowed to have children. Hans had told me that living was hell, and death was heaven. Unfortunately, I had never taken him seriously.

I recall a time when the telephone rang in the middle of the night. Hans picked up the receiver, listened, gave a brief response and came back to bed. I asked him who had called. He turned his back to me and said, *My dad has just died.* I jumped up and said that we had to go at once to his family's home in Rheineck. He replied no, it can wait; we can go in the morning.

Why should he act that way?

Hans had always told me that his ashes should be dumped in the slums of Lourenço Marques (now Maputo) in Mozambique. I never understood why until after his death, when I met with two of his friends from his earlier days. They told me that back when they and Hans lived in South Africa, on weekends they would go to the shantytowns of Mozambique and have sex with child prostitutes. That alone might have made Hans wish for burial in the slums. It certainly explained to me why the presence of my friend Agnes and her dark-skinned children in our home brought back such disturbing memories for him. But there was more.

Hans and his friends had to drive many hours between Johannesburg, South Africa, and Mozambique. One time, when they had all been drinking, Hans got behind the wheel, even though he didn't have a driver's license. While the others slept, he lost control of the car and crashed it, killing one of his friends. To carry this knowledge with him through his life must have been a horrendous burden.

I suppose what Hans's old friends told me about his demons should have made it easier for me to get over the fact that he had killed himself, but I still felt very sad. Sad and confused. His past was no excuse or explanation for why he was unfaithful to me throughout our marriage.

I had been married for ten years to a man I did not know at all.

I got in touch with attorney Töndury and mentioned the fact that I wanted to use my maiden name again. In May 1986 he brought me the necessary documents, which he had prepared for me at no charge. I was Frau Wouters again.

THE SCATTERING OF ASHES

Although it had been Hans's wish, I couldn't bear the thought of scattering his ashes in Maputo. Instead I flew with them to the Seychelles, where we had been happy during our honeymoon. I had to obtain special permission to take the ashes outside the country, so it wasn't until two months after his death that I finally flew to Mahé.

I arrived early in the morning and took a taxi to the Beau Vallon Bay Hotel. I briefly entered the lobby, stepped out and walked along the beach for about fifteen minutes, strewing the ashes among huge black rocks at seaside, crying and thinking about Hans and my life to come. After an hour or so I dried my tears, gave a weak smile to people passing, and lay on the beach. I realized I didn't know what to do with myself. I walked back to the hotel lobby, had a soft drink and looked out the window, watching the taxis come and go. Although my flight wasn't due to depart until midnight, I decided to return to the airport.

I went to the taxi stand, got into a cab and told the driver to take me to the airport. He said it was much too early. I told him I knew that, but I wanted to leave now. He turned around, looked me in the eyes and said, *You want fucky fucky?* Shocked, I started crying again and said I had just buried my husband and wanted to leave. The driver, genuinely embarrassed, told me he assumed I had come to the Seychelles for sex; many white women, he insisted, especially the Germans, come for that purpose. I told him I wasn't German and wanted to get out of his taxi. He apologetically asked me to stay, and said he would show me the Seychelles as no tourist had ever seen it. It was around 2 P.M., and I still had ten hours before my flight. I looked at him. He honestly seemed to regret his previous words, so I agreed.

We drove around to view stunning beaches, tea plantations, mountains and waterfalls. We also stopped to see his family. At that time there were few tourists on the island of Mahé, so I felt fortunate to have had this experience. Around 8 P.M. I asked him to find a good restaurant for dinner. He stopped in front of a local restaurant. I asked him to join me for what became a memorable meal. I was given a sample of everything on the menu, and the friendly chef joined our table. After two hours I paid the bill, and the cab driver and I left for the airport.

When we arrived, I asked how much I owed him. He shook my hand and wished me a good flight, saying, "You owe me nothing. I feel very ashamed about what I first said to you. I'm happy I could give you a beautiful day in the Seychelles." We embraced and I left. What had started in grief had ended with a smile.

MAURO

After Hans's death, I lived with Dickie and Zdravko for a short time while looking for a new apartment. My friend Sylvia lived in Zürich, and as it happened, the apartment next to hers became vacant, so I moved in immediately. She was long divorced from her ex-husband Mauro, an Italian wine salesman and singer, but he kept in close contact with their children, Sabrina and Melissa. The girls often visited me in my apartment, and when they did, Mauro would phone them there. During one of these calls, Sabrina told Mauro I was spending too much time alone, and wouldn't he take me out? He invited me to see him perform that evening in Winterthur. I dressed up and drove to his street, where he was standing on the sidewalk. He was of medium height, dark-haired, with dark brown eyes behind John Lennon-style glasses. His cheeks dimpled when he smiled, and he smiled at the sight of me. We looked at each other and it "clicked."

Mauro Ilario Bandinu became one of the most important people in my life. Although I'm writing relatively little about him here, the influence he had on my life was immense. He taught me to *see*, he taught me to *live*, and he enjoyed life to the fullest. He taught me that it is the little things that matter. He showed me how to find the beauty in nature during every season of the year. In winter, we shared long cross-country ski tours; in summer we walked up the Üetliberg, Zürich's landmark mountain, which offers breathtaking views of the city and its namesake lake. Mauro taught me that I could be and do anything, and that our love was a gift that we should not take for granted. I yearned to leap over the mourning period and leave it far behind. What better way to do that than jump into a new relationship? I fell deeply in love with Mauro; he was a very charming man.

Mauro had sung professionally for Radio Svizzera Italiana with the orchestra of Mario Robbiani and now performed weekends with a band called Bagatelle. To my ears, he sounded like Frank Sinatra with a touch of Joe Cocker. From the stage he would sing to me, making me feel very special.

During the day he worked in the wine business, driving cross-country through the most scenic parts of Switzerland. Sometimes I would meet up with him for a weekend when he had a wine tasting. I especially liked traveling to the French region of Switzerland around Lausanne, where there were many lush vineyards. I bought a new car, a white Mazda RX-7, in which we drove to Italy to visit his family. Everyone warned us not to take that car, advising us to use Mauro's instead, as Italy is famous for car theft. If crooks didn't outright steal the car, they'd dismantle parts they were able to sell. I told everybody there were no Mazda RX-7s in Italy, so it was of no use to steal parts! I was correct: Mauro took very good care of the little *bijou*, and everywhere we went people complimented us on it, wanting to touch it, drive it, be photographed in it, but definitely nobody thought of stealing it.

Mauro was the "star" at my parents' fortieth wedding anniversary. We sang and danced together in an event the village would never forget. Everybody loved him.

Unhappy that I now dated her ex-husband, Sylvia blew up at me during a one-sided argument. I decided it was time to move out of the next-door apartment. I settled into an apartment in Mauro's block, on the Burstwiesenstrasse in Zürich.

My parents came to visit. They slept at my place during the night, and most days while Mauro and I were at work they spent in his ground floor apartment, enjoying its small garden. One evening I came home and I found them both wearing grumpy faces. I asked what was the matter; neither would explain. Then Mauro returned and finally it came out: while going through Mauro's videos, searching for a film to watch, my father had discovered some soft porn, which he of course wanted to see. My mother, not really knowing what was going on (after forty years of marriage) reluctantly agreed to watch it with him. For my father, it was like discovering the moon: he'd never known that foreplay existed, nor did my mom. She had never liked sex, seeing it as a duty to one's husband, a common attitude at that time. Mom felt shy and upset and ashamed to look at it, while my father became very enthusiastic and wanted to put it all into immediate "practice." My mother absolutely refused. They fought, and Mauro and I found them in a silent standoff. I looked at mom and dad both and sat with them after dinner and gave them a lecture in sexual education. I told them when two people love each other there is nothing to be ashamed of, as long as they both enjoy it. We all went for a long walk in the Üetliberg forest before each of us went to his or her own bed.

The next day Mauro and I went to work as always, but when we returned home the reception was quite different from before: both my parents wore big smiles. They had slept in and tried what they had seen the day before on the video. It was a big success, and everybody was happy.

It was important for Mauro that I looked good. It made him proud to be seen with me. After two years of looking like Jane Fonda, however, I got fed up and wanted to change my image. I went into town to the first hairdresser I found and told the person at the entrance desk that I wanted my hair to be cut very short. She looked at me and advised I try a medium cut first. I left and talked to other hairdressers, but couldn't find any willing to make such a drastic cut. They were all afraid I would be disappointed and would blame them. Finally, I took a pair of scissors and cut a big lump of my hair myself. Now there was no reason to refuse. I always was and always will be a person who, when I decide something, after thinking long upon the pros and cons, will act on my decision. In this case, my decision had been to cut my hair short. I was very happy with the results: I looked like a porcupine, my hair no longer than two centimeters long. It felt great!

It was Monday and rehearsal time for Bagatelle, which met in its practice space, a double-padded basement in the center of Zürich. All the band members were there except Mauro. When I opened the double-padded door, everyone looked at me with questioning eyes, until my friend Nicole, the wife of Kurt, the organ player, started laughing.

"Oh my God, is it you? You look so *herzig* (cute)! OMG, what will Mauro say!"

Everybody admired my new extreme hairstyle, and Nicole and I finally sat down to listen to the band rehearse. We kept waiting for Mauro, who was late, as usual. The door opened again and Mauro stepped in. He looked around and asked Nicole, "Is the Chichotella not here yet?" I was sitting next to Nicole, and he had overlooked me completely. She pointed her finger at me. Mauro looked, looked again and started laughing, reaching over to rub his hand over my head and kiss me. He made it very clear before he picked up the mike to sing that he loved my new hairstyle.

America was Mauro's biggest dream. It was told in his family that the brother of his great-grandfather, for a reason nobody knows, left

Sardinia and shipped himself on a boat to America, in those times still the country where dreams came true. Nobody knew what happened to him, only that he ended up in Boston and was never heard from again. Mauro had told me this story many times, so when he and I decided to go to the USA the following summer, I had enough information ahead of time to secretly track down the great-uncle's descendants.

There are many Bandinus and Bandinis in the Boston area, and I had to phone them all. These calls were placed on evenings when Mauro was with clients; his job required him to try and sell his Italian wines to restaurant owners, which often meant he dined out. Good for me! I started with the Bandinus, as Bandinu was the original name. No success. I continued with the Bandinis. It took me about four days until I had a "bite." I had now extended my search to cities around Boston. A lady answered the phone, and I asked her if she had a great-grandfather who had come from Sardinia. I told her I was calling from Switzerland and was looking for the family of my boyfriend. She asked me to call back in an hour. Her father would be home then, and he would be able to answer all my questions.

My heart was pounding, and the hour of waiting seemed terribly long. When at last I called, a man answered and told me that his name was Albert Bandini. I asked him the same questions I had put to his daughter. He replied yes, his great-grandfather's name was Alberto Bandinu, he arrived by boat, and after a few years he met his great-grandmother, also Italian. Alberto Bandinu never spoke Italian; what's more, from the moment he set foot on American soil, he never wanted to talk about his family back in Italy.

I told Albert Bandini that Mauro and I were planning a trip to America and that it would be a wonderful surprise for Mauro if we could visit him and his family. I also told him I'd like to keep it a secret as long as possible.

I continued to plan the vacation. New York City—Niagara Falls—Boston (which included Lexington)—Long Island––Washington—Nashville—New Orleans—Napa Valley and San Francisco. I remember telling Karin, my colleague at the clinic, "Somehow I have a strange feeling, as if this were our last vacation together."

Time came to leave on this grand tour; it was difficult to keep my secret to myself. We arrived in NYC, where we went to the Empire State Building and the Statue of Liberty on Liberty Island. In the evenings we had great food at the restaurants in Little Italy. Mauro would ask the owners to visit his table, where after they both spoke Italian. This would result in fabulous food that Mauro requested but was not on the menu, as well as a Montepulciano d'Abruzzo, a wonderful red wine from the region of Abruzzo. The owners loved Mauro, we were fussed over, and instead of just us two at the table we were now three, including the owner, all for a reduced price. We would mostly conclude this culinary treat at midnight, an hour when Mauro was at his best, for he would always find places where he was able to sing.

The next day we flew to Niagara, where we were picked up by a limousine with a chauffeur of Italian descent and driven to a hotel with a Niagara Falls view. While Mauro and I were strolling on the promenade, I suddenly had the feeling again that I needed to make the most of this vacation, as I was going to lose him. I knew with sudden certainty that after the summer holiday, our relationship would be over. I was shocked. Why this revelation now? I kept it to myself but was quiet the whole afternoon. Mauro never noticed...he was too happy realizing his American dream.

At Niagara there was a pavilion where people could give a kind of karaoke performance that would be recorded and five minutes later played for everyone to hear. Of course, Mauro was in his element! We met a man from Canada who also was a very good singer, and an excited audience soon gathered around them. Heaven for Mauro! I had to finally pull him away to get dinner before all the restaurants closed.

The next day we flew back to NYC where a rental car was waiting for us. Now came the part of our trip that was unknown to Mauro. He kept asking where we were going, but I wouldn't reveal my secret.

I drove him to Lexington and found the street where the Bandinis lived. I parked in front of the house with the number I was given. As we got out of the car, the whole family came outside, and I introduced

Mauro to his long-lost family. The surprise was tremendous—he couldn't believe his eyes! He kissed and hugged every family member, he and Alberto shedding tears.

We went inside the home, where we were treated to coffee and pastries and asked many questions, while we asked questions back. For dinner they took us to a beautiful restaurant where the food was very American. The daughters in the meantime had arranged a hotel room for us, as they did not want us to leave yet. After we came home from dinner, Albert and Mauro sat in the kitchen and tried to retrace the great-grandfather's steps. Their conversation continued into the early hours of the next day. Mauro's English was not that good, and he wanted to ask and tell so much in so short a period of time that I found it almost overwhelming to translate. I recorded the encounter, but I'm sorry to say I have since lost the videotape. Without a doubt, the family meeting in Lexington was a huge success and the high point of Mauro's vacation.

We traveled from there to Boston, staying one night. The next day we left for Long Island to see Grace, arriving in the late afternoon. Frank, Grace's only brother, had cleared his little apartment above the garage, and Mauro and I stayed there a few days. Moira, Grace's mom, could listen forever to Mauro singing, and he loved to perform for her. It was a joy for me to see all of Grace's relatives again.

We continued our trip with a stop in Washington, then on to Nashville where we attended the Grand Ole Opry. In New Orleans we strolled along Bourbon Street, admiring a *pizzaiolo* (pizzeria artist) throwing the pizza dough in the air. We sat and savored the playing of musicians in bars and restaurants, our hands wrapped around beer mugs.

Our next stop was Mauro's friend Bill in California. Bill, an American, had lived in Switzerland and been a member of Bagatelle. We stayed with him and his wife, Bettina. From there we journeyed to Yosemite National Park and Napa Valley, where Bill and Bettina joined us. We went from winery to winery, having a great time wine tasting and listening to the stories of owners and salespeople.

One story a salesman retold, which you're welcome to verify on Wikipedia, is this: The Champagne coupe or stem glass is a shallow, broad-bowled drinking glass. It's commonly used at wedding receptions and often stacked in layers to build a champagne tower. Champagne is continuously poured into the top glass, trickling down to fill every glass below. Legend has it the shape of the glass was modeled on the breast of Marie Antoinette, the young wife of Louis XVI, king of France. The salesman looked at us with a naughty smile and added, "What would have happened if they'd modeled the glass on the breast of Dolly Parton?" Everybody laughed.

We soon drove to Los Angeles, where naturally Mauro and Bill found a studio where they could sing together. Bill and Bettina returned home, and Mauro and I went for dinner in a small Italian restaurant, where a lady was playing the piano and singing jazz. The food was promptly forgotten while he and she sang their hearts out.

On our way to San Francisco, we stopped at a beach where young people were jamming on conga drums. Being the conga player in his band, Mauro couldn't resist joining them. I practically had to drag him away to reach San Francisco before dark.

My second visit to San Francisco was far better than the first. Now I was with a lover, and the sun was shining. We walked the city during the day, including famous, twisting Lombard Street. We admired flowerbeds in full bloom and explored historic Pier 39. We searched for jazz places at night, and do I need to mention that Mauro performed at as many as he could? Musicians are like bees: they home in on each other wherever they are!

Vacation over, it was time to return to Switzerland. Rumor had it our flight was overbooked, and we hadn't reconfirmed our reservations. Worried he'd miss the flight, Mauro squeezed in front of me on the line. He'd be punished for that. He got his seat in Economy, while I got mine in First Class. Lucky me!

BREAKING UP WITH MAURO

Back home, we slowly fell into our old routines. One day, having offered to look at Mauro's business account while he was out, I struggled to understand a telephone bill and some unidentified numbers that added to his expenses. I called a number that had appeared many times on the bill. It was telephone sex. I was unable to talk to Mauro about it, and after two years of great happiness, I started spiraling into a severe depression. My friend Nicoletta offered a shoulder to lean on, and as before, Dickie and Zdravko were there to comfort me. Sometimes I hated Zdravko, he always knowing better than I and sounding like my father, but I must now admit that most of the time he was right in his advice.

Part of my distress was due to my finances. I had a terrible setback. Swiss tax laws did not take into consideration that my bank account was empty after the death of my husband. For the next two years, I was taxed for the equivalent of two salaries. I was soon fed up with Switzerland and my life. Mauro couldn't deal with all my problems. He broke up with me, advising me to "find" myself before pursuing another relationship. It seemed cruel to me at the time, but of course, he was right.

I felt quite sorry for myself. After speaking to my old friend Dr. Stocker, asking him for advice, I bought myself an electronic piano, a Yamaha, and tried to comfort myself with music therapy. It wasn't as if I were completely alone…my cat Seppie was always with me. I spent Christmas in Holland and was planning to return there permanently, but my brother-in-law Henny advised against it.

"No, that's just running away," he said. "Work through your problems. If you then still want to return, do so, but not now. That would be in my opinion a wrong decision. You have a great job, a great life. Work through it!"

My misery lasted for months, never seeming to end. Living so near Mauro, hearing his voice from the balcony, made me suffer even more, so I played the Yamaha as if I needed to play competitions. One night the doorbell rang. It was a neighbor; I thought she was coming to complain, but she asked which radio station I was tuned to. I told her the music was mine. We had coffee, and she stayed and listened. Within three months I had successfully gone through six levels of *How to Play the Piano*.

Then one sunny morning I woke up to a bright sky and a lot of snow on the road. I put on my ski clothes, took my skis, put them on top of the Mazda and away I drove, Bruce Springsteen's "Born in the U.S.A."

blasting. I skied in the mountains the whole day. From that point on-wards my life improved.

Once my taxes were paid, I decided to leave Switzerland. I gave Zdravko a year's notice. He and I had worked together for thirteen years, successfully he had believed, so he thought I had gone mad. I started saving my money for traveling the world, writing to friends all over the planet, promising I would come and visit.

HANS II

In 1988 another Hans came into my life.

My Dutch friend Trudy had talked about her brother Hans, who lived in the United Arab Emirates. He had just been released from jail where he had served three years of a sentence for his involvement in one of the biggest drug busts ever prosecuted in the UAE. He had convinced the government—and us—that he was innocent of the charges. Of course, it never occurred to me to investigate the case for myself. I've always been attracted to any living thing that needs help, and after talking on the phone with Hans a few times, I felt that he needed me. He said that he planned to come to Switzerland, so we started writing and calling each other often.

I went with his family to greet him at the airport. When I saw him coming down the stairway at Zürich-Kloten Airport, he struck me as a bon vivant. In his mid-fifties, dark haired, clenching a pipe between his teeth, he sported a cap and a Chuck Norris-style beard. I had an inkling this would not go well. Hans was not my type at all. Then again, who was my type? They had all been the wrong men. Perhaps this time I should not go for looks.

Hans collected his suitcase, came through customs, looked around the arrivals hall until he found us, and embraced each member of his family. They hadn't seen him for many years. Then he looked at me and took me in his arms. I had felt lost and insecure, and the embrace was warm. Since his sister and their parents were already living together in a crowded home, we decided Hans would come to my place.

He was exactly the type I shouldn't go for: a dominating male, very good with words, charming when he wanted to be. To be fair, he loved me in his way. He could get jealous, which made me feel good; it had been a long time since a man had made me feel like a beautiful woman.

Hans stayed with me for six months. We vacationed in Switzerland and France. It was a wonderful time, but an anxious one too, for me at least. I worked and he did nothing. Admittedly, Hans tried to find work in both Switzerland and Holland—he had experience as a chartered accountant—but at his age the opportunities were few. It didn't help that his expectations of compensation were unrealistically high.

After my parents met him, they told me to be careful: they sensed he was a manipulator. They were right. Hans would take my car, a small Mazda RX-7, a vehicle I treated as lovingly as a child, and drive it everywhere. He even took it to Holland. I no longer had a car just for myself. I paid for the expensive gas that went into the car, and the expensive food that went into Hans's mouth. He liked to go out and never stopped to consider the cost. I didn't see reality, however. I was in love again.

One day Hans got a call from Dubai: there was an opening in a travel agency for a safari driver, and he wanted the job. What did I know about Dubai? Only the stories he had told me, and as I mentioned, he was a good talker, so they were very entertaining. Since I had decided even before I met Hans to travel the world, I instantly agreed to go with him. I quit my job. Zdravko said nothing, but I sensed his opinion of Hans was very different from my own. I packed my essential stuff together and shipped it to Dubai.

THE UNITED ARAB EMIRATES
(1988-2003)

A VERY DIFFERENT LIFE

When I arrived in October 1988, Dubai was a beautiful city just starting to take off. The tallest building, erected in 1979, was the thirty-nine-story Trade Center with its distinctive "beehive" design. It was the first high-rise on Sheikh Zayed Road, which was just a fraction as wide as the six-lane highway it is today. There were only three big hotels: the Hyatt Regency on Dubai Creek, the Chicago Beach Hotel in Jumeirah (renamed the Jumeirah Beach Hotel in 1996) and the Jebel Ali Hotel on the road to Abu Dhabi. In those times, the Jebel Ali Hotel was not even considered within the city limits of Dubai, but in a small village named after a towering sand dune called Jebel Ali or Mountain of Ali.

The United Arab Emirates comprises seven emirates: Dubai, Sharjah, Ajman, Umm al-Quwain, Ras al-Khaimah, Fujairah and Abu Dhabi. Initially, Hans and I lived in the capital of Sharjah, also called Sharjah. The city was small and slowly expanding. Its charming airport, built in the middle of the desert, looked like a mosque surrounded by a green oasis. Located on the Persian Gulf, Sharjah was the first bustling commercial center in the UAE. I liked Sharjah's old wind tower houses (homes with towers atop them that were open to the air on all four sides), the city's harbor and friendly people. In Sharjah many women still wore a *niqab* (face mask) with a black veil and *abaya* (robe-like dress). I discovered that a surprising number of women were in business; they took good care of themselves and were remarkably independent.

Computers had not yet come to the UAE, so I had to pay our utility bills at their respective places of business. To my surprise, there were always special counters for women, who were never kept waiting. At first I thought this was out of respect, but no. Women were waited on promptly because men wanted to get them out of the building as quickly as possible. Otherwise the males, ninety-nine percent of whom were Indians and Pakistanis, would be constantly eyeing them.

We went straight to Al Khan, a suburb of Sharjah, and moved into a room in the apartment of Ching, Hans's best friend. Ching was a gentle, cynical Englishman in his mid forties. One of his parents was Asian, and he looked Chinese, hence the nickname. He had helped Hans whilst he was in jail, surrendering his passport as bail so Hans could get out. Having recently gone through a divorce, Ching appreciated our company, becoming my confidante and friend. Hans's safari driver job disappeared—poof!—so there we were, living in someone else's house, no jobs, but lots to talk about.

One autumn day, Ching and I found a puppy on the stairs of our apartment building. Somebody had dropped it there, knowing that Europeans would take care of it. Of course, Hans was absolutely against it, but what could he do? It was Ching's place, and Ching wanted to adopt it. Me too! We called the dog Polar because he looked like a miniature polar bear. I would take long walks with Polar to the Sharjah Creek, more like a lagoon, while Hans went job hunting. Seppie, who had adapted to being an indoor cat, tolerated Polar.

Life was totally different from what I had expected. I was used to the Swiss way: strict routines, punctuality. Instead I did a great deal of sitting and waiting. Hans slept until ten in the morning, sometimes noon, then left the house and returned late in the evening. Just as he did back in Switzerland, Hans refused every job offer, claiming everything was beneath him. He told Ching and me that he was no Indian and would not work for an Indian's salary. That's when I discovered Hans was a racist. I was fed up with him, and yet…here's why I didn't leave him:

I had only a tourist's visa. To remain in the UAE, I needed a residence visa. The law said one could be obtained either through a job or marriage if a spouse was already in possession of a residence visa. Life without this document was a trial. I couldn't open a bank account, get a driver's license, or remain more than a maximum of two months in the country. Since I couldn't have a bank account of my own, my money went into Hans's account. He dove into my funds and bought a Range Rover. It was registered in his name only—because, you see, Hans *did* have residency. I couldn't find work, no matter how hard I tried, so what was I to do? What's more, people had noticed Hans and me living together in Ching's apartment, and if they talked about it, that could cause Ching problems. The UAE is a Muslim country. Unrelated men and women are forbidden to live together outside of marriage. The police won't come down on you unless someone files a complaint, but when that happens, you're in trouble. So Hans and I did Ching a favor and moved out.

We found an old villa in Al Riqqa. Hans was still unemployed, and on principle I refused to shoulder the entire rent, which should have been paid in advance and covered a complete year. It was actually very cheap, but even cheap was too much for Hans. The landlord was constantly ringing the bell to get his money, but Hans never opened the door. Nor did he let in the meter readers for the electricity and water. As a result, those bills went up until I could stand it no longer and paid them.

I was not used to a life like this. My parents had raised me in a proper, responsible way, and this man had no dignity, no pride. I started to suspect that his parents and sister were wrong thinking he was innocent in that drug case. Hans used people every way he could to avoid working and live an easy life: sleeping in, drinking his tea, smoking his pipe, and socializing only to con people out of their money.

Since Hans wasn't in the habit of paying bills, always preferring to wait until a notice was served, I kept nudging him regarding my expired tourist visa. A penalty had to be paid for every day it was overdue. I need-ed to go to Switzerland to arrange shipment of my remaining personal belongings, so I wanted to start the paperwork for my residence visa.

We finally went to the Immigration Office in Sharjah, a dirty old building with countless small rooms. Shunted around, Hans and I got separated. He refused to pay the current visa fines, and I was sent to jail. It felt like I was in there for ages. In reality I sat behind bars for six hours, surrounded by Indian, Pakistani and Filipino women, all of whom had visa problems like myself. At last, Hans paid the fine, I was released, and the application for my residence visa was initiated.

MARRIAGE TO HANS II AND WORK…AT LAST!

I was furious that Hans had put me in that situation, showing no re-morse, supremely relaxed, smiling with his pipe in his mouth. But my overwhelming desire then was to get my residence visa as soon as pos-sible. And the fastest way to do it would be…to marry Hans.

We wed at St. Mary's Catholic Church in Dubai with only a few peo-ple present. Immediately afterward, I applied for a residence visa on my Dutch passport. The priceless document was in my hands within days.

In the meantime Hans got involved in the organizing of the Dubai International Rally. For every sponsor he signed up, he received a com-mission, so at last he was bringing in some money. The rally was, and continues to be, the final round in the Middle East Rally Championship, a celebrated event covered by the world press.

I found a job working mornings at Aria Film Production as a secre-tary. It paid little, but it kept me busy. Mr. Aria was an Iranian who held a German passport. He ran all over the country, seeking clients for whom he could produce TV commercials. He had no success whatever until a lone business expressed an interest: a milk farm in Ras al-Khaimah.

Aria wrote a script.

The first shot would feature a beautiful Iranian girl (she was twelve) with long black hair leading a cow from its barn. Cut to various shots of cows. The girl leads her cow past famous landmarks in Dubai. At the con-clusion, the titles read, Buy Our Milk, or some other such exhortation.

We went to Ras al-Khaimah and spent many, many hours filming, as the featured cow didn't care to do what Aria wanted. Then we went to Dubai City Centre, again dragging the animal forward and back, over and over again. (I later posted the comical outtakes on YouTube.)

When the editing was done, I drove two hours up and two hours down to deliver the video to the farmer at Ras al-Khaimah. We didn't hear anything for several days. Finally, we got the verdict: rejected! The commercial was deemed unacceptable as the cow and the girl were too...? My English fails me here, but if I tell you the pre-teen was busty and the cow had a healthy set of udders, you can perhaps supply it yourself. Aria was now broke, so he couldn't pay my salary, and that was the end of my job.

VICTOR, THE GREAT DANE

Hans and I moved to a nicer house in Al Riqqa. It had a small garden for Seppie and Polar to romp in. (The dog had to stay with us because Ching went on leave for four weeks.) I had succeeded in tricking Hans into accepting Polar, so why should I stop there? We were soon joined by another pooch named Victor. Here's how he came into my life:

> One of our neighbors was an Iranian named Mohammed. He had lived in Finland for a while, met and married a Finnish woman, and brought her to the UAE. What happened next was a tragedy I saw replayed time and again. Their relationship changed completely. The wife was expected to adapt to the religion and customs of the UAE, which were, of course, strange to her. She stayed at home within her house or fenced-in garden. She could only go out to shop or visit friends if Mohammed was with her, and even then she had to wear a veil and *abaya*.

They bought a dog for her—being Muslim, Mohammed felt no affinity for the animal, so you wouldn't say they bought it for the two of them—and the dog became the wife's sole source of joy. Victor was a Great

Dane, the best they could find, sired by world champions. However, the woman's life became unbearable, and one night she deserted Mohammed and fled the country. Seeing no way to bring Victor with her, she left him behind, too.

The wife had treated Victor like a child, keeping him indoors, always at her side. Now that she was gone, Mohammed left Victor outside in the garden. The first time I saw the dog he was whimpering, standing in the oppressive heat of midsummer, around 50 degrees Celsius (122 degrees Fahrenheit). His paws were infected and swollen. Taking pity on him, I asked Mohammed if I could bathe and walk him. Mohammed soon saw that Victor would be better off with me, and agreed to give him to me.

I took Victor to a vet, who said he should be kept from licking his paws—it was preventing them from healing—so I tried putting socks on them. The paws would improve for a time and then start festering again. I think he might have been allergic to the desert sand.

My little mutt Polar treated huge Victor like his personal toy. He would jump at Victor's ears, and the Great Dane would whine like a baby. I think he had the sweetest character I've ever seen in a dog.

But he wasn't gentle with everyone. When Mohammed would come to our villa and try to step through the front door without permission, Victor would growl and strain forward, determined to bite him. It took all my strength to hold him back. The silver lining was that now I knew Victor would be able to defend me, if ever the circumstances called for it.

In early 1991, Hans's brother Gerard came to visit with his family. They fell in love with Victor, and since I could see that his health remained uncertain in the UAE, I agreed to let them take him to Switzerland. However, this was a daunting task. We didn't have enough money to fly him there. We couldn't even afford the extra-large pet carrier Victor needed. Mohammed kindly agreed to foot the bill for the crate. As for Victor's airfare, I wrote to Imholz, a Swiss travel agency that chartered flights in and out of Sharjah. Imholz agreed to fly Victor for free, on condition that I accompany him. Victor's huge crate was lifted onto a truck, and he was driven to the airport, taken out and placed in the hold of the plane. Everyone along the way quaked at the sight of him!

We flew to Zürich, where Victor was examined at customs in the cargo area. At last, he was given permission to pass through the cargo gates into the arrivals hall. The crate proved too big to pass through the sliding doors, so I had to take Victor out, and he did what I had dreaded. He sat himself down and made a huge pooh in the cleanest airport in the world. All the passengers who witnessed the event regarded me with disgust as I pulled him on his leash toward the exit, he gliding behind me on his four paws, pooh extruding after him. Luckily, the van rented by my in-laws was ready and waiting nearby. We put Victor inside, and he was off to his new home.

I'm sorry to say that Victor lost some of his sweetness in Switzerland. Trotting through the streets of his new home village in the mountains, he noticed the other doggies cowering before him, and started enjoying the role of bully. Susy, my sister-in-law, decided Victor needed obedience training.

The dog training school was sixty kilometers (about thirty-seven miles) away from Susy's village. Victor made good progress. Often after a long day of instruction, he would accompany Susy into the cafeteria of the school, where she would relax with a cup of coffee. One time when Susy was seated there, a young woman with a Siberian husky joined her. The other woman said she also lived about sixty kilometers away, but in the opposite direction. She looked at Victor and told Susy she had a friend in Sharjah who owned a Great Dane, or did until recently. Susy said the world was a very small place. Might the friend be Marilyn?

The next day I received a fax, a drawing showing two women sitting at a table, a husky and Great Dane beside them. My friend Monika Lenzin wrote the caption: *Meeting with Victor.*

THEFT AND CENSORSHIP

While in Switzerland I took the opportunity to get some of my furniture and other possessions out of storage and arrange their shipment to Sharjah. I applied three layers of seals to the shipping container for protection. My Mazda RX-7 I left behind in a garage in Zürich. I had mixed feelings; I didn't want to sell it, but I couldn't see me driving it in the UAE. Perhaps leaving the car in Switzerland gave me a sense of keeping my options open.

On an August day after I returned to the UAE, the shipping container arrived in front of our house in the presence of customs inspectors. Every box was unpacked and checked for dirty books, liquor or other contraband. The laborers doing the unpacking treated my boxes quite roughly, and I told them several times to take more care, especially of my piano. They didn't listen, so I kept repeating myself, getting frustrated, thinking they didn't understand my English. Then one of them looked at me and said there was no piano.

I jumped into the container. No piano. Only the boxes in the front row were full. The ones in the back were empty. The three seals had remained intact, but somehow thieves had rifled through everything and stolen all my valuables. After the death of Hans Number One, I had kept only things of personal value; now even they were gone.

I was terribly upset. I had insured the shipment for a fraction of its worth—about $10,000 USD—never dreaming I'd be robbed. I'd thought the worst-case scenario would be the cargo ship sinking, and what were the odds of that? I sadly put the insurance money into the joint account I'd newly opened with Hans Number Two.

To add insult to injury, the customs inspectors took my books back to their offices to check them against the forbidden list. I was told I could collect the "acceptable" ones a week later. Each book was dear to me, so I was already angry when I showed up at their offices. Most of the books were set aside, to be destroyed later, they said. They gave back some books with individual pages torn out. *Treasure Island* was on the forbidden list and had to be destroyed! I had two novels by Harold Robbins, one in German, the other in English. Funnily enough, they let me keep the English copy, but the German was in the to-be-shredded pile. They had also taken a small Dutch poetry book that I cherished because it was from my old elementary school teacher with a note from her in it. The book was a compilation of cute things students had said to their teachers. The title was *Juf, er Zit Een Naakte Vlinder in de Boom*. This translates as "Miss, there is a naked butterfly in the tree." By "naked," the child had merely meant the butterfly wasn't colorful. The inspectors, however, zeroed in on that word and confiscated the "dirty" book.

Only part of me accepted the absurdity of it; mostly I was furious. I suspected that some customs employees would take the condemned books home with them, and I didn't want to give them the pleasure. I insisted that I destroy all the books myself. I sat in their offices for at least two hours until the last of my treasures disappeared in the shredder.

For the record, I found most Emirati to be kind, decent people. That's one of the reasons I wanted to remain in the UAE.

GOOD CAT, BAD CHECKS

Soon after the customs inspection, I met a Dutch-born woman named Yvonne who had two little children and a cat named Vincent. Vincent was a terror. He bit everyone's legs and toes and incessantly jumped from chair to chair. I took the cat home, where he never gave me any problems.

In June 1990 Yvonne had offered me a job at a tourism company she was helping to open. The owner was a man named Mohammed X, who had a ticket agency. He had known Yvonne as a hard-working member of his staff and trusted her to set up this local company. Little did he know she had hardly virtually no business experience. By the time we should have started operation, she had frittered away so much money on unnecessary details, such as placing big ads in the most expensive magazines and buying land cruisers instead of leasing them, that the company had failed before it even took off. It folded within nine months. I believe the seed money came directly out of Mohammed's pockets; unfortunately, he was increasingly strapped for cash because tickets being bought from him were mostly paid by post-dated checks, which was normal in those times. The jails were filled with owners of bounced post-dated checks. Mohammed had a high post at the DNATA, the UAE's air travel service provider, but apparently he didn't have sufficient savings. The poor man got in trouble with his family, who had to pay his debts. He couldn't pay my salary, so again I was stuck.

A HEALTH EMERGENCY

I started having strong pains below my abdomen. At first I dismissed them, thinking I was simply stressed, or it was "all in my mind." Finally I went to a doctor, who told me I had to have a hysterectomy.

At that time, Al Zahra Hospital in Sharjah was the only decent private hospital in the area. It insisted on cash payments. I had no cash. I did have insurance, but it wouldn't pay up front; it required a hospital invoice, and I could only get that after the operation was performed. Mohammed owed me for months of work, but he said he couldn't pay me; his family had frozen his account. Every day I went to his office and begged for my back pay. Finally, he gave me a post-dated check. I took it to the bank, only to see it bounce. According to the law, you couldn't seek redress against a check-issuer until you had received three bounced checks bearing a certain stamp from the bank. I was tired and scared as hell, worried about the health consequences of delaying my operation, but I went back to Mohammed again and again.

After three weeks and three stamps on the post-dated check, I went to a police station and boldly asked to see the highest in command. Being Western at that time had its advantages. If I'd been Indian, for example, there's no way I would have been permitted to see such a person. I explained my story to the officer. While still listening, he picked up a phone and called Mohammed. Mohammed told him that the account belonged to his wife, and unfortunately she had withdrawn all the funds. I was outraged and showed it. The officer told me I should be patient; Mohammed had promised him that he would pay. And what choice did I have? Pursuing Mohammed through the courts would have taken too long. Besides, although Westerners had some advantages, UAE citizens tended to have more rights than foreigners. A lawsuit could have landed me in even greater trouble.

What is it people say that desperate matters call for?

The next day I drove to the parking lot of Mohammed's office and blocked his car with mine. A friend told me he had slipped out of the office through the back door. I couldn't care less. He had to come back for his car, and when he did, I'd be there! I waited hours. In late afternoon I finally caught Mohammed sneaking into the parking lot, and I let loose the only weapons a woman ever needs: tears. He opened his wallet and gave me the cash.

Knowing we had a history of cancer in our family, I was fearful, but I also didn't want to put the operation off a moment longer than I had to. I called Dr. Krishna Gill, my gynecologist, and scheduled my surgery for that same week. Just days before my operation, Hans told me to hire a housemaid, as he would not look after the cats and dogs while I was recuperating.

A year into my marriage to Hans Number Two, part of me knew I'd made a mistake; another part of me didn't want to admit to myself or anyone else that I was again in a failed relationship. Perhaps the fault was mine: maybe I'd never loved myself enough, and so I never recognized the difference between being used and being loved. Howsoever I had reached that moment in my life, when Hans told me he wasn't willing to care for our pets, all my feelings for him died.

Needless to say, I couldn't find a housemaid on such short notice. I went into that operation room deeply depressed, worried about my cats and dogs and repelled by the coldness of the man I had married. I could not speak with anyone about it. Dr. Gill thought I was scared of the surgery and nothing more. She had no idea what I was going through. The operation went all right, and I got out of bed the next day, much sooner than I was expected to.

The second day I nearly died.

While I was having my operation, the maternity ward was abuzz: a sheikha, the wife of a member of the royal family of Sharjah, was preparing to give birth. The nurses thought that because I was recovering so well the first day, I didn't need further attention, freeing them to admire the new royal baby. Little did they know, I had somehow acquired an infection. On that second day, when my first visitors came to see me, my room filled with a horrible smell. Nurses were summoned. Dr. Gill was at my bedside *stat*, administering infusions of antibiotics. Dr. Gill's husband, one of the handsomest physicians I've ever laid eyes on, helped his wife treat me. It seemed they were hovering over me every time I woke up from a doze. My friends were worried and caring, and even the hospital board sent me flowers, but…the man who should have been most concerned about me was moaning and groaning about housework.

I couldn't handle that, so I told Dr. Gill I'd be better off at home. She asked me if I had a housemaid. I said yes. In the UAE, every Westerner has a housemaid, so she didn't suspect for even a minute that I was lying. I went home with a promise to touch nothing and just rest. The infection was still raging, and I was on high doses of antibiotics.

Hans had hired a housemaid from Sri Lanka who was willing to work for $100 USD a month. He called her Primula, as her real name was too difficult to pronounce. Hans gave Primula the servants' quarters so that she could live there with her husband. Apparently, Primula was incapable of many things, including lifting heavy objects. Hans had brought home loads of young trees and other plants for the huge garden of our new villa, but who was going to put them in the ground? Day after day, he came home and told Primula and her husband to shift the plants to the backyard. Primula seemed scared as hell of Hans, but a week passed and still she had done nothing. Hans complained to me daily about this, never thinking that he, the white human being, could have done the work. It was strictly a brown face job.

I got so annoyed that one morning I got out of bed and carried all those heavy pots to the backyard. As a result, of course, I had more interior bleeding and my infection worsened. My doctor shouted at me. Why didn't I listen to her? Teetering on the edge of a nervous breakdown, I finally told her about Hans. She then had a long talk with him, and for a little while everything went well between us.

My vaginal wounds still weren't healed after half a year, and the cauterizations I was receiving twice a month were horrible. I decided to fly to Switzerland and make an appointment with University Hospital in Zürich. Maybe doctors there could find a better way to treat me. Meanwhile, I would stay with Susy and Hans's brother and have the delight of seeing Victor again.

I had not yet sold my little red Mazda RX-7, and my brother-in-law was taking care of it. He suggested I take the car, drive to the railroad station, and from there take a train to Zürich Central Station, a stop close to University Hospital. I thought it was a good plan, so I climbed in the little car, sped off and arrived at the train station parking lot. I circled and circled but couldn't find a space. Tired of searching, and remembering that Triemli Hospital had a big parking lot (although, admittedly, being situated on the outskirts of Zürich it was farther from my destination) I turned around and headed for it.

I drove and drove, thinking how funny it was that I had adapted so well to driving in the UAE, despite its different traffic-light laws and my relatively brief time there. Now, I was calmly approaching a Zürich intersection on the Birmensdorferstrasse and needed to turn left. The light was green, but…that was the signal to go straight. I hadn't noticed the red light indicating no left turn.

That's why I was completely surprised to find a big blue bus bearing down on me. I remember the driver throwing his hands up in horror, seeing that little red car in front of his bus, knowing he was gonna hit it. He rammed my Mazda on the passenger side at full speed. Again, my guardian angel had picked me up and saved me from certain death. My beautiful Little Red Riding Hood Mazda RX-7, however, was eaten by the big blue Zürich wolf bus. A total loss.

Naturally, traffic halted, people started running around. Somebody tried to wrench open my driver's side door and succeeded after several long minutes. An old man was shouting at me, "Hallo, Hallo!" I registered, but could not react. An ambulance was called. I don't remember how I got into it, but it drove me immediately to the nearest hospital— Triemli. Nobody understood what I was talking about, when I kept saying,

"No, no, no, I have to go to University Hospital! I'm in the wrong hospital!"

They thought I was hallucinating, in shock. Finally, one doctor actually listened to me, phoned the number I gave him and realized I hadn't lost my senses. I hadn't broken any limbs (yet) and had spoken the truth, so after filling out all the insurance paperwork, they let me go.

I continued my trip to University Hospital by tram. After several hours in the waiting room, I was received and had my consultation with an experienced physician. He said the hospital couldn't do anything for me, as only Dr. Gill, who had performed my operation, knew where the internal stitches were. I had better go back to her, he said.

I was not pleased.

I returned to the UAE.

I found a new job that year as a secretary at a German-run law office, Meyer-Reumann Legal Consultancies. I worked long hours, but the salary was good, and I started worrying about money a little less. Although my infection persisted, I felt better, I'd made some good friends in the UAE, and as they say, it was the quiet before the storm.

BETTINA AND SHEIKH X

My Swiss godchild, Bettina, wrote to me that her parents were getting a divorce. She was extremely unhappy being with them, so I suggested she come stay with Hans and me a few months. I felt she could get work helping to organize the rallies; it would also be a fun way to improve her English. There was a problem, though: it would be very difficult to get a six-month permit for a sixteen-year-old girl who was not my blood relation. Immigration offices in Sharjah and Dubai refused my request, as I expected.

I discussed the matter with co-workers. My boss advised me to speak to one of his client's representatives, a man named Moussa who also represented the royal family of one of the emirates. I called Moussa, whom I knew from his visits to our office, and asked if somebody higher up could help. After thirty minutes he called me back and told me to wait for a telephone call from Sheikh X. (At the time, I knew zilch about this man. Today, he is His Highness, ruling an emirate.) My boss and I wondered if he would ever actually call, but at 7 P.M. the phone rang. Sheikh X introduced himself in perfect English and asked how he could help me. I explained the situation with my godchild, and he told me to bring a photocopy of her passport and wait in my car for him the next day in front of the most elegant hotel in the emirate. I told Hans about this, and he was pleased, as now I was creating connections that perhaps would prove helpful one day.

Next day I drove on the near-empty road through the desert in my new car, a black secondhand 4x4 Land Cruiser, bought from the insurance money from the Mazda accident. The trip took about ninety minutes. (By the way, if you're wondering how I could afford to miss work, it was a Thursday, part of the Thursday to Friday weekend in the UAE.) When I stopped in the parking area in front of the hotel, a limousine with tinted windows rolled towards me. The red-numbered license plate bore two crossed flags—one signifying the UAE, the other the emirate—showing the car belonged to a member of the royal family. The driver's side window lowered with a hum, and a man's face appeared. His expression showed that he liked what he saw. Right there, I should have realized this was not going to be easy. What's more, we recognized each other. He was the same handsome smiling man—black beard, big black eyes, full red lips surrounding a generous mouth with shiny white teeth—who had gazed straight into my camera a month earlier while I was at a jazz concert at the community center.

Sheikh X made a sign to follow him. We drove through the center of the city and stopped in front of a government building where two older guards with beards and rifles were standing at the gate. I felt like I'd been magically transported onto some classic movie set.

We stopped and got out of our cars. The sheikh introduced himself, white teeth gleaming. I was wearing my little maroon suit and carrying a briefcase, hoping I looked more like a businesswoman than a nobody seeking a favor. Sheikh X led the way into the building and then into a grand room with a large sofa, some big chairs and a huge office desk. He gestured for me to take a seat, and ordered someone to make tea. I opened my case and gave him the photocopy of the passport. The sheikh, in turn, gave me a resident visa application form to fill out. He told me that at Bettina's arrival, I had to show this form to the authorities in Dubai and come with her to his office, from where she would be taken for an AIDS test, a normal procedure to obtain a residence permit. All I had to do was inform him when she was arriving; he would take care of everything else.

The tea had come and we were left alone. We chatted about this and that, me talking about my experiences in the UAE, when Sheikh X suddenly fell to my feet and started kissing them. I was so surprised I froze for a few seconds. He tried to get under my skirt. I hit him on the head with my briefcase, and his *kaffiyeh* (head scarf) and the black ring around it fell off, while he was also trying to get rid of his *dishdasha* (ankle-length robe). I was appalled and told him to stop, that I had not come for that, and if he wanted to help me that was OK, otherwise I would leave. He apologized, got himself properly dressed again, and showed me the way out. Now, after all this time, I realize that he thought it would be an exchange of sexual favors, as there were many ladies who came to Dubai for just that. I could have been one of them!

Driving home, I couldn't believe what had just happened. Had it all been a dream? Naturally, I told Hans, who just smiled and said that it was to be expected. So now he was a pimp, too! I faxed Bettina the stamped application form so that her parents could book a flight, and two weeks later she arrived.

I called Sheikh X. He told us to come the next day so Bettina could take her HIV test. I was a bit nervous, not knowing what to expect after our little encounter. I had told Bettina the whole story, so she was wary, too. However, the sheikh did what he promised. He called the immigration authorities, and his driver brought us to their offices. Bettina and I had no wait at all; the entire procedure took a few minutes. We were told we could return to Sharjah and that the sheikh would contact us in a few days when the test results were final and the residence visa ready.

Voilà! The sheikh called me at work, told me the paperwork was complete, and I should come to him the next day with Bettina. In great spirits, we went to his office, finding only Moussa there. He told us the sheikh was at a camel racetrack and wanted to show us around it. We followed Moussa's car to the track, where Sheikh X's luxury Land Cruiser was waiting. He stepped out of his car, and I thought, *He's going to kidnap us.* Instead, he said we should follow him, he'd show us around, and afterwards we'd have lunch in his apartment. As long as Bettina and I were in my car, I wasn't too worried, because when I used to help out with the rallies some drivers said I had a natural talent for driving in desert sand.

Sheikh X did indeed show us some scenic parts of the emirate, and he seemed pleasant enough until I got wind of his real intentions: he asked me if Bettina was still a virgin. We ended our tour in the town center and followed him to a nondescript apartment, where a beautiful lunch was waiting for us, arranged by Moussa. Sheikh X started to sit next to Bettina, but I dropped myself in between them. Despite feeling terribly on edge, I assumed a calm demeanor, made small talk and filled any silences before they became awkward. When we finished lunch, I lingered a bit, afraid to announce our quick departure and seem impolite. I could see that Moussa was smiling—he clearly enjoyed seeing me squirm—so I was happy to hear him confirm my excuse that I had to go back to work. Bettina and I said our goodbyes to the sheikh with a kiss on each cheek, promising to see him again soon.

The instant Bettina and I got in the car, we started laughing and never stopped, so relieved were we to have safely extricated ourselves from that predicament. In later years, we often looked back at our memorable time with His Highness Sheikh S.

Would you be surprised to learn that Hans and Bettina couldn't stand each other? Bettina was convinced Hans was a lunatic, even before he suddenly introduced the rule that her bedroom door must remain open at all times. My exchanges with Hans became increasingly heated.

RALLY TIME, SOME CLOSE CALLS, AND RUTH
Fortunately, it was the time of the annual Dubai International Rally, so Bettina and Hans were largely out of the house, Bettina helping at one of the rally offices, Hans out looking for sponsors. Hans was the assistant to the chairman of Al Nasr Motor Club, Colonel Saeed Khalfan, a former rally driver who was now part of the team that created the rally tracks and drove over them daily to keep the desert sand from hiding them. In my spare time I helped in the colonel's office or drove over the tracks in my car. Some drivers started telling me I was doing it so well I shouldn't be a secretary but a competitor myself. Of course, I couldn't possibly have afforded a racecar, but they decided I could borrow the practice car of Sheikh Suhail bin Khalifa Al Maktoum for local rallies. Christina, my colleague at the law office, was my co-driver. We won two prizes as a ladies' team.

And how did the men do? The championship was dominated by Mohammed bin Sulayem, a driver who would eventually win a whopping fourteen times. My favorite competitor was a Qatari driver named Saeed Al Hajdri. I can't begin to convey the excitement of the race in words, so feel free to view the videos I took. They're all up on my YouTube channel.

The rally of 1990 stands out in my memory because it was also the time of the Gulf War. Many foreigners, on advice of their embassies, fled the UAE, but Hans, Bettina and I stayed. While creating stages for the rallies, we found many bunkers in the desert occupied by soldiers of different nationalities, including, of course, American marines. We also regularly saw bombs fall into the sea, and lights from foreign aircraft blaze across the sky.

Meanwhile, at Meyer-Reumann Legal Consultancies, we were receiving applications from young German law students who wanted to do a six-month internship with us. Previously, only male students showed an interest, but this time several young women had applied. As Rolf Meyer-Reumann, head attorney and owner of the law firm, went through the applications, we watched him out of the corners of our eyes. Finally, he called his three female employees to him: Elena, a fellow attorney, and Christina and me, the two secretaries. He showed us photos of all the applicants, and pointed out his selection: a young lady who was leaning provocatively against a tree. All three of us looked at him in astonishment. Was this really his choice? Without hesitation we advised him against it. He thought we were jealous of this beautiful woman and that we were "defending our territory." We told him plainly that it was not her beauty we objected to but how she applied for the job. It was extremely unprofessional...what would be the quality of her work if this were how she chose to approach her first workplace? He rejected our initial impressions and wrote back to her that she was welcome to work at his firm as a trainee.

We were all waiting, wondering what to expect, when Ruth arrived. As I mentioned earlier, at the time Thursday and Friday made up the weekend in the UAE, and Saturday and Sunday were working days. It was early on a Sunday morning when Ruth wandered in, looking rather punk in a leather jacket, leather boots and jeans. We looked through our office windows at Meyer-Reumann and waited for his reaction when she stepped into his office, guided by the coffee boy. His expression was worth seeing. We gave each other knowing smiles.

Once Ruth was settled at her desk and we started to know her, it was clear that her interest was not law but money, and the fastest way to get it. Good times were necessary, too. Immediately after her arrival, she went partying with American soldiers stationed in Dubai.

The stories Ruth would tell each morning upon arriving at work were full of excitement. Elena, Christina and I enjoyed her; Meyer-Reumann not so much. Ruth told us women that she had paid for her law studies by being a call girl specializing in sadomasochism. We hung on her every word, never having heard stories like these before.

Ruth wanted to know where the Dubai money was. We informed her it was not with the American soldiers, but the locals. And if she wanted to meet them, she should go to the camel races on Fridays and change her dress code from punk to elegant. So next Friday while I was relaxing in front of the TV, flipping through the channels, I suddenly stopped. The screen was filled with a woman with long blond hair wearing a tiny tank top, parading in front of the sheikhs' loges. Ruth! My colleagues had also seen her, and we couldn't wait for the next workday to hear all the details.

Turns out Ruth had failed to do her homework, and it cost her. At the races, a local man had approached her and told her he was the secretary to Sheikh Mohammed, who requested she join him in his private seating area. She refused; she had wanted to be invited by no one less than His Highness Sheikh Rashid, ruler and Father of Dubai. Unbeknownst to Ruth, Sheikh Rashid had died a few months earlier. (It was quite a loss. Sheikh Rashid used to leave the Majlis—the house of parliament—early every morning to meet his people on the streets of Dubai and personally learn what was going on in his emirate. He was beloved by his people.) Ruth had no clue that Sheikh Mohammed bin Rashid Al Maktoum, although younger than his brothers, was the most powerful man in the emirate.

Naturally, this blunder upset her, but it was just a minor setback.

The annual Dubai International Rally was again being held. As usual, Hans and I checked in for a week at the Hyatt Regency, transferring the rally office to the hotel. The Hyatt was also where stage one and the press office were located, as well as the prize-giving gala that finalized the event.

It was during the rally that I had two accidents, after which I realized that Dubai was a police state with cameras all over the city. The first accident happened when I had to bring a delivery to the Jebel Ali Free Zone to Sultan bin Sulayem. There is a speed limit in the free zone, but I was in a hurry and, to be honest, I was driving fast. Other than a big truck in the distance, there was no traffic. As I came closer, the truck suddenly made a U-turn, and I realized it had two trailers attached. I slammed both feet on the brake, thinking, *Oh, my God, this is the end*. My car stopped in the nick of time, its nose under the last trailer. My heart was thumping in my chest, blood pounding in my ears. I was one lucky woman. I sat there a few minutes while the driver of the truck continued innocently onward as if nothing had happened. A few minutes later, I arrived at the office of Sultan, where I was received with joy at my survival. Saeed Khalfan had seen everything on the cameras and had counseled the secretary of Sultan to look after me.

The second accident happened when I was on my way back home to Sharjah. As I was in my old, strong, short-wheelbase Land Cruiser, I had a good view of the road in front of me, which led into a small tunnel on the border between Dubai and Sharjah, just opposite the Dubai police general headquarters. I saw that the cars in front of me had stopped, so I also stopped, braking slowly as I had calculated I had plenty of time to halt. Suddenly, I felt a big bang on the back of the car. A truck had struck me; its entire front cabin was covering the spare wheel of my 4x4, which was situated in the back. Thank goodness nothing happened to the truck driver and his passenger. This was going to take a long while to sort out, so I decided to call Saeed. He took the phone and told me not to worry: for the second time, he'd witnessed an accident of mine!

What's more, he'd already called a police car to meet me. The paperwork was completed within five minutes.

But back to the rally...

As I mentioned, I was employed days at the law office and evenings and nights at the rally office at the Hyatt. Ruth asked if she could come with me to the rally's opening ceremony, and I agreed. We stood in the great hall of the hotel as participants and journalists from all over the world and everybody else who had received an invitation were arriving with an air of excitement. While I was greeting people whom I hadn't seen in a year, Saeed Al Hajdri stopped to say hello. He smiled at Ruth, started chatting with her, and after a few minutes they left. I saw them going into the elevator, disappearing most probably to his room. It was not even ten minutes later that he returned alone, she five minutes after him. She said only three words to me: "In. *Prrrr.* Out." Much later she told me that her experience with locals from the Gulf was sexually very disappointing: no foreplay, lift the *dishdasha* and then just in and out. It would be over before she could even get undressed.

It was also at this rally that the prize money for the last day of the event was late. Saeed had tried to contact Sheikh Mohammed the whole day, but in vain. Finally, one hour before the prizes were to be awarded, a local man ran up to Saeed and gave him a big bag. Saeed called, "Marilyn, come quickly, we have to count the money." We raced to the elevator and then went to his room, which was booked under my name so that Saeed could remain anonymous. He emptied the bag on the bed, and thousands of *dirhams* (UAE currency) rolled over the covers. He smiled at me and said, "What do you think everybody who saw us running to the elevator is thinking we're doing?" We laughed and started counting the money, which we found to be around $500,000 USD. It took us quite a while to fill the envelopes for the designated prizes to be handed to the lucky winners of the race.

I'm betting you want to hear more about Ruth. Well... Ruth started "working" the big hotel bars, where she met Ali Obeid, a local business-man. Ali was a nice guy with a lovely house on the beach, which I once visited with Hans. Ali came from a good, reputable family, and he liked Ruth. So Ruth started seeing him. She began showing up less often at work, partying with Ali and his crowd, flying to London and elsewhere for whirlwind vacations. Ali gave her presents, and for a while Ruth was happy.

At this time, several locals were interested in investing in the former East Germany, now dissolved and part of Germany. Since Ruth was a lawyer and German, Ali wanted to invest in *her*. He kept suggesting they partner up, but the proposal annoyed her. She wanted instant money, not distant money, and she wanted a computer. Elena, Christina and I couldn't believe how shortsighted she was. We tried to convince her that hooking up with Ali was the best thing that could happen to her; she'd be able to open her own law office, and forge a great future for herself. Neither Ali nor we could convince her. She demanded her computer; he gave it to her, and the relationship promptly went down the drain. Ruth returned to Germany, but before she did, she slept with several of Ali's best friends. He was livid, and she didn't care.

Soon afterward, we received letters from many different law offices in Germany asking for references that Meyer-Reumann never answered. One day a furious Ruth got on the line, asking to be connected with our boss. He took the phone and listened patiently to her shouting, "Why haven't you replied to any of the reference requests?"

He told her, "I couldn't write a reference about your work because you never worked."

Then he hung up.

CATS, BRAS, AND THE UNDERSIDE OF UAE LIFE

Although no longer young (he was eighteen years old), my cat Seppie was still a roamer, venturing out into the neighborhoods where no expats were living. As temperatures rose through the day, he would regularly return home to enjoy the cool of the house. One afternoon he didn't come back, and I was devastated. Primula and I walked through the streets, calling his name. After one week without result, I made posters featuring a photo of Seppie, my telephone number and an offer of reward money, sticking the signs on palm trees and in the windows of the many little grocery shops in the area. I could only hope that somebody might have seen my precious blue-gray cat, which was unique in the whole of Sharjah.

A few days later, while I was at work, the phone rang and Primula answered. Another house girl, working a few streets away, told Primula she had seen the poster in a corner shop and that her *arbab* (boss) had taken Seppie from the street and given it to his children. He kept it in the garden outside his house. The girl said she would call back when the *arbab* and the family were not there, so she could let us in to take the cat and give her the reward.

When I came home that day and heard the news, I excitedly counted the hours, waiting for the girl to call. Just before dark, she rang. I asked Primula to talk to her, as the girl did not speak English. After getting directions, Primula and I went to the worker's house and collected Seppie. Tears sprang to my eyes as I gave the girl her reward. We all separated quickly, so that the neighbors wouldn't notice the exchange and get the girl in trouble. Poor Seppie. I called the Jumeirah Vet clinic, which had an Australian lady doctor, Kelly, who had a cat that looked much like Seppie and perhaps for that reason treated him especially well. I told her the story, and Kelly had us come immediately. Seppie was completely dehydrated and stayed in the clinic for two days on a drip. After that he came home, but he was no longer the same adventurous cat I had loved. Now he was always lying down, weakened by kidney problems. Every two months he had to return to the vet for two consecutive days of treatment.

Around this time, a horrible murder happened. An Indian family traveling from Dubai to Ras al-Khaimah had car problems and got stuck between Ajman and Umm al-Quwain. A car filled with young local men stopped and offered to help. They stopped another car to take the father to the next gas station to get help for repairs. The young men assured him they would take care of the grandmother, mother and two daughters. The Indian trusted them and left. Returning a few hours later with a car mechanic, he found his family had vanished; the car sat empty at the side of the road. The man flagged all passing cars, a search was started and police informed. All four females had been raped, and only the man's wife survived. Not much sound was made in the press, but the country's CID (Criminal Investigation Department) was working undercover, and the next morning the young men were tracked down. They were openly hanged by verdict of the ruler of Abu Dhabi the next day.

In those days harems still existed. Indian, Pakistani and Filipino houseboys and house girls would be sexually abused, not only by males but also by female members of a family. These miserable servants found it difficult to escape, as their passports were often taken from them. It was also said that tourists staying in one of the hotels would be surprised by an unexpected visit from a woman—or was it a man?—who, unrecognizable in a long black *abaya* with veil, had made note of the room number and followed the innocent foreigner there. It was not until I myself had a disturbing encounter that I heard all these stories. During one of the rallies, while I was sitting waiting for someone in the Hyatt lobby, a local was constantly looking at me and playing with his room key. Then I realized that he was trying to get my attention, glancing from me to the key and back, signaling me to go to his room. Afterward people confirmed to me that this was a common practice in the hotels and that many young women earned good money that way!

While living in Sharjah, I experienced an ongoing difficulty: shopping for bras. The staff at lingerie shops were entirely male, mostly Indians and Filipinos. They always stared at me when I asked for large cup sizes, and just basically made me feel uncomfortable, so I often stormed out empty-handed. I decided to write letters to the Dubai government and to His Highness Sheikh Sultan Al Qasimi, ruler of Sharjah, whose address I found on the Internet. I pointed out that in Arabic culture the ladies are all covered up, while women from my part of the world are not. Ironically, in my country a man would never assist a woman in purchasing lingerie, whereas a decent woman in the UAE could not buy underwear anywhere without being ogled. How might your women, I asked, feel about this breach of intimacy?

I never got a reply from the Dubai government, but Sheikh Sultan wrote back. He said he would look into the matter...that I was totally correct...and thanked me for reaching out to him. Just one month later, the male employees in Sharjah's lingerie stores were gone.

From this time I recall two other happy events. One was receiving my cat Queenie and her brother Pasha, a gift from my colleague Elena. Queenie got pregnant and gave birth to four beautiful kittens. Of course I could not keep them all, so I told my friends to keep their eyes open for anybody who wanted Persian kittens. I was lucky: soon a woman named Ann B. arrived, who took one home. Little did we know that in the near future Ann and I would share in a mutual tragedy.

The other happy memory was the Gulf News Fun Run. It was an annual race organized by one of Dubai's major newspapers, the *Gulf News*. Hans, Bettina and I desperately wanted to attend, but Hans's old Range Rover was being serviced and wouldn't be ready in time. All our friends had already left for the run, so we couldn't hitch a ride, and every 4x4 rental car in Sharjah and Dubai was leased for the event. Unscrupulous Hans decided to go to Mohammed X and ask to borrow his Land Cruiser. I couldn't believe it when Hans actually drove home in that expensive, luxurious car, and our friends thought they were dreaming when they saw us pull up to do the run in it. I guess Hans had made Mohammed feel guilty for making me suffer and beg for my back pay; I can't otherwise explain such a kind gesture from him.

Kittens and the Fun Run. Bright spots in the growing dark.

With the Dubai International Rally over, Bettina and Hans were getting in each other's way and fighting more than ever. Bettina decided to return to Switzerland, unable to understand how I could live with that man.

FEAR OF HANS II

As soon as she left, Hans started psychologically abusing me in new and terrible ways. He didn't work, he was living off me, he never raised a hand to me; I should have felt like the powerful one in our marriage. But truth is I was deathly afraid of him. Even today, I can't explain why.

I became more and more introverted. My life became reduced to my job, the cats and dogs, and taking care of Hans. Sheikh X and his assistant Moussa had returned to our lives, regularly stopping at our home on their way to business meetings in Dubai. Hans told me plainly I should accept Sheikh X's advances. I refused. And then I discovered that Hans himself was putting Valium in my coffee to abuse me sexually. I had lost all respect for my husband. I needed a way out.

REGISTRAR AT EIS

In May 1993 an ad in the newspaper caught my eye. Dubai's Emirates International School (EIS) was looking for a registrar. Hundreds of applications flooded in, but because I was the only person with actual academic experience, I was hired.

Hans drove me to and from school, so I was always under his control. He was extremely possessive, proud as a peacock when men eyed me, but somehow he made me feel unworthy of him. When I would complain about anything at all, he would scream at me to shut up. I had never been shouted at and didn't know how to handle it. I found myself hiding under my own skin.

The job kept me going. I made new friends, "normal" people, who made me realize how shitty my life with Hans was. The director, Martin Kenney, a Canadian in his late fifties, was a gem. He ran the school and did it well. It was not easy to work for the Al Habtoors (the powerful family that owned the school and several other institutions in Dubai) but Martin was the only one who directly communicated with them, so I was shielded from those pressures. I was a member of the administrative staff, which meant my direct boss was Farid Jayyusi, a kind man who would become a faithful friend.

Working as the registrar at EIS was such a pleasure, it was less job than hobby. That's what made going home each afternoon all the more painful. I was scared to eat or drink anything Hans prepared, afraid of being drugged and being his sex slave. I wanted to run, but he had made it clear that it would be very bad for me if I ever tried.

At the end of each school day, Hans would drive me home, after which I'd usually take a little siesta in the bedroom. One time I woke from my nap and saw behind me, reflected in a mirrored wardrobe, Hans rifling through my purse. I was shocked. Why would he do that? My life was an open book; I couldn't move one step outside his view, except for my daily walks on the beach with Polar. I quickly closed my eyes, before he could see that I'd observed him. He took his time, and when he finally slipped out of the bedroom, I was incensed. How could he mistrust me? I didn't deserve this. I thought *if he thinks* I *have something to hide, it must be* him *with something to hide.*

THE SECRET LIFE OF HANS II

I figured that if Hans had secrets, he would guard them in his workroom, which I rarely entered. One day I instructed Primula to tell her husband to ask Hans to go with him to Hole in the Wall to get some beers. This would give me at least an hour alone in the house. (In those times, the UAE made the purchase of alcohol difficult. A permit was required, and the amount one could spend on liquor was limited to a certain percentage of one's salary. However, Hole in the Wall, an infamous dive in Ajman, allowed anyone to buy booze without a license.) The husband asked Hans, and he agreed to go with him.

I told Primula to stand guard outside the house, while I checked the workroom. I came across many papers related to the rallies...I briefly thought I'd misjudged Hans...and then I opened an easily overlooked drawer in his desk. It was filled with papers I had never seen. I copied each and every one with our copier machine, then hid them in my office briefcase. Just in time, too. Primula came running, screaming, "Madam! Madam! Sir is around the corner!"

She and I quickly went to the kitchen and acted as if we had just started cooking.

The next day I gave all the papers to Ayman Khouzam. He was the school's public relations coordinator, handling all work having to do with the government: visas, permits, etc. Ayman soon got back to me. He asked if I knew that my husband was a Muslim. And did I know he was still officially married to a British woman named Evelyn Coates?

Rather than being upset, I was jubilant. I finally saw a way out of my horrible marriage. Ayman translated all the paperwork, including Hans's Muslim conversion certificate. The documents made clear that Hans had never divorced his second wife. This was a lot to digest, and it took me time to gain the strength to confront him. At last, alone with him in the house, I told him I wanted a divorce.

He went mad, flinging things everywhere. I thought that he would hit me, but no. Instead, he disappeared. Five minutes later he called to me, his voice strained, high-pitched. I found him standing naked in a bathtub full of water with a hair dryer in his hand. He looked at me and said he would drop the dryer if I left him. Thinking of Hans Number One and his suicide, I looked at him with cold eyes and said:

"Do it."

Hans had made an empty threat…this time. But I could not assume that he would allow me to divorce him without repercussions. He could stalk me or physically attack me. I needed more help before I could leave this wretched marriage.

CHANGO

In the summer of 1993, school was closed, students off on vacation, teachers away on leave. Only I and a few other administrative employees were at our desks. Despite Dubai's excessive heat and humidity, this season was my favorite time of year. The streets were quiet and empty. Most expats had left for their home countries, and many Emirati had transferred their households to London, Geneva, Paris or the USA. The only noise and bustle were produced by newcomers. There were fathers whose working contracts brought them to the fast-growing city, mothers anxious to find a school for their children. When I wasn't tidying up my office or updating my filing system, I was meeting new students and their parents in a relaxed atmosphere.

On this particular day in early July, as my favorite recorded music was softly playing in the background and I was sorting papers at my desk, Ibtisam, our beautiful receptionist, called me and said,

"Marilyn, there are some people for you in the waiting room."

I had no appointments for that morning, so I got up and almost bumped into two men just walking into my office. One looked like an Egyptian. The other, well, that was difficult to say. He resembled a gypsy with his shoulder-length gray hair and green eyes. His was definitely a face with character, wherein every line had its meaning and story to tell. The way he moved, and the way his eyes caught mine, confused me. I had a feeling of déjà vu…and yet, I was sure I had never met a man so charismatic and interesting.

Instead of sitting in one of the chairs in front of my desk, the stranger came and stood beside me, introduced himself and his colleague Magdi, and asked for forms to register his son in our school. He took the papers, and the two men left. A week later, on July 11, the stranger returned with the completed forms. I scanned the documents and compared them to the copies of the passports and report cards. I checked the father's name: Juan Carlos Peralta. No mother's name. I checked the son's name: Juan Marco Peralta. I spoke the name out loud. The way I pronounced the "J" inspired Juan to comment, "Ah, you know Spanish."

"No, a bit of Italian." Not looking at him, without thinking and without any reason, I continued, "Once I had an Italian boyfriend, a wonderful man, but for me no Latin lovers anymore, *basta*." Having raised my head, I saw him looking at me. He merely smiled. We continued talking about the enrollment and residence visa for Marco. Registered for the 1993-1994 school year, the boy would enter the eleventh grade in the fall.

It was not until September 1993 that I would start to know the man who would change my life—Juan Carlos—who preferred to be called by his nickname, Chango. In the meantime I had bought myself a new car (cars were relatively cheap in Dubai, as they were tax free) a Land Rover Discovery, the first one sold in Dubai. The car had actually been used for marketing videos and I had got it at a good discount, so Hans no longer drove me to and from school. What's more, Hans had started working again for the Al Nasr Motor Club and the rallies. Following some flirtatious phone calls, Chango and I agreed to meet after school in the Metropolitan Hotel lounge. He was a contractor for an Italian company that designed the roads in Dubai. Chango was supervising the Abu Dhabi Highway, but his working hours were flexible, so it was easy for him to get away. While we talked, I felt a strong, passionate connection to him, a kind I had never before experienced. I felt like I was on fire and sparks were flying from me to him and back.

We met several times after that, and started a sexual relationship. When I told Chango about Hans, he agreed that I needed to develop a plan, one that would set me free and prevent Hans from ever harming or threatening to harm me again.

Some old words of advice swept to mind, something Dr. Antelj had said: "If you are planning to do something against another person, never assume he is stupid. Always assume he's smart. Never underestimate your enemy."

Hans was my enemy, so I carefully started preparations for my escape with the doctor's counsel in mind.

I had to find someone with whom I could go into hiding, a person Hans would never suspect.

I couldn't take any possessions with me; anything missing from the house would raise his suspicions.

I needed a new residence permit.

I needed to start a court case to annul the marriage.

I needed to fly outside the country and come back on a new residence permit.

I discussed everything with my friends at school, Martin, Farid and Ayman. They said the school would take care of my residence permit on my Swiss passport. I called one of my rally friends, Rita Bufton, who lived alone and worked at Dubai TV. I told her my story, and she agreed that I could stay with her, but I couldn't bring my dogs, only my cats. This was acceptable to me, as Rita was living very close to Farid, who agreed to take me to and from school, once I made the move. I anticipated a violent response from Hans, although I was also aware that some people felt I was overreacting.

As chance would have it, my escape would be executed earlier than I had planned.

LAST HOURS WITH ANNE-LIES; FREEDOM FROM HANS II

My family gave me terrible news of my sister Anne-Lies: she had been diagnosed with ovarian cancer and had only a few months to live. I told Hans that I wanted to go to Holland during the Christmas to New Year break to say my goodbyes to her. He gave me permission and decided he would travel abroad also, visiting his family in Switzerland. I bought a round-trip Malaysia Airlines ticket Dubai-Amsterdam, as that carrier flew to both Amsterdam and Brussels, and my parents' home lay exactly in between those two cities. I wanted access to two airports to expand my options for the time of my return, thinking Hans might check my flights.

I spoke to Ching, who agreed to go to the house while we were gone, remove my Swiss passport and jewelry, and hand my passport over to the school. (By the way, if you're thinking Ching was a treasure, you're right. Was and is. Today he is living happily with his American wife in Florida.) When I landed in Dubai, Rob Geurten, a Dutch phys ed instructor at EIS, would bring me to my house to collect my cats and some clothing. Once the residence permit was applied for, the passport had to be handed to someone at the Dubai airport. My friends assured me this would all be taken care of.

Hans and I had agreed that we should fly back the same day; this is how our tickets were booked: his Dubai-Zürich round trip, mine Dubai-Amsterdam round trip.

At the airport, Hans and I said our goodbyes.

When I arrived at my parents' home, I told them the whole story. They understood and told me they had never trusted Hans. We went to see Anne-Lies, and although we had initially agreed I would spend the day with her, her husband allowed me only thirty minutes. Her treatments had left her fragile and ill, but her face was serene. She calmly told me that her leaving this world would be more difficult for us, the ones left behind, than for her, as she had already seen departed loved ones waiting for her to come HOME.

I spent a subdued Christmas and New Year's with my parents. I changed the date of my return flight; I called Malaysia Airlines, said I had an emergency, and had to fly back through Brussels to Dubai. No problem. I was re-booked and informed the school, so that the residence permit would be waiting for me. I called Rita and told her I was coming the next day, one day before Hans would be back.

When I arrived at Dubai International Airport, Ans, a blond Dutch woman in a Swissair uniform, whispered my name and secretly handed me my Swiss passport. I went to the visa counter where I received my papers before proceeding to customs. Everything went smoothly.

Outside I met with Ayman and Rob. I still had a full day before Hans was due back, but I kept Dr. Antelj's advice in mind. I wouldn't un-derestimate Hans. I called Ching before driving to my house and asked him to check the house. Ching drove there and gave the OK.

Primula was very surprised to see me. I told her I was going to run away and that she never should mention to Hans seeing Ching or Rob, only me. While I gathered some clothing and the cats, she burst into tears. I could see she was upset to see me go, but also relieved that I finally had the courage to do this.

"What happens to me now?" she begged.

I said, "Just do your job. He has nobody but you and your husband now, so he needs you." I told her to take good care of Polar, and assured her once I was settled I would come and take her. Then we cried together.

Rob drove me to Rita's home, a small villa located between the Dubai city communities of Satwa and Jumeirah. I settled in a small room with my cats Seppie, Queenie and Pasha, and kitten Pluisje. I was so nervous about what might happen. I had finally taken the first step to freedom, but I knew that Hans would create a big mess. I just hoped he'd leave my friends out of it.

Aware Hans would arrive the next evening, I moved quickly. First thing the next day I went to the shari'a court with all my papers and applied for an annulment of the marriage. I also bought a new sim card for the phone. What I forgot to do was block my bank accounts; they held all my money, and they were shared accounts that Hans could access. This omission would later cost me dearly.

I met up with Chango, who told me to be courageous and believe in myself. His words put me on cloud nine…but they couldn't prepare me for what was to come.

Farid and his family lived two minutes from my hideout. The first day after the Christmas holidays, he and his children, Husam, about six years old, and Natasha, a teenager, picked me up to take me to work. The kids thought it was fun to see me crouching out of sight in the backseat of their four-wheel drive.

Nearing the parking lot, we saw Hans's white Range Rover in front of the school.

Farid changed tactics. We slipped within the side entrance of the school. I went to my office, while Farid told security that Hans was not to enter the school premises. One guard kept an eye on me. Farid went outside and told Hans to move his car. He refused, so Farid called the police. The police came and removed Hans and his car from the school grounds.

This farce was repeated every day for the next two weeks. Enraged, Hans had made a T-shirt featuring a large picture of my face. Wearing the shirt, he went from building to building in Dubai and asked if anybody had seen me.

At the start of the third week, the workday drawing to a close, Farid, his children and I piled into his car. Pulling away from the school, Farid spotted the Range Rover in his rear mirror. Farid accelerated. Hans kept pace. They raced like maniacs, up one street, down another. They reached the Trade Centre Roundabout, Farid driving the inside lane, Hans right behind him. They were speeding about a hundred miles per hour. Suddenly, Farid turned right and cut several cars to exit. His kids were shouting and laughing, finding it all very exciting, while my heart pounded with fear. Hans failed to follow; we looked back and saw him still circling the roundabout. Farid veered into an alley and then into the driveway of someone's home, where we wouldn't be visible. Finally, after about ten minutes, Farid pulled out of the driveway and drove to his home using side streets only. We arrived there safely, and the children eagerly recounted to their mom, Maha, the action story starring their hero father. The others soon relaxed, but I was slow to stop trembling.

Seeing the coast was clear, Farid drove me to my hiding place. Of course, I told Rita the whole adventure. Luckily, she wasn't the sort that scares easily.

The next day's drive to work was without incident, but trouble lurked around the corner.

Farid and I could see into each other's offices through a big window with a hallway in between. Since he was the administrative manager who often dealt with the school's owners, it was not unusual to see locals in his office. This morning, however, his room was thick with them, all dressed in *dishdashas*. I called him and joked, "Farid, do you have the CID in your office?" Farid said, "Shut up!" and slammed down the receiver. This wasn't like him at all. He also wouldn't look in my direction.

He stepped out of his office. The locals stayed. He returned to his desk, his face like stone. Farid talked with the men, and after a few minutes he and they left together. I still didn't make anything of it, thinking they were perhaps members of the Ministry of Education come for an inspection. Then my door opened, and Farid entered with the whole bunch. I was told to pack my things and come with them. It was indeed the CID from Sharjah, accompanied by the CID of Dubai. They were there to return me to my husband.

Someone, perhaps Farid, said my removal wasn't legal without the agreement of the local CID, so I must next be taken to Dubai's CID headquarters. Farid told me he and Ayman would follow in his car, never letting me out of their sight. As we walked out of the school building, I saw Hans standing next to his Range Rover, triumph in his eyes.

During that tense drive to Dubai CID headquarters, I tried to call the director of Central Police Headquarters, traffic department, Saeed Al Kamda, known by me through the rallies, and the chief of police,

Saeed Khalfan, chairman of the Al Nasr Motor Club. Saeed couldn't stand Hans, but he and I had become good friends while I was involved in the rallies. Unfortunately, both powerful men were on vacation and couldn't be reached. Hans had chosen the perfect time for this maneuver, when my few friends in high places were scarce.

At headquarters we stepped into a spacious office, where the chief of the Dubai CID was waiting. He asked Farid, Ayman and me to be seated, then requested the door be closed; Hans was forced to wait in the hall. The chief asked Farid what was going on, and he explained in Arabic that I had a court case in Dubai against Hans, who was still officially married to another woman. Then Hans was called in. He shouted at Farid and badmouthed EIS. Farid jumped to his feet, shook his fists and told him if he ever tried to smear the school's good name he'd kill him. It was all quite dramatic, but the chief had no desire to start a political feud between the two emirates. He permitted the Sharjah CID to take me to their police station. Hans immediately left, wanting to have the upper hand and reach the station first. I was escorted back into the police car, and again, Farid and Ayman followed. I used the long drive to phone the Swiss ambassador, Bernard Meier, who said he would hurry and meet me in Sharjah.

I wasn't surprised to see Hans waiting for me in front of the station, but I was shocked to see his sister Trudy there, too. The two of them hollered curses at me when I got out of the police car. I couldn't understand why Trudy, who'd been my good friend in Switzerland, would treat me this way. I was upset beyond words.

The ambassador was waiting for me, the calming presence I needed. He, Farid and Ayman, as well as Hans and Trudy, were asked to remain in the waiting room, while a uniformed policeman who spoke a little English brought me alone into a small room.

His first questions were simple enough. What was my name, where did I live? Then came a slew that had clearly been instigated by Hans. Did I work at EIS? Did I know a Mr. Farid Jayyusi? Yes, I said, he's out there in the waiting room.

"Are you having a sexual relationship with Mr. Jayyusi?"

I looked at him in shock. No, I stammered, of course not, he's my boss, and I'm very good friends with his wife and children.

The officer continued with some less inflammatory questions and then handed me a statement to sign. I refused, saying Ayman and Farid needed to review it first; it was written entirely in Arabic and I couldn't read a word. The officer got permission from his supervisor to step out to the waiting room and hand the men the document.

Farid's face went from white to red as he read and re-read the accusation of us having a sexual relationship. At last he exploded, shouting at Hans that he would sue him if he didn't take back the allegations. Ambassador Meier, Ayman and the police quieted him down by providing an addendum to the document that stated I was a plaintiff in a case against Hans, who was still married to an Englishwoman; that our marriage had no contract and was therefore invalid; and that an annulment had been filed with the shari'a court in Dubai.

The police came around to my side, realizing Hans had misled them with false information. They now warned him to keep away from me. With great relief I signed the statement, left the station, got into Farid's car and was driven away, Hans and Trudy again screaming foul things in my wake.

The court date for the annulment came soon after: May 12, 1994. My heart was beating wildly as I entered the shari'a court building in Dubai, Farid and Ayman at my side. Thank God for these men, my Arabic translators and friends. Ayman figured out which courtroom we needed to be in, and when we arrived we found Hans already waiting, a sickeningly confident grin on his face. A judge sat behind a desk in the simply furnished room. Ayman, Farid and I seated ourselves on the left side of the judge, while Hans sat in front of him.

Speaking in Arabic, looking at both of us, the judge of the shari'a court, Ahmad Bin Hamad Al Mazrouh, stated that the case was actually very simple. Marriage in Islam is a legal contract between a man and a woman, aimed at safeguarding the rights of the couple and their children. Law demands that the contract be registered in a shari'a court in the UAE. Since I could prove with official documents that Hans had converted to the Muslim faith before we wed, our marriage was never valid. We had never registered the contract in Dubai or any other part of the UAE. Indeed, there was no contract at all. Therefore our marriage was officially annulled at once.

On November 27, 1994, I received an official document from the Swiss consulate in Dubai stating the following:

> The Consulate of Switzerland hereby confirms that the certificate dated February 26, 1989 regarding the marriage between Petronella Maria Cornelia Wouters and Hans Peereboom cannot be accepted by the Swiss authorities. Certain details in the Application of Marriage (February 9, 1989) and in the Marriage Certificate are incorrect. Thus according to Swiss law the marriage is not considered legal.

Hans and I were given official copies of the ruling.

That priceless document in hand, a few days later I returned to the police station in Sharjah, seeking security backup while I went to the villa in Al Riqqa and reclaimed my personal items. A few CID men piled into a police car and followed my own. My earth angels Ayman and Farid drove there with me. I had also hired a truck to convey away my belongings.

Arriving at the villa, we found the gate in the perimeter wall latched. We knocked and called out Hans's name. My dogs started barking, but neither Hans nor Primula emerged from the house. The CID men jumped over the wall and found Hans on the other side of the gate. They ordered him to open it. He could not refuse.

After six long months, I could finally hug and pet my dogs, with the exception of my favorite, little Polar. Hans held her on a short leash and wouldn't let her come near me. It was an absurd power play. I felt sorry for the little creature, forced to remain in his possession, but at least she appeared healthy. Primula had been looking after her properly.

We went inside the house, and I pointed to all the items belonging to me. (Most of the furniture was mine, but I had decided in advance not to take any.) I had wisely brought photographs, taken during my first marriage, which showed that most things were definitively mine. Hans resisted letting go of anything. He insisted he should have the expensive

Dutch dinnerware, one of the wedding gifts when I married my second husband in Switzerland. I protested, but the police let him keep it. Hans even tried to claim the sewing machine. I said to the police, is he starting a tailor shop now? They gave it to me.

Hans had squirreled away many things: photo albums, personal videos, cameras and other electronic devices, all of which I had acquired before I met him. Again, it was a power play, an ugly one. I showed the police a bill of sale for my piano. The instrument was carefully loaded onto the truck, and the police and I left.

I soon discovered I was penniless. Hans had emptied our joint bank account in the UAE, as well as an account we held in the UK. Still, I tried to stay positive: I had a good job and people who loved me.

LOSS OF ANNE-LIES AND SEPPIE

While I was still living with Rita and looking for an affordable place of my own, Anne-Lies's husband called: my sister had passed away. She died February 16, 1994. I was devastated. It was impossible for me to attend the funeral, as I already had so many absences from school due to the case with Hans. I also had no money for the flight. I felt I couldn't ask my parents to lend it to me; I was too proud, and I didn't want to distress them by revealing the extent of my problems. Anne-Lies's husband shouted at me over the phone. *This is your sister! And you're not coming to her funeral?*

I was overcome with grief and guilt.

Increasing my distress was Seppie's illness. Now twenty years old, he had to undergo treatments every month. When I went to pick him up and saw him lying in the big cage, he would look at me while I petted him and softly meow. I understood what he was saying: "Please let me go." I called Kelly the vet and told her Seppie's decision. She asked me if I was sure. I told her the decision wasn't mine: Seppie wanted to go in peace. Since Hans had been good to Seppie and seemed to have loved him, I called him and told him that if he wanted to say goodbye, he should come right away, as Seppie was in a very bad state and wanted to leave this earth. We waited, and Hans was there within ten minutes.

Unbelievably, he stood behind me and whispered in my ear, "Murderer!" Already in shock over what was happening to Seppie, I turned around, stared at Hans and told Kelly, "I made a mistake. Please take this man out of the clinic." Cursing loudly, Hans left.

I told Kelly to wait a bit longer, as now I was confused, upset and angry. I had to let go of this energy without transferring it to Seppie. Kelly and I went outside and drank a coffee. Then I went back and took Seppie in my arms. He kept looking at me as I whispered, "It's OK." Kelly gave him an injection to fall asleep. I fought back tears. Seppie had been my "child" for twenty years, had gone with me through thick and thin. With him the past left me, the past that had been so difficult to handle, the past in which this cat, who had been my marriage present, was always there to give me peace. As Kelly gave him the final injection and his last breath was felt in my arms, I cried out loud, unable to hide my pain. Some people might say, "It was only a cat," but what Seppie had given me—unconditional love and trust—no human ever had.

A couple of months passed. Rita, who saw I was still suffering, told me that a psychic, a friend of a friend, was visiting from the UK. Perhaps this woman could get in contact with my departed sister? I thought it was worth a try, and when I told my sister Marijke my intentions, she asked if I'd also be willing to try contacting her firstborn son, Matthijs, who had passed away at seven months from SIDS (Sudden Infant Death Syndrome). Chango, who was supportive of the effort, suggested we invite the medium to his apartment.

The woman walked in, looked at me and immediately said that someone was giving me a red rose.

It was my birthday that day, so I told her that it could be my husband who had passed away. The woman then looked at Chango and told him that an old lady was unhappy with him, and that he should first finish his relationship overseas and only then start something new. It was obvious to Chango that the psychic was referring to his beloved grandmother and his partner in Canada with whom he had lived for many years. His grandmother, speaking to him after all this time... It was a powerful moment.

The medium continued to hear messages from other spirits whom I recognized, but every now and then she would speak of the rose again. The spirit offering the rose didn't want to go away, nor did it care to deliver any other message. The medium couldn't even tell me if the spirit was male or female. I gave up, greatly disappointed, wishing I had heard from Anne-Lies so I could apologize for not coming to her funeral.

Once the psychic had left, I called Marijke in Holland and told her that Matthijs had not spoken to me, but there had been another constant presence, a spirit who almost seemed bent on disturbing the session, insisting on giving me one red rose.

On the other end of the line, my sister went silent. Finally, she said,

"Didn't you know that the invitations to the funeral had one red rose on them? And that everybody at the funeral, before entering the church, received one red rose?"

I had never received an invitation or a thank-you card. Anne-Lies had organized her own funeral with exquisite care. I was the only one to whom she personally delivered that one red rose. She knew I was with her that day and ever since.

The psychic, by the way, refused to accept a penny for her services.

HARASSED BY HANS II

I was still looking for a place to live. The most affordable complex was Jebel Ali Village. Chango was also eager to move there, and he had used his connections to be atop the waiting list. When I heard there was wriggle room in the application process, I immediately called Mohammed bin Sulayem, the frequent rally champion, good friend, and brother of Sultan bin Sulayem, chairman of the Jebel Ali Free Zone. I was given the villa meant for Chango; it seems the free zone administrators called him, told him an urgent matter had come up, and he had to wait a little bit longer! He took the news gracefully, and I happily moved into villa 225, Road M, Jebel Ali Village.

I had registered myself at the village under my Swiss passport residence permit, received after I returned to the UAE earlier that year. What happened next I can only offer as hearsay. My "non-husband" discovered I had found a house in the village and went to the village administration office. He announced that he was my husband and wanted to see under which passport I was registered. Because Hans was a foreigner, had a big black beard and looked imposing, the poor Indian lady working there showed him—against my expressed wishes—my Swiss passport with the residence permit. Of course, he went straight to Immigration and reported my crime.

If I had received the call from Immigration directly, that would have been upsetting enough. However, since I was employed on a work visa with EIS, school administrators received the call. This was bad news for EIS as well as for me, as this could be grounds for my deportation.

I called Saeed Khalfan, whom you will recall was the chair of the motor club rallies, and Mohammed bin Sulayem. I asked them if they would do me the favor of informing the director of Immigration about my case. I think they were glad to do it, as they disliked Hans. Next, I phoned the Swiss ambassador and Dutch ambassador, and asked for their support. Calls completed, I made an appointment with Immigration.

I arrived at the entrance of the Immigration building in the reassuring company of Farid, Ayman and the two ambassadors. Hans was waiting there, staring at me with his usual eerie smile. He tried to follow the rest of us into the glass-walled office of the director, but this was denied, and he was visibly angered.

We were invited to take a seat. I explained my case to the director, after which the Dutch ambassador took my passport and ripped it apart. He looked at the director and said, "For me, she is not Dutch." The Swiss ambassador held my Swiss passport and said, "She is Swiss." The director pronounced that good enough for him, wished us a good day and escorted us to the door. Outside the building, Hans screamed at the Dutch ambassador that he was Dutch, too, and deserved representation. Nobody listened. We hugged, and each of us went our own way.

Two weeks later I received a replacement Dutch passport.

Yet that wasn't the end of it.

Hans decided to make my new life miserable. He had cut a hole in the wire fence that enclosed Jebel Ali Village, slipped inside and started stalking me. Fortunately, Arnold Corpeleyn, a tall, hefty Dutchman who lived on a street behind me, came to my rescue. Whenever I sighted Hans, I called this man's family, and he would come stalk *Hans* until he ran off. Hans also tried to drive into the village, but security guards blocked his advance.

Gradually, very gradually, Hans stopped harassing me.

I MEET MY "SISTER"

When I moved into the villa, I had very little besides my piano, my sewing machine, some clothes, and a framed photo of Anne-Lies that hung upon my bedroom wall. Some parents of students at EIS, including the parents of friends of Marco's, heard about my difficulties and gave me chairs, a bed and other items for the house. Chango also found a villa soon after this, and Marco spent much time in both our places. He was my spiritual son.

A few months passed. Grateful for all the kindness that had been shown me, I decided to "give back" and throw a party for single mothers who were having problems getting residence permits for their children. One mother called me at the last moment and explained that she couldn't make it, as she had to deal with an emergency, some problem related to the marriage of her friend Evelyn.

Evelyn?

I asked if by any chance her friend's surname was Coates. Yes, she said. Did I know her? "No, I've never met her," I replied, "but if she has long, strawberry blond hair, you can tell her that she has worse marriage problems than she thinks, because she's not even married to her current husband, she's still married to my non-husband." The woman was speechless. Me too, actually, as the words had simply dropped out of my mouth.

The party that evening was successful, and I went to bed late, thinking I could sleep in the next morning. But no. Around 6 A.M. the doorbell rang. I opened the front door and saw a tall, beautiful red-haired lady standing in front of me. Evelyn! Before she finished introducing herself, we were hugging each other.

Those first days Evelyn and I knew each other, we sobbed more than we hugged. Evelyn cried because the sight of me brought back so many memories of Hans, and I cried because, well, he was a man who had given me hell. However, it seems that Hans treated Evelyn even worse than he did me. She ended up in a hospital on one occasion. She even served jail time on account of him. Evelyn had been with Hans when he was arrested for what turned out to be one of the most infamous drug cases in the history of the UAE. This is not my story to tell, but she was definitely innocent and had nothing to do with the crime. She was only *guilty by association*.

Evelyn and I discovered many similarities between us, including being born under the same star sign, Taurus. We immediately felt like sisters. So... Evelyn left her current husband, who was gay, and moved in with me. This worked out perfectly, because I had the house and she had the furniture, curtains and household materials.

Did you think we were done with Hans? Not quite. When he heard Evelyn and I were sharing a home, he squeezed himself through that hole in the fence again and spied on us. With nothing exciting to see, he soon disappeared.

Evelyn shortly after made the acquaintance of a sea captain named Dauphine. They became a couple and were very happy. Neither of them liked Chango. They didn't think he treated me the way I deserved, and said they were sure he was f---ing all the Italian women in the village. Evelyn and Dauphine wouldn't listen to me when I tried to explain I needed to remain a secret in Chango's life, for my own safety—Hans could still be a problem—and ours. Remember, living together without marriage was expressly forbidden in the UAE. Still is.

One night on the way home from the Jebel Ali Club, having drunk a good deal, Evelyn and Dauphine passed by Chango's house. They saw the lights on and shouted at him to leave me alone, even picking up and throwing stones. Chango quickly dimmed the light, and they walked on. He didn't discuss the episode with me until much later.

I had a great time living with Evelyn, but great times rarely last. Evelyn and Dauphine decided to move to France, and I had my villa to myself again.

EMPLOYMENT AT SWISSAIR

Through Chango I met Yvette, a woman who worked at Swissair's offices in Abu Dhabi. She told me there was an opening for a ground hostess at Abu Dhabi International Airport. The job required only a few evenings a week, and the airline was looking specifically for someone Swiss. Since I finished school each day at 4 P.M., I thought I might manage it. The pay was quite low, but if I were hired I'd be eligible for virtually free flights.

MARCO AND HIS PALS

Because of Chango's working hours and frequent trips overseas, I spent much time with Marco and we became close, especially because I was accident-prone and he had chronic digestive problems. We brought each other regularly as emergency cases to the doctor's office, where I would get a cast applied and he would get injections. For years, doctors couldn't determine the source of Marco's pain. It turned out to be a huge tapeworm.

Marco and his friends used to hang out at my place to study and party, more party than study, really. I decided I should take the boys on educational field trips on the weekends instead of them being bored doing nothing or watching TV. We would pile into my Land Rover Discovery, and the boys would chat about anything, as if I weren't present.

One day I decided to take Marco and his pals Mike and Daniel B. to Ajman to see the oldest dhow yard in the UAE (dhows being traditional Arab boats). While we were traveling the Dubai-Sharjah road, the boys started talking about their sexual encounters and their orgasms. They were all fifteen years old. As Marco was describing his experiences loudly and noisily, his friends laughing and completely absorbed in his story, I said, "That is exactly like your dad."

Awkward silence. Nobody spoke. I looked at Marco beside me and in the rearview mirror at the other boys. They regarded me with disgust, so I asked them, "What? I am sitting here behind the wheel, you know, I'm not wearing earplugs."

Marco said, "Ewww, Mer! Old people don't do things like that. You're not supposed to talk about what we young people do!"

I just replied, "We do it better, believe me, guys!"

At that moment, I had to hit the brakes hard not to hit the car in front of me, which had also suddenly braked. I glanced in the rearview mirror and saw a Land Cruiser behind me whose driver had not paid attention and tried to avoid smashing me by yanking his steering wheel too abruptly to the right. His car veered from the road and rolled twice. The boys turned around in their seats, watching the spectacle and calling out, "Mer you killed them!" several times. I was still driving away, but slowly, observing the whole thing in the mirror. No other cars stopped to help, and why should they? The doors on the sidelined car opened and two men got out, no harm done.

Relieved, I continued the drive to Ajman. We arrived at the largest dhow-building center in the world, where the boats are still built by hand using traditional tools and techniques passed down through generations of craftsmen. Most of the workers were Pakistani and Indians, and the boys did not know anything better to do than to ask them for ganja (marijuana). I told them if they couldn't mind their manners they'd end up in jail, and quickly left with them. They'd had enough "education" for the weekend.

I imagine our initials and the year—M.M.D.M. 1994—can still be found where we spray-painted them on one of the rocks of Jebel Hafit in Al Ain. The boys amused themselves jumping into small sand tornados, which were on top of the mountain. I was forty-seven years old at the time and thoroughly enjoying myself. The guys kept me young.

On the way up the mountain, I suddenly tripped between two rocks. Luckily, I got stuck between them and did not tumble to my death, as there was a sheer drop of several hundred meters straight beneath. Losing sight of me, the guys started calling my name and ran back to where they'd last seen me. Finally, they spotted me hanging about one meter down, legs dangling. It was a dangerous situation, and they took quick action. Marco lay on the ground to pull me out, Daniel holding

Marco's legs and Mike holding Daniel's to prevent all of us falling off the mountain. I believe we were all scared, and when they finally managed to pull me up to safety, I was not allowed to walk behind them any more. I had to walk between them where they could see me at all times.

One Thursday afternoon the boys decided they would do three things with me that I had never done.

1. *Surf.* We drove to Chicago Beach Village and walked to the end of the pier. The boys had their surfboards, and I had a body board strapped to my wrist. Standing on that pier, I thought the sea looked awfully rough and far below me. I was delaying and delaying, waiting to jump, not admitting to myself that I actually was too scared to move, when Marco shouted, "A wave, Mer! Jump!" He pushed me off. I flew through the air and plunged into the water. Virtually drowning, I swam to the surface to hear Marco shouting with excitement, "Get on your board, now, now!" I was happy to be alive and was like a fish above water, catching air. A big wave came. Under I went again, Marco flying over me with his surfboard, yelling, "Go, Mer, go!" I have no idea how I reached the beach in one piece; maybe it's because I'm a good swimmer. However I survived, I promised myself to never ever again leap from a pier with a board on my wrist.

2. *Eat fast food.* I had never tasted fast food, so we decided to go to Burger King for lunch. I was not impressed with the burger but liked the curly fries.

3. *Jet ski.* I had never been on personal watercraft before, so we drove to Dubai Creek where the boys rented three Jet Skis: one for Mike, one for Daniel and one for Marco and me. I sat behind my Marco, and we all rode happily around on the creek until Marco decided it was time for me to give it a try. We swapped places, and Marco told me how to handle the machine, explaining that the kill switch was attached to my wrist; if I fell, the engine would stop. The creek was wide enough for us all. I gave the ski gas and there we went, faster and faster. I soon realized that

I didn't really have control over the whole thing, the steering handle seeming very heavy, so I decided to just fly straight over the water and not try a turn or anything else. As I mentioned, the creek was broad. Daniel was having fun on the right side of me, Mike on the left. They were far enough away that I didn't worry about them. I just went *brum brum brum* enjoying myself when Marco shouted at me to turn right. I hadn't realized that Mike's Jet Ski was having engine problems and had stopped dead in the water. I tried, but the steering handle didn't turn, so I continued straight towards him. Marco shouted again that we were approaching Mike too fast. I thought him still at a safe distance. *Brum brum brum*, we kept moving happily forward. Suddenly I felt Marco jumping off the back of my Jet Ski and saw Mike coming up straight ahead of me. We collided, and I flew right over his Jet Ski like a professional. I got my Jet Ski to stop and sat in shock before slowly turning around to see Marco swimming towards me, fast as a shark. I then saw Mike burst up from under the water and swim towards me. Daniel pissed in his pants laughing on top of his Jet Ski, watching the whole thing. Marco later told me that Mike was furious. Luckily, Marco was a faster swimmer than Mike and saved me from a sure death, as Mike was really ready to kill me.

Marco decided to return to Canada at the end of the school year, as there was not much for young people to do in Dubai in the late nineties. He also wanted to look up his first love, who had been heavily into drugs.

To our surprise, Marco decided to come back for the new school year, and Daniel decided to apply to the aviation college. Daniel called me one day and asked if I could help him with his German, as there was going to be a test end of term and he wanted to do well. I went to his home and sat with him in his bedroom at a study desk where I dictated him a little scenario in German. It featured a German couple entering a hotel asking for a room, and Daniel was to take the role of the reception desk clerk. When I saw him writing down the dialog, I asked him, "Daniel, are you dyslexic?" He confirmed this, and I decided at that moment that we were going to change tactics. I told him that for the next week he was going to call me a few times every day, the two of us trading roles of guest and clerk. The exam came, and he got the highest grade in the class. Although his dyslexia was taken into account, the teaching faculty believed he had been cheating and somehow known the exam questions ahead of time. He told them I had been helping him, yet still they didn't trust him. A new date was set for an exam covering different vocabulary. Again, Daniel called me several times a day for a week. When he sat for the second exam, he once more had everything correct. We were both very proud.

Typically, I worked through the school's summer break. Parents would be coming and going from my office, discussing admissions matters with me. One day late in the summer of 1994, a couple came to me asking if they could speak to a particular teacher. I had spotted that instructor a moment earlier, heading for the teacher's lounge, so I told them to wait and quickly ran out my office and around the corner, where I slipped and fell. I knew at once I'd broken my leg. The teacher who saw me fall came running, lifted me up and brought me back to my office. The parents, still sitting in their chairs, looked at me in astonishment. "What happened?" they asked. I replied that I had broken my leg and needed to go to the hospital. They continued their talk with the teacher while I called Marco, who had returned one week before school started and was surfing with friends. He came together with Daniel, and although Marco didn't yet have his driver's license, he knew how to drive, so together they brought me to the Iranian Hospital (a major hospital in Dubai). There x-rays were taken, which confirmed the fracture. I needed a cast that couldn't be applied over my leggings. I took my leggings off and asked Marco to give me his jeans. Grimacing, he pulled off his jeans and put on my leggings. He looked like a ballet dancer!

After the cast was done, we were hungry, so we decided to go to an Indian restaurant in Satwa. Marco forbade me to walk: he carried me out of the car, clearly enjoying my embarrassment as he danced with me into the restaurant. Of course, a broken leg did not stop me from working. My neighbor Liz Duquenoy, secretary to our director Martin Kenny, drove me every morning to school. Why not Marco? Too often he couldn't drag himself out of bed. I finally got so fed up that I warned him that if he didn't get up and take me to work the next day, I'd throw a bucket of water on him. He didn't believe me, of course, but before I went to wake him the next morning, I filled the largest bucket I had with water and put it beside his door outside in the hall. I knocked on his door and sweetly asked him to get up, as it was time to go to school. I heard him mumble something un-understandable. Five minutes later I knocked again with more force. Not a sound came from the room. I opened the door and looked inside. Marco slowly opened his eyes, coming out of a deep sleep to the sight of me shuffling through the door with the bucket in my hands—it was very heavy, so I couldn't walk fast—and as I lifted it above his head his eyes grew larger, and before he could jump out of the way the water splashed all over him and the mattress. He had to sleep a few days on the sofa, while his mattress dried in the garden.

"I HAVE NEVER PRAYED SO MUCH IN MY LIFE"

Daniel and Marco started working part time for a clothing company called Diesel and hanging out with their new boss, Damien, a Belgian entrepreneur. I remember mentioning to Chango that I was wondering why this Belgian guy was hanging out with these two kids.

Chango used to call me when he'd arrive home. I'd go to his house, and we would cook and have dinner together. One late afternoon, while Chango was still at work, Marco called his dad to inform him that he would be late, as he was with his boss and Daniel. Chango had a vision; he told Marco to stop what he was doing right there and then and come home immediately. Marco told his dad not to worry and promised he would call again later.

When Chango got home, he told me about the phone conversation and his premonition. He was very preoccupied with this call. This surprised me, as Chango wasn't the kind of guy to overreact. We ate and heard nothing from Marco, which was strange because father and son usually phoned each other several times a day. Chango called Marco repeatedly, but the boy's cell was switched off. Chango kept looking at his watch. Finally, we went to bed.

Around 2 A.M. Chango's phone rang. It was Ann, Daniel B.'s mother, crying and telling us that Sharjah and Dubai CIDs were on their way to our house with the kids in chains. The CIDs had searched her house and Damien's apartment and charged the boys with drug trafficking.

At that time, an enlarged newspaper cutting hung above Marco's bed, detailing the law that had recently introduced the death penalty for drug trafficking. Until this moment, I suppose all three of us thought of the law as simply words to be applied to others.

Chango and I had little time to get our act together before the doorbell rang. While I hung back, Chango opened the door. About ten men in white *dishdashas* entered, Marco standing in the middle in chains. I saw how ashamed he was, not daring to look us in the eye. He came and hugged me, saying, "I'm so sorry, Mum." His words immediately erased the fact that I was not his mother and didn't belong in that house. Remember, shari'a law forbade unmarried people to live together. The UAE was a strict Muslim country. I was so grateful to Marco for his white lie. The CID searched Marco's room thoroughly, but fortunately there was nothing to be found. Before they left, they informed us that Chango could see Marco the next day in court in Sharjah.

Chango could not share the pain he felt during this period of his life, and instead of our relationship getting stronger, we slowly grew apart. He forbade me to talk about Marco with his daughters. He had two: Claudia, who was backpacking and travelling the world, and Alejandra, who lived in Argentina. I visited Marco in jail as much as I could. He started writing me, and I wrote him. This was the first time Marco wanted to know about my life, so I started writing him about my childhood. In fact, this was the start of my "autobiography."

Until he was sentenced, Marco was kept in the crowded police station jail, squashed with the other prisoners like sardines in a tin. Marco sent me a drawing of the conditions there; the boys always had to be on their guard, especially Daniel, who was a small blond boy and wanted by his inmates for sexual reasons. Marco made sure he was always next to him while sleeping!

During the religious holiday of Eid, parents were allowed to bring food to the jail. I made my special meatballs in gravy—there must have been fifty of them—as well as about 150 of my delicious Indonesian chicken drumsticks, Marco's favorite. It was a feast for the prisoners in Marcos's cell.

It was a difficult time for everyone involved, mostly for Marco, who now realized that the jokes had come to an end. Still, he kept up his spirits. He asked me to bring books, he who was not a reader at all. In those times, most of my books were by Harold Robbins, Sydney Sheldon and other easy-reading authors who tended to write about romance and sexuality. Of course, I never stopped to think about the content, but Marco told me later that some of these books made him feel uncomfortable, considering the circumstances.

In those days embassies and consulates didn't want to get involved in drug cases. Nevertheless, Chango was in contact with the Argentine embassy in Abu Dhabi, Ann with the UK embassy in Dubai, while Damien's parents sought assistance in Belgium. Ann hired a lawyer; she had to take a loan and went deeply into debt. I invited her to stay in my villa, as I spent most of my time at Chango's, one street up in the same village.

I have never prayed so much in my life. One time I went to the police station to get permission from CID to see the prisoners. When I arrived I saw several mothers, including Ann, crying because they were not allowed to see their children. Holding my cross and praying to Jesus, I knocked on the door of the CID office. An officer opened the door. I held my cross and kept praying, while telling the man I wanted to see Marco Peralta. He told me to wait and came out a few minutes later with the permission slip. I was so relieved. Visitors were the prisoners' vital lifeline to the outside world; they craved contact, even if only a few words were exchanged. During the time of the trial, none of us involved used our telephones, as they were all bugged. We lived the lives of saints, all of us feeling oppressed.

In 1995 the sentences were handed down. Damien got ten years in prison and a suspended death sentence. Marco got four years in prison and a suspended death sentence, as did Daniel, but without suspended death sentence. We were all devastated, living in a nightmare. The boys were transferred to the central prison in Sharjah. Visiting hours were on a regular schedule, but we were only allowed to view the boys from afar. They would stand alongside each other in a corridor, their heads shaved, faces partly obscured by steel bars and mesh, while we stood side by side opposite them in another corridor fifteen meters (fifty feet) away, also covered by bars and mesh. When I visited Marco, I used to block everybody else out and focus only on him, standing there, looking back at me, trying to smile and make me feel better. I would stay strong until I left; driving back to Dubai, tears would pour down my cheeks. Police jail had been heaven compared to central prison.

From his side, Chango worked to get Marco out as soon as possible. I started working from my side and met with Mahmood Al Redha, one of Meyer-Reumann Legal Consultancy's clients, with whom I had a good relationship. I met with him a few times, while he had contact with his brother, who was a judge. The last time I saw Mahmood he told me to relax, that everything would be OK.

A NIGHTMARE ENDS

It seems that during the summer holidays, judges of different emirates would help each other out in different districts. Al Redha transferred himself to Sharjah as a temporary replacement. He knew the whole story. Once the boys went into appeal, Marco got his sentence reduced from four years to one. I decided that when he got out, he should go to my parents' place. There, he'd have the opportunity to take long, quiet walks in the peaceful forest and recover from the unspeakable things that had happened to him in prison.

Meanwhile, Chango was making plans with the ambassador. Judge Al Redha had composed a letter permitting Marco to be released to the ambassador and deported. I was on standby with an ID90 from KLM when Chango called: *Tonight* was all he said. I got my ID90 confirmed and went to Dubai airport, where I waited, my blood pumping in my veins. From the outside I looked cool and confident, but inside I was almost breaking apart. A police van stopped in front of the Dubai airport, followed by another car. Police got out, and I saw Chango and the ambassador get out of their car. The backdoor of the police van opened, and Marco came out, his hands and feet shackled. The police came into the airport with him and went straight to airport security, followed by Chango and escort. After some talk Chango went to the check-in desk and arranged Marco's boarding pass. I did mine. I passed security and customs and waited anxiously. A short while later, after checking all documents, a Sharjah policeman took Marco to the gate, his foot chains removed but hands still manacled. From the gate we were immediately escorted into the aircraft. We were the only passengers inside. Finally, half an hour later, the first passengers started coming into the aircraft, and the police removed Marco's handcuffs. Marco and I looked at each other, almost not daring to breathe until the door closed behind the last passenger. When the plane left the tarmac and the wheels left the ground, we embraced each other. The nightmare was over: Marco was free.

We slept for most of the flight until we arrived in Schiphol Airport, Amsterdam. We had a busy day in front of us, as Marco, with my advice, had decided to apply to a hotel management school. My first choice was Den Hague, not too far from Dorst, so that he would have a family to fall back on. I had made an appointment with the admissions office. The school was impressive, and Marco was excited when a young woman asked him to join her for an application interview. Unfortunately, we had not considered one thing: Marco, being a young Latin lover deprived for many months of any female contact, was speechless just staring at her and could not concentrate on any question she asked. When he came out of the building, I asked him eagerly how the interview had gone. He replied, "Horrible, Mer. I acted like a fool, but I couldn't help it, she was so beautiful, that was the only thing I could think of." Needless to say, we could not go back to the interviewer and explain that he was fresh out of jail. The school turned him down.

Before driving home to my parents, we went to Scheveningen to take a stroll on the beach with the wind blowing around our ears. We found a nice restaurant and ordered lobster. Neither of us had ever had it before; it was a new experience, for both us and the restaurant owner. We were the only guests, which was fortunate, as bits of lobster were flying around, and our fingers and faces were disgustingly smeared with all parts of the poor creature.

We went home by train where my parents received us with open arms. Marco spent lots of time with my father in the garage, where they did some craft project in quiet tranquillity. I guess my father had always missed having a son. Marco later told me it had done him a lot of good. We took long walks talking about his experiences, accepting that he still kept mostly to himself, not ready to open up to anybody yet. Still, it was the start of a new beginning. We discussed other hotel management schools and decided to try one in Neuchâtel, Switzerland, where we sent all his documentation with a reference letter from me, as the registrar of EIS. He was accepted, starting in January 1997. He would spend the few months remaining in Argentina with his family. We both went to the airport and flew to different corners of the earth, Marco to Argentina and me back to Dubai. There I would have to deal with my problems with Chango, which I had put out of my mind the past few years.

PROBLEMS WITH CHANGO

At the beginning of our relationship, Chango had made it clear to me that he was his own person and would not allow me to interfere in his way of living. That this would include infidelity did not even touch my mind, as I had had no experience with Latin lovers. Therefore I was fated to suffer again.

It happened that while Marco was still in jail, my parents would be celebrating their fiftieth wedding anniversary, which I think is a big deal for every married person. I really did not want to leave Marco, but Chango insisted I should go and enjoy myself with my family. In the meantime Yvette and I had become good friends, and she said that she would schedule a party over the same weekend and invite Chango, so he would not be alone. I promised her that I would call at that time.

I flew to Holland and joined my family for the preparations for the celebration, which would be marked on Sunday, April 25, 1996. Many people were invited, including everyone who lived on our village street, as well as every member of our very, very extended family. What's more, my brother-in-law had arranged for Pierre Kartner to perform for us. A Dutch musician who sings under the stage name "Father Abraham," Kartner has written around 1,600 songs.

Friday afternoon (which you'll recall is part of the weekend in Dubai) I called Yvette. She said her party was going well, thanks to its good food, including barbecue. Then she gave the phone to Chango. The way he spoke to me sent telepathic signals to my brain. After we finished talking, I asked him to give the phone back to Yvette. I asked her if he had come alone. She replied, yes. I asked if he was with a woman at the moment. She said, "Yes, one of my friends also came alone, and they are chatting now." I felt something strange coming over me. Was it only jealousy? I said my goodbyes and looked forward to my own party on Sunday with my family. Need I mention it was a great success? We sang and danced deep into the night, "Vader Abraham" making the evening unforgettable.

When I returned to Dubai, life seemed to go back to normal. Ann was still living in my house, as Daniel remained in jail, and the appeal with the lawyer was costly. When I'd come to the house I'd often find Ann crying, feeling lost and desperate. She had taken out loans, and even received a charitable donation from an organization working with the embassy. Her daughter had also moved in with her Great Dane. Ann had years ago taken one of my kittens, now an adult cat that did not like my cat, so I had to lock my cat in my bedroom. For all these reasons, plus the fact that it was my house and I was staying home more, I was happy when Ann told me she was looking for her own place.

Marco was still in Argentina, and Chango called him almost daily. One weekend I was helping out with the Terry Fox Run, a charity run that our school participated in every year. I was assisting with the water stands and expected to be back home in the late afternoon, which I had also told Chango. As it happened, the whole event was over at 2 P.M. I went home and decided to call Marco. Not having his number and Chango not replying to my call, I remembered that he had called his son the night before. Thinking that the phone would not have been used between then and now, as Chango typically used his cell, I hit redial, expecting a Spanish-speaking person to answer. To my surprise somebody mumbled something like Video blah blah blah. Flabbergasted, I hung up. I sat there for a moment, hundreds of thoughts rushing through my mind. Hadn't Yvette said that her lady friend who had been talking with Chango owned a video shop? I redialed and listened more carefully this time. Yes, it was a video rental shop.

I immediately called Yvette and asked her if she knew if her friend was in Abu Dhabi. She told me that her friend travelled back and forth from Austria to Abu Dhabi, as her husband and kids lived in Austria, but yes, as far as she knew, Sissy S. was currently in Abu Dhabi. I told her my redial story and asked if she could call her friend and check where she is. A few minutes later, Yvette called back to tell me that she had been unable to reach Sissy. When she had called the shop, they told her Sissy was in Dubai.

Furious at this point, I kept on calling Chango. Finally, when he answered his phone hours later, I bombarded him with questions. He knew he was caught and told me to relax; he'd be home in half an hour. That was the time he needed to get his story together.

Of course, when he got back he made me look like a fool with my jealous insinuations. He went calmly to the bathroom to take a bath, while I sat next to him on the toilet seat. He told me that he had just met up with a friend and nothing else, but if I chose to stay jealous he would give me a good reason to be so. That was it; he didn't want to talk about it anymore. I felt silly, and although part of me wanted to forget about it and go on as we had, after my night shifts I now slept at my own place, and we basically lived apart.

ANOTHER CLOSE CALL

It was then that my third, and hopefully last, accident occurred. It happened on a stretch of the highway still under construction between Abu

Dhabi and Dubai. The Dubai side had only two lanes, while the Abu Dhabi had four. Remember, I worked three nights a week at Swissair as a ground hostess at Abu Dhabi airport. The job was easy and I loved driving. I lived on the outskirts of Dubai towards Abu Dhabi, and typically encountered little traffic during my nightly travels. I had a fast car, a Mercedes 280 SL sport cabriolet, the kind with a removable roof that stores during the summer. The car was an old timer, a heavy piece of German-made steel, not a thing to be pushed around lightly. Every night at around 2 A.M. I used to drive home from the airport far above the posted speed limits, at 220-250 kph (135-155 mph). There was never anybody on the road, although a police car was usually parked on the border between the two emirates. Sometimes I stopped to give the police some of my packages of Swissair first-class food, left over from the incoming flight from Zürich, which they always appreciated.

So there I was, "flying" towards home on the two-lane highway, looking forward to a warm bed, when suddenly a large truck loomed ahead of me. I overtook it at full speed, until…wow! The lanes disappeared. There had been no warnings posted, no signs. My car shot between large cement boulders that divided the two lanes into one on each side of them. I spun the steering wheel, circled around myself and faced a car that was coming straight towards me. I turned the wheel again, too fast, and the wheel turned around its axle once, and again I zoomed between another set of cement boulders back to the correct side of the highway, the road to Dubai. While circling and circling, I actually let go of the steering wheel, wondering if it ever would stop, grateful for my rally experience and grateful for my angels watching over me. Finally after seconds that seemed a lifetime, the car stopped in a drainage canal, its nose turned in the wrong direction, toward Abu Dhabi.

I sat in the pitch dark in shock; I couldn't even find the button to press to operate the wipers and clear the thick mud from the windshield. I closed my eyes and told myself to loudly count to ten. Slowly I relaxed and gave a deep sigh. I found the wipers switch and turned it on. It worked. I got an even bigger shock when I turned on my high beams and saw where I was. The car was in a canal so deep that it wouldn't have been visible from the road. I again caught my breath and turned the key in the ignition, praying the car would start. Yes, the Germans had done a good job with their Merc engine. I put it in gear, and slowly the vehicle moved forward to where I hoped would be an exit out of the mess. I was lucky; after what seemed a hundred kilometers, which were in reality not more then 200 meters (about 218 yards), the canal abruptly ended. I knew I couldn't climb up on the left bank, so I looked to the right. My car was not a 4x4, and I'd be driving through mud. Still, the engine was strong, and I had rally driver experience. After about five minutes of mentally speaking with my guardian angels, I gave the car a little gas and climbed like a snail out of the ditch, back onto the highway.

My car was facing the wrong way. I pulled into the breakdown lane. I got out of the car to assess the damage, the headlights offering me the only illumination in the heavy darkness. The bumper was loose, the back tires sagged, but miraculously, that was all. Still dazed, I continued home at a very slow pace. As I was driving along, a car passed me. I couldn't believe my eyes. It was the Dubai police, who never noticed the flat tires or bumper loudly scraping the road. Maybe they had more important matters to deal with than little ol', miraculously alive me!

I arrived home safely after an hour, a trip that usually took me fifteen minutes. Despite it being 4 A.M., I called Chango, who was in charge of the construction work, and vented my frustrations. First thing in the morning he came and looked at my damaged, once-precious-now-ugly Mercedes. Then he accompanied me back to the site, so he could assess it for himself. I was right: there were no signposts at all to show the detour. The tire tracks were still visible; Chango couldn't believe I had shot between those lanes with the cement boulders separating them, not just once but twice forth and back. In fact, the space between those boulders was exactly the width of my car, and skid marks were still visible. Angels had been carrying me, for sure. It was not yet my time to leave this earth.

In spring of 1998 I sold the Mercedes for a good price to a collector in Abu Dhabi, and then bought a white Mazda RX-7, the first one ever owned in the UAE. When I drove it for the first time and the Abu

Dhabi police saw me flying by, they followed me at high speed with lights flashing and sirens going. They stopped me, looked into the car and said, "Oh, it is you, *jallah* (hurry), go!"

I continued my "flight" on the road to Dubai.

LITTLE AHMED

I would look after a local family's little dog during their holidays when they went on their yearly Hajj to Mecca. The Hajj is a pilgrimage that Muslims should make at least once in a lifetime. The gathering during Hajj is the largest annual convocation of people in the world. The word Hajj means "to intend a journey," which connotes both the outward act of a journey and the inward act of intentions.

One day the father of the family, a celebrated rally driver, called and told me he had problems keeping his twelve-year-old son Ahmed under control. If we would accept the boy at EIS and I could look after him, no problem, but first he had to sit the admissions test. He passed, and Ahmed started at the school. Ahmed was spoiled but could be nice, visiting me during break times to chat.

From what you've read of my life this far, you know I've always tried to be open-minded. As Ahmed grew to be a young teenager, he started asking questions about sex. Sexual education is not common in Arabic countries. I've been told that, for many boys in those earlier years, their first sexual experience is with other boys or with animals, certainly not associated with love, as most marriages are arranged by families when the boys are very young. Knowing this, I tried to explain the sex act emphasizing the importance of love. I told Ahmed to respect girls and not just use them, as was common for young local men who have lots of money and nothing to do. Ahmed seemed to understand and, pleased with this new knowledge, drove home in his father's very expensive car without a driver's license. Who needs a license when you're the son of a rally champ!

A few days later Ahmed called me, sounding very excited and saying he needed to see me immediately. Fifteen minutes later he entered my house and told me he'd figured out the right way to lose his virginity.

"You told me," he said, "that I should only make love if I actually love the other person. Well, this is very easy. I love you, so you and I can make love."

I was speechless. He'd trapped me with my own philosophy! I told him that this was another kind of love, the one from a mother towards a son, or a friend for a friend; the love for a partner was different. He accepted this and left. We never touched on the subject again. It had come from his heart, and I never felt anything dirty in his thoughts. It came out in innocence and was accepted as such.

I MEET CLAUDIA

Meantime, Marco had enrolled in the School of Hotel, Hospitality and Design Management (IHTTI) in Neuchâtel and would start January 2. I rented a house in Neuchâtel and secretly made plans to bring his family together and surprise him. Alejandra, whom I came to call "Ale," would join us with her fiancé, Sebastian. Chango arranged a week off. By email I invited Claudia, who was still backpacking around the world and now in Europe. I had never met either daughter, so it was very exciting. I agreed with Claudia to meet her at her flight's designated meeting point at Frankfurt Airport, as it was cheaper to rent a car and fly to Frankfurt than to do the same in Zürich. Before she arrived, Marco also flew in to Frankfurt. I told him that we had to wait for a friend of mine who would join us on the drive to Switzerland. We were sitting in the restaurant near the meeting point, looking at people passing by, when Marco suddenly got up and cried out, "There's Clau!" Laughing almost to the point of tears, he watched her approach. I only saw a big backpack, a pair of feet below, the top of a head above. How he recognized her I have no clue. He shouted her name, she turned around, and I met for the first time Maria Claudia Peralta. I liked her the moment I laid eyes on her, although I knew from stories other family members told that she was not the easiest person to know.

We all hugged and went to the car. We drove through Germany and the German and French parts of Switzerland. Claudia and Marco, although tired, could not stop talking, they were so happy to see each other after many years. We reached the rental home and settled in easily.

The next day we were joined by Ale and Sebastian, "Sebas" for short, as well as a travelling friend of Claudia's. While waiting for Chango, we made plans for Christmas Eve and New Years, trips into the snowy mountains. Each day Chango would tell us, "I'm delayed, I've changed my flight," and although the kids told me not to expect him, I could not believe he would let them down. They had not been together as a family for years.

I got sick with the flu, and on Christmas Eve everybody shed a tear for a man who most probably had never even booked a flight to Switzerland. After I recovered, we toured through the cantons and visited several of my friends, who lived throughout Switzerland. All were very hospitable, especially Jacqueline and Hans Andretto, the parents of my godchild Bettina, with whom I was still in contact, and the Novara family in Chur, who also had young adult children. It was a great time with lots of laughter.

When we returned from the trip, I invited Bettina to join us in Neuchâtel for New Year's Eve. She came and became friendly with Marco. A day later everybody packed their bags, and we drove together into town to Marco's new school. I stayed outside, as I had seen the school before and knew it was important for Marco to enter IHTTI with his two sisters at his side, to be officially admitted and start his new career. Never a word was spoken about the Sharjah affair. An hour later I drove to the airport, from which we all went our different ways. I was a disappointed woman on my way back to Dubai, although Chango picked me up as if nothing had happened.

Ale and Sebas came to Dubai. We had fun sightseeing in all seven of the emirates, crisscrossing the country in my little Mazda RX-7. I called my friend Mitch, whom I knew from my rally days and was now working with a tour company. He was a natural desert driver, able to master any conditions behind the wheel of any car, reading the different colors of sand as if he were born a Bedouin. He agreed to take us on a daytrip in the desert. We rode camels, saw a baby camel being born in a Bedouin camp, and in the evening enjoyed a barbecue with a belly dancer for entertainment. Mitch showed us landscapes we had never seen before.

BECOMING MS. HANNIGAN

The yearly play at EIS was scheduled for February, and casting began in January. I had put myself on the list for helping backstage. While sitting in on the auditions, I was asked if I could sing and dance. I replied, "Of course I can!" I had never been on stage, only sang and danced in front of the bathroom mirror. Shortly afterward, I was invited to play the role of Ms. Hannigan in the musical *Annie*.

The character of Ms. Hannigan is clear: she's a man-loving drunk. However, scripts must go to the Ministry of Education for approval, and the UAE frowns on drinking, so we had to modify my role. Instead, I would be a clumsy, nasty person. I felt I could only do this properly if I didn't know what the other performers were doing; then I would be naturally clumsy. Therefore I never rehearsed with the kids. Ale helped me run through my lines constantly until I "became" Ms. Hannigan. I was in character day and night, even during my hours at the admissions office. I owned the *Annie* video, so I practiced all the dances and songs by myself until the day of the final rehearsal. I left little notes on each side of the stage to help me remember my lines, even leaving a page on my office desk on stage with the words to a long speech.

At last, it was show time! Everything looked great—the art department had created three major sets, and the backstage crew skillfully assisted with actors' makeup and costume changes. Things sounded great, too, the school orchestra playing to perfection.

We had three performances. I sang my songs, danced like a crazy woman, and slapped poor Annie (a student named Lilly Kandalaft) pretty much for real. It was a thrill to look out at the audience, throw the dolls of little orphan girls into onlookers' laps and sing angrily, "Little girls...little girls!" Yes, I felt a star was born!

There was a dance I had to do with Rooster, Ms. Hannigan's brother. Played by Saif Al Flasi, Rooster led the way, and I followed. At one point, we bumped our hips together. I heard and felt a cracking in my back, but ignored it. The show must go on! I danced through to the final scene, and again for the next two performances. You can guess that *Annie* went over big. We all had fun and worked like a team: the backstage crew, the actors, the orchestra, the background singers, everybody involved. The credit goes to one person: Kate Taraniuk, director of the play.

When the show ended, and Ms. Hannigan disappeared from my life, I felt empty, as if I had lost something. It was difficult to become myself again. Was the problem all in my mind? Not really. I went to the doctor and had x-rays taken of my ribs. I had broken three during that first-night dance with Saif, and because I bumped him with less enthusiasm over the next two performances, nobody ever saw me grimace. When Saif heard about the fractures, the sweet boy brought me flowers. For me, *Annie* was never to be forgotten, a milestone in my life.

VISIT TO MARCO

I went to see Marco in Neuchâtel during the weekend of Valentine's Day. We had a major matter to discuss: adoption. I was considering adopting Marco because that would solve an ongoing problem. He was born in Italy but had an Argentine passport, which meant he always needed visas for travel in Europe, and obtaining them was both time-consuming and costly. I sent a request for information to my *Bürgerort* (town of original family residence) and promptly received a letter back. It indicated that if Marco signed the papers before his eighteenth birthday, I could adopt him. I told him this, and then Marco did something he had never done before: he called his mom. He and she had no relationship at all at that time. He told her about my suggestion to make his life easier, but she strongly opposed it. Marco felt bad for her, so he never signed the papers, a decision he still regrets to this day.

I stayed in Marco's room while he stayed with his girlfriend Kristina, a Danish girl whom I liked immediately. All his friends were nice young people, and I didn't feel out of place with them for even a moment. The evening of Valentine's Day, the students had arranged a party. The girls dressed as men, and the men dressed as women. The preparations as the girls put makeup on the men were hilarious. I laughed so hard during this "pre-party" that tears were rolling down my cheeks. The men took their roles very seriously, styling their hair, shaving their legs and armpits, plucking their eyebrows, trying on many outfits and choosing the ones that suited them, with matching stockings. How vain they were! The evening went off splendidly, and when I left the next day it was with a big smile on my face. I felt reborn and happy with all these newly made friends, who had made me feel welcome despite the considerable age difference.

JEALOUSY

My positive feelings didn't last. When I returned to the UAE, and settled back into my usual routine, I would find myself looking to God for guidance, asking Him to show me the way. I had become very insecure with Chango. I didn't trust him, and my feelings of jealousy would overwhelm me.

One day, Chango called me to say that his car was stuck on the side of the road. He had left it there, and could I please get his stuff out of it, as the car was being towed to a garage? I drove to the vehicle and collected everything from the glove compartment and off the floor. His wallet was there. I couldn't resist opening it and looking inside. Behind his credit cards was a business card with no name, just a picture of a rose and a telephone number. It looked like a call girl's card. I had tried to push Sissy S. to the back of my mind, but I was thinking of her when I dialed the number. It was disconnected. Still, that didn't stop me from feeling betrayed. I thought about the hours Chango kept; since he worked late and often came home during the afternoon for a nap, it would be easy for him to have several affairs without me knowing.

I called Yvette and asked her if she knew Sissy's cell phone number. Annoyed, she replied, "Marilyn are you still thinking about that woman? There is nothing, believe me." I told her about discovering the strange business card and gave her the number. Yvette went quiet on the other end of the line, then said, "Wow, yes, it is her number, but I did not see her in Abu Dhabi. I don't think she's here." We were both speechless, me thinking, *well, God is showing me the way.*

Late that evening I spoke to Chango. I had to confess that I had gone into his wallet, but I didn't care. He replied very calmly that he, Sissy and her husband were just friends. I told him I didn't believe him. If she and her husband were his friends, why didn't he ever invite them for dinner? Of course, this never happened, but many phone calls flew between them, while he was standing in the garden or on the street, times he claimed to be speaking to a client.

Weeks later Chango decided to see Marco. He planned a one-week vacation, never asking me to join him, which of course disappointed me. But more than that, I felt something was going on. Blame it on my jealousy or woman's intuition. When he returned from Neuchâtel, he showed me photos of him and Marco. Happily, they had lots of sunshine and enjoyed each other's company. One photo was particularly nice, both of them sitting on a bench. I asked Chango to make me a copy on several occasions, but he always seemed to forget. One Friday afternoon (which was the weekend, remember) I was bored and decided to make a copy myself. I went looking for the negatives and found them easily; I knew where Chango kept his stuff. I put them up to the light to see them better. I saw a woman with long brown hair and wondered who it could be. It couldn't be one of Marco's friends, as I knew them all. It was difficult to tell the woman's age, which might have been a clue to help me identify her.

I numbered the negatives and went to Carrefour, the only mall open in Dubai on Friday afternoons. I had to wait until 4 P.M. when the photo shop opened, but it was worthwhile. I had the beautiful photo of Marco and his dad on the bench, but...also the photo of an unknown woman with long brown hair. I called Yvette and asked what color hair Sissy had. Brown, she said. I drove to EIS and used the school copier to send Yvette a fax of the photo. A few minutes later she called. She couldn't believe what she had seen: the woman was Sissy. It was like the world was coming down upon me. It's one thing to harbor a suspicion, a whole other thing to suddenly have that suspicion confirmed. The man

I thought was the love of my life was destroying me by his behavior, and I was unable to break free.

Sundown. I was sitting in the dark in the living room of his house when he came to the front door. I heard him outside calling me on his phone. I did not answer. When he came in, he regarded me with surprise. I had left the Sissy photo on the coffee table. He noted it and said, his face expressionless, "I told you I would pay you back. Blame your jealousy. This is what happens."

Speechless, I went to my own home and stayed there for several days, begging God to not show me the way anymore, as it was too painful.

As so many who have been in my situation will know, I was suffering and unable to remove these feelings of utter pain. One week later, the doorbell rang. Chango told me to come with him and have dinner. Our lives continued as before, with the difference that he tried to come home earlier and spend more time with me, but he never kissed me anymore. I was somewhat happier, but confused once again. I had called Marco's girlfriend Kristina, who told me the story of Chango and Sissy. Chango had invited Marco and his friends for dinner. When they arrived at the restaurant, Chango and a woman with long hair were already seated. Marco went to his dad and said, "Who the f--- is that? Does Marilyn know about her?" His dad answered that this had nothing to do with me. Marco looked at him and left the restaurant, his friends following him.

CHRISTMAS WITH MARCO AND CLAUDIA

The year sped by. Claudia was still trekking through Asia, so Marco and I decided to join her in Bali over Christmastime. I would also reconnect with my friends Vivienne and Richard, who vacationed there regularly. I met with them in Kuala Lumpur, and together we flew to Bali. We spent some wonderful days together, sightseeing and reminiscing. Marco and Claudia arrived a few days later. The three of us had an outing to the Ubud Monkey Forest that I'll never forget: while I was shooting a video, I suddenly heard Marco shouting, "Be careful, Mer!" But it was too late: a monkey had jumped on me and didn't want to let go. Marco was gleefully taking photographs; nobody even thought of rescuing me! Finally, the monkey let go and I was free. We all laughed until we cried.

A PAINFUL NEW YEAR'S EVE

Just like the year before, Chango promised to spend New Year's Eve with us. Faxes were shot back and forth. Finally, the day before year's end he said he had too much to do and no time to come. I decided then that I would take the next flight back to Dubai, so that he would not be alone on New Year's Eve. Claudia and Marco told me it was a foolish idea, I should stay with them and enjoy their company. I did not listen. I wish I had. I flew back, first sending Chango a fax to tell him I was coming. He was waiting at the airport, and said when he saw me, "Que imbranata tu sei." ("What a clumsy person you are.") I smiled, as I thought he was teasing me, accusing me of being too romantic. In other words, I felt it was his way of saying, I love you.

In the car he told me that he would be dropping me off at my house, as he was going to his company's New Year's Eve party, and I was not invited. I have no words to describe my disappointment; I just looked at him. He left me and went. My mind reeled with images of Sissy S.

At 10 P.M. I dressed in black and slipped out of my house, unseen by anyone. I crept through gardens to his house. The lights were off. I stayed there for ten minutes, noticing no movement inside. I would have stayed longer, but I was exhausted from the flight and my situation, so I slipped back through the gardens to my house, where the phone was ringing. I picked it up. It was Chango, asking where I had been; he'd been trying my number for a long time. I told him that I had been in the bath. He told me that he had spoken to Alejandra, and she had told him she would call me to wish me Happy New Year. Only later did I realize that was rubbish; Ale had never said any such thing, but he knew I loved his children, so he used her name to keep me at home. I fell asleep waiting for the call, which never came.

The next morning I went to Chango's house. The key was inside, so I had to ring the bell. He came and let me into the kitchen. I knew there was somebody in the house, I felt it. I walked to the bedroom, he directly behind me. I don't know where the woman disappeared to, but I couldn't find her. I was so frustrated that I shouted at Chango and threw my camera at his face. It fell wide and crashed through the window. I ran out of the house. Again, as always, Chango came to my house a few days later and hypnotized me to come back. That is the only way I can explain my stupidity, pathetic me.

CLAUDIA IN THE UAE

Claudia arrived from her adventure trip, complete with backpack. She and I got along very well. A strong, intelligent and beautiful young woman, Claudia expressed an interest in remaining a long while in Dubai. I spoke with my friend Rita, the one who had sheltered me while I was hiding from Hans II. She worked at Dubai TV, and I thought somebody like Claudia should be doing something in that field. Rita arranged a meeting with the director, and soon Claudia was a co-presenter on the weekly show *Where 2*. When the shows were filmed outside Dubai, Claudia invited me to come along as a chaperone. She soon started going out and meeting people her age. She would ask to borrow my little Mazda when I didn't need it. I was happy to lend it; I'm not really the materialistic sort, and I trusted her to take care of it.

One night I was watching the news when the front door opened. Claudia entered and sneaked in softly to her bedroom. This was not like her, so when she didn't come out after ten minutes, I went to see her. She was huddled under the bed sheets making little sounds. I slowly pulled back the sheet and saw she was in tears. Surprised, I asked what was the matter. I couldn't understand a word she was saying, as she was crying too much. I told her to slow down, and then the story came out. As she was driving home, using Al Diyafah Road, a Land Cruiser was in front of her. The traffic light changed to red, which Claudia had not seen, because my car is so low. She bumped into the Land Cruiser. The driver came out: a pregnant woman. Claudia was horrified that something could have happened to the baby, but the lady quieted her down, saying everything was OK, the Land Cruiser had sustained no damage. But the Mazda…? Claudia and I went outside and looked at the little car.

Only its headlights needed repair. I told her it was OK. Poor Claudia, such a shock.

I introduced Claudia to little Ahmed. Once while we were in the Mazda, Ahmed sitting in the back, Claudia and I in front, the two of them were joking around using double entendres. I was only half-listening when Ahmed uttered a general slur against girls. Claudia told him to shut up, as he and his "mini penis would not be able to do anything anyway." He acted very upset, but I think he actually liked the attention. Little Ahmed was a product of his macho upbringing and not an exception at all.

THE VARKEY GROUP

During these hectic, emotional times, a woman named Raheela Ashraf called me on my cell. She offered me a job as a registrar for a new school to be opened September 1998 for the Varkey Group. I looked into the Varkeys, and this is what I dug up: Mariamma (a teacher) and her husband, K.S. Varkey (a teacher working at a bank), came to Dubai in 1959, at a time when there was no electricity, water or schools. They started teaching English to Arab students, including members of the ruling family of Dubai. With Arabic-English and Persian-English dictionaries, they made themselves understood to their students. They lived in a very small house; Mariamma used to teach in the front room.

The gossip in Dubai tells us the following: K.S. Varkey told his fellow Indians living in Dubai that if they gave him their money, he'd invest it in their home country and make them rich. Many Indians gave him all their savings. He went to India, invested the cash and lost everything. At least, that is what he said; nobody believed him. Soon they came to know that he had secretly bought lots of properties in India. With their money? No one knew, but after that no Indian trusted him anymore. This is also the reason why the locals and old settled Indians have never respected the Varkey name. The Varkeys may try to improve their reputation by owning schools, but it's a fact that schools are one of the best moneymakers as a business. I'll give "Mamma" Mariamma her due, however. She was respected as a teacher and is a good lady. I met her several times.

I told Raheela I would love to take the job, but I was loyal to Martin Kenny, director of EIS, and the administrative manager, Farid Jayussi, who had helped me through hard times. She understood but told me that the offer remained open, as she had heard I was the best registrar in Dubai. I thanked her for the compliment and hung up. She called me several times afterwards, but I always turned her down.

"LEAVE THE PREMISES IMMEDIATELY"

It shows that God or the universe was looking out for me, because it happened that Martin had gone to the Al Habtoors for a pay raise for the staff. When he returned I asked him how it went. He looked at me in surprise.

"Oh, my God, I forgot the administrative staff!"

I looked at him with concern and asked, "How could you forget us?"

He said, "Well, we can't run a school without teachers."

I asked him what he would do if we administrators did not come in the next day. He looked at me in disbelief. "Exactly, Martin," I said, "you cannot run a school without administrators." I left him standing there, strode straight into Farid's office and told him what Martin had said. We both went to Martin's office. He called Liz, his secretary, to make an appointment with Khalaf Al Habtoor for the next day to ask for an increase in our salaries.

When he returned from that meeting, he did not look into my office, as he would usually do. I thought that strange, but was too busy with new admissions for the next school year to pay much attention. As a registrar, I had to be honest and straight with the parents about curriculum and facilities in the school. The Al Habtoors had made many promises, many came through, many not, which was very difficult for me as a registrar to handle. At one point I must have said something to somebody about this in a not very happy tone, because now it had come back to bite me. As I mentioned before, Martin and I had a good relationship, but now he ignored me for days. When I had enough, I called Farid and asked what was wrong. He said he could not tell me. I told him that I needed to know if I had done something wrong to Martin. He said he would call me.

Five minutes later Liz called me and asked me to come immediately to Martin's office. He sat there with a serious expression. Farid was there, very tense. They told me to sit down. It was a dramatic moment. Both men had tears in their eyes when Martin told me that I had to take my things from my office and leave the premises immediately, per command of Khalaf Al Habtoor. Martin told me that he had gone every day to Khalaf en Mohammed's office, begging to keep me, as the school needed a registrar and I had proven to be the best. All his pleading, however, was without success.

At first I looked at Martin in shock. Then I started laughing. Finally, I was free! Martin and Farid did not understand. I thanked Martin, hugged them both and told them not to worry, because for months I had been approached by different schools to come and work for them, but I was loyal to Martin and Farid, as they had helped me in my difficult times. I did not like the Habtoors at all; they had no principles. It was not easy for directors to run a private school in Dubai, as most educational requests were ignored. It was all about budgets and money. I know how frustrated Martin was when he returned from the monthly meetings with Khalaf Al Habtoor, and time and again essential requests were denied.

In 2011, when I heard that Martin had died, I offered my condolences to his wife, Lynn. She wrote back the following:

> Dear Marilyn,
>
> I am so very happy to have heard from you, and especially to read your "Martin story," Marilyn. I distinctly recall the day that he came home to our Al Diyafah Street apartment after he'd had to tell you to leave EIS within minutes. Again, he had tears in his eyes in telling me the story, and having to face helplessness in a situation that he could not change.

I went home without a care. I had some savings, and I still had my Swissair job, for which I could arrange additional shifts, if necessary.

I went to bed that night knowing I could handle whatever the future brought.

The next morning I was still lying in bed when my cell rang. I looked at the time: 8 A.M. I picked up the phone and recognized the number of Raheela Ashraf.

"News travels fast," she said. "You're fired from EIS?" I confirmed this, and she replied, "Very good, so now you can start here."

A NEW SCHOOL, A NEW LIFE CHAPTER

An hour later I met Raheela, an elegant Pakistani lady known to the Varkey Group by her educational background. They had asked her to set up an American international school in Dubai they would call the Modern American Private School (MAPS). The school was established in a big villa, easily accessible and located in a good expat area of Al Quoz. We aimed for the school to open September 1, 1998, with a small staff that included Raheela as initiator; Dr. Harold Fleetham, director; Wendy Gutenkauf (Harold's wife), librarian; Geety Kazerouni, kindergarten teacher; Hilmi Ahmad, assistant; Arun Kumar, accountant; and I, Marilyn Wouters, registrar.

A new chapter of my life had started.

We all liked each other and worked well together as a team. Harold was an intelligent man who had connections to a network of teachers around the world. He and I hit it off immediately. It took him a little time, though, to get used to my Dutch directness, to which he would often respond, "Good Lord, woman!"

Most good schools in Dubai were full, so parents started coming in to look at the school and its curriculum. In addition, my friend Ghada, who had stepped into my shoes after I left EIS, sent me students when she had no space for them.

Soon it was known in Dubai that I had changed schools, and many Europeans, especially the Dutch, came to Modern American Private School. Of course, we needed to get rid of that name immediately: it sounded Indian and did not suggest the kind of school the Varkey Group was looking for. One of us proposed Dubai American Academy, and it went for approval to the group's chairman, Sunny Varkey. It was accepted and submitted to the Ministry of Education, which accepted the name Dubai Academy, only. However, we did not give up, and two years later the school was called the Dubai American Academy (DAA).

When I was hired, I had to hand over my passport to the public relations department of the Varkey Group. This didn't make me happy, but my residence visa had to be renewed by Varkey, so I had no choice. I could not work until the Ministry of Education accepted me as registrar.

MY MOTHER HOSPITALIZED

One night while I was working at Abu Dhabi Airport, I received a phone call: my mother had suffered a stroke and been rushed to the hospital in critical condition. Immediately, my station manager contacted KLM and made a reservation on the next evening flight out of Dubai with an ID90. I was lucky the flight was open. A huge problem arose, however, as my passport was with an Egyptian gentleman in the Varkey office. I didn't have his number. I called Harold, who found him after contacting the chairman himself. The Egyptian called me back, and we agreed to meet at the Dubai airport at check-in. My heart shook when I saw him standing there, as deep down I was expecting that it would not work out, but he handed me my passport. I got on the flight with a heavy heart, thinking of my mother and hoping she would be alive when I arrived, as I had another few hours to go by train to Breda, where she was in the hospital.

I found Marijke and my father already sitting beside my mother's bed. She was in a single room. I asked the nurse to bring a mattress or stretcher, as I refused to leave my mom alone that night. I held her hand while talking to her, remembering times we went camping, good times and good memories. I stayed with her for several days, and after a meeting with the family, it was decided to take her off life support, respecting her wishes. The machines were switched off while we were with her. She remained alive, half paralyzed, half blind, and what was worse, not knowing who we were. We decided to keep her at the hospital until a nursing home in Breda could accept her; my father would not be able to take care of her at home, as she needed round-the-clock help. Unable to do anything more, I flew back to Dubai. We all remained concerned about my mother, however, as the hospital could not keep her, and no nursing home had a room available.

Soon after this, I read about a controversial Dutch New Age guru who called herself Jomanda or "The Lady of the Light." Apparently, an entire soccer stadium in Utrecht was full every weekend with people who sought out her healing gifts. One could go to her website and ask for help. My family and I were desperate, as the hospital demanded we take my mother out. I googled Jomanda's website. There was a brief prayer, which I said aloud. I turned off my computer, put on my bathing suit and lay outside on a lounge chair. As I closed my eyes, thinking of my poor mother, I dozed off to a half sleep. Images appeared in my mind of Jomanda and a young woman, whom I recognized as my mother at a younger age. I did not dare to move. The rest of the afternoon I waited, sure I would receive a telephone call from Holland saying that my mother had died. Hours later, my sister called with the good news that my mother had been transferred to a nursing home in Breda. Thank God, she was now in good hands. From that time on, I have regularly seen images of people passing by my "inner eye." It's clear to me that they're spirits trying to get in contact with a loved one. I know they need help, so I pray for healing.

A CALL IN THE NIGHT
When I thought my relationship with Chango was going well again, a woman came back into his life, ending everything there had ever been between us.

In the early morning hours, while we were fast asleep, Chango's phone rang. He sleepily picked it up, then suddenly sat up in bed and asked, "Who is this?" The answer must have been a big surprise. He replied immediately in Spanish and went to the living room, where he continued the conversation. When he returned to bed, he did not say anything. I saw that he was digesting the call, and asked if something had happened in Argentina. He said, no, someone from his past, an old friend from the university, had been trying to find him for many years and now succeeded. Someone once very important to him...

CHANGO'S STORY IN HIS OWN WORDS

I was born February 2, 1944, in Santiago del Estero, a city in one of the poorest provinces in Argentina. Santiago del Estero is the country's oldest, continually inhabited city founded by Spanish settlers. I am quite a mix of nationalities. My grandfather on my mother's side was Syrian, my grandmother on my mother's side was Spanish, my grandfather on my father's side was Spanish, and my grandmother on my father's side was French Basque. Until the age of eight I was considered a delicate child because I had asthma, but my determination to be a normal child and play with other boys cured me. As a child of five, I moved out of my mother's house and went to live with my grandmother, a wonderful woman. She did not speak very much, but she was an extremely hard worker, made of steel, hardened to face whatever life sent her way.

I always enjoyed school and knew from a very young age that education was the only way out of poverty. My passion was to study medicine; I would have done anything to start a medical career. Unfortunately, coming from a technical secondary high school, I had not taken the courses necessary to enter medical school. What's more, I couldn't afford the required extra year, so better to be an engineer than nothing. Besides studying I had also worked odd jobs during my last three years of high school, earning money so I could afford to leave the impoverished North. Having passed all my exams, I left the house of my grandmother, bound for Buenos Aires. I took only a small satchel that I had filled with a few belongings. In those times I was a lean young man, just turned twenty. With long black hair and skin darkened by the sun, I looked like an outcast. I had decided to go to La Plata, the capital city of the province of Buenos Aires, my goal to be accepted at the National University of La Plata and study engineering. I had only a few pesos in my pockets and no clue how to get into the university, but I knew that I could do it. Travelling by train would give me many hours to think about my next steps, and I was bent on succeeding and learning whatever was necessary to make something out of my life.

Arriving at the train station, I met my cousin Turko, also carrying a bag and ready to start the big adventure to the big city. We bought our tickets and felt each other's excitement about boarding this train into our future. As we entered a compartment and took our seats, the train slowly started moving and we both looked back at the station. The familiar sights of Santiago, where we had grown up, passed by faster and faster. I leaned back and made myself comfortable, thinking of the things I would do as soon as we arrived in the capital. I saw the villages passing by and looked at Turko, who was fast asleep. It would be our first time in La Plata, in fact the first time ever that I had traveled such a long distance, and I was too excited to sleep.

Around nine o'clock in the morning, the train pulled into La Plata. It was summertime, the air was humid, the temperature hot. I woke my cousin, and with stiff bones we left the train and mingled with the crowds of people coming and going. We had no idea where to go. We only knew we needed a room to sleep in; whatever room we found would be good enough. We bought a newspaper and started to walk, reading the advertisements and searching for a boardinghouse or hostel, something cheap, as we couldn't afford anything luxurious. We paced the streets without rest. I cannot remember how many times we lost our way in this beautiful, pulsating city, with its diagonal streets all ending in squares every 500 meters [about 546 yards]. Sweating heavily, moneyless, not stopping to eat or drink, we walked on as the hours passed. Growing depressed, we knocked on more doors and gazed at ads posted on windowpanes. No luck. Ten hours of running around, ten hours with hungry stomachs.

Finally, at 6:30 in the evening, I fell exhausted on the front steps of an old house. I'll never forget where I was: at the intersection of Street 46 and Street 1. The home was just opposite the Engineering Department of the university. Fate had played a role. Turko and I discussed the fact that we would not find anything cheap close to the university, and it was getting late. I wanted to have a look at the department, see the place where I could make my long list of dreams come true. Now, sitting there on these steps, my first dream had been fulfilled. I, Juan Carlos Peralta, had finally arrived in La Plata. While my thoughts wandered, Turko complained that he was hungry, thirsty and deathly tired, and that we needed to get hold of a room **somewhere**. At that moment, the door opened and an elderly lady asked, "What are you doing on my doorstep?"

"Looking for a room," I said.

"What kind of room?" she asked.

"Just a room for sleeping and studying," I answered, "for two poor students who don't have money to spend and just arrived this morning by train from the North." She looked at the two longhaired, exhausted creatures in front of her and opened the door.

"Come in, I have a small room left, I can rent it to you but it is nothing special. It's in the attic, no toilet, just two beds, a table and two chairs. That's it, take it or leave it."

Immediately we rose and followed her up an iron stairway that seemed to lead to heaven, and at the top of it, finally, there was the room. Small, but a room. We dropped our bags and fell on the beds. The woman explained where the shower and kitchen were located, but we were sound asleep before she could finish her sentence. She left us, shaking her head. Tia Elena would be our landlady for many years to come.

The next morning Turko and I woke up energized. We bought bread, ate, and went straight to the university.

When I signed up for the admissions tests for engineering, I found myself among 1,200 applicants, of whom 640 managed to pass. Here I was, the "pretender from the North," nervous and doubtful, and yet I finished with some of the highest results. I have passed every exam I've ever taken, and not because I was clever, but because I simply couldn't afford to fail. I didn't have the money and time to lose. Of the 640 students, only five finished their degrees in April 1970, and I was one of them.

During my first year at La Plata, I lived the normal life of a student. I partied, smoked, drank and had girlfriends. One stood out: her name was Graziela, and she came from Misiones, the area of Iguazu Falls. She would become the mother of my children. The first year came to an end, and so did my money. I had to take a job, like most other students.

When I was in the third year of my studies, June 1966, there was a military coup. The first thing the dictator did was to attack the universities. That is when I got involved in the student movement. No one pushed me into it; I had my principles, convictions and ideals. If anything pushed me, it was injustice. From the attack on the university until I finished my studies, I was a worker, a militant and a student.

Prior to the coup, I had not been much involved in politics, as my studies were important to me. And there had been no reason to be involved: Arturo Illia, elected in 1963, had devoted 25 percent of the national budget to education and culture, and brought unemployment down from 8 percent to 4 percent. The problem was that big corporations and the political opposition did not like this, so they started an "anti-Illia" campaign. May 29, 1966, La Noche de los Bastones Largos—The Night of the Long Sticks—constituted a critical turning point. It marked the first violent interruption of Argentine academic life by a military regime, and opened the path for more tragic things to come. The result was the military coup in June 1966, led by General Juan Carlos Ongania.

The new government of the dictator with its military regime abolished the National Congress and declared all activities of political parties illegal. The leadership of the university officially opposed the violation of the constitution, with the result that the new target was, of course, the university. On July 28 the new military regime cancelled the autonomy of all universities and their right to self-governance (their political power had been divided among students, professors and graduates). The university was given forty-eight hours to accept the new rules. At those times the University of La Plata had an excellent international reputation. In the Department of Sciences (Ciencias Exactas), the faculty council decided to reject the orders of the military that had violated the constitutional order. This council, led by Dean Rolando Garcia and supported by several internationally recognized researchers such as Juan Roederer, was one of the most prominent divisions of the University of

Buenos Aires. Professors and students of most departments started discussing possible responses to the ultimatum. One day before the deadline, on July 29, 1966, the army and police moved to the Department of Sciences. The professors and students closed the doors of all the university buildings and remained inside. With great violence the military and police destroyed the entrances and attacked students, professors, researchers and staff. They injured many men and women and took about 400 students and professors to jail. The most prestigious scientists of Argentina were victims of beatings. Laboratories and libraries were completely destroyed. After the incidents, all deans and 1,400 professors resigned. Three hundred scientists went into exile, most of them immigrating to the US, France, Chile and Brazil.

This was the time that changed my life. I got involved right after the night of the military coup, not so much in politics as in the manifestations of protest, assemblies and meetings with the labor class. Everybody was scared. Very few had the courage to talk. The university was the main bastion of the resistance. Political parties were banned, and former politicians played it safe and kept quiet. Few labor union leaders had the courage to speak up; they were followed day and night by the military or were thrown into jail. The injustice pushed me to get fully involved. Remember, this was "Cold War" time: Cuba, the Iron Curtain, and not to forget, Vietnam. It was the time of the Baader-Meinhof Gang in Germany, and of Che Guevara, whom I met on several occasions. Each university department had its own student center. At that time, Engineering was the only one that had its own building, library, bar and restaurant, print shop with machinery to make books, etc. It was like a "bunker" and the most attractive target for Ongania's army. Studying as we had known it became nearly impossible at the university. Who could attend classes during the day and fight during the night? The majority of professors who remained at the university were scared and/or apolitical. Only a few who had not fled the country had real principles, convictions and ideals. They were fighting beside us.

Unlike most other students, I had the opportunity to get away from Argentina's troubles for short periods. In 1968 I received a scholarship to the Sorbonne in France. In the summer of 1968 I attended Florida University and Columbia University, where I met Elvis Presley and Werner von Braun. In the winter of 1969 scholarships brought me to the universities of Rio de Janeiro and Sao Paolo.

Still, my heart was in La Plata, and I joined a group that ran for student center elections. We won with 75 percent of the vote. Suddenly, Chango from the poor northern province was the leader of the student opposition at La Plata University, where I remained until 1973. They were beautiful and hard times. I was one of the many students attending the now regular political meetings, where many words were thrown around, but no actions taken. The crowd, including myself, became restless. I was fed up with just words. Words wouldn't give us the freedom we wanted. I felt myself getting up, standing on my chair and shouting all the feelings that had been locked up in my heart from the moment our rights were stolen by the government. At first I was too excited to realize that the crowd had grown quiet, listening to me. Before I knew what was happening, people had carried me to the stage, where I continued my speech, spoken from the heart. Not long after that I was elected president of the Student Party.

That was the time that I learned to know Raquel, also a student at the university. Our relationship was very intense, most probably because of the times we lived in. We were students who boycotted the military when we could. Many of us were captured and never seen again. We hid our weapons in churches or other places the government would not think of. We were now organized and a strong union.

In 1970 after I had finally finished my exams, I received a scholarship for graduate study in Germany and moved there for my own security. Germany drove me mad. I was a young Argentine man who thought of nothing but sex, fucking around to the point that I looked at myself and thought, this has to change. I decided that it would be best for me to get married, so I wrote to my longtime girlfriend Graziela and told her I wanted to marry her. I researched how this could be done without bringing her to Germany, as I was on a student visa. I was told about an old Dutch way where the bride or groom is represented by someone with a power of attorney, and the marriage takes place as usual, with the exception of the kissing of the bride! Originally, a glove was displayed to signify the absent party, which is how the procedure got its informal name "Trouwen met de Handschoen" (Marriage with the Glove). The formal name is "Trouwen bij Volmacht" (marriage by power of attorney). It requires a license from the Department of Justice, and it is not issued lightly. Graziela agreed, and we got married. When she flew to Germany and I collected her from the airport, she hardly recognized me, I was so worn out from living the life of freedom and excesses in everything. Slowly I got myself under control, and we lived a simple married life.

When my graduate studies were completed, we returned to Argentina, where the political situation had not changed and I found myself again speaking out against injustice. I never classified myself as a Marxist, anarchist or anything else. I simply fought for what I thought was the right cause. I fought for what every person wants: Freedom. It was officially called "The Dirty War." Many freedom fighters were abducted or illegally detained and kept in clandestine detention centers where they were questioned, tortured and killed by the Argentine military to obtain intelligence. Some of the ones taken by the government were heavily drugged and loaded onto aircraft, from which they were thrown alive over the Atlantic Ocean in the so-called "death flights" (vuelos de la muerte), their bodies never found. The forced disappearances (los desaparecidos) were the military junta's attempt to silence the opposition and break the determination of the guerrillas. The number of people believed to have been killed or "disappeared" range from 7,158 to 30,000 in the period from 1976 to 1983 during this military dictatorship.

I had to be careful now. I had a wife, and my first child was on its way. I made sure that nobody knew where I lived, always alert not to be followed. This time my involvement in the cause was more dangerous than in my times at the university. I worked for a foreign-owned engineering company and moved around a lot, leaving behind destruction and attacks on many military projects. Nobody knew about my secret underground life as a guerrilla, not even my family, although they suspected something. More and more friends of mine disappeared, people who were considered political or ideological threats to the military junta.

The victims of the violence were left-wing activists and militants, including trade unionists, students, journalists, and Marxist and Peronist guerrillas. Their support network in the Montoneros [a leftist urban group] was believed to be 150,000-250,000 strong, with approximately 60,000 in the ERP (People's Revolutionary Army), as well as untold numbers of sympathizers. Leftist guerrillas caused at least 6,000 casualties among the military, police forces and civilian population.

Graziela spent most of her time with her parents in Misiones, while I organized and executed attacks against the army. One time I was captured by members of the junta. I would not have given a penny for my life, yet torture could not break me. (These are memories I would rather erase from my mind.) I got freed during a rescue mission; a few weeks later the car I was driving was bombed. Wounded but alive, I was now one of the most wanted men in Argentina. Life became very dangerous for my family as well as me. I asked my engineering company to transfer me overseas. I knew now there was a price on my head, and I had to disappear if I didn't want to be one of the disappeared myself. My company finally found me a job at its headquarters in Italy. I fled through Misiones to Brazil to Italy, where my family followed soon after.

You, *imbranata*, deserve happiness and a beautiful life. However, it is the hard and difficult moments that are important and make a person grow. I was seventeen years old when I severed my ties with religion. I simply decided to follow what I think and what I feel. If God exists, one day I'll face him with all that I did on this planet. If he doesn't exist, it doesn't matter. I choose to live my life intensively, and no one can tell me how to do it. Raquel was at my side during my most difficult, never-to-be-forgotten years. And that is why she remains an important part of my life.

End of Chango's memoir.

"WE'RE OLD FRIENDS"

Raquel called the next day. The following week a package came for Chango: a CD of songs by Celine Dion. Raquel wrote that he should listen to one song in particular: "It's All Coming Back to Me Now." I could see on his face he had no clue who Celine Dion was, nor had he ever heard the music. I knew both the singer and the song, and I told him Raquel loved him. He looked at me and said, "No way! We're old friends from a long time ago, nothing more." The two of us sat and listened to the song.

Over the next few weeks, Chango and Raquel spoke on the phone at least once a week. He did not hide this from me; he enjoyed talking about their mutual friends and their days at the university. I was not surprised when he told me she was coming to Dubai with her son and his fiancée. I did not really know what to do with this news and told Claudia about it. Her instant reaction was to move out of the house, wanting nothing to do with this woman. The day before Raquel arrived, Claudia packed her suitcase and left to move in with her boyfriend Morgan. When her dad asked her to join us in picking up Raquel from the airport, she refused.

So, on an early morning in March 1998, Chango and I got in the car and drove. I was silent on the way, not knowing what to expect. We did not have long to wait for Raquel, her son and his fiancée. They collected their luggage and walked into the arrivals hall. We all went then to the airport hotel to have breakfast. Considering it from the viewpoint of an outsider, it must have looked funny. I sat on the right side of Chango, Raquel on his left, her son and fiancée opposite us. I saw on the young people's faces that they were a bit surprised, but we all talked about little nothings. The breakfast seemed to last a lifetime before we finally left the table. When we went to the car, I sat in the front seat, so she, her son and his fiancée had to sit in the back. I had taken ownership.

Driving home to Jebel Ali, Raquel asked where they were staying. I had already tried to discuss this with Chango, but he had always ignored the subject, so I offered them my home. Looking over the steering wheel at the road ahead of him, Chango now said, "I have one guestroom for your son and fiancée. Raquel, you'll stay with me in my room." In the rearview mirror I saw her looking at me. I was completely in shock, but I kept quiet, not wanting to make a scene. I saw her son whispering to his fiancée and sensed their discomfort. Chango dropped me at home, after which I went to work. Of course, I couldn't concentrate at all. How dare he put me in this strange, horrible situation?

After work I went home, feeling sorry for myself. The phone rang: it was Chango, asking why I hadn't come to his house. I told him I didn't feel very welcome. He said rubbish, come and make your *pasta arrabbiata*, which was his favorite dish. Everyone gave me a hug on my arrival, we all had a drink, and I prepared the pasta the way Chango liked, with extra peppers thrown in. Raquel set the table and helped me with the serving. I was sitting at the head of the table, Chango and Raquel on my left, her son and fiancée on the right. I took my first bite and almost burned inside out, but kept my face straight. Her son and fiancée took a taste and looked at me with glitters of a smile in their eyes. Raquel took a mouthful and ran to the kitchen to get more water, as the water glass on the table was not enough. Chango looked around, not understanding our reactions, as he loved the spiciness.

By this time, everyone with the exception of Chango understood my feelings about the sleeping arrangement. It was also clear that Raquel's son did not like his mom sharing Chango's bed. After all, he had a father at home. It was impossible to discuss this with Chango; he simply didn't want to listen. Chango made coffee. I drank it outside in the garden, and while they were washing the dishes, I quietly walked back to my house.

The next morning, as if nothing had happened, Raquel called me in her bad English and asked me to come and have breakfast. I went. We ate without much talking, and I left for school. When she called me in the evening to come for dinner, I told her that I would never again return to that house, and hung up.

COSTA RICA, GUATEMALA, MEXICO
On my computer that evening, after googling many locales, I decided I'd go to Costa Rica for a vacation. I needed a break from everything. I had not started yet at MAPS, as my residence visa was still not approved, so next day during my shift at the airport I asked for two weeks' leave, and booked ID90s to Costa Rica. When the telephone rang, I didn't answer it. I packed my suitcase, and the next day, March 10, I boarded a flight

to Amsterdam. There I changed planes to fly to San José. My ID90s worked out well; I had a seat on every flight and experienced no delays.

I had arranged to stay the first night in a hotel in San José run by a Dutchman. The plane arrived early in the morning, and the gentleman picked me up and took me to the lodgings. After a rest, I started planning the remaining two weeks. I would buy a property in Costa Rica: it would have a sea view and fit my budget. The Dutchman and I discussed my plans. He knew a Dutch-born woman who was a real estate agent, Saskia Delic-van der Neut. He called her, and we decided I would go by bus to San Isidro, continuing to the province of Puntarenas on the west coast of Costa Rica. She would wait at the bus stop in Dominical, a town well known by surfers, where she would arrange a guesthouse for me.

Early the next morning I boarded a bus together with many locals, goats and chickens. The ride from San José lasted about three hours. In San Isidro I changed buses and had lunch. The rides were fun, as locals were very friendly and talkative, especially one young man, a student who told me he was a native of Costa Rica. He said that Costa Rica is one of the few countries that did not support a military; tax money was used for free education for everyone. I was happy with this newly gained knowledge, and we parted exchanging addresses.

I finally arrived in Dominical around 6 P.M., where a blond woman was standing at the bus stop. I got out, and we greeted each other in Dutch. She brought me to my guesthouse, a cabana on property that bordered the jungle. I was the only guest, and I loved it. We agreed that she would pick me up the next day to see some properties. I went to have dinner, which was prepared by the owner's wife. The guesthouse belonged to a family consisting of a father, mother and daughter, the mother being the cook. Every morning I enjoyed a wonderful breakfast of fruits and delicacies.

Saskia came as expected the next morning, and we drove to Uvita, where I met her husband Sasa, daughter Claire and son Sam. Her house, which had an open design, crowned a mountain and featured a breathtaking view of the sea. We drove around for days. I met many of her friends when we relaxed on the beach in Dominical. We went from

Uvita to Hatillo, where while we were relaxing at a bar, a man overheard us talking about my wish to buy property. He introduced himself; he said his name was Richard Abrahams and that he had a piece of land I might like.

Richard invited us to his villa, where I met his wife, Diane. We discussed the property for sale over a pleasant drink. He explained that the entire mountain belonged to him and a friend and was registered under the company name Dos Gringos Limitada. Richard explained that he had been a musician in the US and left many years ago to live in Costa Rica.

The next day Saskia dropped me at Richard's house, and he and I drove off to see his land. We got off the road in Hatillo, where we passed a horse shed. Slowly the car climbed the mountain up a dirt road. The land was divided into four properties. Richard showed me the first, which I did not like. The second I didn't care for, either, nor the third. The fourth I loved immediately. It was atop the mountain, with a full view of the Pacific. The land was a little over fourteen square meters (about 150 square feet) and the price was $55,000 USD. I sat myself down and meditated. In my mind, I saw wigwams with native Indians walking all around me, a good spiritual place. Richard and I walked through the jungle on the back of the mountain where he showed me the boundary lines, one of which was determined by a stream flowing from the top of the mountain. I saw there a wild horse enjoying the cool water. I made the decision there and then and bought the land. It would be a good investment and a retirement site, as I could not stay forever in Dubai.

I celebrated with Saskia and her family on the beach in Dominical and returned to the guesthouse, where I sat and enjoyed the sounds of a natural "choir." Exactly at 6 P.M. the crickets would start singing in the jungle, their loud cries rising to a pitch, then suddenly stopping after about twenty minutes. I found it enthralling.

On my last day at the cabana, Saskia and I drove to San Isidro to see a notary public, Casimiro Vargas. We prepared all the paperwork, and I gave Saskia a power of attorney to finalize the deal in my absence.

The property was officially registered with the Registro Nacional June 4, 1998.

Having fulfilled my dream, it was time to begin the return trip to Dubai. It turned out to be an adventure in itself.

I chose to take a taxi instead of the bus to Quepos. There I bought a ticket for a local flight to San José. The flight was cancelled at the last moment, but luckily the owners of the travel agency where I had bought my ticket had also intended to be on that flight, so they decided to drive to San José and invited me to be a passenger. I arrived at the airport on time, but…the KLM flight was full, and I would be unable to fly out of the country for the next few days, as all flight were overbooked. I tried other airlines flying to Europe, with no success.

I started looking into other options. There was a flight out to Guatemala with Sansa Regional. I left the airport and went to their office. I tried to explain to people at the front desk that I needed an ID90 to fly to Guatemala, as all flights out of the country were fully booked. Nobody understood what an ID90 was. The manager arrived, and he was familiar with it. He sent a telex to Swissair in Abu Dhabi to ask for authorization. A return telex came, an ID90 was prepared, and March 20 I was on my way to Guatemala City.

In the aircraft I was seated next to a young German who was backpacking through Central America. He was carrying a portable radio with huge speakers. Together we decided to look for accommodations, as I was uncertain what my next steps would be; I was now traveling on a budget, and neither of us had Guatemala currency. We walked and walked until we finally arrived in the city. On a small street in what looked like a red light district, we found a tiny place that called itself a hotel. We rang the bell. A full-bodied lady opened the door and confirmed that she had two rooms. We agreed to the price and settled in.

Next day was a Saturday. We had a good breakfast and left to get some local money from the bank. It was impossible; no ATM accepted my cards, and the banks were closed. The German and I looked at each other, not knowing what to do, so we decided to go sightseeing until we again had to leave for the airport. It was actually a very nice day, and we saw a lot of the city. We went back to the hotel to settle our bill. The mamma did not want our dollars or German marks or Dutch guilders. However, she was willing to accept the radio in exchange for payment. I told the poor German that I would pay him my share in US dollars. He was clearly unhappy parting with his radio, but I hoped he at least appreciated having less weight to lug around.

We returned to La Aurora International Airport, where I went straight to the KLM desk. We were hours early, and the gates were still closed. As soon as the KLM desk opened, I presented myself and asked for a space on the flight to Amsterdam. Misfortune still dogged me. The flight was overbooked. However…there was a seat on the first leg of a flight to Mexico City. Again, an authorization request was sent by telex to Abu Dhabi for an ID90. This time I had to wait an hour for the reply. Everybody in the Swissair office in Abu Dhabi was growing concerned about me. I messaged back that I would do everything possible to return ASAP.

March 21 at 10 P.M. I flew to Mexico City. The instant I arrived, I went to the transfer desk to ask if there were any flights going out to Europe. Nothing. I took a taxi to a hotel recommended by the cabbie, and after studying a local guidebook I found there, I reserved a city tour for early morning the next day. I was glad I did. I was impressed with the tour guide and found the city fascinating: its history, the fact that it is sinking, the dramatic murals of Diego Rivera. I bought a Mexican carpet, which I still own today.

In the early afternoon, I took a train to Xochimilco. Located on the southern edge of Mexico City, Xochimilco was built upon a lake at the time of the Aztecs and now features a vast system of canals and gardens. Having taken a leisurely walk through the village, I boarded a boat on the river. We drifted past many other boats, some with wedding parties on them, colorful and inviting. People danced as mariachi bands played. My day had been wonderful, and full of happy anticipation, I went to Mexico City International Airport hours before the KLM check-in desk opened.

I started chatting with the staff, who told me the next flight was full. I went to the Lufthansa desk; again, the flight was fully booked. I waited until all passengers were checked in, hoping that somebody would not show up. I turned away feeling bitterly disappointed, as I was told that the next day was shaping up to be the same. Then the Lufthansa station manager stopped me. He told me there was an empty seat in their morning flight next day. Immediately we sent a telex to Swissair Abu Dhabi for authorization, which came by return telex. I thanked the staff and returned to the hotel, relieved. The next morning I boarded a flight to Frankfurt, and from there I made connections to Zürich and Dubai without further problems. At midnight on March 23, I finally arrived back in Dubai, satisfied with my unexpected adventures.

DUBAI'S FIRST WOMAN REGISTRAR

Upon my return, I had a meeting with the Ministry of Education. There I learned that EIS had not designated me as a registrar, but as a secretary, possibly for convenience of paperwork. The woman in charge of my case corrected this error. Now I am officially the first woman ever to be a registrar in Dubai, and from what I hear I remain the only one officially registered with the Ministry of Education.

Being back home was harder than I thought it would be. Although Ann was still living in my house and keeping me company, and Claudia passed by as often as she could, I felt lonely. Claudia told me she had always tried to adhere to her father's principles and expectations, which was not easy. For years, she had adored him and put him on a pedestal. Now she had a long talk with him and expressed her disappointment with him for treating me so poorly. Chango did not know how to respond to this criticism coming from his beloved daughter. He said nothing at all.

On April 26, I would turn fifty-one years old. Claudia asked me what I was going to do for my birthday. I told her I didn't know. She said perhaps a handsome young man would serenade me at my bedroom window. When I told her no one had ever done that for me, she looked surprised.

On the night of my birthday, Ann and I were watching TV when the doorbell rang. I opened the door to see my friend Sonia standing there with a birthday cake covered in candles. I was happy to have Ann and Sonia there to celebrate with me, and when I went to bed, it was with grateful thoughts for having such dear friends.

Something woke me in the middle of the night: a soft voice outside my window, singing. I got up, looked out the window, and there was Claudia standing with a huge stuffed dog in her arms. As she finished her song, I took her in my arms and we laughed. What a memorable birthday! That beloved dog would travel with me everywhere until I went to Spain, where sadly he met a tragic end following rough play with my newly acquired puppies.

My focus was now completely on my work. I increased my shifts at AUH airport, and this meant I needed a new car, as my Mazda was in the shop too often and too long, spare parts being hard to find. Ajman from EIS told me about friends who had a Mercedes convertible 300-24CE sitting in a garage. It was the family's third car and never been used. Ajman and I went to see it: it was a handsome maroon color and everything was electronic, a dream of a car. I negotiated a price, and the gem was mine.

Ann at last found a small affordable house in a compound nearby and moved there with her daughter and the huge Great Dane.

A WEDDING "REHEARSAL"

My friend Sonia told me that she and Jean-Luc were going to get married in just a few months, and that I was cordially invited to the wedding. I was not very confident I could handle that, as I was still suffering a lot over my separation from Chango, who was also a wedding guest. Then I received an invitation to the November wedding of Alejandra and Sebastian in Buenos Aires. I told Sonia I would come to her wedding as a kind of rehearsal for Argentina, where Chango would again be present.

The day of Sonia's wedding came and I went, despite nursing a bad cold. The affair was celebrated in the Jebel Ali Club garden. Sonia and Jean-Luc were seated at the entrance and surrounded by big tables overflowing with people. Sonia is Italian and Jean-Luc French, so there was a nice international mix of friends present. At one long table there was a young man; his eyes and mine briefly met. I congratulated the happy couple and was then shown to my table, where Chango was already seated. I greeted Chango shyly, not really knowing what to say or do, so I concentrated on the guy who came around with the drinks.

PASCUAL

Soon I felt another presence at the table. I turned around to see the young man with the penetrating eyes. He introduced himself as Pascual and proved an entertaining speaker, sparking several animated discussions at our table. It turned out that Pascual was half Venezuelan and half Italian He had brown curly hair and big brown eyes. He wore an Armani suit and gave the air of someone who always dresses fashionably. It did not take him long to realize that Chango and I had been a couple. He said to me, "You know, we in Latin America have one big heart, which is for the one we love at home, looking after our children and us. But inside that heart are many, many little hearts, all for the flowers around us."

I told Pascual I could handle only one heart, with no other hearts inside it. Then I rose and said my goodbyes to the happy couple.

My flu worsened during the evening. Feeling horrible, I checked my very high temperature and decided to stay home the next day. I collapsed onto my bed, relieved to think I could sleep in the next day.

It was not to be. At 7 A.M. my telephone rang. A voice I didn't recognize asked me how I was.

"Who is this?" I asked.

"Pascual from yesterday."

I was sick, and on top of that, not a morning person. I grumpily asked him how he got my number. He replied that he had been impressed with me, and had asked Sonia for my number, convincing her that he had only good intentions towards me.

Pascual would be a fresh breeze blowing into my life.

An hour after he called, Pascual arrived at my home bringing medicine for my flu. He made me tea and toast, I aware the whole time that I looked terrible. He returned at lunch and dinnertime, making me soup. After a week in Pascual's caring hands, my health had improved to the point that he decided we should…go out dancing. He ignored my protests and told me to dress comfortably, as I shouldn't be sitting at home bemoaning a lost love, but out having fun.

Before he and I went to a salsa dancing place called the Savage Garden, we headed out for dinner. We went to the Cactus Cantina in Satwa for Mexican food. There I met Claudia Gonzalez, who was waitressing for some extra pocket money. Later she and her husband, David, would become my good friends.

Pascual orchestrated the next few weeks; he was a butterfly, and I flew at his side. We spent all our free time together. When I would get home from work at the airport around 2 A.M., he would pass by my house from his late night dance escapades to ensure I was safe and well. Another who would regularly pass by my house was Chango; it had not escaped his attention that I had a new beau. Finally, he called and announced that he and I should meet. I agreed to see him at a gas station near the beach. He was already waiting when we pulled up. Pascual demonstratively got out of my car so that Chango could see him. Chango's green eyes were sparkling. Was it from anger or…? His face said it all, but he controlled himself. We talked, I forget about what, and Pascual and I continued on our way to the beach, where we typically spent time with friends on lazy Friday afternoons. After those hours in the sun, Pascual would drop me off at my home on the way to his, and we both would have a rest before meeting up in the evening, if I didn't have work at the airport.

On one such afternoon, as I was lying on the sofa in my living room, I couldn't stop thinking about Pascual. I phoned and told him I had a terrible sunburn (which was true) and that I needed his help to apply the sunburn cream. He came to my house and sat beside me. As his hand slowly and sensuously wandered over my back, my whole body became extremely sensitive to wherever he touched me. We moved to the bedroom, and it was then that we went from friends to lovers.

We spent many more hours together during the following weeks, making love as if our bodies had known each other always. Pascual never stayed overnight, but of course his car would be in front of my house all the time, a fact that did not escape Chango. One Friday morning, as I was waiting for Pascual to pick me up, the doorbell rang. Thinking it was Pascual, I opened the door and gazed in surprise at a soaking wet Chango, who strode inside without asking. He said that he had been to the gym and wanted to dry his clothes. He undressed and took me in his arms. We did it there and then.

In the quiet that followed, he told me that Claudia had mentioned my new property in Central America. "Why did you buy the land in Costa Rica?" he demanded. "We could have bought the farm of Che Guevara in Argentina!" I looked at him in astonishment and thought: *WE? There is no WE!* My heart ached. He was and is the love of my life, but I would no longer allow him to confuse my feelings. It was there and then that I followed one of his own sayings: "If there is something in your life that hurts you, cut it out. It will hurt even more at that moment, but gradually the pain will disappear and you will heal. If you fail to do this, you will suffer forever." I cut, it hurt, I suffered; but yes, gradually the pain inside disappeared.

Again the doorbell rang. I called to Pascual that I was coming, dressed and ran out the front door, leaving a speechless Chango behind in my living room. I felt like a slut. When Pascual asked if it was Chango's car in front of my house, I said, "Yes, I left him inside the house," keeping the details out of my story. It was the last time I met Chango in my house or his for the rest of my time in Dubai.

Pascual and I became very close. We saw each other every day. He was proud to be with me, and thought I was beautiful; he could never stop gazing at my legs. Never in my life had I been so admired. It did me good, and yet it scared me very much. He was so much younger than I, and it was impossible for me to simply live in the moment, so I did what I always do: worry and feel guilty.

One afternoon while resting after work on my living room sofa, I had a dream. Or did I? Half awake, half asleep, I saw a swing standing in a green meadow. On the swing was a teenage girl in a crinoline dress dating to the 1800s. A boy around six years old, dressed in a dark velvet suit, was pushing the swing. I recognized the girl as myself and the boy as Pascual. Then the scene shifted. I now saw a casket and a young man walking behind it. The girl had died, and the grieving boy was bringing her to her grave. I knew this dream told our story, and it had given me the answer I sought.

I called Pascual and told him what I had seen. Clearly, we had met in a past life, and this was the reason we felt so familiar with each other. I told him that we could be friends but lovers no more. I was relieved. We didn't see each other for several weeks, which hurt us both, but afterward we became really good friends. I never regretted this little episode of mutual admiration and intimacy.

ALE'S WEDDING AND A TOAST TO 1999

November was drawing closer, and I had to decide if I would go to Ale's wedding. The children kept asking me, and I didn't want to disappoint them, so I got myself an ID90 on KLM to Buenos Aires. I had bought a nice dress, and was now looking forward to the event.

Marco and Claudia were there to collect me from the airport. Chango's family was all in one hotel, and I stayed at another, but most of the time I stayed with the kids in Ale's apartment, where we laughed and joked. Chango did not speak to me; he actually ignored me completely, but then, I wasn't there for him. We had a pre-wedding party at the house of Sebastian's parents, whom I remember as very nice people. My suitcase had not arrived and was not expected anytime soon, so the young people helped me shop for new clothing for the wedding.

At last, we gathered for the ceremony in a small chapel in a park in Buenos Aires. While we were all waiting expectantly in the pews, Chango made a dramatic entrance with Claudia and Ale at his side. I filmed the whole event, so it kept me busy. After the ceremony we went to the hotel where the new couple had a room. While they changed their clothes, drinks were served. Although Marco and Claudia were trying to involve me, they were all with family and I felt lonely. Not many people there spoke English, and I suspect, as they kept glancing at Chango and me, that they guessed I was his ex.

After dinner a band played. The bride and groom danced to the title song of *The Godfather*. While Chango was talking with friends and professors from his university days, I saw him sometimes turning and looking at me. I guessed he was thinking of introducing me, but then deciding against it. Fifteen years later, he confirmed that my suspicions had been correct.

Around 10 P.M. I decided to leave. I spoke to the doorman, who called a taxi. I couldn't give the cabbie my hotel's name or address; I only remembered the road it was on, so after many turns and U-turns I recognized the place and arrived safely. I went to bed, happy for the couple but unhappy for myself. The telephone rang. It was Graziela, Chango's ex-wife. She asked if I was OK, and urged me to come back to the party. I thanked her for her kindness but said I was tired and preferred to sleep, so she wished me goodnight.

The next morning Marco brought me to Ale's place. We were making breakfast when Chango came in, ignoring me. Graziela asked me when I had to leave for the airport; I told her after lunch. She was offering to bring me, when Chango interrupted and said I could take a taxi. Graziela just stared at him and said that she and her husband would have lunch with me, show me a bit of Buenos Aires and then bring me to the airport. I was relieved. It was a pleasant drive and a very good meal in a typical Argentine restaurant. As Graziela dropped me off at the airport, I had the feeling she was feeling sorry for me. I did too! She was a kind woman who probably knew what I was going through.

It had been an eventful year: changing schools; ending my relationship with Chango; meeting Pascual; attending the wedding of Sonia and Jean-Luc, as well as the wedding of Alejandra and Sebastian; and last but not least, visiting the newlyweds Evelyn and Dauphine in the south of France. It was wonderful to see Evelyn again, since our lives had been so similar, even having been married to the same man. Both born under the star sign of Taurus, we felt like sisters and still do. It made me happy to see Evelyn so relaxed. She and I took long walks in the scenic countryside.

Nineteen ninety-eight was quickly drawing to a close. I decided to hold a little New Year's celebration with my new friend Margarita

Castillo, the manager of La Parilla, a restaurant at the Jumeirah Beach Hotel. Offering authentic Latin American cuisine and live entertainment, La Parilla was one of my favorite spots. We planned to have our party for two on the Jebel Ali beach on December 29 because both of us would be working New Year's Eve—she at the restaurant and I at the Swissair counter, where I had offered to take the shifts of my colleagues who had families, so they would be able to celebrate with them.

Margarita bought a small tent, we picked up wood to make a campfire, and drove to the Jebel Ali beach in her Ssangyong 4WD. We parked the car directly on the beach and set up our tent beside it. We swam in the sea, which was quiet and lovely at sundown. To have the beach to ourselves, no human voices, no droning cars, only the sound of the waves, was close to paradise. The evening was cold, so I was glad I had brought my boots, jeans, ski jacket and warm pajamas. Our noses were cold preparing the fire, but finally flames rose up from under the wood, Margarita proving an expert campfire builder. We had an excellent barbecue, and at midnight, with recorded music playing in the background, we toasted the year 1999 with good champagne.

For a long time we lay in our sleeping bags outside the tent without talking, just enjoying the moment, the clear starry night, reminiscing about our lives and the people in it. We fell asleep and woke with the sun. It was just beautiful. We ran into the sea and let our bodies float on the soft waves.

This part of Dubai life I loved and remember fondly. If you were lucky, you could find an empty space under a wooden sun cover on the beach and spend the weekend there from dawn until dusk. The seashells were pink, the corals cream. Walking into the water, you'd see fish swishing around your ankles. You'd feel peaceful and at one with nature...

Then development started. The dredging was a continuous, annoying drone for us above sea level. No wonder the pretty shells disappeared, the cream corrals dissolving into a smashed, gray mush. Marine life vanished, too. Funky shaped islands and flashy hotels are progress!

Margarita and I re-heated the fire and made coffee for our breakfast. Then we leisurely cleaned up and packed everything in the car, leaving no sign that a tent had ever stood on the beach. We drove off, and Margarita dropped me at my home. We both considered it a perfect New Year's Eve and never forgot it.

My next few birthdays I would throw myself a dinner at La Parilla. The Latin band would serenade me and my colleague Shauna Richardson, who shared the same birthday. A scrumptious birthday cake would top off the gourmet evening.

MYRTHA

Margarita introduced me to a Swiss woman staying at the Jumeirah Beach Hotel. Her name was Myrtha, and she had owned a gardening business. Her husband had died of a brain tumor, and she herself was diagnosed with alveolar cell carcinoma. She fought it, but it seems it had been in her system for many years. After doctors told her that her time was short, she sold everything in Switzerland and got herself a room at one of the best hotels in Dubai. She didn't tell the staff she was ill, as she didn't want pity. She simply wanted to enjoy her last days on this planet.

Myrtha and I became friends, and sometimes I stayed over at the hotel when she was not doing well. Her condition went from bad to worse. She had to get up at 4 A.M. and beat herself on her back to loosen up the fluids in her lungs and cough them out. At 8 A.M. she finally would be ready to have breakfast and lie in the pool, after which she would be exhausted again and take a rest. The staff at the hotel started observing what was happening, and guessed at her secret.

Finally, I suggested Myrtha leave the hotel and move into my house. She loved gardening and my garden was a mess, so whenever she felt up to it she plopped a hat on her head, took a rake in her hands and went to work.

It had been Myrtha's custom to travel out of the country every six months to renew her visa. I advised her not to return from her next trip to Switzerland, as her dream of dying in Dubai was not possible. She needed very strong drugs that no doctor in Dubai would prescribe for her. It would also have been difficult for me to explain a dead body in my villa, although it was a matter we realistically discussed and prepared for somewhat.

We went for one last time to the Jumeirah Beach Hotel for a meal. There Myrtha ordered thirty-six oysters. The waiter stared at us and asked if we had made a mistake. Myrtha replied, no, we like oysters. It was our last dinner together. For years afterward, I kept the oysters in Myrtha's hat (which she left behind).

Myrtha flew to Switzerland, and I followed a week later. Accompanied by my friend Nicole, I visited her at a luxurious hotel on Lake Zürich where she was staying. We said our goodbyes, and two days later, on August 24, 1999, Myrtha died peacefully. She had left the world on her own terms.

The experience with Myrtha made a deep impression on me and made me start thinking about life after death and other spiritual matters. During her many stories about herself, Myrtha used to tell me:

> *Schmerzen sind die Sprache der Seele*
> *Und wenn die Seele in Ihrer Not schreit, entsteht Krankheit*
> *Um dem Leiden letzlich ein genädiges Ende zu setzen.*
> Pain is the language of the soul
> And when the soul cries out in distress, illness occurs
> To ultimately end the suffering gracefully.

When I looked at the people around me who were suffering from cancer, I must admit I was struck by how many of them were overly reserved. Most of them were the quiet, brooding type, suffering inside.

EXPLORATIONS WITHIN AND WITHOUT

Nineteen ninety-nine became a year of spiritual awakening and travelling. It was also the year that my Swiss friend Nicoletta, with whom I had remained in contact throughout the years, introduced me to Ursi. Ursi is the mother of a friend of Nicoletta's, and when she came to visit Dubai, I met her and we clicked immediately. Ursi and I are still friends today. She follows me wherever I move, and I look forward to each and every time she visits.

Whenever I went to Switzerland I would meet up with Nicole and stay a few days at her home, where we would reminisce and relax. Her husband, Kurt, would fire up the barbecue, and we would enjoy great food with even greater wine. Nicole and I shared an interest in the "unknown," so we signed up for a workshop run by Richard Unger, founder of the International Institute of Hand Analysis based in Marin, California. We were excited to learn that hand analysis, as developed by Unger, uses traditional hand analysis as well as practical formulas for living your life to its highest potential as revealed in the map of your fingerprints. The workshop made sense to us, and we were glad we went.

Upon returning to Dubai, I read all the fingerprints of my colleagues and friends. However, I realized I could not do the readings while I was actually sitting in front of people. While holding their hands, I received impressions of their lives, and depending on how strong the connection was, the warmer my hands became, the energy flowing freely. Immediately after they left, I would go to the computer and type like a wild woman my report on what I had just read from the prints. Suddenly I saw spirits everywhere. When photographing mosques in the region, I would see orbs or bubbles floating in front of the pictures, one moment here, the next gone. Other people could not see these images. One evening I went to the old parts of Sharjah and Ajman and took a photo of an abandoned house. It was empty and dilapidated, its windows broken, no electricity, of course. But in my photograph, one of the rooms glowed. It was spooky! Nights I would think of sick people and send them healing thoughts, hoping it would lessen their pain, even just a little. Since my experience with Jomanda, I started reading books on spirituality, clairvoyance, etc. It was then I realized I had gifts I had never explored.

Modern American Private School continued to do well. It relocated to another huge villa in Jumeirah. There we were one big family, staff, parents and students.

This year I would make time to visit many friends in Europe, starting with my friends Rosanna and Cipriano. They lived in Bergamo, in northern Italy, and collected me from the Milan airport. They had a guest room ready for me, but when I tried to sleep there, I tossed and turned and woke the next morning a physical wreck. When they asked if I'd slept well, I replied, no, you have water under your house. They looked at me as if I were crazy, especially Cipriano. I told them that my uncle was a dowser, and people in our village had asked him to walk with them to find water. I felt there was a lot of water under the house and had to sleep elsewhere. After we went sightseeing in Bergamo, Cipriano, curious now, researched the matter and discovered that an underground river passed beneath the house. That night I was moved to a guestroom on the other side of the house and slept like a baby for the rest of my stay.

We hiked the beautiful mountains surrounding Bergamo and ate Rosanna's delicious home cooking. Feeling refreshed, I left my friends and headed for Holland, planning to visit my mother as much as I could.

A VISIT HOME

When I arrived at my parents' home, my father was sitting as always in his recliner before the front window with a view of the street. He was quietly watching everybody coming and going. Sometimes people waved at him and he would wave back. Sometimes he stepped out to chat or merely say hello. Dorst was still a village where everybody knew each other. I settled in my old room and decided to make the most of the week I would be staying there.

The next day Dad and I drove to my mother's nursing home. Upon entering, I saw her sitting with a group of other people at a big table. I embraced her, but she didn't know who I was. When my father embraced her I had the feeling there was some recognition, but most probably because he visited three times a week. I felt very sad in the presence of the residents: some were deaf, some paralyzed, some mentally impaired, some blind. Her stroke had rendered my mother blind in one eye, deaf and partially paralyzed. She was a body; the spirit was gone.

I asked my father if he had ever taken my mother home for a visit. The look on his face told me the thought had never crossed his mind. After visiting hours he and I went to see the head nurse and arranged a wheelchair-accessible taxi to bring my mother home in two days. I felt terribly sorry for my mom. Deep down, my sisters and I had always believed that it would be Dad who would go first. To see Mom in this state was extremely sad. Who deserved to live like this? Dad and I did not have much to say to each other. Over the years our relationship had cooled. It was increasingly obvious that he was a selfish man, and I could see that he suffered by doing his duty towards his wife, my mother.

The next day I took my mother alone on an outing in the city of Breda. My mother had been properly attired in a nice dress with a jacket over her knees in case it became cool. I pushed her wheelchair to the marketplace where we sat in a restaurant and ate pancakes and ice cream. Of course, despite my help she made a mess of it, but she smiled the whole time. Then we went shopping in a mall. She looked at me, smiling, grateful to have such a nice nurse; she had no idea who I was. After a few hours exploring downtown Breda, we stopped for a cappuccino and a piece of fabled Dutch pie. As we walked from the eatery, the wheelchair suddenly slid from the sidewalk cobblestones, and Mom and the chair tumbled sideways. Luckily, a passing gentleman on a bike rushed to help. He and I helped her up in the wheelchair. She was unhurt; in fact, she was laughing. The man and I were both relieved. Five minutes later, I returned her to the nursing home. I felt sad again to leave her there, the woman who had given birth to me and taken care of me for so many years.

When I arrived home I sat down with my dad and asked him to sell the house and come with me to Dubai. He looked at me as if I'd gone mad, refusing to even think about my proposal.

Whatever our differences, he and I eagerly looked forward to the next day. It would have been my father's day to visit Mom, but now she would come home after a two years' absence. Dad had fetched pie from the bakery, the coffee was ready, and we were gazing out the living room window when the big wheelchair taxi arrived. I saw curtains moving behind the windows of houses on the other side of the road, the curious taking a peek; in Dorst, everybody knows everything about everybody, so why hadn't they known this! My mother rolled down the little ramp in her wheelchair. Then my father wheeled her through the gate onto the porch and into the garden, where a table was set. Dad and I knew she loved sitting outside in the garden. She would stay half a day and be collected at 3 P.M.

Dad brought the coffee and pie, which she enjoyed, but we both could see that she had no memory of where she was. Yes, she liked it, but that was all; it was unfamiliar to her. I suggested to my dad that we go for a walk, as the day was sunny. We could take a pleasant walk in the woods bordering the village. He agreed, as he preferred to be doing something to sitting and staring at her and me in silence. His love for her was gone; mere duty had replaced it. I had the feeling he was just waiting for her to die.

We rose and prepared ourselves for the long walk, me with a camera, Dad with his hat and jacket. The moment we reached the sidewalk, people came to say hello and greet my mom, shake her hand and chat with us. It was clear she was loved by neighbors and friends. We wheeled her towards Surea, the natural pond where I got married the first time and where my sisters and I used to skate and swim as youngsters. More people stopped us and asked about my mother's health. Unfortunately, the restaurant we had planned to dine at was closed, so we continued our walk, now in the direction of Oosterhout. At the crossing we turned back toward Dorst, where we stopped at the small chapel just outside the village. My mother seemed to have enjoyed the walk, my father quietly pushing the wheelchair, all three of us savoring the sounds of nature. We bought ice cream, which my mother loved. I saw on my father's face that he didn't like the way she spread it all around her mouth and cheeks. He looked away; either the sight hurt him too much or he was just tired of it.

After the taxi came and collected Mom, my dad promised to bring her home regularly. He didn't. The visit with me was the last time my mother ever entered her house.

I had phoned my German friends Peter and Ute and invited them to visit. Their village was only a two hours' drive from Dorst. We reminisced about our teenage years, camping in West-Kapelle, and their wedding. Then we chatted about our travels and their son, Pascal. Peter and Ute joined me in a visit to the nursing home.

My last day in Holland, Dad and I brought Mom down to the entertainment hall, where people were dancing, eating and singing to live music by an "oldies" band. I loved to see my mother happy and laughing, but knowing that she didn't know who I was hurt me very much. Tears in my eyes, I said my goodbyes, not knowing if I would ever see her alive again.

While registrar at EIS, I met a woman named Dr. Michaela Prinzessin Wolkonsky. She had (and still has) a dental clinic in Munich, and she planned to open a clinic in Dubai featuring cosmetic specialists. Therefore she came to EIS to inquire about schooling for her children. It never materialized, but we remained friends, and I had promised to visit her in her holiday home in Spain.

Michaela and her four children collected me from Barcelona airport and took me straight to their house. We took in the sights, strolled on the beaches and talked about life in general. She mentioned a medium in Marbella named Barry Lee. She thought I might be interested in meeting him, as she had heard many good things about him. We phoned him, and I was delighted to learn I could schedule an appointment on short notice. I was excited to know that my future would soon be revealed to me...hopefully.

BARRY LEE

I purchased a ticket to Malaga. From Malaga airport I walked to the railway station and took a train to Marbella. I had never been to the south of Spain, and at that time there was no Internet, no Smartphones. I found my way by consulting a roadmap and asking strangers for help. I continued by taxi, which dropped my two suitcases and me in front of an apartment building. I rang the bell and was buzzed in. A man came and introduced himself as John. He glanced at my suitcases, and I told him not to worry, I wasn't moving in. He smiled and asked me to wait in the living room. Barry was coming soon, he said.

I saw a man walk onto a terrace. He gestured me to follow, and when I reached him he sat and said he was Barry. The reading started immediately. He looked at me and said:

> "Your mother loves you. She knows what you did for her, her body is still on this earth plane, but she is gone and wants me again to tell you that she loves you and she appreciated your coming to see her."

Even if there had been nothing else interesting to hear, this alone was so important to me—to hear that my mom had recognized me—that I cried and cried from happiness. He told me that I was living in the wrong place; it was unhealthy for me. He told me that the man I loved, loved me too, but that we would never be together, as he could never be faithful. Barry told me that although I had no children there was one son, the son of the man I loved, who was my spiritual son and that he would always stand by me. It would be a lifelong relationship. Barry said I should continue to use my healing powers each night before sleep and continue sending them to people who needed them and…he told me something no one except my immediate family knew, and which I had heard about only recently.

When my sisters and I were young, we heard through gossip that my grandparents on my father's side had to get married because my grandmother was pregnant. Most of my father's brothers and sisters had mental problems. My father had told us this was because Grandma and Grandpa were related. Years later, when I was in my thirties, I asked my sisters if they had ever feared having mentally ill children because of this incest. I had read that mental illness usually jumps a generation, and my sisters and I were normal. For this reason, I had my tubes tied to make sure that I would never have children, additionally since Hans, my second husband, turned out to be psychologically unbalanced. Their reply was that my father was not a product of incest, and then the story, which I had never known, came out: My great-grandfather owned a stud farm before World War I. He, his wife and children had a good life. The story goes that he was a handsome womanizer. His wife died, and it was decided that the very young sister of his wife would come and help him look after the children and the farm. Soon she also looked after him and his needs and got pregnant, which was a deep shame in those times. Her family decided that my great-grandfather's oldest son, my grandfather, Jacques, would wed his aunt, who was close to him in age. The young couple had no say in this and got married. In 1918 they moved to the house next to my mother's. My father had always felt less loved than his brothers and sisters; by listening to the village gossip, he put the pieces together and understood.

Here now in Marbella was a man, Barry, who said he was in contact with the Spirit, and the Spirit told him that my grandfather, my true grandfather, was proud of me and wished he could have known me, as he had not been a good person during his time on earth and I would have set a proper example for him. I was ashamed of his behavior with others, Barry said, looking deeply into my eyes. "I am talking about your real grandfather, not the one you used to call grandfather." I nodded that I knew what he was talking about. Then he told me that my grandmother on my mother's side was also here. "She wants to embrace you, she says she is always with you." I knew this; I had always felt her spirit near me. She loved cats, and from childhood I loved them, too. Barry said more things that I have since forgotten. He then started talking about my past lives. I had come as a healer from the star system of Sirius to Atlantis, where I also had been a healer.

It was very strange he mentioned this, as a few months earlier I had gone to a stone workshop given by Simona Juchert in Dubai. The stone I had intuitively chosen was moldavite, which was thought to have fallen to Earth during a meteor shower some 15 million years ago. In ancient Asian chronicles, the crystal was said to have come from the Sirius star system. Moldavite, it was believed, was a talisman of Tazlavoo, the one-time emperor of Atlantis. Legend has it that this same crystal was sent to King Solomon in Israel, who split the crystal and made a ring out of one piece. The other pieces, according to lore, were sent to a monastery in Tibet. Centuries later, it is said that Mohammed took three pieces to Mecca. Nicholas Roerich, a Russian artist and mystic, theorized that moldavite crystal is charged with Shugs, currents of psychic force. He speculated that, like an electrical accumulator, the crystal might release the energy stored within it. For instance, it will increase the spiritual vitality of anyone who touches it, infusing the person with knowledge or enhancing healing abilities. A friend of mine, Simona Hejlova, a native of the Czech Republic, gave me two moldavite stones. She had found them near the Moldau River Valley, north of Prague, while she was visiting her family.

Barry told me I had experienced many past lives. He chose to describe only those he thought I would find particularly enlightening. They included a Chinese woman living as an artist in the 1400s and an Austrian composer who gave all his earnings to poor orphans. In the 1600s I was a mother superior in a convent in Northern England. Extremely religious and very strict with myself, I died praying on a prayer chair. In the 1800s I was an African healer, a huge, powerful woman who preferred to heal animals and was known for her hearty laugh. Following the first World War, I was a German man—bad karma for me, as he was a scoundrel with no respect for women. He died an alcoholic. Before he told me about my most recent incarnation, Barry asked if I had any problems with my feet. As he explained:

> "You must have problems with your feet, as just after WWI you were a German farm woman working the lands. You did not want children, as in your previous lives you had many miscarriages. This is also the reason why you did not want children in this life. One day, while working on the land with a horse, the horse panicked and trampled you to death, your feet completely damaged."

I looked at Barry and told him that I was born with clubfeet. I was impressed. Again he looked at me and asked if I knew that this was my final reincarnation on this planet. I returned his look and confirmed with a "Yes." He said, "When you chose this lifetime, you made your choices how it would be. You also know that there will not be any more love relationships for you." Again, I agreed, as this was what my intuition had told me over the years. I did not feel sorry, I did not feel sad;

it just **was**. I knew that there was so much more to life, and that mine had just begun. I left Marbella with a good feeling in my heart, thinking about my mother. Her "coming through" had been an enormous relief to me. Now I knew that she was just waiting to go. I hoped she would not suffer pain.

SCHOOL AND *ELFSTEDENTOCHT*

Returning to Dubai, my life revolved around school, my tutoring, and work at Swissair. I was very busy admitting students. Most were Dutch, Scandinavians, other Europeans, Koreans and Japanese, who had no chance to be accepted at the American School Dubai (ASD).

One day I was walking on the first floor when I met one of my favorite parents, Els Carlsson, a mother of four. She showed off her newborn son Kai to me, and I offered to hold him. While she went down to the main floor to see other people, I followed her slowly, being extra careful carrying the baby. Despite wearing high, squared-heeled shoes, I descended the first stairway safely, walking slowly. But coming down the second stairway, while Els was chatting with other parents, I slipped and fell, instinctively folding my body around the baby. We both flew down about fifteen steps. Everybody came running. Me, I was just worried about Kai. We were both fine. My angels were working overtime again. How lucky I was! And it was lucky for Els that staff and parents were like a big family. Soon after this near-accident, Els phoned me in distress: she was unable to collect the children at the end of the school day. Reason? There had been a power failure at her home, and her gate could only be opened by remote control. Solution? Ms. Marilyn brought the children to her doorstep.

Around this time I moved offices. As the student population was growing rapidly, and my office was the biggest in the school, I offered to let my office be converted into a classroom. I found myself a space under the stairs from which I had so gracefully taken my tumble.

Third grade teacher Martin Reinsmoen liked to drive pirouettes outside the school gates with my car. He would also regularly plop little drops of water on my head, then hide himself and his giggling students in the hallway. I would act as if nothing had happened, but when

Christmastime came and Santa came to school, he personally punished Mr. Martin for being so naughty to Ms. Marilyn...!

Many of our students were Dutch, which gave me an idea for a special school event. Students would play the role of journalists covering the famous *Elfstedentocht*, acting as if their news coverage would be broadcast on local television.

The *Elfstedentocht*, or Eleven Cities Tour, is a nearly 200 kilometers (120 miles) long skating race. It is held in the province of Friesland in the north of Holland, passing through eleven historic cities. The ice along the entire course needs to be at least fifteen centimeters (six inches) thick. That means sometimes the event can be held on consecutive years; other times the intervals between tours can exceed twenty years. When the ice is suitable, the competition is held both as a speed skating match (with up to 300 contestants) and a leisurely excursion (with around 16,000 skaters). Since the first tour in 1909, only fifteen official Eleven Cities Tours have been held. The last one was in 1997. Every year, right after the first frost, the Dutch suffer from "Eleven Cities Fever," hoping for one of these unique and spectacular events.

Our school would do mock news coverage of the event and broadcast through the fictional DNN (Dubai News Network), invented by Ms. Marilyn. We scheduled it during a morning assembly. I wrote a script for each journalist based in each city through which the skaters raced, and invited "dignitaries" to attend, including the president of the committee (played by a student) and the Dutch queen (played by Cheryl Rowlands, the head of one of the Varkeys' British schools). Our school nurse, Louise Fisk, represented the medical team on site.

The students and staff were chosen, and several months of practicing and creativity went into the project. Someone rustled up a sound system and a microphone for each journalist, too. On November 28, 1999, the *Elfstedentocht* was on, to the great excitement of parents who attended. The students did a fantastic job. Not only was the presentation educational, but it also brought our school community closer together. You can view the show at my YouTube channel.

LALITA

Working days, evenings and nights did not allow much time for house-work, so I decided to hire a house girl. Her name was Lalita. She was Sri Lankan and very outspoken, a bit bossy, but hardworking. I found my house and garden clean. I was also pleased with the food on the table (my diet consisted of first-class Swissair meals).

When Lalita had worked for me a year, she returned to Sri Lanka to visit her children, who were college students. I traveled to see her there. She picked me up at the airport, than we rented a bus and did a three-day tour of cultural and religious sites. I briefly considered buying land in Sri Lanka; the white beaches were beautiful, very affordable, and foreigners were at that time permitted to buy property there, but I never took the step.

A FINAL VISIT WITH PASCUAL

Pascual had left the UAE and moved to Madrid to work for a UK com-pany. We remained in contact, and in April I went to see him in his little apartment. It was Easter, so he had time to show me around. The first evening we dined in a restaurant downtown with his girlfriend. She did not speak English well, and it was the language Pascual and I commu-nicated in. He sat opposite me, and she sat next to him. She broached a subject that she probably thought I would back her up on: she said that she and Pascual had a great time together, but that he wasn't seri-ous about their relationship. Why wouldn't he buy a ring for her finger? Poor girl. He looked straight at her and then at me and replied cruelly, "Because you're not the one." She demanded to know how he could know that, and he said, "For sure I know," looking at me. From there on they both acted as if nothing had happened, but I felt uncomfortable. As soon as we returned to his apartment, we each went to our beds to be able to rise early to see Madrid.

We had a fantastic day sightseeing, stopping to eat light meals. The weather was sunny, but not too hot. I found Madrid exquisite, and af-ter I posted my photos on Worldisround.com, I received many warm compliments from people in Madrid, writing that I had caught the heart of the city. This was my last visit with Pascual; although we both had a great time, we had our own paths to follow. He is happily married now with two children.

A MUSICAL INTERLUDE

The Dutch embassy issued a special request to all Dutch people living in Dubai: if you have room in your home, please house members of the Dutch Youth Orchestra. The Princess Christina Competition had organized the effort to send these gifted young musicians around the world to raise awareness of classical music. Frederieke Saeijs, now one of Europe's eminent violinists, and Saskia Plagge, now playing cello with the Brabants Orchestra, settled into my home, and we got acquainted. Soon musician Michiel Bot moved in, too, as it seems the family he initially stayed with was a little too strict with him. I loved to hear the three practice. It was incredible to spend a morning listening to Frederieke play my favorite Tchaikovsky piece for violin. I took the young people sightseeing on days that they did not need to perform, and to thank me for my hospitality (they said mine was the best home where orchestra members lodged) the three came to play at Dubai Academy. After holding a question-and-answer period in the classroom, they went to the theater and performed a two-hour concert. It was a miracle that the kids could keep quiet for such a long time. I have a video of Saskia on my YouTube channel, but Frederieke asked me to remove hers as she thought it didn't represent her current level of skill.

MARCO SHUTS ME OUT

I had been writing to Kristina, Marco's girlfriend in Neuchâtel, sharing my news, such as what was happening at school. I visited the two of them regularly. One day I received an alarming email. Marco had learned that his former boss Damien, the one with whom he went to jail, was currently in Belgium, and Marco planned to visit him. Kristina did not know the complete story, so she couldn't know how much this worried me. I was extremely upset and put this in many,

many words, telling her to please stop him, as nothing good could come of it. Marco had been sober until then, and I didn't want anything to come between his studies and new life. I still can't believe it happened, but when I finished the email and pushed send...I saw the mail flying to Marco's email address. My heart pounded in my head. I didn't know what to do. I called Kristina and told her what happened. She said she would let me know Marco's reaction as soon as she knew it. She said...he took it calmly. If I had never told her about sending the email, she never would have guessed that he had gotten it. However, Marco's demeanor hid his true feelings. He called his sisters and his dad and told them never to be in contact with me again, as he had cut me out of his life. That was it. I did not hear from him for many years afterward.

THE CHILDREN OF ANNE-LIES

Around this time images or "photos" started coming back to me at night before I fell asleep. Most of the time I did not recognize the people depicted; I simply looked upon them as spirits passing by to say hello. One photo kept coming back. It showed a man with a beard, who said to me: "Tell my son not to be like me. He has to go to his children, they are in trouble." I had no clue who this man was, yet he persistently returned about five nights in a row.

Then suddenly it dawned on me. I called my sister Marijke and asked if she knew how Wendy and Maikel were, the children of my sister Anne-Lies, whom you will recall passed away from cancer. Anne-Lies's husband had moved on, remarried and lived in Ireland, while he had left his young adult children to themselves. Marijke and I had drifted apart and were no longer close; when I would visit Holland I would stay with her for a few days, but we had little in common. She did not think much of me, and I thought she was a materialistic snob. Now, however, I put aside those feelings and pressed her to check on our niece and nephew, which she promised me to do. We both had lost contact with these young people, me because I lived so far away and my sister because personalities clashed.

A few hours later, Marijke called me back and told me that she had heard that there were problems, but she could not tell me what exactly. I asked for the phone number of Henny, my brother-in-law in Ireland. I dialed it, and Henny's new wife, Ineke, came on the phone. I told her who I was and asked to speak with Henny. I heard her call him, telling him who it was. I heard movements and then there was his voice, hard and distant. He had never forgiven me that I had not come to the funeral of Anne-Lies. I greeted him and said before he could get nasty: "Henny, you should listen now before you start shouting. Anne-Lies has forgiven me." I told him the story of the red rose. It was quiet on the other end of the telephone line, then gentle crying. I said,

"But this is not why I am calling, Henny. I have had visions, five times now, of your father telling me to tell you that you should not be like him. You have to go to your children, they have problems."

It was quiet again on the other end of the line. I waited for a response. Finally, he asked me what I know. I told him that I knew nothing, but that for five days this man with a beard, whom I eventually recognized as his father, had been sending me this warning. Perhaps, I said, I was the only one the grandfather could reach spiritually. Henny was skeptical. "Oh, sure, you know nothing!" I pointed out that I wasn't in contact with his children, and that I had to call Marijke to get his number. To be fair, Henny's father had not been close to his oldest son, so I can imagine how Henny must have felt. I suspected he thought I was crazy, until he said, "I'm flying to Holland tomorrow. Yes, there are problems." I didn't ask for details. I simply said I was sure his dad would be happy to know that the problems were being addressed.

NIN AND MAURICE

Now that I was no longer in a relationship, I had more time for myself, so when I was asked to join an organization called Dutch in Distress or *Nederlanders in Nood* (NIN) I accepted. NIN was established to assist Dutch citizens in Dubai who had problems that the consulate was not allowed to address. The idea was the brainchild of Lody Embrechts, consular at that time in Dubai. He teamed up with Jan Demmink, a well-respected Dutch national who had been doing business in Dubai for a long time. Jan modeled the organization on the British Community Assistance Fund. NIN needed volunteers who would give their time and expertise: people with empathy, people of different lifestyles, people who were kind and strong, people with life experience. Although the official launch was February 2, 2002, we started working long before that. Coordinating efforts with the consulate, NIN guides and advises on a variety of issues, including personal, legal, financial, medical, and matters relating to repatriation. NIN is strictly confidential. We volunteers kept to strict shifts, carried mobile phones (this is before everyone in the world did, remember) and took our job very seriously.

The teenage son of a family I knew from EIS called and asked if he could stay with me a while. I contacted his mother and asked what was going on. Before I relate what she told me, perhaps I should give you a little background.

While I was living there, the UAE was a young country. Tax-free zones were springing up in each emirate. Foreigners assumed that locals knew what they were doing when they opened a business. Abu Dhabi, in particular, had a reputation for business sense. However, many locals did not know how to deal with the newly found possibilities. For that reason, many foreigners were taken for a ride. They were given promises that were never kept, with the words *Insha'Allah* (if God wills it) or worse *Bukra Insha'Allah* (tomorrow if God wills it). Now, these expressions were not intentionally used to deceive. Their usage was simply a fact of life in the emirates. Do you remember Moussa, the financial adviser to Sheikh X? He once explained to me:

> "I have a meeting. I leave the house. On the road something happens with the car, I get stuck, I need a garage. This takes hours, so *Insha'Allah*, through no fault of my own, I cannot go to the meeting."

Personally, I never believed any Arabic-speaking person who told me *Bukra Insha'Allah*. I intuitively knew that whatever had been promised would never happen. But there were foreigners coming to the UAE who were not well enough self-informed, either about the country, its people or its business opportunities. It also often happened that some foreigners were too stingy to pay a lawyer, a decision they would later regret as debts piled up.

The case of this EIS family was, in some ways, typical. The father, Renier, had a great job at Philips. He, his South African wife, Estelle, and their two children, Mory and Maurice, lived happily in Eindhoven, the Netherlands. But Dubai was starting to boom, and its new business opportunities were advertised all over the world. Renier came to the UAE with the idea of building a bulb factory. I met him at EIS when he was considering sending Mory and Maurice to the school. I warned him, as I warned many exploring parents, to be careful; never spend your own money. Renier didn't listen. He sold their house in the Netherlands, gave up his job and moved the family to Dubai. He was dealing with people of Ras al-Khaimah, I believe, but months passed and nothing materialized. The family lived on savings for years, plus money from Renier's occasional consulting jobs. Renier found somebody to make them visas so that they could stay in the country. Probably in desperation he started making contacts with somewhat shady business people everywhere, especially ones in Abu Dhabi. It was in those times that Mory reached out to me and stayed for a little while with Chango and me, as she couldn't handle her mother anymore. I should add here that Estelle was a lunatic, manipulative and possessive of her friends and children. One would be kind to say her wardrobe choices were strange. People stayed away from her, which she did not seem to realize. Hundreds of years ago she would have been burned as a witch.

I did not hear from the family for a while until Maurice's phone call. He asked if his family could see me, and they arrived that same evening. I asked what was wrong. Renier and Estelle told me that they had to take the children out of EIS as they could no longer afford the tuition. They had moved to Sharjah into a cheaper house, and Maurice was now in a school in Sharjah. Maurice and Mory were gifted children. It was particularly difficult for Maurice to adapt, as he was placed according to age but was much brighter than the other children in his class. He became the perfect target for bullies. I told Renier and Estelle that if Maurice were to stay with me, it would not be possible for them to visit him. I didn't want the overpowering mother, whom he was trying to escape, in my house all the time. When Mory stayed with Chango and me, Estelle had gradually taken over the house, even staying there when we were out, concocting the strangest excuses as to why she would do that.

Soon I discovered that Maurice was a nice but disturbed young man. He studied online and helped around the house as much as he could. When I asked him to wash the dishes after dinner, however, I observed that he had no clue how to do them. He simply stood there with the wash brush in his hands, looking at the water running down into the sink. Finally, I asked him what was wrong. He told me that he didn't know how to clean the dishes, so I showed him what to do with the dishwashing liquid, brush and water. That's a genius for you. Einstein couldn't tie his laces, and Maurice couldn't wash dishes.

Maurice and I started talking about how to spend New Year's Eve. I remembered the great time Margarita and I had celebrating on the beach, so at the last minute, I asked Maurice if he'd like to go there. He agreed. It was already getting dark, so we quickly gathered warm clothing and blankets and drove through Jebel Ali Village to find wood. Maurice grabbed some, and away we went. The beach was beautifully empty. Maurice knew exactly how to make the fire, as he had learned with the Boy Scouts, I guess. Soon we had food on our plates and champagne glasses in our hands. We swam in the sea, and at midnight we gazed at distant fireworks, sparks in the sky. It was a wonderful start to the new year, 2001.

Maurice's parents needed to find a solution to his problem, as he couldn't stay with me forever and do nothing, although he would have loved that. For a while I heard nothing from the family. I had already discussed the situation with my colleagues at NIN and the consul Lody Embrechts, especially since rumors were going around that Renier was taking his daughter to the locals in Abu Dhabi, trying to marry her off to the highest bidder. I couldn't confirm these stories, but knew that Mory had slowly turned into a local girl, donning long dresses, a black *hijab* and veil. She was reputedly a favorite with young men in the royal family and their friends. Her mother also had adopted the local dress code.

Eventually, the parents brought Maurice home. Some time afterward, they rang my doorbell. On my doorstep I found Renier, Maurice and two ladies covered in black. I tried to hide my shock. They were on their way to Abu Dhabi, just stopping by for a chat. They soon left.

MY MOTHER PASSES

On May 17, I got the call that my mother was dying. I phoned Abdullah Richa, my station manager at Swissair, and he arranged an ID90 with KLM for that same night. I called Harold and told him that I would not be at school for the next few days. I packed a carry-on and arranged Lalita to look after the cats. From plane to train to taxi, I kept hoping I would arrive at the Breda hospital in time to see Mom alive. I found Dad and Marijke gathered around a bed where she lay, still breathing. The priest had given her the last rites. My father and sister had been there the whole day, so we decided I would take the night shift and they would go home; I would call them if there were any changes.

After they left, I made myself comfortable next to the bed and took Mom's hand in mine. The nurse had shown me her body and the blue coloring of the toes and fingertips, clear signs of the body giving up. As I held her hand, I felt her fear spreading through my body. Tears sprang to my eyes. I spoke to her as if to a baby: "Mom, you can go now, don't be afraid, all are waiting for you—Anne-Lies, Ome Janus, your parents and other loved ones."

I felt her spirit hovering above me, and I even looked up, holding her hand. Hours passed. No change. Her body was fighting against the light, and I think I understood why. My mother had been very religious, even considering becoming a nun at the fragile age of sixteen. Then she fell in love with Louis van Dorst, the friend of her brother Piet, who had tuberculosis. She even went on trips with Louis to different parts of our country. Then the war came. There was no work. Louis and his friends joked around, daring each other to go to the Nederlands-Indie (Indonesia, our colony) to fight the Japs. Louis was the only one who enlisted. He died in 1943 as a prisoner of war doing forced labor on the Burma Railway. Surely it had not been easy for my mother, expecting him to come back and marry her. Now I imagine that they had been intimate, because when she married my father three years later, giving her vows in front of God in church, she was not dressed in virgin white but silver gray satin. She had made the gown herself. It was beautiful but gray. Nobody thought much about it; the war had just ended, and she probably told her parents and guests there was no white satin available. Knowing my mother, she had to live with her sins deeply buried in her mind for sixty years with nobody to talk to. Now preparing to face her judge, God almighty, she could not imagine that he would forgive her.

As I held her hand, all this was going through my mind, as if she were telling me her story. I cried and cried, not because she was dying, but because she had had to live with so much pain for such a long time with no one to hold her and understand her. She was carrying so much guilt that now, in her most important hour, she was unable to believe that God is Love and that He would forgive her. I told her the words that God gave to me, talking to her with her hand always in mine, until she finally stepped over and left. It was a great relief. The battle she had fought against herself was finally over. I needed some minutes with her alone in peace. I kissed her and slowly left the room and walked to the nurses' station. I told the night shift nurse that my mother had gone, and we both went back to the room. From there I called first my father and then my sister. My father came to collect me. He seemed relieved; finally, after all these years, he was free. I left immediately after the cremation. My sister collected the urn a few months later and left it in her house until we knew what to do with the ashes. Later we buried them in the garden of the house my mother was born in, after getting permission from the new owner, a lady we knew from our childhood.

MORE TROUBLE FOR MAURICE

Back in Dubai, I became increasingly active in NIN. While the group was still getting off the ground, we met to discuss the Maurice case. The family had contacted Lody, trying to get air tickets from the consulate. They wanted to leave the country but were now penniless. The mother was a regular guest at the consulate, and Lody had to spend many annoying hours with her until they found a solution.

Our group decided that because Maurice was still a minor, we would pay for his ticket. He told us that his parents had arranged for family friends in the Netherlands to take care of him and enroll him in a local school until his sister and parents could join him. Because of his age, he needed to be accompanied by an adult on the plane. I had been in contact with my Swiss friend Ursi and was going to spend the summer holidays with her at her vacation home in Corsica. I had all my tickets in place and promised NIN that I could make a simple detour and bring Maurice to the Netherlands. Everybody was happy with this solution, and at the appropriate time Maurice and I boarded a plane to Amsterdam. From there we took the train to a city, I've forgotten which, and from there a taxi to the host family's village.

We arrived at the address we were given and saw a car standing in the driveway with a fully packed trailer. It was obvious that the family was preparing for a trip, and if we had arrived just fifteen minutes later, they would have been gone. Maurice and I walked toward the car while the family came out the front door. I looked at them; they looked at me in shock. I could tell they recognized Maurice. I introduced myself and asked what was going on. Wasn't it agreed that Maurice would stay with them? They stared at us both and said very cruelly: "We thought about it and cannot take Maurice. We like him, but if we take him, soon his mother will follow, and we don't want to have anything to do with her." I'm seldom at a loss for words, but this was one of those times. I stood there flabbergasted. I felt so sorry for Maurice, who had to experience all this. In a way, I could understand this would-be-host family, but they had so brutally insulted him. Luckily, the taxi driver was still there to take Maurice and me away. I do not think he and I said goodbye. We just left, very disappointed and sad.

My thoughts now ran in fast mode. I needed a plan. I couldn't leave the boy alone in a country he barely knew. Calling NIN would not help; I had to solve things myself there and then. We got on a train to Breda, and from there we took a taxi to Dorst to my childhood home. I was thankful that my father was still living there and had not yet moved into an assisted-living apartment, as he had contemplated doing. Assisted-living would have helped him meet most of his daily needs, with nursing care available if required. After all, like my mother, he was now eighty years old. But at that moment, Maurice needed a refuge, and the home in Dorst was it.

When my father opened the back door to us, his eyes opened wide. I signed him to not ask any questions in front of Maurice. I had always spoken English with Maurice, and was doing so when my dad rudely ignored my gesture and demanded to know what this boy was doing in his house, etc. I told him that Maurice was Dutch and understood every word. My father quickly shut his mouth. I showed Maurice his room upstairs and told him that I needed to speak with my dad about the situation; he could join if he wanted. So we went down to the garden, where we all three sat together to discuss things. Maurice himself did not know what to do; somehow his mother again had messed things up. He knew he couldn't rely on his actual Dutch relatives: they weren't interested in taking care of him. Maurice started making a list of everybody he knew, all his friends, finding telephone numbers. We called his mother, and she gave us more numbers to call. Calling for two days did not help. I felt so sorry for Maurice. He was unwanted everywhere because of his mother, who was co-dependent on her children and made them have the same feelings towards her.

After the two days, I explained to Maurice that we had to find a solution that didn't depend on family or friends. I asked if he truly wanted to stay in the Netherlands. When he assured me he did, I called Lody in Dubai, who suggested I get in contact with the *Raad voor de Kinderbescherming* (Council for Child Protection) in Breda. Lody could not do anything from Dubai, which I understood; the matter had taken a bad turn, and I had to follow my gut. I called Ursi and cancelled my holiday in Corsica.

I had worked part-time with Child Protection Services before leaving for Germany in 1969, so I called an old colleague who arranged an appointment with a social worker within two days. It was during summer break, so this was akin to a miracle.

After two days at home, my father was questioning why Maurice was spending so much time in the shower. He had looked at the clock, and it took the teen two hours to wash himself. At his request I asked Maurice why this was. He told me he was accustomed to washing every centimeter of his body, which took time, of course. My father was not happy with this wasting of water, and his face showed it. I knew he would soon be palpably angry, so I took Maurice out as much I could on little trips. My sister Marijke liked Maurice, and promised once to keep an eye on him.

The appointment with the social worker was relaxed and simple. I told her my story, Maurice told her his story. Then she asked what he wanted; even though he still was a minor, he had rights. He made it clear he didn't want to go back to Dubai and his parents. The social worker contacted the consulate in Dubai and confirmed our stories. Within three weeks Maurice was enrolled in one of the best colleges in Breda, and a place for him was found in an assisted-living commune of young people supervised by an adult who would teach them how to live on their own. The timing was great—it was still summer break. What's more, the social worker had discovered Maurice's computer skills. She arranged for him to teach retirees how to use their computers. Maurice was happily busy, and because he was consistently polite, people found him a pleasure to have around. I was kept apprised of his progress and heard only good news. At his wish, his living situation was kept a secret from his parents; he knew his willpower was not strong enough to resist them.

It was too good to last.

His mother somehow found a way to Holland and settled in a village close to Eindhoven. There she got social services to pay the rent on a cheap townhouse for her. She made it her life purpose to find Maurice, never considering what would be best for him, only what would be best for her. She walked around Breda for weeks and finally went to Child Protection Services, where they breached confidentiality after listening to her sob story. A perfect actress, she blamed me for estranging her from her child, whose mother she was and whom she loved with all her heart. They gave her Maurice's address. She went there and collected him like a package. I was told that he left with her without even a peep.

It was Mory who told me the story. I nearly had a heart attack and immediately called child services, insisting on speaking with the social worker
on the case. She now believed that I was the world's worst human being
and told me that I should be happy not to be charged with kidnapping.
Had they forgotten that they had confirmed our story with the Dutch
consulate in Dubai? No one would listen to me, and I anticipated the
worst for Maurice.

I almost couldn't wait for my next holiday break at school. I obtained
ID90 tickets and flew to Holland, took a train straight to Eindhoven,
and called Estelle, telling her I was on my way to see her. She spoke
sweetly, purring like a cat around a mouse, an act that I ignored. I arrived and was allowed into the home, which I found poorly furnished.
She offered tea. I asked where Maurice was. She said that he was still in
bed, sleeping, although it was early afternoon. I asked where his room
was and went straight up the stairs. I found a room with a mattress in
it, nobody there. I looked in the other rooms; nobody there. I went back
to the room with the mattress and looked more closely. I saw a body in
a fetal position under the blankets. Heart breaking, I lay myself beside
Maurice and held him, asking what was happening. He turned around
and, looking at me through his tears, told me she had come and made
him feel guilty for leaving her, thereby making him co-dependent again,
following her like a puppy. He looked me straight in the eyes and said,

"One day, Marilyn, my mother will be gone. Don't go looking for
her, because I'll have cut her into little pieces and put her in the freezer
and gotten rid of her piece by piece."

My heart ached for the young man. I asked him if he would come
with me and go back to Breda. He shook his head and said that she
would take him away again and again. I told him this was up to him, but
he had lost all strength and given up. I left. That was the last I ever heard
or saw of him, poor Maurice.

RISKY BUSINESS
The year 2001 marked the beginning of the notorious 419 scams flood-
ing the Internet, as I learned personally...the hard way.

In April I received an email from one Kadaba Mpenza. He claimed to be the son of King Dokatu Mpenza of Congo, who in 1998 had brought 19 million dollars to a security company in Abidjan, Ivory Coast. In 1999, rebels killed the king. Kadaba the son (the prince?) could not deposit the money in an Abidjan bank and needed help getting it out of the country.

After reading this rubbish, I hovered my finger over the "delete" key...before writing back, asking for more information. Kadaba Mpenza gladly obliged.

It won't surprise you to know that Mpenza the son had suffered through a series of problems, including a case of hepatitis in June. He asked for money to pay his doctor bills, passport, visas, etc., which stupidly enough I sent him. Our email relationship grew intense. He called me his sister, the only one who could save him. He soon delivered the millions by diplomatic mail to Spain, so that I could collect them from there. However, my greed for money was as real as my belief that this was an unethical scheme, and I put off taking action.

Before you look down on me, you might consider that the Internet, email and email scams were just in their infancy, and I—I was just born!

In addition, as I've mentioned, I'm a Taurus, and we Tauri need financial security. If anything threatens our monetary wellbeing, we get all grumpy and nervous, unable to focus on anything else. (I must mention here, that those times are past. I wouldn't say I'm financially secure, but I flow with the wind, and God has allowed me to relax in the best place ever.) So I was struggling with my conscience, security versus lust for adventure.

The plan called for me to collect the money from Malaga and travel to Switzerland by train, where I would open a bank account for Mpenza and deposit the funds in our accounts. I was expected to pay the couriers, Mr. Harkness and Mr. Johnson, the fee of $10,000 USD for this risky transaction. That amount just happened to be all my savings. I couldn't speak to any of my friends about this matter, because deep down I knew it was illegal and possibly dangerous. I wrote Mpenza about my nagging reservations, but of course, because he was a crook, he was a genius at turning everything around. Today I know that it is not a single crook but a group of them who compose the emails and that a special unit of the CIA was stationed in Nigeria to help foolish Americans like me.

That summer, my friend Nicole called me from Switzerland. She said Richard Unger was returning to do some workshops on fingerprints; if I were interested, she would register the two of us. *Ahah!* I thought. I'll fly to Switzerland and afterward take a side trip to Spain. I confirmed with Nicole, and happy the decision was made, prepared myself for this daring excursion. I took $10,000 from the bank, got myself ID90s for Switzerland and Spain, and packed my suitcase.

I had arranged one overnight room in a Malaga hotel. I sent Mr. Harkness and Mr. Johnson the name of the hotel. All that remained was to send them my room number.

My first stop was Zürich. Nicole took me to her friend's house where the workshop was held. It was scheduled to last two days, but on the second I left a little early to go to the airport to fly to Spain. I said my goodbyes to everybody, Unger last. He took my hand, looked at me and said, "I know what you are planning. Do not go. It is dangerous." I had told Nicole about Mpenza. When she brought me to the door, she said, "Marilyn, listen to him, I don't have a good feeling about this." I ignored her and Unger and went.

Sitting in the aircraft I talked to my angels, begging them to keep me safe, as they had done so many times during my life. I asked them to cover me in their wings. Arriving in Malaga, I took a taxi to the hotel I had chosen. I called the couriers and gave them my room number. They said they would come the next morning at 8 A.M. I walked around town, had dinner and went to bed.

The next morning after breakfast, I returned to my room where I waited nervously, praying to God and my angels, definitely knowing now that this was not right. A knock on the door made me jump from my bed. Why I had been such a fool to agree to this? On paper, on email, everything had seemed so simple.

I opened the door and two black men were standing there, one with a small black briefcase in his hands. Before entering, they opened the door wide. (Now I know it was to check if there was anybody else in the room, and yes there was—my angels!) The couriers introduced themselves as Mr. Johnson and Mr. Harkness. They sidled up to my windows and looked through them (ensuring they hadn't been followed or watched by police). Once they felt safe, they got down to business. Taking a key from a separate courier envelope, they unlocked the briefcase so I could confirm it held the money. On top of the bills was a small plastic bag with a syringe and some powder.

While I was praying and praying, the men told me there was a problem. They explained that the king had stamped the money, most probably for security reasons. They assured me, however, that the powder would remove the stamp. One man went to the sink and mixed the powder with some water and pulled it into the syringe, while the other took a $100 bill from the case. The mixture from the syringe was dropped on the $100 note, and the inked stamp was washed off. They repeated this procedure with other bills from the case. They gave me the $100 notes and told me to go to a bank and check if the money was real. They would come back the next day and hand me the rest. I paid the $10,000 courier fee, and they left.

I had seen the money with my own eyes; I knew it was there, and the bank confirmed for me hours later that the $100 bills in my possession were real. The problem was that Mr. Johnson and Mr. Harkness couldn't seem to find a chemist with enough powder to clean the rest of the money. They kept me in Malaga for another week, calling me almost daily with updates. They needed more time, they said. I had no time, so I left, lucky not to have been killed during this silly but perilous operation.

For two weeks I heard nothing from Mpenza. Finally, he emailed me, asking what was going on. We continued making plans to recover the consignment from Spain, but my holidays were over and he needed more money, which I didn't have. We continued corresponding through December, his tone becoming increasingly desperate. Here's an excerpt from one of his emails:

GOOD MORNING AND HOW ARE YOU TODAY?
IT IS WITH GRIEF THAT I WRITE YOU THIS
MAIL. THE MANNER THIS ISUUE IS BEING
HANDLED NOW IS FRUSTRATING ME. HOW
CAN I AT THIS STAGE BE A LIVING DEAD? I
MEAN DO YOU PREFARE ME TO DIE?

I felt bad for Mpenza, but I had my own worries. I had lost four years of savings for my retirement, and wasn't sure I could pay the next month's rent. For a while I couldn't even drive anywhere, as I couldn't afford insurance payments on my car.

AN INVITATION INTO THE UNKNOWN

This was right around the time that Trudy called me. You remember her—the sister of my non-husband, the Swiss woman who shouted obscenities at me in front of the Sharjah police station. Yes, her! Over the ensuing years, we had made peace, and I considered her a friend again. She had moved to Dubai with her daughter Natascha. Trudy told me that Sheikh Moussa would like to see me, the next evening if possible.

Who was Sheikh Moussa? She gave me an answer that made me curious:

> "We know an old Iranian man named Baba who owns a shop selling herbs and traditional medicines in Dubai's Heritage Village. He also gives healing massages. Nobody knows that he comes to see us, but when my daughter and I were having problems, he helped us and we became friends. Baba has four spirits who speak through him, Sheikh Moussa being the most powerful. Sheikh Moussa came through last night and said that he needed to speak to you."

How could I resist this invitation into the unknown? I headed to Trudy's apartment the next day, feelings of excitement and distrust mingling within me. When I arrived, I found that Trudy had already prepared tea and laid down cushions for us to sit upon. A small burner was lit with coal, and incense filled the air. Baba had not yet appeared. Trudy went to the balcony to check if he was waiting in his little old blue car. There he was! She called to him, he came to the apartment building's entrance, and she brought him up to the apartment. I gazed upon an old local man whom I guessed was between sixty and seventy years old.

Over the next several days, Sheikh Moussa, speaking through Baba, gave me advice for dealing with Mpenza. He told me the millions were not clean, and Mpenza himself was *harami* (a bad one) who deserves no good. Unfortunately, sometimes it was difficult to understand Moussa because he spoke Arabic exclusively, and neither Trudy nor I were fluent in the language. To guard against Mpenza's evil, Moussa told Trudy and me to tell Baba to go to a *nabi* [prophet] to collect water for me to drink. Baba did as we instructed, and I drank the water, while saying again and again, "Too much money for this lady."

One evening while Baba and Trudy were at my home, Moussa left Baba's body, and Baba himself asked about Mpenza. Was he planning to see me, he wanted to know? The question irritated me a little.

"No, of course not, Baba, why should he come? I don't want him here."

Baba angrily replied that Moussa had taken him by the throat as he entered my house. Mpenza, he explained, was practicing black magic and trying to do me harm because I wouldn't send him more money. In the next breath, however, Baba assured me I was safe because Moussa had earlier given me a silver ring with protective powers, and I had drunk the *nabi's* water. I didn't say it aloud, but I was thinking that I would be safe even without all these sources of protection. My angels and my belief that God is more powerful than the devil would keep me from harm.

One night, when Trudy and I were alone, I asked her to lay out a deck of tarot cards. I asked her to pray or try to keep her mind blank, while I prayed about my relationship with Mpenza, but asked no question aloud. Here's how the cards turned out:

center	prosperity-co-operation, withdraw-retract, woman > loving;
up	faithful-loyal-true, power > man > outside town, shock;
down	solution, satisfaction, trip overseas;
left	dominating person, optimistic, money;
right	passing problems, theft, documents

Reading: prosperity and co-operation > faithful-loyal-true > solution > dominating person > passing problems > withdrawal > power-man-outside town > satisfaction > optimistic > theft > woman-loving > shock > trip overseas > money > documents.

The cards had exactly painted the story of this part of my life at this moment in time.

I wrote to Mpenza and begged him to send no more emails. By the end of December, the seemingly ceaseless flood had stopped.

I continued to consult Moussa on other matters, however. My cat Rakker was unwell, and the vet had told me he had problems with his kidneys. (Trudy thought perhaps Mpenza was doing black magic on him. Since the man couldn't touch me with my ring and water, maybe he was attacking the next thing I love, my cat.) I asked Moussa for help. Having looked at me pitifully and praying intensely, he waved his hand, showing that I should "let go of my worrying about Rakker." A few days later, it seemed to me Rakker was looking better, his fur softer and shinier. I gave Moussa the credit.

Poor Baba had some bad luck of his own. He spent two days in the Rashid hospital with heart pain. He had been treating a woman with a chest tumor. As the cancer did not go away with massage, Baba had sucked it out of her. Somehow he could not protect himself and had a severe attack. I promised to send him healing thoughts.

Soon afterward—too soon, I thought; Baba hadn't really had time to recover—Trudy invited him to her home for another spirit session. It did not take long for Moussa to come through. He was furious: he refused to listen to us or to help heal Baba. He told us very clearly that he had warned Baba many times not to massage bad ladies. Even during Ramadan he had not listened! He, Moussa, would not lift a finger to help Baba, but Banyan (another of Baba's spirits, a healer) might be willing, so Moussa disappeared and Banyan came. We begged Banyan to please help, and he started massaging Baba.

After briefly "disappearing," Banyan returned, requesting a cigarette and an egg. Trudy gave him both, and when he touched the egg, turning it around and around, a ring slowly appeared around it, as if one egg had moved over another one. He opened it and showed it to Trudy. She said that the egg was vertically split in two; he had made two eggs out of one. He took the egg, opened his mouth, and sucked it in one go inside himself. He then vanished and left us in astonishment.

Baba woke up and went to wash out his mouth, disgusted by Banyan's egg eating. When he came from the bathroom, he appeared totally refreshed, so Trudy had been right. It had done him good to come to us so that his "friends" would be able to heal him. I saw very little of Baba or his spirits after this encounter.

COMINGS AND GOINGS

Trudy and I went to Oman during Eid al-Adha, driving from Dubai to Hatta to Al Ain, which are two oases in the UAE. We had to get visas to enter Oman and did not have to wait long, as there were not many tourists interested in going there. From the border we drove from Ibri to Nizwa and finally to Muscat. I took many photos, and it was re-energizing for me. I made a promise to myself to take more of these excursions, and kept it. I drove alone a few months later to Khasab on the Gulf of Oman. The scenery on the drive was spectacular, all along the coast from Dubai to Sharjah to Ajman to Umm al-Quwain and then Ras al-Khaimah. In Khasab dolphins were just swimming about, and civilization had stood still. An army of small fishing boats flew across these open waters to the coast of Iran, smuggling items forth and back, and the authorities did nothing. The boat engines sounded like big flies, buzzing around my ears as soon as the sun went down. I went back several times to enjoy the simple local life and the act of driving an open car through these beautiful countries, which I knew I would leave soon.

Since the passing of a new law, there was no future for me in Dubai. People over sixty years old would be forbidden to obtain a work permit. I was fifty-five, which meant there would soon be no visa for me. Maybe by using my connections I could wrangle a way to stay, but my heart wasn't in it anymore. Slowly I started to look around and consider my options.

I was used to being on my own now and happy, not looking for a new relationship, satisfied with the ways things were. Dubai Academy now was approved by the Ministry of Education to become DAA— Dubai American Academy. Parents, staff and students were happy with our move to the new campus in Al Barsha, Dubai.

My sister Marijke, her husband and son came for a visit. On weekdays they borrowed my Merc and enjoyed the attractions of Dubai. Over a weekend, I joined them on a trip to the Empty Quarter, which is what the locals call the expansive desert in the southeastern interior of the Arabian Peninsula. Accessible from the Liwa Oasis, a two-hour drive from Abu Dhabi on excellent highways, the Empty Quarter is the largest continuous body of sand in the world. It's tempting to call it "no man's land," but that's not quite correct. Nomads do in fact inhabit parts of the Quarter at various times of year, and camels thrive there. The territory is spoken for: the interior borders of Saudi Arabia, United Arab Emirates, Oman and Yemen are in here...somewhere. It's just that no one has bothered to actually *draw* those lines in the sand.

My boss Harold was not happy with the fact that my sister and her family never even once came to see where I worked, the place where I was loved. I was disappointed too, but I knew my sister: the world revolved around her and her family, and I was not part of that.

But...guess who did pass by? One day the school's factotum, Mr. John, called me and asked me to come to the front gate, as someone was waiting for me there. Puzzled, I stepped out and spotted a young man in local dress standing next to what I believe was a Maserati. He turned around and came to me with a big smile. It was little Ahmed, now a full grown, good-looking man. I hadn't seen him in years. We embraced and chatted for a while.

He didn't want to come in, as it was an expat school, and he dreaded being stared at. Actually, it was happening anyway, as break time had started and all the kids had come to the gate to ogle the spectacular car. We said our goodbyes, and he drove off. It was the last time I ever saw Ahmed, although we regularly talk on the phone and connect through Facebook.

After ailing a long time, my Persian cat Rakker finally died, and I was devastated. Not long afterward, I saw an ad in the newspaper: Persian kittens free to a good home. I called and was told that there was still one left. I gave my address, and two hours later a woman covered head-to-toe in a black *abaya* handed me the poorest-looking little creature ever. I asked her what had happened to it. She acted as if she didn't understand, but a small lock of blond hair slipped from under the veil, so I knew she was bullshitting me. I took the kitten, and waved her out. The kitten had clearly suffered through something horrible. It took two months for it to look normal and jump happily around my house. My friend and colleague Colleen named the kitten Chispa (Spanish for "sparkle") for her big, shiny eyes.

Now, let me backtrack a little and tell you who else came into my life...

My friends at DAA all knew I was looking for a new kitten, so parents, teachers and students kept their eyes peeled. One day Nurse Louise came and told me that the European Veterinary Centre on Sheikh Zayed Road had a white Persian. After school I drove straight to the clinic. A white Persian yes, but not up for adoption and no Persian kitten. None of the other pure bred or mixed-breed kittens clicked with me, so I left, disappointed.

DESTINED TO BE MINE

A few weeks later, a member of Feline Friends came to me: "Oh, Marilyn, the European Vet Centre has Persian kittens." I told her that I had gone there, but I would check again. After school I drove to the clinic, which was not far from the school. As I entered I was recognized and told, no, no Persian kittens. I shook my head and left.

Then one Thursday I went to tutor my Japanese student Mariko. Her dog was limping, and the family was not familiar with any vets in the area, so I took mother, daughter and dog to my own. He said an x-ray machine was needed, and he didn't have one. We would have to go to… you guessed it. The signs were undeniable. I MUST go to the European Vet Centre! Still thinking God or the fates wanted me to have a kitten, I looked at all of them, but didn't feel that "click" as I had with the other pets in my life. Now I was really feeling frustrated. I peered into every cage, convinced that something was in that clinic for me, something that had been waiting three months to be collected. I asked if there were any stray animals lingering there that long, waiting for a new owner. I was told no. With a heavy heart, I headed for the stairs. I stopped half-way down, looked at the vet assistant and asked what was behind the dishtowel hanging against the side of the stairs. Without waiting for an answer, I moved the cloth away and peeked.

There was a young husky, lying in his own pooh, all diarrhea. I was told that he was brought in by a boy who had found him in the desert with a double fracture of hip and leg. The dog had been malnourished, to boot. Vets had operated on the dog and were waiting for the boy, who had left no address, to collect him. The child never returned and the animal had been with them now for three months…the three months since I had been coming there. The husky wasn't recovering from the di-arrhea, so it had been decided to euthanize him that evening. I had come in the nick of time. I told the vet assistant I would take him. Regulations in Dubai dictated that a dog could not be adopted unless it was neutered, so I agreed, and I soon collected Aztec, as he was called. He would stay with me for the next twelve years.

I would guess that Aztec was about one year old when I took him. It was not easy to care for him. There were moments I wanted to bring him back to the clinic to be put down, as his diarrhea would not go away. One vet advised me to give the dog Purina, but there was no change. I went to Choitrams (a chain of malls in the UAE) and bought many different kinds of dry foods for large dogs. Nothing worked. Every morning we went for a walk, and a running pooh would appear. It was frustrating for both Aztec and me. I decided to buy the cheap-est food available, not looking at large, small, vitamins, whatever. One early morning two weeks later, Aztec and I were dancing on the street in Jebel Ali Village. A big round sausage of pooh had come out of him. Hurray, he could stay!

Aztec loved to drive with me in the convertible. When we went to the airport for my work, he would come with me and wait in the car until I finished. He would sit in the passenger seat, and we would drive in the night back home to Jebel Ali. Whenever a car passed us he would bark, angry that somebody else was faster. Typical husky!

Although doctors had advised me not to take long walks, Aztec loved to run, so lazy me, I took my convertible with Aztec in it to the desert behind Jebel Ali. I would let him out, and he would run in front of the car on the track, and I would follow. It was then that he found a friend, what appeared to be a husky mix. Somebody must have dropped the dog in the desert. Once he got used to me, I coaxed him into the car, and he came home with Aztec and me. I thought it good for Aztec to have a friend.

The next morning both dogs greeted me, eager for a walk. However, when the new dog stepped out, it bared its teeth and made threatening noises toward Aztec, preventing him from following. I called to the stranger, and he came back inside with me. Then I let Aztec out and quickly closed the door. Aztec and I enjoyed our usual morning walk. Returning, I let the stranger out, and everything was OK. Leaving the dogs to play in the garden, I went to school.

There I received a phone call from my house girl, Lalita: "Madam, I cannot go in the house. There is a strange dog in the garden with Aztec, and he does not allow me to enter." I told Harold that I quickly had to go home to rescue Lalita. Fortunately, Jebel Ali is located close to Al Barsha, so I was there within minutes. There was poor Lalita standing before the gate, the stranger grinding his teeth at her. When he saw me he wagged his tail and jumped up on the gate, which I opened to allow Lalita in, no problem at all. I left Lalita with the promise to come home in time to let her out. She was so scared of that dog, who had decided he was my protector.

The next morning Lalita arrived earlier, so I could let her in before I went to school. One hour later I received her call:

"Madam, you have to come home. No one is allowed to pass your house on the street. The dog is standing in the middle of the road, growling at everybody who wants to pass."

Again I asked Harold if I could go, and I sped off. Now, I could see it for myself: a dog, big as a wolf, looking extremely dangerous. Village administrators were there, and we discussed what to do. I saw that I could not keep the animal: he was a one-person dog and dangerous for anybody who came close to the owner. That was probably the reason why the dog had been abandoned.

I would have to do something I really didn't want to.

I called the school and asked Tina, the receptionist, to find the number for animal control. I then informed Harold that I would be staying away some time longer until I had resolved the problem, which I briefly explained. Tina gave me the number. I called it, and thirty minutes later a truck from the Dubai government came with two dogcatchers and their nets. Feeling horrible, I told the catchers their nets weren't needed: I would control the dog. I told everybody to go away and let him cool down. Some people worried about me drawing near him, thinking he had rabies.

I went to the dog and petted him. He looked at me, wagged his tail and snuggled himself to me. It broke my heart. I took him by the collar, an old one I had taken from Aztec, and slowly we walked to the back of the truck, while the police officers stepped back and let me through. Onlookers held their breath, fearful that the animal might suddenly attack me, which I was sure he would not do. I felt so sorry for the dog. As I sat down in the truck, I asked him to jump up to me, which he did. I signed the catchers to stay away. I got up and walked inside the truck to an open cage and softly pushed the dog into it. I had a lump in my throat as he gazed at me. I felt like a deceiver, and he must have known it, but still he allowed me to imprison him and let him go to an unknown fate, which I really didn't want to think about. I jumped from the truck and cried, while the catchers closed the doors and drove away. The spectators congratulated me, but I was sad and told them so. With my head down, I went into the house. I needed some time to recover before I went back to work. There I told Tina the whole heartbreaking story.

Not long after this, Lalita told me there was another husky like Aztec in Jebel Ali. She had seen it swimming in a nearby pond, trying to catch the ducks. I shook my head, looking at her pitifully. "That had to be Aztec," I said. "How did he get out?"

Almost offended, she said, "No, Madam, it cannot be Aztec, as when I came home he was sitting in the garden."

Over the weekend I watched Aztec. He never tried to jump over the garden wall. But there was no doubt he had learned the technique from my briefly owned desert dog. I soon got a call from the grocery shop in Jebel Ali Village: "Ms. Marilyn, please, can you come? Your husky has killed a duck in the pond, and now he is sitting in the car of some other residents." I rushed to the scene and saw people standing in front of the shop, all surrounding a 4x4. Were they angry? Not really. They were cuddling Aztec, offering him food and water. Everybody felt sorry for the poor husky who had been "neglected" and therefore forced to kill a duck to eat! They also lectured me for bringing a cold-climate dog to Dubai. I quickly told them Aztec's story, after which their expressions changed, and they became supportive.

Thereafter, Aztec only went outdoors with Lalita or me, or played outside when I was home and could monitor him. Not being used to dogs in the house, I carelessly left everything lying everywhere. Once I put my wallet on top of the hall cabinet and went to the bathroom. Coming back, I found my wallet all chewed up, including my money and credit cards. It was a hard but good lesson for me. Aztec looked sweetly innocent, as if nothing had happened. Afterward I went to the bank, got cash for all my bill payments, and bought more toys to keep Aztec busy.

One night while I was eating, I felt a gold filling loosen from one of my teeth. I tried to catch it with my tongue so as not to eat it with my other food. As I opened my mouth, the filling and a wad of food fell on the floor and yes, Aztec ate it. For the next few days Aztec was not allowed to go out for poohs without me. Each pooh was collected and inspected. After two days, I spied a spec of shimmering gold. There it was, my intact filling. I washed it, dropped it in alcohol, called the dentist, made an appointment, took the filling, and soon, despite its being twenty years old, it was reinstated in my tooth, which had not been damaged. Good old Dr. Antelj had done a good job!

AUSTRIA, EGYPT, MEXICO, AND THE US

DAA was thriving, but Swissair was not. The Abu Dhabi office was scheduled to close down. Quickly, I got myself some ID90s for the Easter and summer breaks, cherishing my last free tickets. I flew to Switzerland to see Ursi and Nicoletta, who always brought me joy. From them I traveled to Vienna to visit a former DAA family, the Dawouds. They collected me from the airport. It was April and snowing, but that never dampened our spirits. We went to a UNESCO World Heritage Site: Schönbrunn Palace or Schloss Schönbrunn, meaning "beautiful spring." This sumptuous imperial palace, built upon what was formerly royal hunting grounds, rivals Versailles for grandeur. Queen Maria Theresa's architect, Nicholas Pacassi, was responsible for its design. The long, symmetrical edifice boasts eighteenth century furnishings and gold and crimson displays drawing on Japanese, Italian, Persian and Indian works of art. The elaborate ceiling frescoes celebrate the Habsburgs. The huge, gorgeous gardens feature a spectacular iron and glass greenhouse called the Palm House, a maze and labyrinth, and a viewing terrace. Since the end of the monarchy, the Viennese people have flocked to these gardens for recreation, including regularly scheduled concerts. As I mentioned, it was a snowy day, but that made our visit all the more memorable.

After Schloss Schönbrunn, we went to Grinzing, a tourist attraction with many restaurants featuring wines of the area. I found Vienna an impressive city, and the Dawouds had been as impressive with their hospitality towards me, but I needed to leave for my third destination, Egypt, where my friend Mervat was waiting at the airport.

Mervat lived with her husband on the outskirts of Cairo, and because she was pregnant I arranged some tours for me alone, so she wouldn't get overly tired. Together we enjoyed strolling through the markets, after which she went home and I went to the Museum of Egyptian Antiquities. Here I spent the rest of the day admiring statues, tables and sarcophagi (coffins) as well as an extensive collection of papyri and coins used in the ancient world. Several languages are found on the papyri, including Greek, Latin, Arabic, and ancient Egyptian. The coins are made of many different metals, including gold, silver, and bronze. The coins are not only Egyptian, but also Greek, Roman, and Islamic. This has helped historians research ancient Egyptian trade. I saw many artifacts from the Valley of the Kings, in particular the material from the intact tombs of Tutankhamun, whom I remembered very well from my history lessons at school.

I took a taxi to Mervat's spacious home. Mervat's husband had been married several times and was much older than she. In my opinion he did not treat her very nicely, although he was hospitable to me, always present for dinner. Otherwise, I never saw him around. That fact confirmed what Mervat told me later: that she was mostly left on her own and was happy to have a friend visiting her. Knowing my vacation would soon end, we relaxed together the next day, just chatting. My third and last day in Cairo I went on an organized tour to the pyramids and the Sphinx, to be followed by a cruise on the Nile. There were many boats anchored in the river, and I was the first aboard mine, a small ship offering dinner and music. Because I sat by myself at a table, the musicians showered me with attention and played as if I were a celebrity. When the sun went down, I stood at the railing and savored the placid beauty of the scene, listening to the gentle splash of water against the boat. It had been a perfect day.

I was running out of free tickets. Goodbye, Swissair! Since I was a part timer, it really did not hit me that much. Swissair had been in financial trouble for months because of losses from a failed attempt to expand across Europe with stakes in smaller carriers. The sharp decline in passenger traffic, particularly across the Atlantic after the September 11 terrorist attacks, made matters much worse. With $10.5 billion in debts, Swissair had to file for bankruptcy in 2002. Switzerland was ashamed and in despair. Two Swiss banks and the government invested in Crossair, a regional airline. It became Swiss International Air Lines after taking over most of Swissair's assets. The flights to Abu Dhabi were cancelled, and I was transferred to Swiss Dubai, where all our passengers bound for Abu Dhabi landed. I had to clear them and put them on a bus to Abu Dhabi. I worked at Dubai airport for about two months. The work was exciting but time consuming, so I was glad when my job at Swiss International Air Lines ended.

I still had ID90s for the summer break, when I planned to visit my friend Patricia Smith, who had taken a sabbatical for teaching at EIS and was now back at UNIS (United Nations International School) in New York City, her hometown. I also planned to see my friends Claudia and David, who were in Guadalajara, Mexico. I decided to fly out of Dubai with KLM July 3. I did this because I figured no one would want to fly on Independence Day, one year after 9/11, and seats would be available. I was correct. I had no problem getting a seat on the connecting flight from Amsterdam to JFK, but the security at Schiphol Airport was unbelievable. Perhaps because I came from Dubai, I was treated like a terrorist. I was questioned and strip-searched. When I finally arrived at JFK, my suitcases weren't with me. They were retained three days for security reasons. Thankfully, I had my carry-on.

Pat had a rent-controlled apartment in Chelsea, small but cozy. From there we arranged small trips around the city. My first outing was July 4 for fireworks, for which we went to UNIS, which is situated on the East River. We sat with several teachers on the terraces, watching the brilliant display. It was an emotional night, especially when one group of fireworks came that honored the 9/11 victims. Many people were crying.

I wrote a poem that night:

> My heart bleeds
> Is this what became of us
> Vengeance, Revenge, Thoughts of evil
> Innocent people dying for nothing
> Is it nothing? What they died for!
>
> My heart bleeds
> Terrorism and Suffering tied together
> Hate and Love tied together

What will become of us?
How will we handle this?

My heart bleeds
Have we lost our values
How cruel to be forced to realize what Life is all about
This living hell
Is this our future
We better think about this very well

My heart bleeds
Thinking of retaliations as a necessity
My heart bleeds
Realizing the difficulty to Love your Enemy
My heart bleeds
Knowing that more people are going to die
My heart bleeds
With this one question: "Why"?

While I stayed with Pat, she introduced me to many friends, all of them gay, even the parish priest. Pat herself had been married and had one daughter and seemed heterosexual. I understood the advantages of a woman like me having male friends who were gay. Interestingly, my flight to Guadalajara was filled with gay people. One young man explained to me that he was flying with his dad, as there was to be a gay conference in Guadalajara followed by a demonstration.

Claudia and David collected me at the airport. They took me to a restaurant in the city, and told me it belonged to friends who were a gay couple. I started thinking that perhaps God was trying to tell me something, as I was never before surrounded by so much homosexuality. I had never firmly decided how I felt about it, but now I live by the motto live and let live.

Claudia and David took me on a trip to Michoacán and the Lake of Pátzcuaro. There the couple had bought a piece of land with a scenic view of Yunuén, an island in the lake, and they were inspired to name their daughter after it. We spent a couple of nights in simple but pleasant hotels. Most of the people in the area looked like Mexican-American Indians. I found everything beautiful.

After my visit to Mexico, I returned to New York City to Pat. When I had stayed in Long Island in the 1980s, I had not been to Montauk. However, after I read the book *Montauk* by Max Frisch, I was intrigued enough to put Montauk on my must-see list. So now in 2002, Pat and I decided to go to Long Island. We drove straight to the southernmost tip of the island, where friends of Pat, a Belgium UNIS teacher and her husband who lived close to the beach, were awaiting us. Pat and I enjoyed the local sights, the beaches were beautiful.

Friends of our hosts invited us over for a barbecue. While we chatted, I seemed to be doing most of the talking, as the others had many questions about life in Dubai. One guest told me I should write a book. I told her that I had started one in 1995, but it was since on hold. She looked at me seriously and said, "No, I mean it. I know an editor who could help you," and gave me the name of Stacey Donovan. I wrote it down and only contacted Stacey years later.

TUTORING

Too soon it was time to return to Dubai, where a load of work was waiting for me, including meeting parents and students and conducting assessments. We now had a full high school program and an International Baccalaureate (IB). The school had a policy that foreigners who did not speak English fluently at the middle school level could not be accepted. I made it my goal to tutor students, especially Koreans and Japanese, in English after school. I had made a deal with Harold, our director: if I could get these kids to sit and pass their English exams after three months of tutoring, they would be accepted. The reason why this was so important to me is because these kids were math geniuses, all of them, and it would be a shame not to accept these kids just because they couldn't speak English. It turned out I was right, and we had some great students accepted to our middle school program. I must say, I ate some terrific meals at the homes of these brilliant kids.

I particularly remember Mariko Ozawa and her parents, with whom I became good friends. One day Mariko told me that her dream was to become an airline attendant. Surprised, I looked at her and asked, "Do you want to be a housemaid in the air? If you can become the pilot, why would you be the housemaid?" I am happy to report that Mariko eventually earned a degree in Science and Business-Biotechnology at the University of Waterloo in Canada.

WITNESS TO CHILD LABOR

Since Mariko and her mother had not seen much of the UAE, and the father was often away working, I decided to take them on a day trip. We were driving through the desert from Sharjah to Umm al-Quwain and Ras al-Khaimah when in the middle of nowhere we saw young children riding camels. I told Mariko and her mom I was going to follow them, but no cameras should be visible. We ended up in a camel camp in the middle of nowhere, far into the desert. The timing was fortunate; it was around 4 P.M., when the children's training for races was to begin. As the camels passed us, I looked into the children's eyes. I saw no joy, only sorrow, big sad eyes. I asked Mariko's mother to take photos but to act as if she were taking them of the older men instead. I joked and laughed with her and the men taking care of the camels, so nobody would question our motives; we acted like tourists. We never looked intensely at the children, but our cameras were doing overtime. When we left, we were very upset. I do not think that at that time anybody had filmed this shocking kind of child labor. I brought mother and daughter home and put all the photos with my comments on worldisround.com. The video I edited and put on YouTube had the following commentary:

> "From a very young age, children are bought in poor countries like Pakistan, India, Bangladesh and countries of Africa to ride camels for camel races. It is child abuse and child slavery. These children will never go back to their home countries and are left without anything once they are too old to ride. The only thing they have left is a crippled body. Many end up on the streets."

Within a week, the photos on my computer and on the Internet, as well as the video on my computer and on YouTube, were gone. I have no idea who hacked my computer and removed my postings.

THE JUMAS ENTER MY "ENERGY SPACE"

The previous year I had met the Jumas, a family that would soon play a major role in my life. The Jumas had come to Dubai from Dar es Salaam, Tanzania. They were Ismailis or Aga Khanis. The Shia Ismaili Muslims are a community of ethnically and culturally diverse peoples living in over twenty-five countries around the world, united in their allegiance to His Highness Prince Karim Aga Khan (known to the Ismailis as Mawlana Hazar Imam), the forty-ninth hereditary Imam (spiritual leader) and direct descendant of Prophet Muhammad (peace be upon him and his family). The Jumas had come to DAA, hoping to enroll their son Hafiz. We did an assessment, after which I told them to wait for my telephone call to see if he had been accepted. The older son Nadeem didn't like the delay. He was an arrogant young man who strutted up and down the halls as if he owned the place. Later I heard that he had called me a bitch. But what could I do? During the day I met with people, and during the night I assessed their papers, so that the next morning I could dedicate myself to informing parents about the status of their child's acceptance to the school. I was busy and didn't care what people called me. Of course, I was in a position of power, but I had never taken advantage of that. I knew my job and was confident I did it well. Years of experience were enough to tell me, even before the paper assessment, whether or not a student would be placed or refused, as his or her behavior and actions told all. However, the school needed paper proof, so that is what I provided. Hafiz was accepted, and the Jumas entered my "energy space."

UNCERTAINTY AT DAA

I still had plans in the back of my mind to leave Dubai when gossip started to whirl through the school that Harold was leaving to be superintendent of the American School of Dubai (ASD). Thinking that Harold and I were good colleagues, working together now for four years, I asked him if the rumors were true. He looked surprised and denied it, but in his eyes I saw he was lying. I was shocked. If it were true, then for sure I was going to leave Dubai.

My problem had always been that I had a big mouth, or as I preferred to see it, I fought to keep promises. The promises had been made to parents either by the Al Habtoors (EIS) or the Varkeys (DAA). When I sensed that parents were being cheated, I did all in my power to see justice done. As Harold had suggested to me once, "Just send the parents to the Ministry of Education," and that is what I did.

When word got back to the Varkeys about this Ministry of Education visit, they would ask, "Whose idea was this?" The reply was not "Dr. Harold Fleetham's" but "Marilyn the Registrar's," so Harold was always covered, and I was the one to be blamed. However, Harold saved me from being fired in order to get the students what they were promised. Now he would be going. He had every right to leave, but why lie about it? Also it was clear that if the Varkeys found out about the move, they would cancel his visa and throw him and his family out of the country. That's how things worked in Dubai. Now Harold was in a difficult situation; he probably did indeed apply for head of school at ASD and somebody had leaked it. The rumors grew louder over the months to come. (But then, there wasn't much else to do in Dubai besides gossip!)

WE ARE THE WORLD (OF DUBAI ACADEMY)

I always looked forward to holding my beloved morning assembly once a month. That fall, I gave myself a difficult task: involve the parents in it. Ask any school administrator, and he or she will tell you it is very difficult to get the parents engaged. However, I had an idea. I decided to change the song "We Are the World" to "We Are the Parents." The students didn't know what I had in mind. I had previously sung ABBA songs with them, so what could they expect?

I stood in front of the stage and started singing the Michael Jackson tune but with lyrics describing the history of our school. Slowly, the mothers walked onto the stage. They chimed in: "We are the world, we are the mothers, we are the mothers of Dubai Academy." Harold, standing at the other end of the stage, started singing, and the fathers lined up behind the mothers. After Harold finished his part, the fathers sang, "We are the world, we are the fathers, we are the fathers of Dubai Academy." The children watched with wide eyes and open mouths, surprised and delighted to see their parents perform. I'm sure the event was long remembered by parents and children alike. (See it on my YouTube channel.)

MEBS, PARVIZ, AND A PROPOSAL

One time while I was walking through the school hallways, I couldn't help overhearing Parviz, the Juma mom, worrying aloud to another mom about the living situation of her daughter Shaista. I decided to interrupt, as both mothers had arrived recently in Dubai, and it seemed to me that they were inexperienced with Arabic culture. Parviz explained to me that Shaista had been accepted at the American University of Dubai. However, the family couldn't house her, because the father's business wasn't thriving, and they would probably have to return to Dar es Salaam. I still didn't know the Jumas all that well, but since the university was close to my home and I had two empty bedrooms, I offered to let Shaista stay with me for a low monthly rent. I made it clear that it was not good for a teenage girl to live on her own in Dubai. Parviz looked relieved. She told me she would speak with her husband, Mebs, and let me know what he thought.

The next day she came in and asked if we could all meet together, and I invited them to my house that evening. Mebs, Parviz and Shaista arrived after dinner. I showed the bedrooms available in my house, and they accepted my offer, including the fee for lodging. We drank some refreshments and started talking about schools in general. Mebs told me that it had always been his dream to own a school, so I asked him why he had never pursued the idea. He said he didn't know how. I replied that it would not be difficult: all he needed was some money, a promising location and a good group of teachers to start with. We changed the topic. Mebs and Parviz told me about their religion and being Ismailis in Tanzania. Their families had come from India several generations ago. They had been outcasts, the poorest of the poor. Many of them had taken harrowing voyages to Dar es Salaam, feeling fortunate to arrive alive. Many of them were business oriented and soon owned little shops and plantations in Tanzania, as well as their own schools, the Aga Khan schools. They considered the native Africans a different culture, living from day to day. Also, in the eyes of the Indians in those times, Africans were a lower caste, so they used them as workers, terms Parviz and Mebs still used when they told their story.

In 1960 Julius Nyerere became the first socialist president of Tanzania (previously Tanganyika). He was a politician of principle and intelligence. Banks, businesses, schools—he nationalized everything, and everyone who had been successful lost everything. The Aga Khan helped his people to repatriate to Canada. Although the families settled and loved the life there, many, including the Jumas, returned to Tanzania when Nyerere retired in 1985. Mebs and Parviz had to start all over again. In the meantime, their children were born, and the family ended up in Dubai, as Mebs was offered a partnership in a business. However, as I indicated earlier, the job did not turn out as expected.

Soon Shaista moved into my home, and the Juma family left Dubai. The monthly payments for Shaista's lodging came in regularly, but school fees for her brother Hafiz were not paid. Harold, knowing that I knew the family, started bugging me to make them pay up. They owed $6,000 USD. I kept on sending messages to Parviz, who did not reply. Finally Mebs was in town and asked to meet me. He suggested that we open a school together as equal partners. He said that he would be able to find financing from good friends in Dar es Salaam. I asked him if he was serious. He told me he had never been more serious in his life; this would be a dream come true. For me, I needed time to think over this adventuresome proposal.

A BEAUTIFUL, UGLY CAT

While walking through the community of Al Satwa one day, I glanced into a shop window and spotted the ugliest feline I had ever seen, a tabby with a nose as big as his whole head. I went inside and asked the shop owner if he was now selling stray cats? The shop owner said that the cat was a Siberian Angora, just imported from Russia. He showed me the import papers, which confirmed his story. I shook my head and left the shop. I went home and googled "Siberian Angora." It turned out to be the Siberian Forest cat, an ancient breed now believed to be ancestral to all modern longhaired cats. It is the national cat of Russia. There are claims that it is hypoallergenic. In addition to being companion pets, they also act as mousers and "watch dogs." Some have been seen patrolling the open-beamed ceilings of monasteries, keeping watch for intruders. I liked the "ugly" cat. I returned to the shop and bought it. I asked my friends and colleagues to suggest a name for him. Having inquired about his personality, the second grade teacher, Colleen, suggested Dominic, for domineering. Dominic it was!

I SAY "YES" TO THE JUMAS

Rumors around Harold were still running high. I asked him again if he was going to jump schools, and he denied it. I went to his wife, Wendy, the librarian, and told her that she'd better advise him to come straight with the staff, as gossip was bad for the work atmosphere, and no one trusted him anymore. About a week later, Harold called a staff meeting and officially announced that he had accepted an offer from the American School Dubai to be their new superintendent beginning September 2003.

I was very disappointed, as I had always thought that Harold and I shared an honest friendship. Now I realized that the only thing he had ever done was look out for himself. On principle that's OK, but he had given me the impression that he would be there for me, professionally. Now I had made up my mind: I called the Juma family and told them we would be setting up an international school in Dar es Salaam, and that they should start looking for investors and properties if they were serious. I approached parents at DAA who had companies who could be of assistance to me. I also started looking for donations for charity organizations in Dar es Salaam, asking parents to please start collecting anything that the poor could use. It was incredible, unbelievable. In the end, I shipped 3 x 40 foot containers, one of them filled with donations. One Dutch parent, a manager of a shipping line, offered to ship the containers for free to Tanzania. The manager of Emirates airline offered me free tickets for my animals and me.

DAA had a bookstore run by the parents. In addition to paying an exorbitant school fee for each child, parents had to purchase a long list of supplies at the beginning of each school year. A committee from DAAPA (Dubai American Academy Parent Association) would go to the big wholesale *soukh* (marketplace), buy school supplies in bulk, and sell them at the bookshop. Additionally they sold books from Scholastic publishing. The first successful book fair was organized by Marianne Kupper McGarrick. The profits generated had been used for anything that the Varkey Group had not granted, extra cash to make life easier for Harold as an administrator. After all, he sometimes had to wait up to a year for approval of items the cost of a pen, as frustrating and ridiculous as that sounds. The shop had been a success and made Harold's life easier. Now that he was resigning, he wanted it closed to avoid problems with the Varkeys.

The regularly scheduled DAAPA parent meeting was held. I was not present, as I'm not a parent. Harold was there in his function as a parent, not as head of school. During the meeting it had to be decided what to do with the items remaining in the shop. Some of the parents, including Els van Oostveen and Boudewien Sisselaar, suggested giving everything to me. This idea got a thumbs-down from Harold, who wanted to hold a sale and then share the money among the parents. When it came to a vote, it was decided that everything would go to me. Apparently, the look on Harold's face spoke volumes. Els and Boudewien immediately took action. They spoke with Mr. John, our school's security guard and factotum, and said they would come early the next morning, and would appreciate him opening the building so they could remove the supplies from the shop. Mr. John felt uneasy about this, but gave in. The next morning Els and Boudewien came and collected everything and dropped it all in Els's maid's quarters until it could be loaded into my container.

When I arrived at the school that morning, a fuming Harold stamped into my office and accused me of being a thief, having persuaded Els to steal everything from the shop. I had no clue what he was talking about, and he gave me no time to reply. It was the end of a relationship, which, in fact, I had only imagined to exist. He now showed who the real Harold was, and I was so disappointed. I should mention, however, that a few months later he would come to me and warn me not to trust the Jumas, after I finally paid the $6,000 USD school fees for their son Hafiz. That, you will learn later, dear reader, was an act of kindness on his part.

My 3 x 40 foot containers were filled up, the paperwork finalized, export documents for the animals completed, checklist items crossed out. I wrote to my editor Stacey, "Now I can finish my book, as my adventures are over." I was so wrong. At age fifty-six I was headed for Tanzania for some of the most exciting—and difficult—times of my life.

TANZANIA—DAR ES SALAAM /ARUSHA (2003-2007)

AN UNPROMISING START

On June 20, 2003, I went to Dubai Cargo and delivered Aztec, my new black American cocker spaniel Murphy, and my cats Chispa and Dominic. The 3 x 40 foot containers were on their way to Dar es Salaam: one filled with my car and furniture, one with charitable items for NGOs in Tanzania, and one containing educational items suitable for starting a primary school.

My flight arrived on time, and there to receive me were all members of the Juma family: Mebs, Parviz, Nadeem, Shaista and Hafiz. We headed for the cargo department to pick up my pets. A custom agent there said they'd have to remain overnight, but I objected, as the animals had been flying the whole day and needed care. Mebs bribed the agent, and my dogs, cats and I headed home. Which was...where? Although the Jumas had had six long months to arrange my housing, they'd failed to find anything suitable, or so they claimed. They said I should stay with them until they found a proper residence for me. I didn't like this, but I was tired and didn't want to start an argument at such a late hour.

Immediately, I faced more problems. The Jumas' garden was not big enough for two dogs. The Jumas were supposedly liberal Muslims, but they would not allow the dogs in the house. Nor was I permitted to bring the cats into my bedroom; I had to leave them out on a verandah. I was particularly worried about Chispa, who had always been fragile and had gotten wet and cold during travel. I wanted to take her into my bed and warm her with the blankets.

By the next morning, Chispa looked pitiful. I asked if there was a veterinary clinic nearby. I was told one was only a side street away, owned by an Australian. I decided to buy pet food, give the animals a meal, and see how Chispa looked then. She and the others ate well, so I tried to relax.

But only a few days later, while the Jumas were at their mosque, Chispa became seriously ill. I had been playing with her and Dominic when she jumped on a table and collapsed. I needed to get her to the vet at once, but I didn't have keys to the house and couldn't lock up behind me. I called Nadeem, who told me where I could find another set of keys. I took Chispa in my arms and started running in the dark—the sun had already set, and I couldn't even be sure the clinic would be open. Unsure of my direction, I asked several people sitting and drinking beer outside their ramshackle homes for the location of the vet. Finally, one man offered to walk with me there.

I was lucky; the vet was in. He examined Chispa and gave her some injections. I said I wanted to take her home and care for her there, but he said no, it was better I leave her with him. When I returned the next day, the vet said Chispa had died during the night of pneumonia. Deep in my heart I have always blamed Parviz for her death, because she had not allowed poor Chispa to stay with me when she was cold, wet and frightened.

I soon made some appalling discoveries. The Jumas had no car. Nor had they found a location for a school. Mebs said he had been meeting with banks, but there seemed to be no money except for *my* money. The Jumas already owed me over $12,000 USD. I was devastated and asked Mebs and Parviz why they had not told me all this before I left Dubai. They kept silent. They didn't tell me that the investor whom they had approached had backed out. The investor himself told me…three years too late…when he came to apologize for never having warned me about the Juma family.

Shortly after the revelation that the school location had not been found, I overheard Mebs telling Parviz that I should pack my things and move back to where I came from. The way they saw it, they were struggling financially as a family, and now there was one more mouth to feed. I was shocked.

In Dubai the Jumas had given the impression they were well off. Now I saw that their rented home was on a backstreet of Mikocheni, at that time a down-at-heel section of Dar es Salaam. The family was dysfunctional; the parents could not talk as normal people. Shouting and hitting were the only way to get things off their minds. Mebs and Parviz bullied each other and their kids, who pulled back into their own worlds.

At that time, I had no problems with the children. Nadeem went to university in Kent, Shaista planned to follow him to England, and Hafiz had applied to IST (International School Tanganyika). I felt sorry for them having to live with these parents, these pretenders. It took me a long time to realize that the apple does not fall far from the tree.

SCHOOL: LOCATION AND LOANS
Nadeem assured me he was not going to give up on our dream of a school. He told his dad he was going to help look for a location, and urged Mebs to continue to search for an investor or a bank that would give us a loan. I was very happy to hear Nadeem say this.

We had three months to prepare for the new school year. I had all the necessary school supplies in my 40 ft container, but we needed money to rent a building and hire teachers. For weeks, Nadeem and I drove around Dar es Salaam, including the districts of Masaki, Mikocheni, Msasani and Kawe, looking for a school site. A good location and a building the right size—it needed to support a growing enrollment for at least two years—were essential, otherwise the project would fail, and I'd have to pack up and leave. On the other hand, maybe Nadeem and I should have opened a real estate company. We came to know just about each and every property for rent in the city!

Our patience paid off. We found two small villas surrounded by a wall on a large plot of land in Masaki, just opposite a small supermarket. The location was very good.

Nadeem wrangled an affordable rent from the owner, and also got him to give permission for us to restructure the buildings to meet our needs. Now it was up to Mebs to convince the banks to invest in our project, which was easier with me being a *mzungu* (white) lady. The Jumas all made sure that this fact was very well known, as it improved their credibility. Eurafrican Bank gave us our first loan.

All banks need securities, so we had to wait for my containers to be released. This too, cost money, which the Jumas did not have. I paid to keep our dream alive. I'll give Mebs some credit, however; he was always there to do the footwork. As a school parent later said, "He could hypnotize people to do things they never intended." We got the building, and we finished the restructuring. Mebs hired a furniture shop to make the school furniture after our specs, convincing the owners to accept payments in installments. Of course, Mebs brought me to the shop to show my white face.

The tension between the Jumas and me eased as the parents saw that Nadeem and I were seriously working towards our goals. We went out on weekends for dinners together, and my relationship with the children deepened. Mebs and Parviz could be very charming and sweet surrounded by people of their community…or should I say, they could fill the roles required.

TELLAN, PATSY, AND THE PASSING OF MAURO
Since "they" were opening a school, Mebs and Parviz were now accepted in the Indian business community of Dar es Salaam and regularly invited to social affairs. They once took me to a rooftop party given by a friend. There I spotted a sexy, dark-skinned man in his early forties with long salt-and-pepper hair, dancing with a *mzungu* lady. They were a great couple to watch. I asked Parviz who the man was, and she brought him to meet me. He asked me to dance. It had been ages since I was on the

dance floor, and I love music, so I had a terrific time. Then I got to meet the beautiful woman who had been his excellent dance partner. That couple, Tellan and Patsy, would become my good friends.

Tellan was born in Tanzania of Sri Lankan parents. Patsy was born in Tanzania but ethnically Greek. We would talk about the Jumas, and they would make me start questioning why Mebs and Parviz were sucking up to me.

I'll never forget the first time Tellan and Patsy invited me out to eat. They met me at a small restaurant where a band was playing. During dinner, my friend Nicoletta called from Switzerland. She told me my ex-boyfriend Mauro, suffering a brain tumor, had passed away in an assisted-dying clinic. I burst into tears. Although Mauro and I separated, we met every time I was in Switzerland, just to catch up and chat over coffee. I went to the band and asked it to play "Stand by Me," as Mauro often sang that song with his band. It was a very emotional evening for me.

WE OPEN OUR DOORS

I was a mature adult and wanted to live my life and move out from the Jumas' home. Mebs had found a house in Msasani for our expat teachers, who were occupying an upper floor. I moved onto the main floor, pleased that it was a big home, although the garden space was limited. My convertible Merc was released from customs, so now I was mobile, too.

In front of a lawyer, an official contract was drawn up between the Jumas and me. Mebs wanted fifty percent interest in the school for himself, twenty-five percent for Parviz and twenty-five for me. I refused, as the couple had not invested anything and had no clue how to set up an international school. A few days later, we signed contracts with terms more favorable to me.

I was the academic director. Mebs and Nadeem forced Parviz to be the administrative director. Father and son would run the finances. Parviz was unhappy with her lot. She was insecure, and I could understand that, but instead of asking me for help, she could do nothing other than shout out her frustrations to anybody who walked in her energy space.

The second week of September we opened our doors with one or two students in each class, a small blond Dutch boy, Kevin van Hoppe, being our first student. During the months to come, we became a big family: parents, students and teachers, all happy except for Parviz, who daily entered the school last and left first. We were all "workers" to her. Whether we dug in the garden, cleaned toilets or had earned a PhD in education, it did not matter. Everybody getting a salary was a "worker."

Despite Parviz's attitude, I loved the first year, meeting parents and watching the children grow under the leadership of their teachers. We offered KG1, KG2, and grades 1, 2 and 3. We began with five instructors. One of them was Ms. Luba, a lovely young lady whom the students adored. Soft-spoken and patient, she was especially good at getting shy young children to open up in class. A few months later we hired three more instructors, all Jehovah's Witnesses, experienced teachers in need of extra pocket money. We soon realized we were very lucky to have them, as they were full of ideas and positive energy. Our library featured books I had brought from DAAPA or ordered from the US. We even had a computer lab for which Mebs had acquired Successmaker, an educational program. Later we learned our students could not be registered for the program because it was a pirated version. Mebs charged us for it; for years afterward we paid him the full cost of the program.

At a little morning assembly that I planned, I brought Aztec and Murphy for "Show and Tell." It went over great. Everybody was snuggling against the two dogs, who lapped up all the attention. Murphy had by now decided he wanted to be alpha dog. Of course, Aztec objected, so Murphy got into the bad habit of barking. It drove me nuts. After the assembly, Annie Nilsen, one of the parents, came to me. She was admiring Murphy, telling me it had always been her dream to have an American cocker spaniel. I looked at her. Annie was heaven sent! I asked her immediately if she wanted to have Murphy. Not believing her luck, she said she had to speak to her husband. The next day she came to school with a smile that meant "Yes!" Annie and I went to my house, got the carrier, all of Murphy's papers, and Murphy himself—who never looked back and never barked again. The world works in mysterious ways.

Because the school was still small and bills had to be paid, Mebs was constantly pushing his poor wife to collect school fees. I had shown her the way to handle this delicately, as we were a young school and the reputation of the staff was very important. However, Parviz did not have the diplomacy to remind parents quietly and decently for a delayed payment. Parents came to me, refusing to deal with her. Later—much, much later—I came to know she had debts all over town.

NADEEM AS PEACEMAKER
Parviz's behavior towards staff and parents soon became unacceptable, and I informed Mebs and Nadeem that I refused to work with her if she could not control herself and properly perform the role of administrative director. While home from the university on Christmas break, Nadeem calmed us all and explained to his mom how important it was for her to become part of the team. Just for the peace and money she agreed. I prepared an admission procedure for her to follow step by step, and each of us was just happy to be left alone.

Nadeem decided that if everything went well with his exams, he would come home to help run the school. This was fine by me, as we had a good relationship at the time and I was very busy doing my job, trying to make Dar es Salaam International Academy (DIA) the best school in the city. We were well on the way.

A TRIP TO SOUTHWESTERN TANZANIA
In March of 2004 we had our grand opening. The 40-foot container with charitable items donated by the parents of Dubai American Academy could now be accessed and its goods distributed. The receiving parties included two charities chosen by me: KidzCare Tanzania, headed by Rob and Mary Notman, and Street Children. Parviz had chosen the third group, a Muslim charity.

Through education, nutrition and medical programs, KidzCare seeks to enhance the care of underprivileged children regardless of religion, nationality or cultural background. For over fifteen years, Rob and Mary Notman have learned the local culture and how best to serve the needs of disadvantaged children. Among many other good works, KidzCare builds and operates preschools, provides surgery to disabled children, and provides for children orphaned by natural disasters. Naturally, I had great respect for the Notmans, and got to know them.

Mary Notman and I decided to go to southwestern Tanzania; she had just learned the rate of HIV infection among orphans there was the highest in the country. We would be staying with friends of hers and visiting local government offices to get more information and looking into the possibility of opening nonprofit schools for these children.

The bus drive was long. We stayed over in a small hotel complex in Kyela where Mary visited several organizations, gathering information and delivering medicine for malaria, worms, etc. The next day we arrived at the house of Mary's friend, a woman who asked us to call her Mamma Davis. Quite the matriarch, Mamma Davis and her son had organized a meeting with the mothers of the village for the next day to discuss their health and education issues. Mary and I settled in the guest room and went to sit in the garden, drinking tea and exchanging pleasantries. In the afternoon Mamma's son took us first by car, followed by a walk, to nearby Lake Nyasa, the natural border between Tanzania and Malawi. On our return we were served delicious food. We went to bed early as by now we were exhausted and needed to rest for the next day.

We slept well and rose early the next morning to the clucking of hens and voices of people roaming around. After breakfast we were all excited to go to the big village tree, where the meeting with the mothers was to be held. A few dignitaries arrived, and then Mamma Davis opened the meeting. The mothers were clearly concerned about the wellbeing of their children, and happy to discuss the details with this *mzungu*. The major problems were malaria and worms, which Mary promised to take care of as soon as she returned home to Dar es Salaam. One of the villagers promised her a piece of land for a small school. After the meeting we went to see it, and hands were shaken on the deal. These were village people, living peacefully together as one family. Corruption was unknown among them, or as I'd put it, corruption was not necessary.

Mary and I returned, tired but safely back in Dar, full of new experiences. As I write this in 2015, the school KidzCare built has three hundred students from all around Ngonga. I filmed all my experiences from this trip, and you will find the videos on my YouTube channel.

THE SCHOOL THRIVES, BUT…

At the end of the first school year, DIA had twenty-two students. The Jumas were not happy, as they thought that number meant the school was a failure. I told them in fact this was a very good result. Both schools in Dubai, where I had worked, had much better facilities than we had, and at the end of the school year each one had between thirty and forty students. This number would normally double the next year, and so on. I was not worried at all, and when a meeting was set with United Bank of Africa, I convinced the bank manager I was right. We received a loan towards the second academic year. Many applications for the school year 2004-2005 came in. Nadeem came home for summer vacation, and he and his dad went looking for a new property.

The second year started well. Nadeem had seriously spoken to his mom before he went back to the university, urging her to ease up on me. Sadly, she soon forgot his words and was once again criticizing me all day long. This was wrong, that was wrong, I should tell my teachers this, I should tell my teachers that, they were not allowed to do this, they were not allowed to do that. It was all little things, not worth talking about, but for Parviz it became mountains, and she just kept on talking and talking, driving me insane. In the meantime there were bigger problems. The books were not paid for, so I could not order more. We needed more desks and computers, but bills were not paid, so nobody wanted to deal with us. Parviz shouted that I should do my job, but how could I when she wasn't doing hers? A few days I actually stayed at home in bed and hid myself from that horrible woman.

As for Mebs, he was developing a pretty terrible reputation among the faculty. He had rented some houses in a compound on the beach for the teachers, including one for himself, where he received his girlfriends. I thought it extremely unprofessional to put himself in such a vulnerable situation, as everybody talked about it—everyone except Parviz, who was left in the dark.

Nadeem was returning to Dar every school holiday. He and Mebs were exploring the creation of new schools. I thought it was way to early to pursue this, but Mebs flew to Arusha, and Nadeem took a business trip with his siblings and friends to Mozambique, paid for by DIA. Suddenly four cars arrived from South Africa: three Nissan Hardbodies for Mebs, Nadeem and me, and a Lexus for Parviz. I was furious, demanding Mebs tell me where the money was coming from. I was told not to worry, that everything was under control. I was too busy running the school and making sure the students had the best education possible to investigate the finances.

NEW FRIENDS, NEW HOME

By Christmas 2004 we had sixty-eight students. We could finally offer our teachers a decent wage; a salary scale was created to reward them for their degrees and years of employment. Our school was producing an annual talent show and musical, and once a year the students celebrated an International Day. I soon made new friends among the school's parents, Yolanda van Hoppe and Beatrix Mugishagwe.

In the meantime I had enough of sharing the house in Msasani with the teachers and searched the Internet for a more proper place for my pets and me. I discovered a villa in Kawe, close to my new friend Beatrix. She was the producer and director of *Tumaini (Childhood Robbed)*, a feature film released in 2005 about the plight of children orphaned by AIDS. The movie received high praise at the Zanzibar International Film Festival and was nominated for the UNICEF Child Rights Award, as well as the Signis East African Award.

I drove to Kawe and loved the house. It looked strangely familiar to me. I saw nobody there, which was good, for if the sellers knew a *mzungu* was interested, the rent would shoot up. I went home and switched on the computer to check Park Villa again and discovered that it was the same way-too-expensive place I had looked at a year earlier. This time I sent Mebs to haggle for me, who got it at a reasonable rate. I paid the landlord to build a perimeter wire fence, and while it was being constructed, I kept Aztec on a long leash. He had gotten away from Davy, one of my two *askaris* (security guards), a few times during his daily walk, disappearing long enough each time to cause me real worry. As a husky owner once advised me, "Never let your husky off the leash, as he will be in his own world and will come back on his own schedule. He might be gone days, and he might get lost." Lost or too naughty. When I moved into Park Villa a month before Christmas, the owner still hadn't completed the fence. My *askaris* got to enjoy barbecued chicken and goat—game my husky "wolf" had run out and killed. Of course, I paid the farmers for their losses.

The school's Christmas party was held at my place, its huge garden making it the perfect location. I left the event planning to Parviz; she loved to commandeer her little army of "workers," who on this occasion included my housekeeper, Mwajuma.

As the school grew, we got into the IB (International Baccalaureate) program. DIA was now a direct competitor with IST, the first international school in Dar es Salaam. People started noticing us. Haven of Peace Academy (HOPAC) was full and we were affordable for many who could not afford IST. Therefore we needed a new location with more facilities and more classrooms. Mebs found an old two-story villa in Masaki, the contract was set up and reconstruction was done. Although it was hard work, I was enjoying every moment at school. It was my life.

"R AND R" IN ZANZIBAR

My friend Pat from UNIS, whom you may remember I visited in New York, was now working in Qatar. She agreed to meet me over a weekend in Zanzibar, a semi-autonomous island region of Tanzania.

Pat and I met in Stone Town, the old city and cultural heart of Zanzibar, little changed in the last 200 years. It is a place of winding alleys, bustling bazaars, mosques and grand Arab houses with brass-studded, carved wooden doors. We spent many hours wandering the fascinating labyrinth of narrow streets. We had booked a night at the luxurious Emerson Spice Hotel. Arriving at the reception desk, we had a delightful surprise. Pat and the owner looked at each other and hugged, New Yorkers in Zanzibar. I thought, is NYC a village? They all know each other! The hotel's elaborate woodwork and stylish, colorful decor took our breath away, and we admired our huge room with its lovely tub. You may not think of a mosquito net as a thing of beauty, but when it billows over a bed in a gentle breeze, it's really an enchanting sight. We had drinks and dined at the fabulous rooftop restaurant offering a magnificent view of Stone Town, while soft music played in the background.

The next day we moved on to the northernmost peninsula of Zanzibar Island to Ras Nungwi Beach Hotel. Overlooking the Indian Ocean, the hotel features a cluster of whitewashed and palm thatched cottages in rich tropical gardens, with walkways between beach, balcony and bar. The gardens drop down onto one of the finest and most unspoiled beaches on the island. Again we discovered that the world was very small. On one of our walks, we passed two elderly men. Pat looked back, the men looked back, then everybody laughed and embraced each other. They were friends from the sailing club in Dubai, stopping on a sailing trip to South Africa. We spent a memorable time on their boat, exchanging many stories. Unfortunately, I had to leave the next day and say goodbye to Pat, whom I never saw again after those days. I did not say farewell to Zanzibar, however. After that visit I regularly returned with all my friends from Europe. This number, of course, included Ursi and her family. They came several times and fell in love with the area.

MALARIA AND AN ANGRY ELEPHANT

Tobias, a Swiss student teacher, came to do his internship at our school and stayed with me for a few months. Our first excursion together was made to Bagamoyo, which was founded at the end of the eighteenth century. It was the original capital of German East Africa and one of the most important trading ports along the East African coast. Later I learned that Bagamoyo, with its crumbling, impressive but ghostly colonial-era buildings, has been nominated to be one of Tanzania's World Heritage Sites.

When Tobias and I arrived at the beachfront Paradise Holiday Resort, I collapsed into one of the chairs in the foyer. I suddenly felt ill, horrible. Could I have the flu? I had a high fever and my body ached, alternately hot and cold with headache, nausea and weakness. We checked in, and I went straight to my room. Toby's room was next to mine. Over the balcony railing, I suggested he just do whatever he wanted, and I would stay in bed.

I could not sleep and my condition worsened. I called the reception desk and said I needed a doctor immediately. After ten minutes I was told there was no doctor around, but my symptoms sounded like malaria. I had never taken preventive medicine for malaria; it has nasty side effects, and when a person is living in Africa, not merely visiting, it is impossible to take medicine constantly. The reception desk people said they would bring me to the Holy Ghost Mission, which had a small clinic. I was too sick to realize that I was put into a car and driven there. The nuns tested my blood and said yes, I had a serious case of malaria and should not be travelling. I was given medication with the advice to stay in bed. So there I was in a beautiful hotel, lying in bed. Tobias was unaware of all this and had acquired a charming sunburn when he checked on me hours later.

Later in the year, by which time I had fully recovered, Toby, two other teachers and I went to Mikumi National Park, the fourth largest park in Tanzania. Driving through the grounds, we spotted a photogenic elephant. I got out of our car with my camera and approached him. Ears flapping, the elephant started charging towards me. I shouted to Toby, who was behind the wheel, "Open the door and drive!" while I raced for the front passenger seat. In my mind I already saw the elephant upending the car with his huge tusks. Fueled by adrenaline I jumped in, and we escaped attack by a hair. I need not say that from then on I was very careful. Peacefully we went to Lazy Lagoon the weekend after, where no adventures happened or were to be expected. We simply enjoying walking on the beach and watching the fishing boats passing by.

ENROLLMENT GROWS, BUT...

The pressures of a growing student body were too much for Parviz, and Leo Mazigo was hired to be head of administration. Leo and I became friends, but he wouldn't respond to my suggestions for an audited report of the school accounts. The Jumas, the ONLY ones who kept these records, sent them to the bank and the government without sharing them with me. I kept insisting Leo take action, and the only thing he said was, "Marilyn, be careful, watch out for yourself, do not believe anything they say." As far as I could tell, Leo was Mebs's friend, but if even Leo talked this way...I realized things were really wrong.

"BULY"

A new student arrived, Kiefer Whitaker, whose father, Neil, was the general manager of Bulyanhulu Gold Mine, located in the Kahama district of the Shinyanga region, northwestern Tanzania. At the time, Bulyanhulu was Tanzania's largest underground gold mining investment. African Barrick Gold, owner of the mine, had upgraded roads and health facilities in the area, developed power and water infrastructure, and provided direct employment to nearly 1,000 people.

Neil suggested we open a small school on the mining compound, as several new expats had been hired, and their families had children. Dollar signs agleam in his eyes, Mebs demanded a ridiculously high budget, but Barrick agreed to it.

I was not involved in any of the discussions, as I had gradually become an outsider. Mebs and Parviz planned to squeeze as much as possible out of Barrick with the least investment. Contract signed, I was directed to find expat teachers. I hired, among others, two new teachers from Canada, Jeremy and Carolyn. A school building was slapped together, parents arrived, school started, one manager left, new managers came.

A DIA board member was expected to come once a week to check on the Bulyanhulu school. The member should have been Mebs, if for no other reason than that he might have gotten the Successmaker computer system running. But Mebs and Parviz refused to make the trip, and I was forced to go. It seems there were several items in the contract that were not fulfilled from our side as well as Barrick's, and someone had to take responsibility. So, there I went, flying into Kahama in Barrick's own private aircraft.

I arrived expecting to stay at the on-site villa the contract had specified: there was none. Did I drive the car the contract had specified? No. There was none. Over a few days, I met the latest manager and sorted out the Harcourt Brace books, whose arrival made Jeremy and Carolyn very happy. Jeremy requested assistance with Successmaker and the computers on a daily basis, but the only people with the skills to help him were Mebs or Shabbar, our computer technician, who weren't there. It was now clear that the Jumas' business plan was a fantasy.

Jeremy and Carolyn, who were far from Dar es Salaam and had their "boots on the ground," became increasingly unhappy. The only bright spot in their lives was the fact that they could travel around Africa and stay in my house for long weekends. Then Carolyn, who had a history of digestive problems, got sick and ended up in the hospital in Dar. She was well taken care of. In fact, for the first time a correct diagnosis was made, and she had a much-needed operation.

During her recovery, Parviz and Mebs pushed me into attending another meeting with the Buly parents, whom they said had requested the meeting. From the moment I arrived, I felt negative energy coming towards me from everywhere, and I was uncomfortable in my own skin. Only Carolyn and Jeremy could fully understand the day-to-day problems of the school, and they were not there. Parents were happy with the couple, who were extremely good teachers, but totally frustrated with "us"—the Jumas and subsequently me—for not fulfilling all promises made. I was guilty by association, as Jeremy later put it. He and Carolyn did not know all the problems and corruption I had to face back at DIA, and I could not bring myself to tell them. It was proposed to the parents that we have another meeting when Carolyn was well again, and she and Jeremy could attend.

Reporting back to Mebs, I lost my temper and shouted at him that Buly was his responsibility. He shouted back that Jeremy and Carolyn were disloyal. He threatened to seize their passports and throw them in jail. I replied that the only one who should be in jail was **him**, for misguiding everybody.

Jeremy and Carolyn returned, and before I knew what was happening, they disappeared. It was all very dramatic. I don't know the whole story, but it seems the couple had heard about Mebs's threats and fled, flown out by Barrick in secret. I later heard that the contract between DIA and Bulyanhulu was terminated, and the wife of the manager (I believe it was her plan from the moment she arrived) took over the fully setup school.

DUPLICITY

Fraud allegations were suddenly made against Mebs by Standard Chartered, which had given him loans. Standard discovered there were four staff members whom he had reported on his audit as a cost, and they simply did not exist. Mebs was taking loans here, taking loans there. He flew to the US for holidays and returned on the "Unwanted" immigration list.

Nadeem had finished university in Kent and returned to Dar. He found an office for a new company that his father had registered. It went through a few name changes before it became E-Fulusi Africa Ltd. Basically, everything in E-Fulusi belonged to DIA. The server with a cost of over $3,000 USD? Taken from DIA (which was forced to make-do with a simpler, $1,000 USD computer). The furniture? Paid for by DIA school fees. Salaries? Paid by DIA. E-Fulusi's audited accounts, like DIA's, were a joke. Next a digital content agency called the AIM Group was formed and financed by...you can guess.

Nadeem was supposed to be in charge of DIA finances. However, after four months, he came to me and begged me to take them over. He said he couldn't control his family, his father in particular, who came to him every few days asking for money. How could he ever turn his father down?

I was confident I'd be able to handle Mebs. By now Leo had come to trust me, and insisted I needed to ask Mebs for audit reports. The company had produced no dividends; however, the Jumas always rewarded themselves with its money. We had hired an international auditing firm to look at the books and interview management on company affairs. The result? The firm resigned!

The Jumas weren't the only ones misappropriating funds. One afternoon, having withdrawn $500 TZS (about $250 USD) from an ATM to cover my electricity and water bills, I came home, took a nap, then awoke. Before I walked with Aztec on the beach, I saw my housekeeper Mwajuma in the kitchen and the *askaris* James and Davy cleaning my home. I really did not pay much attention to my employees. As long as the house was neat, I paid them good salaries and assumed they were happy. Mwajuma went home at the end of every day. Davy lived in the little servants' quarters with a woman who might have been his wife. James went home every night.

The next morning, getting ready to go out and pay my bills, I looked in my wallet and discovered the money was gone. I called everyone to the living room and asked who had stolen it. No one took the blame. I called Leo for advice, and he told me he would come to my house right away. While I waited, I observed the three as they continued with their work. Mwajuma had been with me since I arrived in Dar. She was a single Muslim woman who lived with her mother and was raising two children. I had left valuables everywhere, and she had never taken a penny or a morsel of food that did not belong to her, so I was sure she wasn't the culprit.

Soon Leo came. He had brought with him two cleaning women and two *askaris* from the school. They waited outside while he called my staff into the living room. Leo told them he had brought new staff for me if the truth would not come out. Each employee had to come in separately and recount his or her actions from the moment I had come home the day before until the moment I had discovered the money was missing. He started with Mwajuma. She very calmly reported what she had done and said she had not stolen the money. Davy came in, fell on his knees and swore he had not done it. James, his cousin, the charmer, came in and confessed to the crime and handed the money back to me.

I fired James and thanked Leo for his successful intervention. Believe it or not, while Leo was leaving my house, James, who was walking home, stopped Leo and with a big smile asked him if he would give him a lift. This was Africa: no guilt, no regret, just live in the moment.

Remember the international auditing firm that resigned? Its CPAs told me very clearly that the accounts were fabricated, staff was invented, and the Juma family's private spending was turning into DIA spending. In a word, it was a mess. The firm didn't even know where to start, and therefore had given up. With this knowledge in mind, I secretly hired an accountant who joined me at the school each morning before it opened, and returned after students, faculty and other administrators had left. I now did what I should have done from the beginning: I audited the school and worked my way backwards, often deep into the night.

I could not work at home because mosquitoes had invaded the house. I tried throwing a net over my computer and hiding under it, but it was unbearable. I moved into a new house, closer to the school.

Mebs suddenly became my new best friend. He would visit me around ten o'clock each morning, trying to get money out of me, crying crocodile tears, saying I was the only one who understood him. I now had sympathy for Nadeem. The man was a menace, a crook, and made me feel very bad. I even gave in a little, paying him $1,500 USD for something he had never bought: Successmaker.

I finally asserted myself and told Mebs not to come to my office any more.

Mebs's interruptions aside, running two departments, academics and finance, could have been extremely stressful for me. Thankfully, academics was very professionally administered by Claire Nightingale and Dr. Jeanette Kuder. They worked very hard to make DIA an IB school, a fine one.

SIA

In the meantime, one of my kindergarten teachers, Sia, got ill and was hospitalized. Illness was a big problem in the school in general because of malaria; there was always somebody absent, so we had floating teachers.

Complaining of flu-like symptoms and a cough, Sia had come to me many times over the year to ask permission to go to the doctor. Several times our other kindergarten teacher, Emelda, asked Sia to join her on doctor visits, hoping to nudge Sia into getting a proper checkup. I told Emelda in confidence that I thought Sia had AIDS and should be tested.

In Tanzania HIV does not exist. Everybody dies of pneumonia, refusing to admit that it is the HIV virus that took hold first. This time Emelda told me that Sia was admitted to the hospital, and that her husband had asked to see me. I met him near the facility entrance. He told me Sia's family would neither allow him to see her nor tell him what was the matter with her. I told him not to worry: we both would go and see Sia.

When we entered the hospital room there were no visitors, and Sia looked very ill. She had been a beauty; now it was all gone, only sadness in her eyes. I took her in my arms, as did her husband, and asked her what her diagnosis was. She started crying and saying she did not know what made her sick.

Sure I would get better results than her husband, I went to the ward's head nurse and told her we wanted to see the doctor who was treating Sia. The nurse brought us to a small office room, where we briefly waited for the doctor. When he arrived, I introduced Sia's husband and myself. I told him that Sia's husband wanted to know what was wrong. The physician explained that Sia's condition was very bad: she had pneumocystis pneumonia, severe weight loss and no immune system.

I looked the doctor in the eyes and asked him if he could confirm that she had AIDS. He did not reply and kept on saying she had severe pneumonia, no antibodies to resist the illness. I asked, "Would you advise for her husband to take the HIV test?" The doctor glanced at both of us and answered, "Yes." I advised Sia's husband to take the test as soon as possible.

The doctor left us. The husband tearfully told me that he had not been with another woman since his friendship with Sia, and they had not long been married. I told him that questioning himself and her would serve no purpose, and if he loved Sia we should go back to her and make her as comfortable as possible, as she had little time left on this earth.

We went back to Sia's room, where she was surrounded by family members. I looked at all of them and said with authority in my voice: "I am Sia's boss. Can I please be alone with her and her husband as long as necessary?" After they left, I told Sia what the doctor had said.

We will never know who was infected first, and it didn't matter now. Husband and wife lay in each other's arms and cried. I quietly left them alone and told the family that Sia wanted to be with her husband. Two days later, I received a telephone call from her husband that Sia had died. It was a sad funeral for such a beautiful young lady.

UNHAPPY FAMILIES

Perhaps less tragic but more ironic, the Juma kids came with their suitcases during the holidays and asked to stay in my house. The fights between their parents had become unbearable, they said. Mebs had girlfriends all over the place and would stagger home in the early morning hours, sparking clashes that were sometimes physical.

My sister Marijke emailed me that the family house was now on the market, as Dad was going to a living-assistance apartment. We were all happy. Marijke and I then co-owned the house; ideally, I would have purchased it entirely for myself, since I did not have my own "home" anywhere in the world. Marijke, however, wanted to buy my share, for her children, she said. Her offer was extremely low; at least, that is what I thought when I read it. Marijke had been there for me when I was in need, but this time I felt cheated and disappointed after I googled houses for sale in my parents' neighborhood and saw they were double or triple the value Marijke had quoted. When I informed her about my google results she suggested I get the house appraised by a notary public, so there would not be any dispute later. She felt insulted that I did not trust her. Soon the house was sold to another party, and Marijke and I received our shares.

I LET MYSELF GO

Parviz and I had our offices close together, she dealing with non-academic matters, I with students and parents. One day she stormed into my room, demanding to know why I had not met with the lady who deals with health insurance. Parviz shouted that she had informed me about this and made an appointment for me, and until today she hadn't heard anything back from me. I looked at her despairingly and said I had no clue what she was talking about. She screamed that I was unreliable, that I forgot everything. How could I be running a school? Without her, I was nothing. I stood there speechless. Then I shouted back, "Get out of my room and never ever return!" She lifted her hand, ready to hit me. When she realized what she was intending to do, she let her arm drop but raved on that this was her school too, and I had no idea all the mistakes she was covering up for me. "Mention one!" I hollered. The door opened and Shabbar came and told us quietly to please lower our voices, as the whole building could hear us. "No problem," I told him, then turned to Parviz. "Get out!" I ordered. My heart was trembling as I closed the door. This was the first time I had let myself go in front of Parviz, instead of swallowing everything.

I allowed myself some minutes to cool down, replaying the scene in my mind, before I went to Leo and described the shouting match. "But Marilyn," he said, "you had nothing to do with this. I met the insurance woman. She was asking for **me**." I asked Leo to please inform Parviz. Needless to say, Parviz never apologized.

I moved my office to the other school building.

MAGGIE AND FAMILY

Around this time, a new family walked into my office. The father was Austrian, the mother Maasai. They had three gorgeous children who had studied at the International School of Moshi. After I realized the father spoke German, we continued our conversation in that language as I showed them around the school and showed them the classes where the children would be after passing their assessments.

As I prepared to distribute the tests, I noticed that the two younger children, Resi and Siamito, were smiling, but the eldest, a teen named Robert, was trying to mask his insecurity with a smug expression. "So, you think you are a clever boy?" I teased. It turned out that Robert was sensitive to jokes, and to my surprise he started crying and ran back to the family car. I followed him and, with his parents' help, got him back to the room for the assessment. It took Robert a few weeks, but eventually he realized I was not that bad. Like many teenagers, he had felt pushed around by moving again to another school. His mother, Maggie, would later prove an invaluable friend.

PRICELESS MEMORIES LOST

Although Parviz and I had our differences, we decided to join forces and throw a big bash for Mebs's fiftieth birthday. We used the school property, hired a band, catered the food, and successfully surprised Mebs. The drinks were all stored at my house. I owned a cast-iron wine holder, a wedding present from one of my previous marriages. There was only one bottle in it, labeled "FIFA World Cup 1998 Argentina—Holland 1-2." I had bought the wine after we (Marilyn), the Dutch, had won from Argentina (Chango). I had promised Marco the bottle would be his upon my passing.

When the party ended that night, I came home and went straight to bed. The next morning, I went to the kitchen and realized something was missing, but what? I looked around and couldn't put my finger on it. I made breakfast, cleaned up all the empty boxes, and was putting all the empty bottles outside when I passed the wine holder. Empty. I couldn't believe it. Everybody knew not to touch that bottle, everyone knew it had priceless memories for me. Nadeem and his friends had been driving up and down to the house during the party, collecting beer and liquor (but wine had not been served). Could Nadeem have taken it? I called him at once and told him about the disappearance. He said it wasn't him, he knew how important this bottle was to me. By now I was furious and walked to my gate, looking for the *askaris*, Davy and a new man. Davy was not there; he was still sleeping. I asked the new guard if he had seen anybody leaving the house with a wine bottle. His English was not good, so I waited for Nadeem, who soon arrived and questioned the guard. The *askari* told him that he had seen Davy walking out with bottles in his pocket, and one of these bottles was bigger than the others. After two hours Davy had come back and left again with bottle-bulging pockets.

Nadeem and I went straight to the servants' quarters. I had given Davy a good bed, a TV, a cooker and cooking utensils. (Typically, *askaris* slept on the floor and cooked over a small fire.) He lay drunk in his bed, and it was difficult to wake him. After a long time of questioning, Davy confessed. The wine was less important to me than the bottle, so we asked if at least he knew where the empty bottle was, but he had no clue. I was so mad, I fired him on the spot. He left my property, but the next day while I was at work Davy returned with a small truck and emptied the quarters, telling the new *askari* that everything belonged to him. I let it go, not knowing where he had gone anyway.

THE AUDIT

Parviz came to me and shed false tears, saying that Hafiz and Shaista's school fees needed to be paid, and she and Mebs had no money. Aren't they practically your children too? she begged. I believed this con woman. I paid her with my own money, and within three months my share of my parents' house was gone to the Juma family. I now believe that the Jumas manipulated me into taking the position of finance manager so I could be their "fall guy." BRELA (Business Registrations and Licensing Agency) and TIC (Tanzania Investment Centre) began investigating the school, as there was no audit available and taxes were not paid. And who would be expected to face these inquiries? Me.

Going into the third month of my secret audit, I discovered that for the first fiscal quarter of 2005, approximately $500,000 USD was unaccounted for. It took me two weeks to check, double check, look for payments, invoices, etc. The money was nowhere to be found. I walked to E-Fulusi, which was close by, and went straight to Mebs's office. He was speaking on the phone and laughing. I told him to hang up. "You're a thief!" I declared. He chuckled and tried to charm me. I shouted that I would go to the police and have him arrested if he didn't retrieve the stolen money. In the meantime everybody at E-Fulusi had heard me, and Nadeem was called, who phoned Parviz. Within thirty minutes all the Jumas were present, nervous, telling me that I was wrong, they could prove to me that there was no money taken, etc., etc. I looked at them in disgust and told them to do so, quickly. I left. In pieces.

But that was not all. Every week I received from Parviz an Excel sheet with the names of parents who had paid tuition fees. Now knowing that her husband was defrauding the school, and following my guts, I approached Ethel the receptionist after school after everyone else had gone home. I asked Ethel to describe the procedure of the parents who pay in installments. She told me that parents call and make an appointment with Parviz; the parent shows up, and his or her name is entered on a sheet. At the end of the week, Ethel gives this sheet to Parviz, who then sends the sheet to me. I told Ethel that our meeting was confidential and that I needed that sheet at the end of the next week. Ethel unhappily agreed to do so. The end of the week came. I received Ethel's list, and one hour later I received Parviz's. Four names were deleted, $2,000 USD gone into Parviz's pockets. Of course, I needed to be sure, so I called each of these parents and told them I was doing a confidential internal audit. Those who had paid school fees that week confirmed it and agreed to sign a statement attesting to this. I created an affidavit for each parent, and when everybody else had left the building, I received these people, who each swore that they had paid and not received any receipt. I now was devastated. Not only was the father a thief, but the mother, as well. I was walking on thin ice, as these were con artists, corrupt and very dangerous. I needed to be careful.

Members of the school's parent organization kept questioning the Jumas and me where the funds were going, as the IB coordinators Claire and Jeanette and department heads told them that supplies were not arriving because bills were going unpaid. I met with Claire and Jeanette and some parents and told them about my suspicions, but said I needed more information and had to talk with people at the bank.

From there everything went very fast.

BREAKDOWN

I was at my office desk one morning. Mebs walked in, making small talk. He stood in my door, gazing down the hall, saying, "I think we should put in cameras. I believe people are stealing!" As I write this, I still have to laugh. Unbelievable! Claire and Jeanette walked in, overhearing him. I don't remember which one of them actually said it, but the reply was, "If there is any thief, Mebs, it for sure is YOU." Shouting erupted, back and forth, going on and on. I slowly closed my computer (as I did not yet know that I would never come back, I did not remove my documents from it), took my bag, walked through my door in between the fighters and left the building, slowly walking to my car.

Two parents, my friends Beatrix and Maggie, greeted me. I did not see them. They told me later I was absolutely stone faced. I got into my car and drove away, which was so unlike me that the two women decided to follow me. I drove straight to my doctor's clinic, parked the car, entered the building and fell apart. The nurse, unable to calm me down, brought me to a small consultation room. Very worried, Beatrix and Maggie asked the nurse about me, and she said I had broken down and the doctor was coming. Unknown to me, the women remained in the waiting room. The doctor arrived but could not ease my nerves and asked if I had somebody whom I could contact. The nurse told him about Beatrix and Maggie. He asked them to come in, and when everybody suggested I go home, I cried, "No way, they'll kill me!" I knew once the truth was out my life was not worth a penny.

It did not take long for a white Nissan Hardbody to pull up in front of the clinic, the bush drums banging the news to the Jumas that I had left the school (which I had never done before) and that my car had been spotted at the clinic. Nadeem, who had been sent to explore the situation, was ordered to leave the premises.

I was asked where I wanted to go. The Jumas knew I was very friendly with both Beatrix and Maggie, so they were out of the question. Then I thought of Yolanda van Hoppe, a parent whose child was our first student when our school first opened. I don't remember who called Yolanda, but when asked she said she would be happy to have me stay at her home on the outskirts of Dar es Salaam, where no one would think to look for me. Much later, having told her I was going to write my autobiography, she sent me the following, which I have edited for length:

27.04.2015
Dear Marilyn,

So nice to hear from you after all these years...

Kevin was enrolled in DLA as the first student. We rushed to pay our enrollment fees and first installment. Kevin's first teacher was a stunning young lady, Miss Luba. He adored her. She was soft spoken and encouraged Kevin to come out of his shell and challenged him to be creative. We slowly got to know you, Marilyn. We became close friends, not only because you were running a school, but because of your personality, you were full of enthusiasm and energy and determination to get this school up and running....

[My husband] Hans and I didn't have a high opinion of the Jumas, and certainly not Mebs, who had a bad name in Dar for swindling people in business. But because Marilyn had all trust in them we supported her and just hoped things would turn out well. It wasn't long before we were hounded by Mebs to pay our second and last installment of school fees long before it was due. His reason? He had no money to pay the teachers. Of course, we didn't want Miss Luba to leave, so we paid up, and not long after found out that Mebs had bought himself a gym, and Miss Luba hadn't been paid after all. A few months later, teachers were complaining louder and louder, they were finding it hard to live in Dar financially, and we hear Mebs has started a new venture, E-Fulusi. He was now openly showing off, and his personal life was out there for all to see. He openly had affairs and threw money around as if it was nothing. But we saw the school suffering, Marilyn suffering, she was no more the smiling lady greeting us at the gates.

Marilyn turned up at our house a broken woman. She came with nothing, terrified. She needed a place to hide, somewhere the Jumas didn't know about. And that was us. We live on the outskirts of Dar, and not a lot of people would drive up [to] our area. We took Marilyn in for a week. She had nothing, no clothes, no money. She had left her animals at home. Personally, I don't think

*she even knew she was in our house for a few days. We offered her
a room, she slept for two whole days. She didn't come down, just to
eat and straight to bed again. She was a wreck, but slowly on the
third day she started talking to Hans. One question after another
came out. Later when she discovered the frauds on her contracts,
she showed Hans her paperwork she believed she had rights to, but
Hans told her sorry, Marilyn, your name is not here, you cannot
show you have invested in the school. Everything has been put in the
name of the Jumas. Being the corrupt country it is, the Jumas would
have easily changed everything at the register. Again I emphasize
I believe the children were very much involved. They are not the
innocent party in this whole history. The mother and her children
eventually did the same to their own father, so please don't think
they are innocent in this whole business....*

*Believe me, Marilyn, God works in mysterious ways. You have
gone through a lot of heartache in your adventure in Dar. And we
are very sorry for that, because the dream would have turned out
so different had you not trusted the Jumas. But they will get what
is deserving of them, money does not bring happiness, my dear, and
that is so, so visible in their lives now. You can have all the money
you want, but the love and respect of people is so much more gratify-
ing than anything else in the world.*

We wish you all the best.
Hugs and kisses
Yolanda

SHELTER FROM THE STORM

After one week with the van Hoppe family, I finally had the courage to
return home. I was under strong medication but wanted to be back with
my animals. Maggie had kept an eye on Mwajuma and my two *askaris*,
who took care of my pets. The *askaris* wanted to be dressed as dangerous
soldiers, so outfits were bought, with sticks, whistles and everything that
they needed to deny entry to my house. (The Jumas had threatened to
go to the police if they would not open the gate, as the house was rented

by the school.) Fortunately, my guards did not listen to that rubbish and, except Maggie, nobody was allowed in. At least once a day a member of the Juma family would drive by and peer through the gates.

Maggie decided to play a major role in my security. She collected me in the morning and brought me to her house after she had delivered her children to school, her house girl and guards keeping me safe. In the evening she dropped me at home, where I would go straight to bed to sleep, she giving strict instructions to the *askaris* to let no one inside my home except Beatrix and herself.

The *askaris* had developed a security system with all the guards on the street. When the guard at the first or last house on the road saw a Juma car, they whistled. The whistle was repeated from one house to another, so that by the time the car was in sight, my *askaris* were standing with their "weapons" at the gate, while I trembled with fear in my bed.

I couldn't feel secure in my own home. Maggie had been looking for a new place for herself, so we decided to look for a common property. By good fortune we found two houses in one compound that belonged to Mama Anna Mkapa, the president's wife, at Mikocheni. We moved in together, becoming one family until tensions eased. I loved the little house and the knowledge that I now was not alone, Maggie and her family living in the house beside mine. Aztec and Dominic enjoyed roaming around, and Dominic became a good friend of Siamito, Maggie's youngest son. The boy would come to my place in the morning "complaining" that Dominic had given him many wet kisses during the night.

In the meantime Maggie wanted to move her children to another school, so she went to HOPAC to see if it could take all three of them. It was a bad time, since many parents who had a child at DIA were moving their children, and most of them ran to HOPAC. Luckily, she got a place for Robert. Resi and Siamito could not get a spot, so she decided they would stay at DIA as long as there were still good teachers there.

The Jumas now realized Maggie was the lady keeping me safe. They sent her a note, demanding she pay the children's tuition for the entire school year up front. She went to see Parviz for an explanation. Parviz gave a vague reply, mumbling about the school being in financial trouble. Maggie realized that Parviz was trying to punish her because she was protecting me and had moved Robert out. Maggie politely said she was not going to pay yearly and that Parviz had no right whatsoever to throw her children out of school. As long as her children were still attending DIA, she asserted, if anything happened to them or me, Parviz would be held responsible, adding she had the backing of the police. Parviz looked at her with disbelief. How could she say such a thing? "I am a Tanzanian," Maggie stated emphatically, "and moreover, Prime Minister Edward Lowassa is my brother. I could use his influence to ruin your business."

During this time, my friendship with Tellan and Patsy deepened. They saw how disappointed, tired and depressed I was and tried to entertain me, introducing me to new people. After years of silence, I heard from Marco, who now worked in Johannesburg. I was in contact with parents of the school who wanted to start a new school with me as the head. I had appointments with lawyers, banks, TIC and BRELA.

SASKIA

I wrote to Saskia, the woman who had managed my property in Costa Rica for the past ten years. I told her I wanted to sell, needing money for a court case against the Juma family. My contribution of all the equipment, books, furniture, etc., that came in to start the school had a specific monetary value, and this could be signified by the debenture list we submitted to Eurafrican Bank as collateral when we got our first loan. I would seek a return of these funds and compensation for the Juma children's school fees that I paid. To win back my money would take money. Saskia wrote back that she would advertise the property and let me know the outcome.

BAD NEWS AND AN OPPORTUNITY

In May 2006, the Jumas began a series of acts to ruin my name and submit me to mental strain. I had been forced to resign my executive position, but I remained a shareholder, a fact that enraged them. They talked to consultants and lawyers to concoct grounds for tampering with my shares and having my resident permit revoked, or throwing me out of the country completely.

In the meantime Maggie drove me all over town to all my meetings. It was at BRELA that I discovered I did not own a school. We entered the building and asked for business registrations. We were shown where to go, climbing many flights of stairs. A young man assisted us, and we looked and searched and searched again. There was no business registration. The next day we returned and discovered that DIA filed no annual returns for the years 2004, 2005 or 2006. The registration had been hidden or stolen, and I was no longer a shareholder.

Just when I was feeling most lost—no lawyer wanting to take on my case, DIA gossip all over town—I was contacted by Mikaeli, a close friend of Yolanda's and chairman of the Hellenic Society of Tanganyika. The society, a Greek community group, originated with Greek immigrants who settled in East Africa in the 1920s and 30s. Prospering in agriculture, mining and business, today the descendants of these immigrants, as well as people of many other backgrounds, send their children to St. Constantine's International School (SCIS) in Arusha. The school is owned by the Hellenic Foundation of Tanzania, a nonprofit that ensures the school maintains the highest standards of education.

Mikaeli proposed that I move to Arusha for six months and be a consultant to SCIS, assessing academic needs. The school compound was completely guarded, and a house would be available for my animals and me. I needed some income and was fed up with always looking over my shoulder. I agreed.

Before I knew it, Maggie, Mwajuma, Aztec, Gypsie, Dominic and I had squeezed ourselves into the car, and off we went on a new adventure. I would count on my lawyer Dickson Mtogesewa to further negotiate with the Jumas while I was away. (Negotiate? Mtogesewa told me a Juma relative once tried to force him off the road, resulting in a minor accident.)

ARUSHA AND SCIS

Arusha, a city with a population a little under half a million, is the capital of the Arusha Region in northern Tanzania. Enjoying a temperate climate, Arusha is close to Serengeti National Park, Olduvai Gorge, Mount Kilimanjaro and other scenic wonders.

Maggie owned a house in Arusha, and she would regularly visit and update me on DIA and its latest rumors, which included that many expat students had left the school. To get my mind off things, she and I would take day trips. We had a glorious time exploring national parks such as Tarangire and Lake Manyara.

In the meantime Mebs wrote an email: "Subject: Meeting with Mehboob Champsi-DCDM (De Chazal Du Mée Consulting Accountants and Auditors). DIA will dispose of Marilyn's property before end of October and the revenue derived will be used to offset $12,000 DCDM, $1,600 Markham Hotel, and $540 Latifa." All expenses unrelated to DIA.

My work assessing each student at SCIS produced interesting results. I concluded that Reading was above level, and Mathematics was on level, but Comprehension was far below level. This did not altogether surprise me, as I had observed that Asian and African parents aid and encourage their children to read at an early age, but do not always explain meanings to them. I found this a common problem as well in Dubai.

I liked the friendly community at SCIS, visiting all the classes, evaluating the teachers and becoming friends with some of them. Aztec was happily jumping around as monkeys were all over the place, leaping on trees, and sometimes scrambling into classrooms! If I would go away for the weekend to Dar es Salaam, my cat Gypsie would climb in a tree and not come out until she heard the engine of the Nissan. Then she'd come running to me, crying out loudly how neglected she felt! As for Dominic, he acted as if he'd always lived among monkeys in Africa!

One day Beatrix called and asked if her daughter Kerage could join SCIS and stay with me while enrolled. I knew Kerage well from our adventurous bus ride in 2003 to Bukoba on Lake Victoria via Tanzania—Kenya—Uganda. Lake Victoria, of course, is famous as the source of the Nile, and Humphrey Bogart and Katharine Hepburn memorably camped on its shores during the filming of *The African Queen*. I spent Christmas with Beatrix and Kerage in their beautiful home with a lakeview. Beatrix drove me to locations for her film *Tumaimi*, where I met beautiful people, Beatrix's relatives and friends, and for the first time I ate barbecued grasshoppers, which were delicious. After showing Kerage's transfer papers to Ms. Janet, the head of school, she was accepted. She adjusted well to the school and to living with me.

BRING OUT THE GARLIC

Then I had a spectacular run of bad luck.

I broke a leg.

Four weeks later, I broke a wrist.

Another four weeks later, I broke an arm.

Everybody started getting superstitious. Mikaeli, sure it was black magic or witchcraft, urged me to drape garlic on the fence around my house. I have to admit I was an invalid at this point and needed more live-in help. I contacted Lalita and asked if she could come. Being Sri Lankan, it was difficult for her to get a visa, as this was the time of the Tamil war. Therefore I flew her in through Kenya to Arusha, where Maggie collected her with help from a friend of a friend.

Mwajuma was a kind, soft-spoken lady. Lalita, by contrast, was quite outspoken, a good woman, but life had made her hard. Kerage and Lalita did not get along, Lalita finding fault in everything the girl did. Beatrix and I decided that Kerage should stay at the school dorm, a two-minute walk from my house.

When Mikaeli came for his next visit (he checked on my progress every two weeks) he advised me to send Lalita back. Why? News had travelled to Dar es Salaam that I had a Tamil Tiger staying with me! That wasn't true, of course, but it was a fact that all the casts except for the one on my arm had been removed, and I no longer needed the extra help. Lalita returned to Dubai—but not before she saved the nuns and their ducks from Aztec. One day my beloved husky escaped the compound. The *askaris* ran to the house, where Mwajuma and Lalita were looking after me. The women jumped into a car with me and my teacher friend Pippa. We asked people along the road if they had seen a wolf. They had, and it was heading for a nearby nunnery! We drove through the convent's gate, following the despairing gestures of the nuns to...a duck pond. Yes, there Aztec was, happily swimming and trying to catch the ducks. Luckily, we prevented him from succeeding at that and took him home, where he was washed and cleaned, scolded by Lalita and never forgotten by the nuns.

REUNION WITH MARCO

Around this time I received an email from Marco that he was coming to Tanzania for some meetings and would like to see me. He was flying into Dar es Salaam; I booked a flight to Dar, figuring we would then drive back to Arusha, as he was planning to rent a car. Eager to see him after all these years, I hurried to the airport, only to discover my flight was cancelled. Devastated, I called Maggie, who said not to worry, she would collect Marco from the airport and bring him to my home. She got to the airport, greeted Marco and his colleague Anna and told them about the cancelled flight. Maggie later told me that the first question Marco asked while walking into my house was, "Is there a man in Marilyn's life?" She replied, "No, look around. Whose photo do you see?" The only photo I had in my whole house, other than one of Anne-Lies in my bedroom, was a photo of Marco in Bali, nicely framed on my kitchen cupboard.

With tears in our eyes, Marco and I embraced when he arrived the next day in Arusha. After ten years there he was, still my Marco. Far into the night, long after everyone else had gone to sleep, we stayed up talking, crying and laughing. It was very sweet what he said to me after hearing all the problems I had with the Jumas:

> "Mer, you gave me a part of your life, I can give you six months of mine. If you want me to come and help you solve your problems, I will do that. You just have to say the word."

The next day Marco and Anna left for their meeting in Mwanza, from which they returned by crossing the Serengeti in their car. Marco promised he and I would meet again soon.

DON'T CLIMB EVERY MOUNTAIN

Not long after this I had a serious scare, and from an unexpected "corner."

Maggie's brother Christopher, a priest, joined me on a drive to a summit from which there was a view of a property for sale. First we drove to a small village at the foot of the mountain. I looked at the narrow road going up: trucks were coming down, as it was a mining locale. Some boys from the village came and offered to run before us and inform the trucks that a car was heading up, so there would not be opposing traffic.

Christopher and I waited patiently until the boys came back, and there we went, the boys, who were not older than fifteen, following us. We had almost reached the top, the car slowly driving at a fifty-degree angle, just arriving at a turn, when a truck appeared out of nowhere. I froze, unable to think. I only knew that my foot was stuck on the brake, and I couldn't take it away. Aztec was sitting in the back, Christopher beside me. I couldn't speak; images of us falling backwards from the slope, tumbling off the mountain to our deaths were messing with my mind. The truck could not reverse, and I could not go back, as I was sure I would kill us all.

The car started slipping backwards. My hand shot to the handbrake; I pulled it with all my strength, my foot on the brake trembling from the tension. Gritting my teeth, I told Christopher to take Aztec and himself out, as I was unable to move and for sure would kill us. They hurried out, and one of the boys popped his head in and said he was a truck driver, he knew the road, he would take over.

He hopped in Christopher's seat, which was on the left side of the car, me in the right seat. With his hands, he tried to take my foot off the brake. I shouted at him to please let go, that does not work, we will both die. He saw that I had completely lost it, so he got out and came in from the right-hand side of the car. He sat next to me and pushed me slowly, very slowly, towards the left side of the car, saying in his broken English, don't worry, everything will be OK. My foot was still on the brake when his bare foot came on top of mine. With his right hand he gradually pushed my foot from the brake while he held the brake with his hand, and then replaced his hand with his foot. I slid to the passenger seat, where I dared to breathe again, relieved. I studied the boy: he was totally in control, no sign of stress in his face at all. He quietly put the car in reverse and drove slowly backwards to a space in the narrow road where the truck could pass.

I couldn't wait to get out. I jumped from the car and went skiing down the mountain. The road was covered with a kind of wet red sand, and I was lucky to wear very good sports shoes, but my only thought was, OMG, I am going to break my legs again. I decided to stop my flight by sitting on my bum, hands helping me to brake. The moment I touched down, I knew I had broken my foot. After the car reached where I was sitting, Aztec, Christopher and I piled in, and I told Christopher to drive me straight to the hospital. There the doctors asked me if I'd like my whole body put in a cast—who knew physicians could be funny?—but they couldn't find a fracture. I insisted I had one, and the next day I flew to Dar es Salaam and saw a well-known diagnostician who took an x-ray and diagnosed a fracture on the side of my foot. Again I was in a cast. The next day Maggie drove me back to Arusha, where everybody was shaking their heads and draping more garlic over my fence.

Hopping on my crutches, I crossed school property with Mikaeli at my side, advising him on the day-to-day running of the school. School head Janet Mmari was a nice lady, but not capable of running a school, and she knew it. She practically begged the board of the Hellenic Foundation to replace her, but she had been working with them for many years, and they trusted no one else.

AN OFFER OF HELP

One day Janet called me into her office and closed the door behind us. She said a man had called asking for Marilyn Wouters. He did not give his name but had left a number to call. He had stressed that he did not belong to the Juma clan and was calling to help me. Janet and I looked at each other wonderingly. I dialed the number.

The man introduced himself as Ric Endersby. He said he was working and living at DIS (Dar es Salaam Independent School), that he had experience in the law, and was interested in knowing and helping me. I remembered him attending Mebs's birthday party in the company of the owner of DIS, a woman named Susan Huxtable.

Since a long weekend was coming up, my new friend Philippa (Pippa), who had become best friends with Aztec and Aztec with her, decided to go with me to Dar, taking all the animals with us. Mwajuma would spend the time visiting her mother and her children, who lived in the area.

We arrived in Dar and in the late afternoon arranged to meet Ric at a beach near DIS. He was a tall, blond man, quite attractive. Ric gave me suggestions on how to deal with the Jumas, whom he had known for many years, as the Juma children had attended DIS. He also was prepared to write official letters to all government and official institutions involved. I did not need to retell much of my experiences because he had heard the whole story from different sources, and knowing the Jumas, had translated it to his own version, which was actually quite correct. Finally, he admitted that he wanted to get out of DIS and start his own school and wondered if I would be willing to partner up with him. It was late that night that we left him. Pippa told me it was her impression that there had been a lot of flirting going on between Ric and me.

The next day I met with Tellan and Patsy and told them about Ric. Tellan looked me in the eyes and told me to be careful. From what I was telling him, he said, he suspected Ric was a "player."

I put my feelers out, asking everyone I knew who might have encountered Ric to give me his or her impressions. His reputation as a teacher was good. On a personal level, everybody thought that he was in a relationship with Susan, but there were also rumors of him being gay, as he was regularly seen with young men on his bike.

Before returning to Arusha, I met with Ric alone and asked the questions arising from my investigations. I needed to know whom I was partnering with, determined not to repeat the mistakes I'd made with the Jumas.

Ric told me about himself. He was born in Zimbabwe, where his parents had a farm but lost most of it due to regime change. He always had loads of girlfriends but could never stay faithful, so he never married. He had several children with different mothers. After Susan established DIS, she contacted Ric and invited him to teach there. When he arrived, she brought him to her home directly to her bedroom. Truth was, he wasn't interested in Susan romantically; in fact, he had recently come to the conclusion that he was gay. Ric explained to me that during the regime change in Zimbabwe he had ended up in jail for quite a long time. There his cellmate was an African man. They befriended each other, fell in love and became intimate. He realized how fulfilling this was for him, and never felt the same way for a woman again. His daughter Felicia lived with him, and Susan took care of her, for which Ric was grateful but somewhat resentful to be always in her debt. Over time he and Susan created their own lifestyle and habits. Their grocery shopping, dinners, vacations, and long weekends were spent with the three of them all together, but otherwise they lived basically apart. This was acceptable to Ric until the moment he got it into his mind to open his own school. He wanted to be independent, beyond the control of Susan (whom I had reason to think was actually a very nice lady).

I told Ric I needed to think about all this and would be in contact with him.

A SATISFYING NEWS STORY

The same day I had an appointment with one of the banks that had given DIA loans. Here I discovered that the damage was much greater than I had believed. Faking my signature, the Juma family had borrowed another $500,000 USD against my securities. Anyone looking closely could have recognized the forgeries. And how could a bank give such a loan without seeing me in person? Giving a loan against MY securities? We went through many documents, fake signature after fake signature. Mebs and Parviz had no scruples.

I asked to see the bank manager. I told him my story, and he asked if I could run the school without the Jumas. "Of course I could," I said. It was my school; they were the ones incapable of running it. The manager said he would call the following week, as he first needed to discuss the matter with other parties involved. The week passed, he didn't phone. When I called the bank and asked for him, he was always out. Finally, I gave up, knowing corruption had won again.

I received an unexpected call from the man who supposedly should have been our business partner from the beginning and then had dropped out. He told me I should immediately get the weekly Swahili newspaper, whose name I now have forgotten, as there was a front-page article on Mebs. I called Maggie, who drove off to get it. She returned with a triumphant smile on her face, which alternated with a look of embarrassment. She said she had to go to many newsstands before finally finding this last copy. The front page showed a photo of Mebs, naked except for a little towel, staring in shock at the camera.

The story went as follows: Mebs owed money to a local businessman. Months passed, empty promises were given but no money. Ready to tear his hair out, the businessman picked up a newspaper and happened to see an ad E-Fulusi had placed for a secretary.

He came up with a creative, funny and vicious plan.

The businessman sent his wife to apply for the job. Mebs interviewed her. She was a beautiful woman, and she let him imagine that to get the job she would be willing to be intimate with him. She suggested they go to a hotel in the evening; her husband would be out of town on a business trip. Mebs happily agreed. After all, he deserved a distraction from his difficult life, juggling his relationships with quarrelsome Parviz and his girlfriend (he had moved in with a young Muslim Tanzanian lady).

Smiling the whole day, anticipating a pleasurable evening, Mebs made himself presentable and went to the appointed hotel, where the woman received him in a room. After they exchanged pleasantries, she told him to undress himself while she went to the bathroom to prepare herself for him. Panting with excitement, Mebs got undressed and jumped into bed. Just then, the door to the hall opened. A photographer sprinted in, snapping photos, the husband of the "new secretary" right behind him. Mebs leaped out of bed and covered his erection with a bath towel. The businessman furiously beat Mebs, while the photographer shot countless photos. At last, Mebs was permitted to get dressed, then instructed to be back in an hour with the money he owed. If he failed to do so, the photos would be published in the local newspaper.

Perhaps Mebs truly couldn't get his hands on the cash that quickly, or perhaps he didn't believe the businessman would be so devious as to publish his indiscretion. Whatever he thought, he didn't deliver the money. When nothing appeared in the papers the next following days, Mebs might have regained his self-confidence, who knows? But the next Tuesday, he was there for everybody to see on the front page (the article continuing on the second page). His full name was printed, as well as photos of his nearly naked body. Maggie and I laughed until we cried. Tellan and Patsy passed by to see the photos for themselves. The story was "out there" for everybody to read. The Juma children and Parviz (still his wife) were livid, as the news could harm the school's reputation. I believe it was then that they decided Mebs was not to appear on the school property again.

Mebs fought back. He sued the newspaper, and through his corrupt police connections, got the photographer thrown in jail.

"SO, YOU ARE A THIEF?"

Soon after this, Maggie was driving me to some place when I spotted a big Sony billboard on the side of the road. It jarred my memory: nearly a year earlier, before my nervous breakdown, Mebs had taken my very expensive widescreen TV out to be repaired. He always brought his electronics to the shop next to Gators Gym. Mebs owned this gym, bought with DIA money, which was not far from a police station, and many of the gym clients were policemen, so you can see how Mebs's web of corruption could have spread. I asked Maggie to take me to the repair shop, where I asked for my TV. They remembered the job and told me that they weren't able to make the repair, so Mebs had taken the TV to a Sony service shop. We went there and were told the TV had been fixed and claimed by Mebs. I asked Maggie to call the owner of the tabloid and tell him to come immediately; if he wanted revenge for his photographer's jail time, he could have it now.

Maggie took me to the police to report the theft. Luck was on our side: the head of the Organized Crime Division (OCD) was a person

Maggie knew. He instructed one of his sergeants to call Mebs. That officer didn't even have to ask for Mebs's number: he had it stored in his phone. Everybody knew Mebs! The two of them spoke in Kiswahili, so I eagerly waited for the OCD head to translate their conversation. He explained to me that Mebs was not willing to come, that he had told the sergeant he is not in Dar. The OCD head ordered the officer to call Mebs back, then grabbed up the phone himself and warned Mebs that if he failed to appear within thirty minutes, there'd be hell to pay.

The tabloid owner joined us while we waited for Mebs. The police had no clue who he was; everybody assumed he was Maggie's brother. By the way, Maggie purposely remained in the rear of the room. She had friends in high places to call upon if necessary, but meanwhile let me run the show.

Mebs appeared at the eleventh hour. He seemed relieved when he saw me, perhaps thinking he could charm me once again. When the door closed behind him, though, and he turned around to see Maggie, his face fell. The OCD head asked Mebs if he knew me. Mebs confirmed this, and actually said I was his very good friend, his sister (!) He still had no clue what this matter was about. He was asked if he knew where my TV was. He hemmed and hawed, and finally admitted that the TV was in his house. "So, you are a thief?" the OCD head asked. Mebs said nothing. He was informed that he was now under arrest, and a report was drawn up. Two police officers drove him and "Maggie's brother" in a police Land Rover to his premises, and the TV and accessories were brought to the police station warehouse for stolen goods, where they were registered. After hours of bureaucracy and signing of all parties, I was given back my belongings. Mebs started shouting, threatening to open a case against Maggie. She coolly replied that we were already at the police station. Why not file charges here and now?

Mebs left, tail between his legs.

Maggie and I had confidently stood our ground and enjoyed a laugh at Mebs's expense. My lawyer was Don Quixote, tilting at windmills, but at least now I had one small victory that did me good.

SASKIA AND JOBURG

Saskia wrote that she might have found a buyer for my land in Costa Rica. She suggested I give her power of attorney, and she would arrange the sale and send me the money. As we had successfully made this arrangement once before, I had no objections. Marco flew me out to Johannesburg, where I signed the POA at the Costa Rican consulate. I remember clearly that the lady consul asked me if I was sure I wanted to sign this document, as I gave all power to Saskia. I confirmed that she was a friend, from my home country, and because she had dealt with me before when I bought the property, I trusted her. I signed the paperwork and sent it to Costa Rica.

I went to Joburg and had a great time there with Marco and Anna, journalists who were planning to attend a convention of big shots in the mining business in Africa. While they were in their apartment and I was out on the terrace, they were calling people and making appointments. Marco and Anna were saying there was only one man they had wanted to reach thus far and couldn't: Grant Pierce. I came in from the terrace and said, "Sorry to disturb you, but are you guys talking about Grant Pierce, the Australian mine guy?" They looked at me with surprise as I continued, "I know him. Do you want me to call him?" While I was having all my problems with the Jumas, Grant had offered his assistance. I called, left a message, and not even three minutes later my phone rang: Grant Pierce. I told him that I was in Joburg with friends and that they had tried to reach him, as they wanted to see him at the convention in Cape Town the following week. I handed the phone to Anna, who made an appointment. How small the world really is!

Back to Saskia. She received the POA in January 2007, and we continued communicating through writing. In May 2007 she wrote "no worries," she had a buyer and could sell the property for $160,000 USD, but she needed money for cleaning the property. I wrote to her she could keep $60,000; I needed $100,000 and she could pay the cleaning from her commission. She sent me regular emails until February 2008. Thereafter she did not reply to my phone calls or emails. I had a strange intuitive feeling, so I asked my friend Pascual, still living in Spain and now co-owner of a bar in Barcelona, to check the Registro Nacional of Costa Rica. He did and sadly wrote back that the property had been sold to a company in April 2007 for around $9,665 USD. He added that he suspected that was not the price the company actually paid.

I wrote to everybody I knew in Costa Rica. Nobody could help. Several of the people who have houses around my plot were told that, at the last minute, I chose not to sell; others were told that I was sent the money. Saskia's ex-husband said she did not transfer me the money because she had a "problem" with me.

I got a hold of copies of all correspondence between Saskia, the realtor who was her go-between, the buyers and their lawyer. It was clear I had been conned. Rumors were that Saskia bought her dream place in Panama with my money...this after years of her being a drug addict. I also heard that Saskia's husband was homeless and bumming across Central America doing odd jobs.

CHACLALMA

Marco invited me to spend time with him and the family in Italy in their house Chaclalma, which was named after themselves: Chango-Claudia-Alejandra-Marco. It would be ten years since I had laid eyes on Chango. I was sitting in the living room when he arrived. All the kids went outside to greet him. When he came in I looked back and rose, he coming toward me saying, "Que imbranata!" and we embraced. I think I cried. I still loved him. It was beautiful to meet the whole family again. As always, I was treated like a princess by Marco and his sisters.

Chango and Marco became my advisers after I returned to Tanzania, calling me weekly to be updated. Marco offered again to come to Tanzania and help me solve my problems. I did not want the young man to put his career on hold, and refused his offer.

A NEED FOR GUIDANCE

My lawyer back in Dar es Salaam was costing me lots of money with no results, and what I had earned consulting at SCIS would not last me much longer. I was approached by Ric additional times about starting a new school. Maggie also wanted this project and was ready to put her house forward as a guarantee for a loan.

So should I start all over again? Looking for guidance, I phoned Barry Lee, the medium I had met years ago in Marbella. Here are excerpts from the transcript taken from his communication.

> *Marilyn, I am gonna tell you what Spirits said before you called. They said to me to tell you whether you like it or not, you're actually not living in the right place.... I'm telling you according to the guides that Europe is a much better location for you.... They say you are but one light in a very, very dark place, and they say that one little candle can't do enough because there is not enough people joining you to light up the rest of this place.... [The Spirits] stress that...the southern part of Europe is much better for you. They say don't run away from it again, the opportunities will be there.... Once you're back in Europe, I get everything flowing very smoothly, and remember, as a very old, highly evolved soul, nowhere on earth will be perfect for you. But, I don't know if you were ever told this before, after this life, you are not coming back here, you understand? You're not coming to earth. You're finished. That's good news, isn't it? They are saying here, that will be the end of the journey here.... When you go to Spirit they will say, What did you do when you went to so and so place? You can say, Oh, I failed, they are not interested. They will ask, well did you try? And you can turn around and say, Well, I tried. That's what it is all about, at least you tried. It is not a matter of the outcome with your life as it is at the moment; it's a matter that you have tried.... We cannot battle certain areas and win, people aren't ready, they are not gonna listen, they love power and cruelty. All we can do is just shine a light, drop the seeds, and it is up to them if they will pick up on it. So now you need to come back and take care of Number One, be more selfish for a change and make your life easier. That is what they want you to do. You've done your bit now. Come home.*

Since I had visited the Peraltas in Italy, I was not sure what to do. Stay in Tanzania and open a school again or return to Europe!

Grant Pierce called to tell me he was in Dar, so I met with him in a hotel garden close to his residence. I immediately saw that I had made a mistake to bring Maggie with me, because he had wanted to meet me on my own. The result was a brief but memorable get-together. To me Grant resembled a cuddly teddy bear, but he was actually a tough businessman. He had over twenty-five years of experience in both open-pit and underground mining operations and in a range of commodities including gold, copper, iron ore and rare earth elements. He had extensive management experience, including serving as an executive general manager for Barrick. Possessor of a big heart, Grant was awarded the Order of Australia Medal in 2003 for his personal contribution to social development in rural Tanzania, and in 2006 he was given Tanzania's Zeze Award, the highest accolade for outstanding contribution to Tanzanian culture. There are many more positive things I could say about Grant, but for me, personally, I was very grateful for his sympathy regarding my financial troubles and advice for my professional career.

DO WE REALLY WANT TO DO THIS?
Another DIA parent called me. Her husband was building a boarding school in Shinyanga in northern Tanzania, and she asked if we could discuss it. She, her husband, Ric and I flew out to Shinyanga to examine the plot, which was a good size and surrounded by savannah. For sure it had potential, but it wasn't what I was looking for. At this point, Ric was assuming he would be the principal of the school, I his secretary. Unfortunately for him, the owners asked me to be the boss; they had no intention of employing him at all. A few years later, however, he was hired as a teacher at Savannah Plains International School.

Ric, Maggie and I continued searching for locations in and around Dar. The problem now was that Ric wanted a secondary school, and Maggie and I wanted a primary. For weeks we drove from one side of Dar es Salaam to the other. There was always something wrong for Ric, although some offers were really good. Ric decided he wanted a new-ly constructed, glass-walled building on a main road, what he thought would be a perfect, if very expensive, site for a high school. Over the phone I discussed my dilemma with Chango, and told him I felt uncom-fortable with Ric's ideas. I also felt pushed by Maggie, who is very ambi-tious and wanted to prove herself towards her Austrian doctor husband, who too often made her feel like a loser.

I had sent Ric's business plan to Chango to confirm my thoughts about it. I think Maggie and I were just so bombarded by Ric that we started to believe in him. She and I went to the bank, I deposited my money, Maggie's house was appraised, and we received a bank check for a deposit on a property Ric wanted. The landlord was a man named Aahad, who had set a tight deadline to respond. Maggie and I headed to a hotel bar with the check and waited for Ric to join us. I looked at Maggie and assured her, "Don't worry, Aahad won't take the check, we are too late. When you come back, just act as if you are very disappointed that he did not take it." I felt my angels were there and nothing would happen to us: Aahad would not accept the check. Ric came and gave Maggie instructions on what to do and who to ask for. Maggie left with her head down, as if bound for the scaffold. She and I did not want to take that building, but I knew Aahad would not take the check. We had left him hanging too long. I was sure…but waiting for Maggie to return was torture.

After half an hour, Maggie came back, head up but looking very sadly at Ric. In a graveyard voice she said, "Aahad did not want to see me, and he did not want to accept the check. The building is rented to somebody else." Ric was furious. Maggie and I stifled laughter. Once we were alone in the car, we let it all out!

Coming home, I looked again at Ric's business plan and compared it with mine. I decided his was a fantasy, and mine was reality. Feeling strong, I called him to meet with Maggie and me that evening. I told him what I thought of his business plan, and pointed out that he had almost bankrupted Maggie by trying to manipulate us into renting a building we couldn't afford. Therefore Maggie and I had decided we didn't want to have him as our business partner. Ric left in a furious temper, rejected by two ladies who had finally got their acts together.

That same evening Chango called and warned me not to invest Maggie's house, as she would lose everything. That business plan was a load of rubbish, he said. I told him what had happened that day, and that Maggie and I would look at something that would suit us both.

MAGGIE, BIRIKAA AND I

Clearly, Maggie has been an important part of my life. I asked her to write her memories of a special experience we shared. Here is an edited version of what she sent me.

Onaipanoi's (Maggie's) Story

I am a Maasai, one of the first girls to be educated.... I became friends with Marilyn during the time that my children entered DIA, after I had moved back to Tanzania with my Austrian husband and three children. I liked to communicate with Marilyn in German to practice the language, which I had learned while living in Austria. During her ordeal with the Jumas, I was happy to help her, as I am Tanzanian and she is a foreigner. I was glad the Greek society brought her to Arusha to consult for them and protect her in their school. It was a good opportunity to visit her regularly, as I had a home in Arusha.

During the time that Marilyn was breaking so many bones, I heard from her house girl Mwajuma, who was still in contact with the house girls of the Juma family. Those house girls reported that the family had seen one of the best witch doctors or black magic doctors in Tanzania. Black magic and witch doctors are very common in Africa. The family had fasted for one week to destroy Marilyn and/or get her out of the country. It was a fact that Marilyn's health was not good. In addition to her fractures, she was smoking three packs of cigarettes a day and having nightmares.

I told Marilyn about my uncle Birikaa Ole Kereto. He is a highly respected and powerful Maasai leader, consulted on cultural rituals regarding childbirth, circumcision, the giving of names and other matters. When I explained that he was also a great laiboni *(healer) Marilyn wished to see him. This was not an easy task, as he moved around constantly from one* boma *(Maasai corral or village) to another. I had not seen him for thirty years. Very early one Saturday morning, we drove to Manyara [a Tanzanian admin-istrative region] to a village called Mswakini, where we found him. He was visiting one of his fifty wives, at a* boma *close to Tarangire National Park. When we arrived he was not outside. We met him coming out of one of the huts. He looked at me and put his hand on my head and said, "I knew my blood is here." He invited us to stay a couple of days (one never knows how long that is). We were invited into a hut made of cow dung, which was divided into two sleeping areas and one living area. The hut was dark inside, but one got slowly used to this and saw the figures sitting around. The women were instructed to give us tea and fresh milk from the cows. A goat was slaughtered and prepared in our honor. Normally a woman is not allowed to attend the slaughter itself, the work done by the young men. However, when the slaughter was over, one of Birikaa's sons, Mepukori, called Marilyn and she was allowed to take photos. They were very proud to show her that it is their custom to drink the blood and eat the testicles. The goat's liver was prepared on the fire with herbs, and Marilyn pronounced it the best she had ever eaten.*

Night having fallen, Marilyn and I took our sleeping bags and went into the thatched home of one of Birikaa's wives. The home looked clean but was dark, hot and a bit smoky inside. We were shown a bed made of wood and twigs and covered with a cowhide, big enough for almost four people. We climbed up on the bed and slept. In the middle of the night we felt something crawling on our bodies, and when Marilyn switched on the flashlight, we saw a kind of bloodsucker. We swiped them off, but they were already full of our blood. We smeared ourselves with bug repellant, and the rest of our sleep was peaceful. When we woke up, we hung our sleeping bags outside so that the bugs could crawl out.

After a cup of tea my uncle called us and talked to us. He asked many questions about Marilyn. He called her Naisula *(the Winner) and started telling her about the Jumas and all her sufferings, and how she could recover her investments. I asked my uncle if it was possible to go with him to Dar es Salaam for a few days, where he could perform his magic for Marilyn and get back from the Jumas all that she had lost. He agreed, and we left together, he bringing his bag of animal skins, powders, and other things he needed to heal and clean. He also brought Mepukori and one of his wives. A young man, Mepukori was the chosen one, destined to follow in Birikaa's footsteps and become a spiritual leader of the Maasai.*

Marilyn told me she understood my uncle without talking, as they communicated by mind. While she was driving to Dar es Salaam, my uncle sitting beside her, he told her to shut her eyes and drive. She looked at him, he nodded. She closed her eyes for at least two minutes and continued quietly driving, while he guided her.

On arrival in Dar, my uncle settled into Marilyn's house. He had only been in the city once before, when the late President Kikwete met with him. Word spread that Birikaa was in town. Many Maasai came to visit and pay their respects. We went sightseeing with Birikaa, and people would stare at us. He was like a picture from the past, wearing a little hat, holding a big tusk in his hands. (As a Maasai laiboni, *he had special permission to carry animal tusks; it is forbidden for others to do so.) We headed to DIA. Birikaa entered, nobody stopped him, and he cleaned the whole area. Coming home, he suffered from a bad headache. Marilyn tried to heal him by using her mind, but he looked at her and shook his head. He told me that her healing was too strong for him. Birikaa also told her that her powers were as strong as his, but that she did not know how to use them.*

We all went to bed early that night. The next morning Birikaa rolled out a snakeskin measuring four meters long (approximately thirteen feet). Marilyn had to walk back and forth on the skin while he uttered words in Maa *(the Maasai language). The rest of the day he went through the house, checking under beds and mattresses, under and in cupboards to see if anybody hid black magic stuff there, as this is very common. He did not find anything, so he put his own stuff there. From that moment onwards, Marilyn's nightmares were gone.*

Normally in the evening, Birikaa's wife would go to bed first, then he would follow, and after an hour or so young Mepukori would follow. This night Birikaa went to bed first. Marilyn was sitting at her computer as always, working on proposals, calculations and business plans. She saw that Birikaa had gone to bed, but did not think anything about it, until a voice in her head told her to come to the bedroom. She looked at the wife and Mepukori, who were smiling, not moving. Marilyn shook her head at Mepukori: no way she was going to sleep with Birikaa! So sitting in front of the computer stoically, she telepathically communicated back that she was not interested, and that he should call his wife instead. Five minutes later Birikaa came through the hallway, looked at Marilyn, smiled and called his wife. The smile on Mepukori's face stretched even wider.

Birikaa had stayed four days and felt it was time to leave. The next day we drove him back to his boma *in Ngorongoro Endulen village. It was the last time Marilyn saw him.*

The days that we spent in the boma *with all the men, women and children who had walked many, many kilometers to greet us, were very special to Marilyn. She learned firsthand that the Maasai are a very kind and friendly people. They do not have our luxuries, but they share everything they have. I will always have fond memories of this experience with Marilyn.*
Onaipanoi (Margarethe) Oberressl

THE BLACK BACKPACKER

As you all know by now, I love Marco very much, but the following story must be told. It became famous, or perhaps infamous, in the family, and it has its own catchword: Backpacker.

Marco came again to visit me from South Africa. Having spent the whole day at Bongoyo Island (a popular resort area) with Tellan and Patsy, he planned to join them for some drinks. On this occasion, Manfred, Maggie's husband, went too, and they left in Manfred's car.

I never knew what time they came home, but when I got up the next morning and walked into the kitchen, I sensed something was different. I stepped into my living room, and there on my big leather sofa were two people, one of them naked. I could look directly into her pussy. I think I stood there for several seconds with my mouth open, before walking straight back to my kitchen and out the door to Maggie's house, where Maggie and Mwajuma already had made breakfast for us all, as we were also expecting Tellan and Patsy. I saw on their faces that the women "knew" and were waiting for words to come out of my mouth. The gardener was told, and he stole a look through my kitchen window, returning with an expression of shocked dismay. Mwajuma clearly disapproved; she was a devoted Muslim. Maggie and I did not really know how to react, so we giggled, looked again in the living room and shamefully giggled again. Marco was an adult man, she was an adult woman, and we were sure she was a prostitute. They were both sleeping soundly. As I walked closer, I saw condoms on the floor and sighed with relief.

I got dressed and went back outside to the garden where the breakfast table was waiting, full of good food. While I was still debating if I should wake the couple, Maggie discovered that the front window on the left side of her car was broken. Both Manfred and Marco were still sleeping, so we couldn't ask them what happened. Patsy and Tellan arrived on the scene. We told them about Marco and the girl. Tellan listened and took action. He told us that if she is a prostitute, she has to get out immediately, as she would steal everything in sight. He asked me if I was a crazy woman to allow her to sleep in my living room. I told him that I was as shocked as he was to see them both lying there.

Tellan entered the living room, took a moment to enjoy the view of the pussy, and then shouted in Kiswahili, "Wake up and get out of here!" Marco sat up, blinking, still drunk and disoriented. Tellan escorted the girl off the property, she running to the front gate. Marco quickly dressed and followed. I believe he found her at a coffee kiosk and paid for her taxi. On returning, he saw the expressions on our faces and said, "What is your problem?" Tellan responded that he should not have brought a prostitute into my house. Marco replied, "But she isn't a prostitute, she's a backpacker." As I write this, I'm still laughing. We looked at him with surprise and disbelief. I said, "What kind of a backpacker? There are no black backpackers, Marco! Where would she be from?" He answered, "Kenya." OMG! Tears fell from our eyes, we were laughing so hard, Marco wearing a look of total conviction. For sure he believed it himself, the backpacker from Kenya.

This is the story Marco has to live with for the rest of his life.

So, that problem solved, we all enjoyed our breakfast until Manfred came over and Maggie questioned him about the broken car window. Marco, like an adult, accepted the blame. As he and Manfred had driven from the pub at two in the morning, two women followed them. Manfred could not bring one home, so one was left behind at the pub. The snubbed woman took a big stone and threw it at the car as they drove off, smashing the window. Marco said he would pay for it. That should have resolved the matter, but Manfred started attacking *me* for no reason, shouting, "You are a child!" He, who had previously told me that I was the only one with whom he could truly converse and communicate; he who would regularly come to my house for a chat, now heaped verbal abuse upon me.

Tellan told him to shut up. Manfred lifted his fists and looked ready to hit Tellan and me. Marco jumped in and warned Manfred, "Don't touch her or I'll beat you up!" Manfred calmed down. Maggie and I were happy to escape this turmoil and jump in the car to drive the next eight hours to Arusha, where we had an appointment.

THE DJINNS WITHIN
For a brief while after Birikaa's treatment, my nightmares vanished. Gradually, however, the sleepless nights returned, and I felt as if a stone weighed upon my heart and stomach. Over lunch I mentioned this to my German friend Silke. She advised me to go to Dr. Kombe Sango

Jumbe, a priest who had studied astrology in Tibet. Assuring me he had helped her a lot, she drove us to a very poor area of Dar es Salaam where there were no streets, only huts and sand tracks. The priest was there and agreed to see me at once. He asked my name, wrote many numbers in Arabic on a little board on the floor and ended up with a column on the left and a triangle in the middle. He explained the astrological significance of the numbers, and used them to understand the events of my life over the previous two years.

He said I was bewitched.

Djinns (genies) had been put into me by different people, he said. He indicated their gender and described their personalities, even imitating the way each spoke, so I knew whom he was talking about: the Jumas, no question. The priest told me to come back on Monday at 4 P.M. to be washed. (It was a ritual that could only be successfully performed on Thursdays and Mondays.)

Silke came with me again. I was cleansed in the presence of burning incense. Then I covered myself and went to a room where many men were loudly praying. I had to sit in the middle of them near a small table with four coconuts on it. I was instructed to hold the first coconut and make my wishes, then the second, third and fourth. This all took about ten minutes. Then Dr. Kombe and a pair of assistants gathered up the coconuts and took me to a small stone room, Silke remaining in the room beside it. Dr. Kombe gave me the coconuts one by one and told me to throw them separately in all four directions. It was very important to break them, he said.

Since childhood, I never wanted to have anything to do with ball-games. On the receiving end, I was always scared of the ball hitting or hurting me, and as a pitcher, I didn't have great aim. However, I focused on the task before me. I threw coconut number one. It split into many parts. Coconut number two also shattered. I put all my strength into throwing number three, and it broke into a thousand pieces. I threw number four, expecting it to be smashed to smithereens. No. Hitting the stone floor intact, in slow motion it reversed back toward me.

I couldn't believe it. I heard the priest gasp, his assistants stared, astonished. My eyes were glued to that stupid coconut. I knew just one thing: No way, no way were "they" going to destroy me. (You know the "they" I mean.) I had believed what I'm always preaching, that "God is stronger than the devil," but I was so mad now that I picked up that coconut, brought it to shoulder height and heaved it with all my power, thinking, *I will destroy all of you.*

The coconut exploded against the wall.

I knew at that instant that I had to be the one to battle the dark forces around me. No one else could do it for me.

The priest hugged me and kept saying, "That was unique, that was unique!" He told me (like many others have said before) that I have great powers but I don't use them. He said never in his life had he thought to see this; he had heard of it, but never expected to witness such an event. He asked if he could mention it in a book he was writing. I told him I would mention him in *my* book.

As the priest explained, when a coconut or other object fails to break, typically the thrower runs away in fear, and the curse persists. When I grasped the coconut, threw it back and destroyed it, I returned to my enemies all the evil they had wished for me. I had vanquished the power of the witch/voodoo men.

CHANGES

Feeling a sense of renewal, I flew to the Netherlands to visit my father on his birthday, as I tried to do every year. I unburdened to him all my problems, including financial ones. In a gesture as unexpected as it was kind, Dad gave me 20,000 euros (about $22,000 USD). I was so thankful, especially since it moved me closer to the possibility of moving out of Africa, once I had resolved my problems with the Jumas.

Marco suggested we get together in Cape Town, and I flew in at the same time as Claudia. We really enjoyed each other's company, swapping stories and sharing laughs. A few years ago, Claudia had moved to Marbella, Spain, with her boyfriend Morgan and had her own business, India Exotica, where she sold Indian antiques. She did all the acquiring and spent a great deal of time in India, while Morgan dealt with the business side of it all.

With Marco we tasted wine, visited a cheetah farm and explored the country's coastal areas before flying back to Joburg. There and then Claudia suggested I come to Spain, stay with her and see where my life was going. At this point Morgan had moved out, the relationship was over, and Claudia and I knew each other well enough to know we could handle living together for a while. We both returned to our homes, and I started planning my trip to Spain.

Around this time, Gypsie disappeared. Mwajuma and I searched for the cat everywhere, street in street out, but there was no sign of her. I was very distressed.

The year's lease on my Dar home would soon run out. I asked Mama Mkapa if I could leave the big house and rent the guest wing on the compound. It was more affordable, and big enough for me and Dominic and Aztec. What's more, the security guards would still be there. She agreed to this.

INCONTROVERTIBLE EVIDENCE

I started negotiations with Nadeem Juma and met with him and his crooked lawyer Frederick Ringo. I told them for absolute clarification that I was the plaintiff, and Mr. Mehboob Juma, as the head of the Juma family, was the defendant. I reminded them again that I had agreed to lend Mr. Juma my personal funds, after constant pleading by him and his wife, so that they could pay educational and living fees for their children Shaista and Hafiz. The source of funds was my personal account at Credit Suisse; the method of payment was by electronic transfer; and the destination of the funds was to the respective educational institutions of these two children. The evidence was thus incontrovertible. I expected this loan back, plus the sales of my shares at DIA. I informed them that I was going to Spain and would return soon, to which Mr. Ringo very unprofessionally and mockingly replied, "You'd better stay where you go and never come back." I looked at Nadeem with disgust, and left him and Ringo with my email address.

OFF TO SPAIN

Ric the Zimbabwean had moved to a small house on the beach. He agreed to have Aztec stay with him until my return from Spain. However, I would be bringing Dominic with me, so that I knew it was not completely a holiday, but a trial test for returning to Europe to live there permanently.

I sold my valuables to friends; they especially appreciated my furniture, which was of a kind difficult to find in Tanzania, all antiques from Rajastan. My convertible Merc would be looked after by a mechanic friend. My Nissan Hardbody was with Tellan and Patsy, who would try to sell it. Everything else was stored in my little guesthouse.

Mwajuma, who had found another job but checked in regularly, drove me to the airport. Along the way, she confessed a terrible secret she had kept. I had neighbors who would turn their sound systems up so loud that I could not hear myself talking to friends. It was disco level, really. I went to their house and asked them politely to turn it down. This they did, but the next time they found my Gypsie in their garden, they took her and threw her repeatedly against the wall until she died. This story was told to Mwajuma by another neighbor. Mwajuma had not dared to tell me, knowing I would cause big problems not only for those people but also for myself. Hearing about this brutal act, I cried and cried, glad I would be leaving such heartless people behind. I got on the plane heading to a new life. I was sixty years old, and it was December 2007.

FRIENDSHIP

Claudia and Nika, her little dog, waited for me at the airport in Malaga. We collected Dominic from customs and went straight to Claudia's apartment in a small village called Nueva Andalucía. Dominic established himself immediately and took ownership of Nika's toys. It took a while for Nika to accept this big lion cat, but after a few days the pair became friends.

I quickly felt at home in Claudia's apartment. She was not only beautiful but intelligent, very hospitable, and a friend. She cooked the most amazing pastas. She's the Pasta Queen! At her request I started working at India Exotica and did the accounts. Spain's economy had been hit hard, and it was tough to break even. Morgan, Claudia's ex and business partner, spent all his time in Tarifa, where he was building a restaurant. She went there regularly to help, unable to cut the tie that had bound them together for many years. Morgan did not make the breakup easy; whenever he came to Marbella and saw Claudia's sad face, he used to hold her and tell her how amazing she was. She confused this behavior with love. The situation between them worsened after I discovered there were discrepancies in the accounts, and Morgan had used funds from India Exotica and Claudia's private account to build his business in Tarifa, of which Claudia was not a shareholder. Although her well-developed brain understood the facts I gave her, she tended to act in opposition to my suggestions. Her emotions ran high and controlled her thought processes... How well I knew the feeling!

Claudia and I would walk in the mountains surrounding Marbella or stroll on the beaches. We'd shiver in the winter breeze while Nika gamboled along the shore. Claudia's personal life was not at a high point, so we did a lot of sitting, eating, reading, and listening to the sad songs of Norah Jones, which of course made us sadder. But something good definitely came of my visit. From the moment I arrived in Spain, I did not touch a cigarette again, and my insomnia was gone. I was becoming a different person, a stronger one. Claudia's love and kindness, with the help of CDs by Norah Jones, Louise Hay and Eckhart Tolle, had shown me the way.

Claudia went to see her sister in the US, where she also met up with her dad and brother. As soon as she left, I called Morgan and asked him to meet me. Over a good meal, I asked him if he intended to get back with Claudia. No, he said. I asked him if it was his intention to hurt her. He denied this. "So why," I demanded, "are you hugging her and telling her that she is amazing all the time?"

Morgan looked at me with surprise; he had no clue that he was hurting her. I immediately thought of the book *Men Are from Mars, Women Are from Venus*. How different the emotions of males and females work!

Morgan just wanted to be kind, but Claudia clung to every straw and confused it with "He still has feelings." I told him to stop. I asked him to please not touch her anymore when she returns from the US, not to cause her anymore pain. He understood and promised.

I HEAR FROM BARRY LEE

When Claudia returned from the States, she bought me a Christmas present: a reading from Barry Lee. I made an appointment on my mother's birthday. This is an edited transcript of his reading.

> *Barry Lee 18 Jan 2008*
>
> *A very strong person came in, and the lady said she is your mother. She wants to thank you for your thoughts, especially leading up to now, because it is a special day, but it is not special to her any longer. I hope you will understand that. She wants you to know that she is very happy, extremely happy…. She is awfully proud of you. She says you're doing well in this life and what you are meant to be doing. She does not measure things by what you think you should be doing, it is karma or God what you should be doing…. She has been looking at where you are living at the moment. It is a nice place she says, but not for you, you understand? She talks about living in Spain. You are not living here, but it would be nice if you did…. You are very much alone on this earth, [your mom] is saying, that is the way you feel at times, that is why you don't want to make the changes, because what you've got you got, and when you move on you ask, Oh, what have I got? But you will be moving to a new family. It is not blood, but it is people of whom you'll think, "I know them!" like in a spiritual family together. So if you take the chance, you will not be alone there…. Your mom has just said to me about the book you are writing of your life [that] you're not fully done. She says you gotta get going with that.... She is coming over giving you a great big kiss there, which is on your left side, and she says I always will be around you. I always will be there, whenever you need me, call…. Your mum has chosen your place and as soon as you are*

there you will know, either it is a sense, a smell, a memory, but you will know, it is your mum.

MY DECISION IS MADE

I called Mwajuma and asked her to meet me at my house in a week and help me pack the personal belongings I wanted to ship to Spain. I informed Maggie, Tellan and Patsy that I would be arriving. I called the shipping company, and collected Aztec from Ric. Mwajuma was selling off every small thing that I did not want or need, and everything that was left I gave to her or Maggie. My bed that I'd bought in Dubai—very expensive, super king size, each little spring sewn by hand—went with the Merc to Maggie. She planned to sell the Merc, but before she could do so, her son Robert drove it to pieces. Fortunately, he was uninjured.

I had left all my DIA paperwork with Tellan and Patsy. When their home flooded, they tried to save it, but most was unreadable. They looked over what was left and admitted to me, "Wow, this really did all happen to you. The accounts show that you were right, you were swindled!" I was hurt to think my friends had ever questioned me or thought I had overreacted.

I wasn't planning to remain long in the country, so I wanted to wrap up the negotiations with Nadeem and his lawyer. Mebs and Parviz were no longer in the picture. I had heard they were getting a divorce and that Mebs's new wife was pregnant. He was a disgrace to the family, which was a disgrace to itself. I was sent a contract for a debt payment schedule, but it was riddled with false statements. Nadeem and his lawyer insisted that my expensive computer and scanner, which I had bought in Dubai, belonged to the school, and that the photo camera, which was seen being used by one of the teachers after my departure, was in my possession. Really, very silly things were holding up my departure to Europe. Finally, I agreed to everything, although in my heart I knew I again was being cheated, this time by Nadeem, the family member whom I had once trusted completely. Yolanda had been right, the whole family was corrupt.

The contract called for DIA to pay me $120,000 USD in monthly installments of $2,000 until the debt was paid. This was the payment for me taking care of the Juma children's education, the same children who had not fought for me but dumped me like a rotten apple. This was the payment for DIA, a school that I had started with my money, my collateral and my container full of supplies. When I came to Tanzania, the Jumas could neither pay their rent nor afford their own car. They had been penniless. Three years later they had ascended to high society, each family member driving an expensive car, wearing fine jewelry and traveling internationally. I just could not leave Tanzania without confronting the head of this corrupt family for one last time and telling him my feelings eye to eye.

The day of my departure, I called Mebs and asked him to meet me at a garden restaurant. Maggie and her children would be seated nearby if things should get out of hand. I was already there when Mebs arrived with a big smile on his face. He came over and tried to kiss me. I pulled away. It was then he realized this was not going to be a friendly get-together.

I poured everything out of my heart. It was not the money loss that had hurt me the most, it was the deception by him and his family, the emotional abuse that had broken me. I looked at Mebs and as I expected, he was shedding crocodile tears. I shook my head and rose from my seat. From the corner of my eyes I saw Maggie and the kids getting up from their table and walking away. I looked back at the man sitting there with his head down and wondered if he would ever understand what I had gone through and decided, no, he wouldn't. And I would not care.

I took Aztec and headed to the airport. I had loved Tanzania as a country, but I wasn't sorry to leave my troubles behind. A new life of recovery was beginning.

SPAIN—COSTA DEL SOL / AXARQUIA
(2008-2010)

COSTABELLA

Needing to register myself in Spain, I went to the Marbella police station and waited in line. When it was finally my turn, I found myself in front of a nice policeman who didn't speak English. However, I had my little "Mauro Italian" and "Chango Argentine" knowledge, and we managed things fine until he asked how I would register myself: Dutch or Swiss?

You will remember that during my problems in the UAE with Hans II, the Dutch ambassador tore up my passport, declaring, "She is not Dutch." However, afterward I applied for and was granted a replacement passport, which I never used, just carried with me in case of emergency. Before coming to Spain, I had researched the citizenship question. If I claimed to be Dutch, I'd have all the advantages the EU offered. If I were Swiss, I wouldn't be an EU member, but would enjoy similar benefits.

I lay both passports before the friendly policeman and asked what he thought I should do. He opened them, studied them intensely, then smiled at me and said, "You do not have a choice. You have to be registered as Swiss." I asked why. He smiled again and said, "Because your Dutch passport has long since expired." Problem solved! Now with my registration completed, I could convert my Tanzanian driver's license to a Spanish one. For that I had to go to the police station in Malaga. This also was no issue: I was in and out in thirty minutes.

Although I loved the way Claudia pampered me, her two-bedroom apartment was a tad too small for both of us, especially now that Aztec was back in the picture. I started browsing the Internet for a house or apartment. In January I put a deposit on a beautiful apartment in a complex called Alvarito Playa. The location was fantastic: Costabella, a village on the legendary Costa del Sol. Without a car, though, I'd never be able to move there. Claudia didn't understand why I had taken action on the apartment rental but was letting the car matter "ride." I was waiting to be inspired...

One day early in February, sitting on a bench in a park in Marbella, I had a sudden intuition that Mike, a friend of Claudia's who owned a car dealership, had something for me. I called him, and he asked what I was looking for. I said I'd like to have a small convertible and that my budget was €10,000. His reply? "You won't believe this, but this morning I received a black Peugeot 206 Cabriolet in your price range." Claudia and I drove immediately to his dealership, where I bought my little gem. I drove my pets and possessions to Costabella and moved in March 1, 2008.

LITTLE SOLITO

My apartment had a great view of the beach and a little garden. At that time, the complex was almost completely empty because it was largely a vacation home resort; most of the apartment owners lived in Madrid or other major cities in Spain and wouldn't show up until Easter. Dominic soon became king of Alvarito Playa, wandering wherever he wished. Aztec enjoyed his long walks on the beach, always on his leash, of course, and I was prepared with plastic bags to collect his pooh. There were rules for everything in Spain, and I wasn't used to that.

One Sunday Dominic didn't show up in the morning. I called and searched all over the complex. Alessandro, the maintenance man, was working in the garden close to a big rubbish container when he heard the meowing of a cat. He called me, and we sifted through the trash to find...not Dominic, but a kitten about two weeks old. I brought it home and went again to look for Dominic, whom I found ten minutes later, locked in the underground garage.

Earlier I had brought Dominic to a Dutch vet at a clinic called Pointers, which was a considerable distance away. I called that vet now, and he told me to give the kitten my body heat, so I lay on the bed trying to warm little "Solito" (as Claudia called him). Aztec found enormous pleasure in Solito and wanted to clean and guard him as if he were a jewel. Dominic hated him and refused to be petted while Solito was with us.

On Monday I left for work, trusting Aztec to keep watch over Solito. When I returned, Solito was very cold, despite the hot water bottle I had put in his cat carrier. I put him on my body with warm towels, offered him bottled milk and called the vet again. But there was nothing to be done: Solito died, purring on my skin. Solito was the first "rescue" animal I lost. (I had no way to know it, but there would be many successful saves in my future.) I couldn't help feeling sad, and Aztec was depressed, lying listlessly on the sofa. Dominic came and rubbed against me, happy with the way things turned out. It's a strange world.

VISITORS

I rarely lacked for company in my new place, now that I was living in a prime vacation spot. Claudia often stayed over weekends, cuddling on the sofa with Dominic and Nika, Aztec at her feet. My German friends Peter and Ute came, which made me very happy, but Aztec more, because Ute walked with him for hours in all kinds of weather. She told me once, "Aztec is a great listener. He's like a psychiatrist who listens to all your problems." I guess she told him many. Of course, Ursi came from Switzerland, and she was easy to be with. Silke, who had moved from Tanzania to Berlin, also visited with her boys.

The Peraltas were coming for a vacation, so Claudia rented an apartment in my complex for them. Every day while they visited, Chango and I went for an early morning walk with Aztec, strolling many kilometers on the beach while everybody else slept in. One evening Marco overheard us talking about the next morning's walk, to which Chango invited me for breakfast afterwards. Early the following day, Chango and Marco came to my door. While I was stepping out, and Marco was entering my apartment to use my computer, he gave me a meaningful look—only I didn't catch his meaning! Chango and I set off, chatting, enjoying the wind and sea, making small talk with owners of dogs whom me met along the way. After about two hours, I told Chango I would quickly bring Aztec back to my place and then meet him at his apartment for breakfast. I entered my apartment and asked Marco to look after Aztec. Marco said nothing, but I felt his words inside my head: "Do you really want to do this?" I looked at him and declared, "I am so stupid!" I quickly ran out of my home and shouted to Chango, "No, you'd better come have breakfast here!" Chango flashed a naughty smile. Thanks to Marco, I hadn't fallen into his trap. Later Marco said, "If you wanna get hurt again, go. I'm just warning you!" I was happy I had realized in time that it was not the breakfast that was dangerous, but the "after breakfast," which undoubtedly would have come. Chango, though over seventy, was still a hunter.

Too soon this memorable visit with the Peraltas came to an end, and everybody left except Marco.

A GIFT FROM ANNE-LIES

I had made an appointment with the Dutch vet at Pointers Clinic to get yearly vaccinations for Dominic. In mid July Marco and I got in the car with Dominic and drove off. Upon reaching the clinic, I went to the front desk and announced myself, adding that Dominic was there for his annual checkup. The receptionist looked at me strangely. (I would later learn why.) Marco and I were told to sit down and wait, as the vet was with a patient.

The clinic door opened. A lady entered carrying a box holding two dirty puppies sick with mange. The lady explained to the front desk that she had observed these *poveritas* for a few days in the mountains, where she walked her own dog, and assumed they had been dumped. Noticing the woman's accent, I asked if she was Dutch. She confirmed this, and we continued to speak in my native language. She explained that she couldn't keep the puppies herself and was hoping the vet would suggest a shelter where she could bring them.

Marco lifted one of the puppies out of the box and put it on my shoulder. Big mistake! The lady seized the opportunity to put the other puppy on my other shoulder. There I stood, everybody saying "Oooooohhhhhh!" and "Aaaahhhhhh!" What could I do? I was sold! Suddenly I owned two puppies, breeds unknown. The vet came out and said it is common in Spain to treat rescue animals for free, so he brought them straight to his nurses for shots and care. The pair were cleaned and pampered, and thirty minutes later they were in my car with an impatient, meowing Dominic in the back.

When Marco and I came home, I put down my purse, which fell on its side; the bill from the clinic dropped out. With it came a note from the clinic with an upcoming date on it. I called the clinic receptionist and asked if I needed to come back, as I had found this appointment note in my bag. It was then she explained why she'd been so surprised to see me: I was not scheduled to come in that day. I was supposed to bring Dominic one week later.

I looked at the calendar and realized the date was July 18, my sister Anne-Lies's birthday. Although no longer on this earth plane and long gone, she was often in my thoughts. I'd like to believe that Anne-Lies took me to the clinic to receive the two dogs that would enrich my life so much. I named the pair after my village: Costa and Bella.

PRANIC HEALING

Around this time, Claudia and I took a course in Pranic Healing at a Buddhist temple in the town of Benalmádena. Developed by Grand Master Choa Kok Sui, Pranic Healing is a highly evolved and tested system of energy medicine that utilizes *prana* to balance, harmonize and transform the body's energy processes. Prana is a Sanskrit word meaning life force. This invisible bio-energy or vital energy keeps the body alive and maintains a state of good health. Pranic Healing is a simple yet powerful and effective system of no-touch energy healing. It is based on two fundamental principles: one, that the body is a living entity that possesses the ability to heal itself; and two, that the healing process is accelerated by increasing this life force that is readily available from the sun, air and ground. According to Master Choa Kok Sui, "Life energy or prana is all around us. It is pervasive; we are actually in an ocean of life energy. Based on this principle, a healer can draw in pranic energy or life energy from the surroundings." Pranic Healing requires no drugs, gadgets, or even physical contact with the subject. Physical contact is not necessary because the practitioner works on the body's energy, not the body itself. This energy or aura surrounds and penetrates the physical body, distributing vitality throughout the muscles, bones, glands, etc. The reason Pranic Healing works is that physical ailments first appear as disruptions in the aura before manifesting as problems in the physical body. Prana not only sustains the body but also affects our emotions and relationships, even our ability to handle stress and stressful matters, such as finances.

At India Exotica I had a co-worker named Jesus. His girlfriend Raquel suffered from depression, headaches and many other problems. As Claudia and I were telling Jesus of our experiences in our course, we suggested Raquel come with him to my home where I would do a session on her. (In theory, she did not need to be present. Distant healing is not unknown to Pranic healers.) I invited them for dinner, and when we were all relaxed, I asked Raquel to join me in the bedroom. I started with cleaning her aura. After that was finished, and I had washed my hands and thrown the water away, I told her I would now give her energy. We both felt it. I thought she was going to levitate, as the energy from my hands flowed into her body. Even as I write this, I feel the tingling, warm sparks in my hands. I prayed, continuing to send my love and prayers for a few more minutes. Finally, I "let go," told her to turn around, and asked how she felt. I saw in her eyes that she had been rejuvenated; she said that at one point she actually thought she was going to take off and fly.

This was a good experience for me.

During one of our long walks, I told Chango about Pranic Healing. He reminded me that he had suffered from back pain for twenty years,

and suggested I send him long distance Pranic Healing. I did. Not knowing if it ever arrived, however, after two weeks I quit sending it. Two
days later Chango called and asked why I had stopped. He told me the
healing was working, the pain had lessened. So I continued.

A LITTLE PROPHESY

Through friends of Claudia, I heard of a British psychic named Anna
Pearson, who gave readings in Spain. I went to see her. Pearson prayed,
blessed her cards, and said several things about me but nothing special.
Then she looked me in the eyes and said, "You will move, not just to another country, but across the sea to the East. And I see many animals."

I stared at her in astonishment before saying, "Well, there you are
completely off, as I just moved to Spain. And if I did some charity work,
it might be with abandoned children or something like that. I've never
thought of working with animals, I'm definitely not moving again and
for sure not to another continent!"

Pearson simply replied, "Sorry, but this what the cards tell me."

DOMINIC, THE "PUPPERS," AND TROUBLE

Alvarito Playa slowly filled up with residents. Into the apartment to my
right came a couple with a golden retriever. Into the place on my left
came someone with a mutt with a constant, intense bark. Now the times
of peace were gone. I understood now why so many people I met had
told me they refused to vacation on the Costa del Sol. It was like sardines
in a can, horrible. Now I could only walk Aztec before sunrise and after
sunset. Dominic used to join us on our strolls, but when the beach filled
up with people, he stayed under the *chiringuitos* (small restaurants on the
beach).

For a while it appeared that my puppies Costa and Bella, with their
short legs and long bodies, were destined to be dachshunds, sausage
dogs, the only breed I do not like. They looked cute and awful at the
same time. One rainy day I had to do some grocery shopping. I would
be gone only ten minutes, so I left the pair in the apartment, along with
Aztec and Claudia's dog Nika (who was staying with me for a couple of

weeks). When I returned I opened the front door silently, as I sensed disaster within. I crept through the hallway, but even if I had made noise, the dogs wouldn't have heard me. I could not believe my eyes. Costa and Bella were pulling on my very, very expensive goose feather duvet on one side, Aztec and Nika on the other. Each had a corner in his mouth, and all four doggies were having a blast. My living room looked like it had been hit by a snowstorm. I had to hide my smile, which appeared after I had digested the fact that what was done, was done. I shouted, "What's going on here?" Each dog pulled his head in, dropped the duvet, and stood still as a pillar, all innocence. I sent them outside in the rain as punishment. They stood in front of my window crying for an hour, but I stayed strong, and they were allowed in only after I had cleaned the scene.

A few months passed, and the legs of the "puppers," as I liked to call them, started growing, and their bodies balanced out. Luckily for me they stayed medium-sized dogs and did not grow to be full-blown Labradors or Pointers. It turned out they were a Lab-Pointer mix, with the typical bird-hunting instincts of Pointers. Their Lab qualities showed in their good natures, intelligence, and eagerness to please me. Later I was told they were surely the famous *Deutsche Bracke* (German Hounds) used for hunting both large and small game and known for their acute sense of smell.

As I mentioned, Dominic held regal sway over our apartment complex. Now that people had arrived, they opened their windows to air out their apartments, and Dominic found wonderful beds to sleep on during his morning rounds. The neighbors' garden chairs, which had been his favorite sleeping locations after noisy Costa and Bella showed up, was suddenly occupied by the golden retriever and the mixed breed dog, which always went berserk when Dominic wandered into view.

Neither Dominic nor I could feel the anger brewing.

One early morning my doorbell rang. Three men were standing at my front door, regarding me sternly. They were my neighbors and "il presidente" from the complex. Not daring to come in, the cowards remained on my doorstep. With serious faces they told me there were complaints about my cat (not admitting that it was they, and only they, complaining). In very broken English they made me understand that Dominic was a big problem. He slept in their beds and scared all their dogs. The solution, they said, was to lock Dominic inside. I looked at them and said, "That is impossible, he is an outdoor cat. I will try, but it will not work." I'd worried that complaints might be made against my puppies or Aztec, but Dominic…I never imagined it.

Claudia and her friends took me to see Madonna in Sevilla, and soon afterward Jesus and Raquel got married, throwing a delightful party. I should have been having a great time, but my neighbors were harassing me. I got fed up and called the owner of my apartment, telling her I was breaking the contract and leaving early. I lost my €3,000 security deposit.

I decided I didn't want to live on the beach anymore—too expensive, too much of a hassle. I didn't need luxury, only peace and quiet and space to be with my animals. Perhaps due to a calcium deficiency, my puppers had bitten big holes in the walls of my apartment. If I'd been better treated, I would have repaired these, but now I just let them be.

HOUSE HUNTING IN THE AXARQUÍA

Again I searched the web. I found some interesting affordable houses in the Axarquía, a region of Spain farther to the east, extending along the coast and inland. I responded to some ads and received an email from someone calling himself Juan Marcos. He suggested a place in the Axarquía for us to meet, supplying the make and model of his car so I could watch for it. Marijke was visiting me at the time, so we drove up together into the mountains. We passed a man hauling his crops on a small wagon pulled by a donkey, and the sight made me feel as if I'd been whisked a hundred years into the past.

The higher we climbed, the more I was in awe. We were looking at the Parque Natural de la Sierras de Tejeda, Almijara y Alhama. La Maroma Tejeda is the highest peak in this mountain range, reaching 2,066 meters (approximately 6,778 feet). From here, the views of the Mediterranean coast and neighboring mountains were nothing short of spectacular.

On the side of the road Marijke and I saw a car parked that matched the description JM had given me, and a couple were standing beside it. We stopped and got out. The man introduced himself as Juan Marcos, and his wife as Elisabeth. My sister and I looked at them curiously and asked, "Are you Dutch?"

"Yes, we are!" They were Indos (a mix of Indonesian and Dutch). Juan called himself JM or Don Indo Español, and he and Elizabeth had lived in the Axarquía many years. We laughed, and the ice was broken.

They got into their car, Marijke and I got into ours, and we followed them to a house with a pool that cost a third of the price of my apartment in Costabella. I didn't need to think long: it was cozy, had two bedrooms, and the view was astonishing. Here I would be able to walk and rest and meditate with my animals. I signed the contract and moved into the house September 1, 2008.

LIFE IN SEDELLA

Now I lived in the town and municipality of Sedella, population 500. Sedella is one of many whitewashed villages in the Axarquía. There, time stands still. People still ride donkeys through the narrow, winding streets...the doctor comes to the village clinic only two days a week... and the mail comes by car, as there is no post office. The supermarket is the front half of someone's house (the policeman's) and his wife, the proprietor, sells everything that a villager needs. Many of the houses have Arab-style courtyards and small but sumptuous gardens.

Like most houses for rent in Spain, mine came furnished, which was good for me as I had sold everything or given it away in Tanzania. My boxes from Africa had still to arrive. I would miss Claudia, but I was sure she would visit me as often as she could, and in fact she appeared the first weekend after my move. Nika loved the place, and we all walked on the dirt paths and admired the views of La Maroma, the olive and almond trees. Aztec was on the leash, the puppers running all over the place, Dominic trotting behind, meowing when we went too fast.

I was in paradise.

As I had mentioned, Claudia had trouble ending her relationship with Morgan. He had been coming less often to Marbella, which she didn't like, and she started using the problems with the accounts as an excuse to see him. He pushed back, and their meetings usually ended in a fight. Now I was happy to hear that Claudia was moving to the United States to be with her sister Alejandra in Miami. Naturally, I would miss her terribly, but I was relieved to see her finally put her relationship with Morgan behind her and face a brighter future.

I was still in contact with Grant Pierce. I received an email from him with some photos of the 1,000 wheelchairs he sent from Australia to Tanzania to handicapped children. The gifts allowed the children to go to school, get educated, and have a sense of independence. I looked at the photographs, tears welling in my eyes. I missed Africa and regretted not having fulfilled my dream: creating a village or home for HIV-positive orphans. But who knows? Perhaps there was a reason, still hidden from me, why I ended up in Spain. These moments of looking back did not last long, and became briefer and briefer, until finally disappearing.

My boxes arrived and I could unpack a lifetime of cherished possessions, including books, videotapes and music. I planned to digitalize everything; it would be a long-term project that would keep me a busy bee. I started with the old videotapes, which I threw away after I converted them to MP4. Then I thought, why should I keep my memories all to myself? I joined YouTube and shared the videos.

Looking over all the yearbooks from my schools, I found myself wanting to get in touch with students and staff. It was a wish unfulfilled, until...

...I discovered Facebook!

I created a page, and soon I had to create a separate page called DAA-Memory Lane. I found more and more students and staff and friends from all over the world. We re-connected, and what was even better, many students who hadn't seen each other since kindergarten reunited after as many as ten years. I loved it.

Soon I learned that in Europe, Hyves (which no longer exists) was more popular than Facebook. I started looking for Anne-Lies's children.

I had last seen them at my mother's funeral, and I had the feeling that Anne-Lies was telling me to find them. Yes, there was Wendy on Hyves. I sent her a message and my telephone number. My phone rang at once. Wendy and I were both very emotional and happy that contact was reinstated. She gave me her brother's number, and soon I was speaking with Maikel. He promised he would visit on his next holiday.

I looked on Hyves for long-lost friends. I found the daughters of my old schoolmate Agnes, whom I had last seen in Switzerland. I also found Ruud, the brother of Anne-Lies's husband. I found Lex Bounin, Alex Bultsma, Henri the French teacher and Jitze the English teacher. Ooohhh I found many people, and contacts were re-established. I had time now to nurture friendships on Skype and via email. Marijke came again, but was not as happy as before, because I had moved into the mountains and that was not her cup of tea. Relations between her and Dad had worsened, and she refused to have any more contact with him. Marijke made it clear that if something happened to him, I would be the one to handle it.

I also found Nico, my first husband. We exchanged a few emails. He had two beautiful children.

AN OLD LOVE RETURNS

And then I contacted…Henk Rampen. The man who had made me so miserable in Germany and brought an end to my marriage to Nico. At first Henk had no clue who I was; he had blocked me from his mind, me who had been so much in love with him. I could not believe it. Slowly his memory came back, and he insisted on visiting me in Spain. He came in through Malaga, where I collected him from the airport. When he appeared in the arrivals hall, I recognized him immediately, he being just an older version of himself. We hugged, and thirty-three years disappeared. Long forgotten memories were recalled: our old colleagues, old friends from Hessisch Oldendorf. He was now married and had two children, a daughter and a son. Henk and I took long walks in the mountains around my house.

It was during one of our walks in Parque Natural that I discovered a house and fell in love with it. My eyes traveled from the foot of a steep hill, where an old flourmill stood, up to a house on top. Perched higher than any other home around, it boasted a pool and an incredible view. Unfortunately, Henk and I could also see it was occupied. The next day I called JM, the Dutch real estate guy. He told me "Il Molino"—what the village people called this dream house of mine—would be occupied until July 2009. The owner was the town policeman, and JM would speak with him.

A few days later, I was invited to look inside. I got a shock when I saw the bedspreads on all the beds: they had the exact same pattern as the curtains in my childhood home in Dorst. Was this a message that my mother was sending me? Was this the right house for me?

One week later, in early fall of 2008, I signed the contract. The house would be mine beginning August 1, 2009.

That autumn was unusually warm and sunny. After breakfast one day, Henk said he was going to catch some rays at poolside. No problem with me, I had other things to do. When I was ready to join him, I almost got a heart attack. There he was, stretched out in his birthday suit. I glanced up to the next mountain, where my British neighbors, Jenny and Les, lived. They had a direct view of my pool. Having lived in the UAE and Tanzania, so often among conservative Muslims, I wasn't used to this kind of exhibitionism, and not wanting to be the talk of the town, I told Henk to please cover up. He apologized and threw something on, but when he left he had a beautiful tan!

HERE AND THERE

Now, "I" was an even more popular vacation destination than ever. Nicoletta came with her kids, and Peter and Ute came to look after my animals when I went to see my dad on his birthday. My father had a girlfriend at this time, which wasn't surprising. He was still quite good looking, the cock on the hen farm. It seems the ladies were lining up to be next on his list. Every evening he and I would play Rummikub (a tile-based game which combines elements of the card game rummy and mahjong) with his girlfriend and other ladies, whom he would spoil with coffee, tea and sweets. He was happy, which made me happy, but now trouble came from another quarter. Some of the women had been school-age friends of my mother, and they gossiped about my mother and her brother's best friend, Louis van Dorst, who had died in 1945 before my parents got involved with each other. After all these years, Dad started bad-mouthing Mom, something I couldn't handle. I warned him that if he spoke badly about her again, I wouldn't return. His girlfriends were really nice women, they thought he loved them, but I cautioned them and their daughters to be careful, as he would drop them like hot potatoes, which he did.

FILM FESTIVAL

After seeing some Dutch friends, I returned to Spain, sleeping in my bed for one night. The next day I left to volunteer at the African Film Festival of Tarifa (FCAT), knowing my "zoo" was in the good hands of Peter and Ute.

An NGO called Al Tarab, which was based in Tarifa in Cadiz province, founded FCAT in 2004. The event was designed to promote some of the best film production from Africa and to publicize a new image of Africa to the Spanish public, countering stereotypes offered by mass media. By its fourth year, the festival had become a competition. Located near the Straits of Gibraltar, where the Mediterranean meets the Atlantic, Tarifa offers spectacular views across the water to Africa's Rif mountains.

My week in Tarifa was fabulous. Because I was a volunteer, my travel expenses and housing were free. I stayed with two wonderful young men in a home close to the beach. I met new people and made contacts I hoped would some day be useful to my friend Beatrix, the Tanzanian film producer. However, missing my animals, I skipped the final night's party and drove home to my little house in the mountains.

CAT AND DOG DRAMA

When I arrived it was late, but Peter and Ute were still up, cuddled with Costa and Bella on the sofa. I did not see Dominic. I asked Ute where he was, and she said they had gone for a walk that morning; he had followed them, then they lost track of him. I almost had a heart attack at this news, as it had been a sunny, hot day, and the trail lacked shade. Ute explained that they had walked around the mountain, approximately 10 kilometers (a little over 6 miles). No way Dominic could have walked that distance. Really worried now, I asked Ute if she would come looking with me, then called Costa and Bella into the car. It was a difficult route to drive, as it was less a road than a walking trail, one side the precipitous descent to the valley. Traveling at night made it doubly dangerous.

We stopped on a broader part of the path, where I would be able to turn, and where Ute thought she had last seen Dominic. I let the dogs out and called Dominic's name and told the dogs to look for him. Of course, they didn't understand, but they were sniffing like mad. I had to control myself not to get angry, telling Ute that Dominic had never walked that far with me. I saw Costa and Bella sniffing under a bush, their tails up and swinging like crazy. When I called them, they refused to come, and I knew they had found him. I ran towards them and pushed the bushes aside, Ute illuminating the area with her flashlight. There was Dominic, completely dehydrated, showing no signs of life. I lifted him up, thanking Costa and Bella, and put Dominic in the car. We drove back home, where I forced liquids into the poor cat. Thankfully, he survived his brush with death.

Thefts were reported in my area. I had not socialized much with people in the surrounding hills, but now I was asked if I could possibly take photos of strange cars passing by, as mine was the house with the best overview. I did so, and week after week I handed my photos to the local policeman (my future landlord). Through this, people started to know and greet me, although Bella still bared her teeth at strangers on our walks. She was a real guard dog. Soon I started joining my neighbors on their daily strolls.

Some of these people felt sorry for Aztec, pointing out that he was on the leash all the time, while their own dogs and Costa and Bella were jumping around. I finally gave in, but not before warning these folks that if he disappeared, "You guys will have to go and find him!" Huskies are famous for racing off on their own, preferring their own timeframe and speed. But there he went, trotting in front of us, his tail happily waving in the breeze while the neighbors and I chatted. You can guess what happened: Aztec disappeared. We searched, first on foot, then in our cars. Nothing. Luckily, this was mountain country, no traffic to speak of, so I didn't worry about Aztec getting struck by a vehicle.

We all went home. I sat on my terrace and made myself a meal, but I was much too anxious to taste it, much less enjoy it. I knew I couldn't search when the sun went down, so I got back in the car with Costa and Bella again, calling for Aztec, driving my little Peugeot down all the trails we had walked that morning, letting the dogs out where we had last seen him. No Aztec.

It was twilight when I got back home. I sat out on the terrace, worriedly studying the surrounding mountains. Did I see something high up, or was it just my imagination? It was merely a dot, but I thought it was moving. I hurried inside, grabbed my binoculars and came back. There! Up between the olive and almond trees it moved, taking its time, smelling here, tasting there, looking around, exploring. My heart was in my mouth, as this dog had suffered a broken hip and broken legs. Basically, he was a cripple, yet there he was, coming straight down the steep mountain. What was I to do? Nothing, just be patient and wait. Aztec was patient too, carefully coming down the *bancadas* (mountain "beds" or terraces with orchard trees on each step) stopping when he pleased, savoring his freedom. I went inside, as it was dark now. Around midnight I heard him barking. He stood in front of the gate, his tail wagging a joyous greeting. I was so happy, but I never left him off the leash again.

The puppers gave me problems, too. Behind my house was a small farm where sheep grazed. One day while digitizing videotapes, I heard a commotion. I ran outside and saw Jenny on the hillside above me, shouting at me and making signs. I had no clue what she was agitated about, so I headed up the steep mountain, much more slowly than I would have liked. At last I saw Les entering a corral where Costa and Bella were chasing terrified sheep from one corner to the other. Fortunately, Les had taken some ropes with him, and the dogs always wore collars, so he could catch them. Les was huffing and puffing as he came down the mountain, furiously yelling at me to control my dogs. Poor Les. Jenny was even worse, angrily shouting that I was lucky she and Les had heard the sheep bleating and gone to take a look. In my defense, Costa and Bella were getting weekly obedience lessons from a Scandinavian dog trainer. He had taught them some tricks, but they hadn't learned how to fetch a ball. An object like that just couldn't excite them, but when they heard a "baaa" or a "cluck" they'd be off on the hunt, and there was no way of controlling them.

One day I even thought they had killed themselves.

I had gone to collect water from a spring that was popular with the locals; even people from as far away as Malaga came to drink it, so I had stopped buying water and always collected from there. This spring bubbled up beside a road at the foot of sheer cliffs. Aztec had to stay in the car as Costa, Bella and I went out to collect the water in several bottles. Suddenly, the dogs were gone. I looked several hundred meters up and saw mountain goats and deer nimbly prancing up the cliffs. To my horror, I also saw the puppers chasing them, climbing the rocks with ease, balancing themselves on their naturally long nails, farther and farther from where I stood, until they were out of sight. I heard a cry that echoed through the mountains. I imagined the worst: one of my dogs falling down the cliffs. What should I do? Call the police? I desperately shouted, "Costa, Bella!" Aztec yowled, his instincts telling him something was wrong. My calls and Aztec's yowls echoed crazily through the mountains.

I remained there for an hour, then drove back a kilometer where the mountain was not so steep, hoping I could persuade the dogs to come down the safer way. Aztec was the first to hear them; tail wagging, he stared at a point high up. I tried to see where he was looking, and finally

I spied some dots moving down between the trees and rocks, very carefully. Bella was the first to jump in the car, Costa following, both panting heavily. I was so happy to drive them home, safe and sound. Needless to say, I never took them to that spring again.

A RARE AND BEAUTIFUL SNOW

Winter was colder than I had expected. The previous one, which I spent on the coast, had been mild. Now the altitude was at work. I was 690 meters (2,264 feet) high in the foothills of the Sierra Tejada. No fan of the cold, I stayed mostly inside for the season, working at my computer. My uploading to YouTube increased, and my supply of videotapes decreased, slowly but surely. I loved the coziness inside, my pets keeping me warm at night.

On the morning of January 9, 2009, I woke up, walked to the kitchen to make coffee, glanced out the window and saw….snow! I had not seen snow since 1988, when I lived in Switzerland, and it was the first time it had snowed in Sedella in fifty years. I looked at my two Siberians, Aztec and Dominic, ran to the front door and opened it. Wow, soooo cold! The world around me was white and beautiful. I raced to the bedroom where I changed into my old ski jacket and ski pants with boots. I had kept them, just in case. I stepped out with my animals, and they flew all over the place, loving their first encounter with snow. I couldn't resist videotaping them, and of course, my YouTube channel shows their fun.

Playtime over, I went back inside to finally brew my coffee, and… no electricity. I went outside and saw Jenny and Les beside their home, admiring the bright white world. We waved to each other, and they came down to check if I was OK, a particularly nice gesture because the trail was not visible and it could have been easy for them to slide precariously down the mountain. When they at last arrived, I told them that I had no electricity. They did, as they were on a different line. They invited me to breakfast. Costa, Bella, and Aztec came with me.

Les and Jenny were good neighbors, as you can tell. Jenny was a homebody who enjoyed knitting, weaving and other crafts, the kinds of hobbies I enjoyed when I was younger. I would give Jenny Aztec's fur, which he lost in big hunks, for her to weave into slipper-socks. (Jenny loved Aztec and was happy to do this.) The soles were made from the covers of my old leather-bound photo albums, which, since I was digitalizing everything, I no longer needed.

The snow fun and power outage lasted for days. Fortunately, I had stocked enough food in the house to last at least two weeks, so the dogs, cat and I never went hungry.

LINCE

One day later that month, I had to take Costa and Bella to a vet clinic in Caleta for spaying and neutering. I was sitting in the waiting room when I spotted a binder on a small table in the center of the room. My hands moved towards it. I knew I was making a mistake, but I nudged that thought aside as I slowly flipped through the pages showcasing doggies looking for a home. I moved on to the cat pages, but they didn't show me any sort of cat I would like to have until…the last page.

There was a beautiful adult Maine coon. I couldn't believe it. It brought back memories of three years ago, when I had bought a Maine coon kitten from a Belgium cattery. I had flown from Tanzania to Belgium to collect him. He was gorgeous and lived with me in Dar es Salaam for six months before he was diagnosed with Feline Calicivirus. For the next six months I tried all kinds of medications to treat him, but I finally realized the poor guy was suffering, and I had him put to sleep.

Seeing this huge, handsome seven-year-old Maine coon made my heart leap. I asked the receptionist what ailed the cat. Unsure, she called the owner, who turned out to be a young woman who had lost her job and could no longer look after her cats, the Maine coon and a Persian kitten. I told her I wanted the Maine coon, and the receptionist said she'd like to see the Persian, and we made an appointment for the next day. I was all excited when I arrived at the clinic the next morning to collect Caparos de Campo, Caparos of the Fields, nicknamed Lince (lynx). I assured the woman that Lince was in good hands.

Caparos de Campo was born August 3, 2003 in Asturias, Spain, expressly to be a show cat. His certificate featured a long list of breeders from the US to South Africa. His papers proved he was a successful show cat, but they also revealed that he had changed owners five times…had chronic diarrhea…and could no longer be shown. I don't know how his previous owners treated him, but from the moment he entered my home, Lince did not exhibit normal cat behavior. He didn't know how to jump, play or defend himself against Dominic, who was very jealous of this newcomer. Lince would cower in my bathroom and refuse to come out. Cat owners will know what I mean when I say, "I seldom saw him smile." He was much like Aztec when I first adopted him: seriously depressed.

Lince's fur was in bad condition, so I tried to shave him, but the noise of the shaver nearly gave him a heart attack. Who knows how much he suffered to be beautiful on stage! I had to bring him to the vet to be shaved under anesthesia, so he wouldn't be traumatized.

After lots of love and attention from me and my dogs, Lince eventually jumped, lay on my bed, sunbathed in front of the windows, had an occasional difference with Dominic, asked loudly for food, and enjoyed lying on my lap where he purred happily. Lince slowly explored the house and realized that there were no threats for him there. He even walked outside a little.

The bedroom became Lince's territory, and he would call for me to come to bed when I was watching movies late at night. "Turning in" was always an event for my animal family and me. Having followed me into the bedroom, the dogs and Dominic would jump up on the bed and find their places, each of them touching one part of my body. Lince would wait until everyone else was settled, then decide that the best spot for his furry belly was my face, or he'd cuddle on top of the doggies. Every morning I'd wake up and there he'd be, lying next to me on the pillow, always touching me.

Behavior-wise, Lince had come a long way, but his diarrhea remained a terrible problem. I noticed the movements in his belly and saw that he did not really digest his food; he'd rush to the litter box the second after he'd eaten. He was on different medications, but nothing helped. For a while I gave him one spoonful of yogurt in the morning, which seemed to help a bit, but after two weeks it was back to diarrhea again. Someone suggested I give him raw meat; that didn't help. I tried everything for nearly a year until I found an angel.

In December 2009, on Les and Jenny's recommendation, I took Lince to *veterinario* Mario de la Torre at Puente Don Manuel Clinic. Wow! Not only was Dr. Mario good looking, but he also fell instantly in love with Lince and spent exactly seventy-five minutes with him, while people and their pets growled impatiently in the waiting room. Dr. Mario told me that he had studied at the University of Limburg in the Netherlands, so of course, we had to spend some time talking about **that**. Then he got down to business and told me to come back with a stool sample from Lince so that he could send it to a lab. He would not give any medication unless he knew what poor Lince was suffering from, apart from depression. I did as Dr. Mario instructed, and one week later we had the result: Lince had a virus rarely found in Spain. Fortunately, it could be treated with medicated tablets. Lince also developed an infection on his cheek. It had started with a small crust, which his previous vet had guessed was eczema, but now it worsened, and Dr. Mario gave him a medicated cream. Oh, Lince hated both tablets and cream, but after a week I could report to Mario that Lince now could hold his stool for many hours. The bloody "eczema" wouldn't respond to anything, and finally I just allowed the wound to dry out, it taking two months to heal completely. Ruud and his wife Els, who were my dog sitters that year during Christmas while I was in Chaclalma, treated Lince with tender care, changing his bandages and giving him special foods.

SASKIA IN PANAMA

That winter, while cleaning out my email boxes, I came across Saskia's old correspondence. I again wrote her, hoping she would reply. Nothing. I surfed the web for my old contacts in Dominical and reconnected with them. Finally, I found someone who sent me copies of all the emails sent from Saskia's computer. Now the theft was proven, but how to get my money back? Saskia had apparently run off to Panama, as I was able to trace one of her children to an international school there. I put an ad on an Internet PI site, but everybody wanted money up front, which I didn't have. I also found additional "victims," including her old friend Caro Dinant and two Dutchmen who had entered into a business contract with Saskia (again, both parties being Dutch inspired trust). They gave her money to set up a business: she registered it, closed it down and vanished. Discovering all this was very bad energy for me, so I decided to let it be for a while.

VISITORS TO IL MOLINO...AND ANOTHER GIFT FROM ANNE-LIES

I realized my little Peugeot wasn't built for the rough climb to my new house on the Molino. Since Claudia was staying in the US and her Toyota Land Cruiser 4x4 was rusting in the garage, we agreed I would buy it. And not a moment too soon: my policeman landlord let me move in a few days early, and before I knew it I was gazing down from the Molino upon breathtaking Sedella. On clear days upon the Molino I could see Morocco and Gibraltar. The mountains, the blue sea, beauty surrounded me. I felt I was in paradise and wondered, "If I don't have a fortunate life, who does?"

Contact between my nephew Maikel and I had intensified, and he decided to spend his summer holidays with me. He would arrive August 1, which was another reason I was pleased I had moved in early. I'd had time to unpack somewhat and get the house ready for him. I still felt very strongly that Anne-Lies was encouraging me to be in contact with her children. In the meantime, I had also extended an invitation to Maikel and Wendy's uncle Ruud and cousin Kyle. Kyle and his mom Els would visit later in August. It would be a busy month.

The first or second day after I moved in, I went out to inspect the garden. It had not been looked after, dried out from the hot, rainless summer.

On the third day in my new home, Maikel arrived. Now in his mid thirties, he was a slim man whose face often bore a serious expression. Tired from driving from the Netherlands across Belgium and France to the south of Spain, he was happy just to do nothing for a while. The next day while Maikel and I were having breakfast on the terrace overlooking the Mediterranean and the sparkling white Andalucía villages, we saw a red flower next to the fence that surrounded the house. Maikel and I got up to admire the only flower blooming in the hot sun, and discovered that it was one red rose standing proudly before us in all her beauty. From that morning we spoke to her as if it—she—were Anne-Lies. I knew she was with us. It was her message to us, *I am here with you.* Every morning at breakfast, the rose was there, blooming and beautiful. Summers in Spain are scorching, and we had expected that Anne-Lies (the rose) would disappear after a few days, but she remained exquisite. I watered her and the other rose bushes, but no new buds appeared.

Els and Kyle showed up, and together we enjoyed long strolls in Parque Natural. There was a footpath down to Sedella, and I started taking it instead of driving my car on the road. Maikel, Els, Kyle and I would walk past olive and almond trees, Dominic padding along until just before we reached the village, where he would wait for us to return.

One day Els and I set out alone from my house for what we thought would be a brief walk. We decided to take a shortcut down a mountainside, planning to cross a ravine and then make our way back. As we were following the tracks of goats or sheep, Els stumbled and fell a few meters down. She appeared to be unconscious, although she still gripped Aztec's leash. Frightened, I called her name, but she didn't respond. I realized an ambulance would never be able to reach her; if Els were seriously hurt, she would have to be rescued by helicopter. Holding on to Costa, I slid on my butt down toward her. Bella ran around freely, unaware of my tension and worry. It seemed to take me many, many minutes to reach Els.

When at last I did, she opened her eyes and looked startled and surprised: she had no idea what had just happened. I told her to stay still, that we should both try to relax. Aztec seemed to understand the situation, sitting beside Els as if to keep her from falling any farther. I assured Els that when and if she felt ready, I could lead her out of the valley by a quick and secure route. After about ten minutes, she told me she was well enough to walk. I looked for the easiest track up and spoke to Aztec, urging him to pull Els up. Slowly, he did so. I did not say it, but I was quite afraid for myself, for as you've learned, my bones are not particularly strong. Keeping a hold on Costa, clutching the low, dry bushes that I passed, I pulled myself up the trail, all while keeping an eye on Els. Being a mountain hunting dog, Costa moved with steady ease, his long nails gripping the soil of the rocky terrain. Both Aztec and Costa seemed to know that any slip could cost us our lives, while Bella remained unaware of our predicament. Upon reaching level ground not far from my house, Els and I stopped to cuddle and thank our dogs. I had always known that Aztec, the alpha dog, would prove to be a rescuer if circumstances called for it. That day, I was surprised and pleased to learn I could also rely on Costa.

The weeks drifted by, the weather hotter and hotter, and still Anne-Lies my rose bloomed on. After thirty days, it was time for Maikel to go. We rose early that morning and went to see our flower together. I said to him, "Tomorrow she will be gone." We said our goodbyes to her, and Maikel departed. Soon after, Els and Kyle left, too. Alone, after everybody was gone, I asked my sister to please replace the rose with another when she leaves. That evening, the rose dropped its petals, one by one. I looked at all the bushes for new buds, to show me she had heard me, but nothing. The next day she was gone, leaving no sign that she had been there to greet us every morning. But next to her, a bush that I had thought was dead soon produced the most wonderful red roses, one in the center and ten surrounding her, all on one stem. My sister thanked me for taking care of her son. Thank *you*, Anne-Lies.

NEW DOG TROUBLES

I made friends with the shepherds coming from the village, bringing their sheep and goats to the soft green slopes of the mountains surrounding me. There was one single hill (I called it my mountain) just behind my house, and the dogs and I would go up there and watch the shepherds come from far away, the bells upon the herds jingling like Santa's sleigh. One old shepherd with a face burned by the sun passed by my house regularly. He had a new dog, a white and fluffy puppy named

Maria. He told me that it would be huge when full grown, as it was a Kuvasz, a Hungarian shepherd dog. Aztec loved the puppy, and I would take Aztec outside the gate to play with her. Costa and Bella hated poor Maria and barked at her as if she were a marauding lion. Gradually, Maria matured into a lovely, giant, gentle-natured dog. Costa and Bella never treated her any nicer.

One time Peter and Ute were visiting from Germany. Early risers, they set out to take all the dogs for a long walk. I had told them the evening before to put Costa and Bella on the leash as soon as they heard the sound of bells. I was still deep asleep when I heard shouts. I looked out my window and saw Peter and Ute in the Parque Natural, only Aztec with them. Dressing fast, I ran outside to them, and they pointed down the mountain. Costa and Bella were there attacking Maria.

I ran downhill as fast as my legs could handle it and pulled Costa and Bella away. Maria was lying on her back, blood flowing from everywhere, although it looked worse than it actually was. I told Peter and Ute to put Costa and Bella on their leashes. I checked Maria, who got up and licked my hands. When the shepherd came, I told him I would take Maria to the vet, but he said her wounds were minor and he'd just keep an eye on her. An hour later I saw Maria running around her herd of sheep as if nothing had happened. I was relieved, but very upset with my Costa and Bella.

Shortly after that, signs went up everywhere at the Parque Natural: *Dogs to be walked on leash only,* with a hefty fine if a dog was found roaming free. The shepherds told me flatly that if they found Costa and Bella walking near their herds, they would shoot them. One dog isn't a problem but two are a pack, killers. Hunters came to my door and offered to buy my dogs, having got wind of their reputation. The dogs who were my babies, slept in my bed, and slept with the cats now suddenly were known all over the area as aggressive hunters. Thereafter we limited our walks to "my mountain" next door.

SASKIA'S SWINDLE
In the fall the Costa Rica swindle came back to my mind. I went through all the emails in my possession regarding the purchase of the property.

These included correspondence that took place between the marketing agent (Anders Gustavsson), the seller (Saskia by POA), and the buyer, a California woman who had no clue that I was never paid. Here's what the marketing agent sent me:

Hatillo Property Investigation
All information provided as a courtesy from Anders Gustavsson on 10/15/2009
Statement by Anders Gustavsson

At the beginning of January in 2007 Saskia Delic came in to South Coast Real Estate and wanted to show and sell a property owned by her friend (Marilyn Wouters) that lived in South Africa. Her friend was not able to come sign any documents, so a full power of attorney was required for the sale to happen. Saskia said that this POA was on the way. We took her word for it, and followed the proper procedures to see the property, clean up the property, make copies of the plot plan, and then we listed the property for $170,000.

A client for this property was found around the 20th of January by 2CostaRica Real Estate & Anders Gustavsson, and Robert Solano closed on the property 28th of March 2007. The selling price was $160,000, an 8% commission was paid to South Coast Real Estate, and 1/4 of the commission was given to 2CostaRica for their cooperation.

Beyond the 8% commission and legal fees, no other money was earned by any of the 3rd parties involved, and I had no knowledge of Saskia doing anything illegal at any time. Due to Saskia having a legal Costa Rican power of attorney no parties were in touch with the actual owner, because all rights to sell the property were given to Saskia. To my knowledge, no one involved in this deal had any idea Saskia never paid Marilyn Wouters any money.

I first found out about the crime on October 13th 2009 from a forwarded email by Scott Williams of 2CostaRica Real Estate.
Anders Gustavsson

I contacted a Panamanian lawyer who informed me that I was not the first one to charge Saskia with a crime, but when court dates were set, she never showed up. I found Saskia's husband, Sasa Delic, and sent him a message. He replied that he had asked Saskia why she hadn't paid me, and she had said because she and I had problems. The only problem we had was that I sent her a POA and she kept all the money from the sale! I never heard from Delic again. A new victim showed up: Caroline Dinant, a friend of Saskia's from Holland who had given her money to invest in Costa Rica. She had written to Saskia to please return the funds. Saskia had never bought a property for her or responded, so Caroline went to see Saskia's parents, who refused to discuss the situation and threatened to go to the police to report Caroline as a "stalker."

I hired a private investigator, Alin Tod Atodiresei. I found him through Google. Romanian born, he had studied private investigation and counter terrorism in Spain and Israel. I gave him all my info, and he went to Panama. He saw Saskia's children go to their school, and noted a man was living in their home, but he never saw Saskia herself. The address and phone numbers Saskia had given were not valid. Alin tried to talk to staff at the children's school, but they wouldn't give info to a stranger. I couldn't afford to retain him longer, and it seemed like a lost cause anyway.

THE "COLD" TRUTH

Winter came. I now lived higher than before, so it was colder. I turned on the gas heater and electric heater, piled wood in the fireplace, snuggled with the cats and dogs and STILL I was freezing. Even with my Land Cruiser, it was difficult to go down the mountain, so to be safe I stocked up on a month's worth of food. The storms around my house were scary; I had never heard such enormous sounds in my life. Sometimes I felt it was a miracle my little house was still standing. Houses in Andalucía were built for hot summers, not cold winters. The wind would gust through the window seals, and I would shiver on the sofa covered with cats and dogs. When there was snow on the ground, and visitors asked me to drive down and collect them from the main road, I did it with my heart in my throat; the trail was only wide enough for one car, the mountain to one side, a steep ravine to the other.

One winter day, needing provisions, I headed for Torre del Mar. Driving slowly, I managed several sharp turns before a truck suddenly appeared in front of me. I slammed on my brake, remembering Tanzania, Christopher and the mountain. My Land Cruiser and the truck would not be able to pass each other. I knew my haunting memories would not allow me to back up, so I pulled up the handbrake, jumped out of the car and walked quickly to the truck, the driver coming out to meet me. I told him a bad experience a long time ago prevented me from backtracking. He smiled, got into my car, and easily reversed it a hundred meters to a corner where the road was wider. Leaving my Land Cruiser about one meter from the ravine side, he returned to his truck and squeezed it past my car and the mountainside, waving as he passed. I continued on my way, always fearing what might come around the next bend.

Winter passed and I went to see a doctor for a checkup. He told me I had a high degree of osteoporosis, and when he saw my address and learned I lived alone, he suggested I move to a more accessible area, in case I should fall and break anything.

I liked where I lived. It was absolutely beautiful. Still, I had to admit it wasn't practical to remain, and the fact that my dogs couldn't roam anymore made the decision to move an easy one, but...move where?

WHERE TO?
My friends Peter and Ute came again, and I told them I was going to move and why, and the question came up: Where to?

Ursi came. We took a fabulous trip to Granada in the foothills of the Sierra Nevada, admiring the medieval architecture dating to the Moorish occupation of Spain. Granada is best known for the Alhambra, a sprawling hilltop fortress complex encompassing royal palaces, grand courtyards and reflecting pools from the Nasrid dynasty. Ursi and I lunched in a small restaurant with a magnificent view of Alhambra, and again the topic came up: Where to?

Ruud and Els came to my place. We sunbathed and relaxed in the pool. There Ruud told me that he had been in love with me a long time ago, when I was a teenager. I remembered I liked to visit his parents with my sister Anne-Lies and Henny, her then boyfriend and eldest of three boys. Ruud and I would tell jokes and watch TV. On one occasion his dad came up to his room and said, "You'd better forget her, she's too old for you." I had never caught on, and Ruud and I laughed about it now.

The subject of conversation changed to my move. I didn't want to go through another winter in the mountains of Spain, so: Where to?

My old school friend Agnes came, this time without her children. We went with JM and Elisabeth to watch a soccer championship match, Netherlands versus Japan. Agnes brought orange flowers to wear so everybody knew we were Dutch.

I had another Tanzania-Christopher-Mountain moment, this time with Agnes in the car with me. While driving through an unfamiliar village, she and I arrived at a dead end. I got out, looked at the situation and knew I could not drive in reverse all the way back on this narrow, winding road with a ravine on one side and mountain on the other. I did some mental calculations. I measured the car and the road and how much the spare tire in back stood out, and told Agnes to guide me to turn the car around. I had about one meter to play with. I almost pissed in my pants, expecting every second that the front tires would lose their grip or that the side of the road would crumble down. Spare tire touching the mountain, it took me about fifteen minutes to turn the car around. Agnes and I were soaked with sweat. When it was finally done, she jumped in and we drove away, never looking back.

Agnes is a much more serious-minded person than I am, so when we later talked about my move she suggested I make a list of the pros and cons of each destination. A good idea…but still, I didn't know where to go!

I had been unable to sell my car, as the worldwide recession had hit Spain hard, and there were few people in the area who could afford a Peugeot. Deciding to rent it out, I found a taker and made another friend: Robert Sibony. Robert is a Canadian drummer and percussionist who has shared the stage and studio with internationally acclaimed artists. Of Spanish and French Moroccan descent, he had come to Sedella to find his roots. Robert liked to hang out at my house and talk about music. From my area he went to Granada, finding like-minded people there: gypsies who were natural musicians and played flamenco. Robert moved to Granada, enjoying his new musician friends and learning as much as possible from their music and his roots. When his money ran out, he returned to Canada.

My lifetime of experiences both wonderful and sad, desired and undesired, resulting from the choices I had made each step of the way, had been digested completely. The ghosts of my past had been dealt with, and I felt rejuvenated and free. I had meditated, taken long walks and deeply enjoyed the natural world around me. Spain had healed me. Now I decided that my three years of solitude, the reclusion I had sought, would come to an end.

I didn't want to experience another cold winter, so the move had to be done before October.

What did I want?

- My animals needed to be able to come with me and have surroundings where they could roam freely.
- A single house with a protective wall, so that my animals could not escape and endanger themselves or other animals.
- A rent and lifestyle that fit my budget as a retiree.
- A house girl, as I did not like to do housework.
- A beach, as I needed the sea to look at. It energized me.
- Sun. I need sun, it makes me happy.

Everybody told me I was crazy to move again at the age of sixty-four with three dogs and two cats. I did not care. I spent a long time researching possible places all over the world. I considered, then rejected, South America. It was too far from Europe, where my father and many of my friends were living. I narrowed my focus to South Asia, studying ads offering houses for rent. (Some countries do not allow foreigners to purchase homes, and I didn't have the money to buy anything, anyway.) It turned out that I couldn't go to Indonesia, as it refused to import dogs. Malaysia and Thailand had no good houses for my purpose; they were all in compounds, which wasn't what I was looking for. Besides, most were too far from an international airport.

AND THE WINNING LOCALE IS...
My destination was certain now: Sri Lanka.

On hearing my choice, some people asked if I wasn't afraid of "the tsunami." The tsunami?! Guys, it was thousands of years before a tsunami reached Sri Lanka, and now it suddenly would happen again after six years? Should I huddle in my house, scared a tsunami will pour onto my doorstep? Not understanding the thinking process of these folks, I shook my head and went forward with my plans.

After checking out many ads for Sri Lankan rentals, I found a great-looking, colonial-era style house in the town of Kochchikade. A real estate agency was offering it for $250 USD a month. My paperwork was easy, as long as I applied through the "My Dream Home" program, which required a one-time deposit of $15,000 USD to Sri Lanka and proof of an income of at least $1,500 USD, which then has to be transferred into a Sri Lankan bank monthly. I also had to show proof of health insurance and a police report from Spain that verified I was not a criminal.

Next I had to fill out documents for my pets. The dogs were no problem: all their vaccinations and permits were arranged in a few weeks. Their travel with Emirates airline was going to cost me €4,000.

The cats were a very big problem, however. As I went through the requirements for importation of cats into Sri Lanka, I found at the end of the document the following note: "Sri Lanka is in the process of declaring its BSE (Bovine Spongiform Encephalopathy *Mad Cow Disease*) free status. Therefore import of cats from BSE-infected countries have been restricted at present." All countries in Europe were on the list of BSE-infected countries. What to do now? I wrote a long email to

Dr. H.M.S.P. Herath, Sri Lanka's Director General of the Department of Animal Production and Health, explaining that my cat came from Dubai, and I had lived for three years on top of a mountain in Spain, where he had not been in contact with cows.

By that time I had decided that Lince would not come with me. The odds were too great that he would have diarrhea in his cage or the infection on his cheek would flare up again—I'd seen stress do that—and he would be returned to Spain to be put in a shelter, or worse, put down. I needed to find a good home for him.

I asked Dr. Mario if I could put a flyer in his window. He agreed to this and promised me that if no one showed an interest, he would keep Lince in the clinic. We didn't have to wait long for an angel to appear. Her name was Lynn Paver, and she lived in Arches, not far from Sedella, in a picturesque home with a big roof terrace. I brought Lince there with a heavy heart, worrying how he would adapt, but when I visited after a few days, I saw that Lince was growing accustomed to Lynn. In fact, he was happy, having made the bed and terrace his own.

I was still awaiting word from the Sri Lankan Department of Animal Production and Health about bringing Dominic into the country. I called and was connected to a woman vet who said emphatically I could not import my cat from Europe. I lost my temper and shouted at her that my cat would come to Sri Lanka whatever the rules were, by ship or by plane.

Since Dominic originated from Dubai, I contacted a parent at DAA who was a Dutch vet. She told me she couldn't get involved in an illegal transaction, as she could lose her license. However, she knew a woman in Dubai named Allison who ran a kennel called The Doghouse and had experience in animal transport. The vet suggested I call her.

I spoke with Allison, and she and I decided that Dominic would travel to Dubai under "an assumed identity." He'd need to stay in Dubai for at least forty-five days, with new vaccination books created for him. It was costly, but I saw no other way.

Dickie and Zdravko wanted to see me before I moved to Sri Lanka. Dickie was allergic to cats, so she and Zdravko got a room in a hotel in Torre del Mar. They rented a car and drove up to my little house on top of the mountain. During their visit, Dickie told me that after all these years, at age seventy-four, she was in the process of divorcing Zdravko. He had accused her of cheating on him, stealing from him, etc., etc. He reminded me of my dad, and I realized they were the same astrological sign, Aries: one who is stubborn, jealous, suspicious and possessive, and always needs to be right. Dickie discovered that Zdravko was the one who had the girlfriend, and soon she would move into her own apartment. Having shared a dinner with me at the end of a memorable day, Dickie and Zdravko got into their car, Zdravko behind the wheel. His foot hit the gas pedal, the car accelerated and smashed into my gate. Of course, I didn't get mad at him, but I had to repair my gate, and he got a new rental car.

I gave away many of my things. All my winter clothes went to charities—I never wanted to see them again. I gave away thousands of my books, keeping only biographies and ones on spirituality. My videotapes and music cassettes were gone, as everything was now digitalized.

Alin, the PI for my case in Costa Rica, had moved to Spain and said he was interested in buying my Peugeot. He would fly into the Malaga airport, and I would drive him up to my place where he could see the car. I had never met Alin in person and was curious to meet him.

I drove to the airport, entered the waiting area and sat on a bench, my faithful bodyguard Costa beside me. I loved watching people and could have sat there for hours. Alin's plane touched down, and people started streaming out of the arrivals hall. I looked at each passenger, but none looked like the Alin I had imagined. I dialed him on my cell, and while we talked I noticed two men sitting on a bench not far from me, one of them on a phone. I said I thought I was looking at him and that I had a dog with me. The guy made eye contact, smiled and hung up. He and the other man stood and walked toward me. One was average height and build. The other was a gorilla! A bodybuilder, tall, almost exploding out of the suit he wore. Alin (the bodybuilder) introduced me to his brother. We all left the airport and got in my car and drove to my house, discussing the Saskia-Panama case. When we reached my home, they looked at the little Peugeot, which Alin was buying for his wife. We agreed on the price, they paid and wanted to leave, but…Alin couldn't fit in the car. He had to adjust and adjust until finally he felt he could drive away, cooped up in the shoebox.

A farmer living to the south bought my Land Cruiser. Both cars were sold at a loss, but I needed the money before I left Spain.

I had arranged for a moving company to get my belongings. A truck came, and its men tossed in my things with stuff from other people. *Uh-oh, will that go well?* I wondered, but I didn't say anything. The truck was so full that the co-driver barely squeezed into his seat (but he was no gorilla).

Early on the morning of October 1, I put all three dogs, Dominic and my luggage into a rental van. As we drove off, I looked back and knew I would never return. The house had been good to me, I had been happy, but now it was time to go.

We arrived at the Madrid airport in good time. I sent Dominic off to Dubai, and the dogs went to a pre-flight kennel. I boarded an Emirates jet that would take me to Sri Lanka via Dubai. Arriving in Dubai, I went to the station manager and requested to see my dogs. (I knew I could trust Allison to collect Dominic.) I was asked, "What dogs?" I said that my animals had boarded in Madrid. The manager looked at me as if I were crazy and said he'd get back to me. Half an hour later, I was told Costa, Bella and Aztec were still in Madrid: the air conditioner in the hold was broken, so the animals were not allowed to travel. Fuming, I contacted airline authorities in Madrid and told them to give my dogs food and water, as they had been imprisoned in their cages all day. Still furious when I arrived in Colombo, I went straight to the Emirates desk, asked for the cargo manager and station manager, and lodged an official complaint.

SRI LANKA
(2010-PRESENT)

KOCHIKADE: LESS THAN IDEAL

Brian, the owner of the real estate agency, picked me up from the airport. He and his wife took me to dinner at a small restaurant in Negombo before bringing me to the door of my new home in Kochchikade. I dropped my bags directly upon entering, went straight to bed, and fell into a deep sleep.

The next morning I opened my eyes to see a Sri Lankan man standing in the bedroom doorway, mouth agape. I told him to get out and close the door; he had no clue what I'd said, but after I made a few gestures he understood and left. I dressed and was now able to see the house in daylight. It had two floors, the kitchen on the ground floor and an upper floor with a living area and a terrace offering a view of the sea. However, the home hadn't been cleaned or maintained, and the garden was too small, absolutely unsuitable for my dogs, who would easily jump over its walls. As for the man in the bedroom, I realized that he was the houseboy and lived there, and had no plans to move out. One more "minus": the furniture was horrible. I was told that before I arrived the house would be refurnished, but obviously nothing had been done, so I called Brian and told him we must meet. He came to the house and heard my complaints. He said he would call the owner (who lived overseas) and discuss the furniture with him. Brian then drove away, and now I could concentrate on my dogs.

I phoned the cargo manager of Emirates to see what was happening. He told me that Aztec, Costa and Bella would be on the afternoon flight going from Madrid to Dubai, information I passed along to Allison of The Doghouse. I met up with Brian again in the afternoon. He gave me the import documents for my dogs and what turned out to be some very good advice regarding the taxes I'd have to pay for them. (I didn't know I owed any taxes at all.) Brian also helped me hire a truck that could hold three huge dog carriers. I was all set to leave for the airport when the cargo manager called and said Aztec and the puppers were still in Dubai and would arrive on the night flight. I felt so sorry for my dogs. I asked the manager to send a telex to Dubai instructing them to be given water, as they were now traveling for a third day. I called Brian to change the rental time for the truck, then phoned Allison to see if at least Dominic was OK. He was, and had been directly transferred to Linda, his foster mother for the time he would spend in Dubai.

When I arrived at the airport that night, I should have been happy and excited at the prospect of seeing my pets again, but bureaucracy got in the way. First I had to go through certain paperwork. Then I proceeded to the cargo area to identify the dogs who, at the sound of my approaching footsteps, instantly started barking and yowling. I asked for water to give to them, then returned to where the rest of the paperwork waited. Upon signing the vet check, I was asked to pay the taxes. Brian had warned me they could be steep, but I wasn't prepared for the figure: a whopping 60,000 rupees, at that time about $600 USD. I had 5,000 rupees in my purse, that was all. My tears flowed. I told the desk clerks I didn't have that kind of money, opening my purse and showing them what I had. I took off my plastic watch and told them that they could have that, too. (Of course, I had not put on any jewelry and was very simply dressed.) I told them the truth: that all my dogs were rescues and I had spent all my money to bring them here to Sri Lanka, where I came to retire. Their response was that if Emirates and the shipping company earned money on my dogs, they had every right to be rewarded as well.

I could see they were scared of my dogs, especially Aztec, so appeals to their better natures having failed, I tried a little gambit. I turned my back and muttered in a cold voice, "Then keep them."

The men called their manager.

In about thirty minutes I was taken into his office and given a seat. Again, my tears ran freely, this time out of frustration and anger. These people thought I was a stupid foreigner who would accept their corruption. I told my story again, opening my purse, waving my watch, throwing everything on the manager's desk and saying that I had no more money.

"Show me the regulations for the import of live animals!" I demanded. "Where is it written that taxes are required? I have never read such rules!" I was now really upset. I rose and said, "I love the dogs, but I spent my last cent to bring them here. You can keep them, and I hope you will be happy."

A long moment passed. The manager looked at me as if I were a cockroach, then called to his assistant, "Take this woman out of my office! I do not want to see her again. And get her dogs out of the airport." With my head down I left his office, trying to hide my smile. Back at the cargo office, the assistant asked for 5,000 rupees. I told him to give me a receipt, which he did. All paperwork cleared away, I brought my dogs in their cages to the truck, then gave all onlookers heart attacks by letting them out. Costa and Bella jumped and barked and danced. Even Aztec joined in. The truck driver was as unnerved as the midnight crew. Telling him not to worry, I got in the truck and called to the dogs. Costa and Bella jumped inside. I had to get out of the vehicle again and carry Aztec in, as his hip didn't allow him to jump up to the seat. It was easy for me to dismantle the carriers and put them in the truck bed. In high spirits we arrived home, me giving the driver an extra big tip, as the dogs were dirty. Brian phoned and asked how things went. I told him the story, and we both laughed, relieved it went OK, I particularly happy I had listened to his warning. The dogs were in a horrible state: they were hungry, dehydrated, and smelled of pee and pooh, as they had been cooped too long in their cages. You can be sure I set to cleaning them up.

Allison of The Doghouse wrote to me:

> *If I had the contact info for the agent you used in Spain, I would have given him a piece of my mind—he never, not once contacted me! Totally unprofessional. I've never known an agent—even for general cargo—to not contact the consignee personally! It was just as well you were so involved or else I wouldn't have known that Dominic was arriving—let alone delayed. Even when I went to collect him, the Emirates staff were "surprised" that there were live animals on board! Don't worry, Dominic was totally fine & I had him out & settled very quickly. He is getting on well with Linda & she has the list of his likes/dislikes/habits to guide her. His onward journey will not be the fiasco that you have just experienced, I can assure you.*

I emailed a lengthy complaint to the general manager of Emirates airline, who wrote back with an apology and assurances that Dominic would not encounter the same difficulties.

Soon after waking the next morning between my beloved dogs, I took them for a walk on the beach. Not a good idea. Brian had set me up in a house where the nearest beach was rocky and littered with paper bags, bottles and food waste. The dogs also discovered very quickly that the garden had big possibilities and yes, the wall could be leaped over, so I had to keep them inside.

I went back to the house, called Brian and told him to look for another house as soon as possible, better today than tomorrow. A few hours later he called to tell me that there was a house in Kaluwapitiya with a swimming pool that was not on the beach but a few kilometers inland. Would I like to see it? Well, I had nothing to lose. When he came I had suitcases and dogs ready. He looked at me in surprise, and I said, "Anything is better than this!" We all got in his car, and there we went.

KALUWAPITIYA

The two-story house was back from the main street and surrounded by a high wall. It had a huge garden and a swimming pool. The house belonged to Albert Philpin, a British man who was away in the UK and not planning to live in the home for the next few years. The house had two bedrooms upstairs with a bathroom in between and a sitting area with Wi-Fi. Downstairs was an open kitchen, living room and master bedroom. The house was perfect, and the rent was within my budget. The security guards/houseboys/gardeners, Morris and Sumane, were included. I signed the contract there and then. Brian called a *tuktuk* driver named Milroy (a *tuktuk* being a motorized rickshaw or three-wheeler) and told him that I was his new client. Milroy agreed to collect me every morning to have a walk with the dogs on the beach in Negombo. The dogs loved riding in the *tuktuk*, Aztec claiming the driver's seat when he could.

From Dubai came good news: Dominic was doing very well. Now I needed to pick up the import papers from the Department of Animal Production and Health in the city of Kandy. On a Friday Milroy drove me there in the *tuktuk*, a three-hour trip. Upon arriving at the department, I was sent to see a lady doctor, and when I started to explain why I came, she impatiently asked where I was from. I realized with horror that she was the same woman to whom, before I left Spain, I had sent my angry email, not to mention shouted at over the phone. I quickly mentioned Switzerland (not Spain) and showed her my Swiss passport. She studied it, tapping her finger on her nose, and said, "Ah! You have imported the three dogs. I will have to take a look at the file. Please come back tomorrow. Although it is Saturday, I will be here. Come in the morning before noon."

For sure, I knew, she remembered.

While Milroy and I were returning to Kandy the next day, we passed Keels supermarket. Having earlier noticed many scrumptious-looking cakes in its bakery section, I asked Milroy to stop, and I purchased a big, lovely cake. The doctor was already sitting at her desk when I arrived at the department, and I could feel my heart pumping in my throat. I greeted her and sat down. She looked at me, again tapping her nose, and asked, "So what is the story with the cat?"

I knew it was time to bring out the cake.

As I slipped it out of its plastic Keels bag, I said I realized she was making a special exception for me to be in the office that day, so I had brought her the cake to enjoy on the weekend with her family. Tip-tapping her nose, she asked once more, "What's the story with the cat?" I told her I bought Dominic in Dubai in 2002. When I left for Tanzania, he stayed behind with British friends of mine. Now I had moved to Sri Lanka and my friends were returning to the UK, so they asked if I could take Dominic back, and that is what I was doing now. The doctor examined my file. I was sure she had already read the letter and knew exactly what was going on, but she would find no evidence of Dominic ever living outside the UAE. If she had simply glanced at my Facebook page, the jig would have been up! The woman looked at me and said, "We are not here to create problems. Go and take your cat," then signed my import papers. I stepped around the table, hugged her, and traipsed from her office on happy, dancing feet.

Allison called to reassure me that Dominic was on his expected flight and was being treated as a VIP, for the staff had showed her written instructions from the general manager to treat him with utmost care until his arrival in Sri Lanka. The next morning I went to the airport, girding my loins for another battle over taxes. However, the people on the day shift didn't try to cheat me (and I suppose it helped that Dominic was deemed a VIP). I made the normal small payments for this and that, and after the vet had seen him, I was permitted to take him and go. The total cost for flying Dominic, boarding him in Dubai, paying for his new papers, etc., had cost me $4,000 USD.

As always, I visited Dad on his birthday, April 3. This time he was single (just for a few weeks) because his girlfriend Riet had been moved to the care department of the retirement facility; she could no longer live independently. To my surprise Dad expressed no regrets about this and coldly refused to visit her. He said that she did not recognize him, which was a lie, as when I went to see her she knew exactly who I was.

Dad had bought a computer. I had asked him to wait for my arrival so we could buy it together, but no, he didn't have the patience. He called my friends Vivienne and Richard, who lived close to him, to help him do it. Dad said he was going to take a computer course, so I loaned him my expensive $1,000 USD leather computer travel bag in exchange for his cheap computer rucksack. An old man going to computer classes should look respectable! I also added music to the computer and showed him how to play it. He was a busy bee with his new toy.

THREE WEEKS IN TANZANIA

Upon my return to Kaluwapitiya, Dimitri Mantheakis, new chair of The Hellenic Society, phoned me. He asked if I could come to Tanzania for about three weeks to assess the students again and give a full report on the school. My houseboys Morris and Sumane had gotten accustomed to my animals by then, but for added assurance I asked Milroy if he could pass by daily and check on them while I was away. He agreed against good payment to do so. Of course, Maggie, who now lived permanently in Arusha, got the good news I was coming.

Delighted to be returning to Africa, I was collected from the airport by my old friend, the driver of the school, who brought me straight to SCIS. I was shown to my room in the guest wing and then met with Mama Janet, who had been transferred to administration. I went directly to work, as I had no time to waste. I had already prepared the paperwork at home, after receiving class lists from the heads. The actual assessments did not take long; what was time-consuming was compiling the grade results for math, writing and reading, work I could do in my room on my computer. I checked in daily with Milroy, and my cat and dogs were OK.

I planned to meet Maggie for four days in the Serengeti. She was now a consultant for ENJIPAI, an NGO working on behalf of the Maasai. The brainchild of Lekishon, a Maasai warrior intensely worried about the future of his community, ENJIPAI aims to improve the living conditions of children and families through providing for their basic needs and ensuring they have access to healthcare and education. As its website puts it, ENJIPAI is a smile in the middle of the savannah.

I drove with an employee of Thomson Safari to Loliondo, a village situated in Ngorongoro District of Arusha Region in northern Tanzania.

From there we continued to Sukenya, where Thomson Safari had set up a new, luxurious tented safari camp. Maggie was waiting for me at the site. We fell into each other's arms and cried, it being four years since we had seen each other. I was especially emotional because Maggie had been the one to ensure my safety during my difficult times with the Jumas. We had a drink, then continued in her car to the staff quarters, where she had her own tent. Wow! I'd never seen one so elegant and comfortable.

Maggie was advising women on using their newly built, ENJIPAI-supplied stone ovens. She was also teaching them how to make their jewelry and other decorative items more attractive to tourists. The Enyuata Women's Collaborative had progressively established several small businesses under Maggie's leadership. Thomson Safari supported these initiatives to attract tourism, and that is why we were staying at their first-class camp.

The next morning after breakfast, Maggie and I drove toward a distant *boma* where she was to hold a meeting with Maasai women. I felt I'd been swept onto a movie set, as the two of us drove through the Serengeti savannah. We saw giraffes, antelope, and huge vultures picking apart the leftovers of a leopard's or lion's kill. They were like dots in the universe—grassland and baobab trees, birds and animals, all living peacefully together—until the moment that one of them got hungry. Then the moment of killing would strike!

We passed *moranis* (unmarried Maasai warriors) herding cows, and lonely corrals where Maasai children played outside huts. All the way from Sukenya, Maggie would stop to speak in her native language to every Maasai walking the road or standing beside it. It seems that she knew everyone, and everyone made me feel welcome. I filmed like crazy.

We arrived at a corral of three huts where ENJIPAI had just finished building a communal oven. Bursting with pride, the women showed it to us. They offered us a kind of yogurt, made from the milk of their cows. The milk is kept in a calabash (they have no refrigerators) and shaken until it thickens. I got accustomed to this drink, as it was offered at every visit Maggie and I made to the Maasai, and refusing it would have been considered impolite. One lady gave me her calabash, which still hangs in my house and still has a whiff of the milk that filled it five years ago.

Maggie and I continued our drive to the meeting place. As it came into view, I saw colorfully dressed women and men approaching from all corners of the savannah. It took a very long time until all of them were finally gathered. As in meetings all over the world, everyone had something to say; even in this small community, there were many different opinions, so many that at one point one of the elders had to interrupt to remind the rest that they didn't have all day. The big subject of discussion was where to sell their traditional jewelry to tourists. Each group of families wanted the sales booth to be close to its own corral, and one had to be very diplomatic not to insult one party or the other. Maggie now and then lost her temper, which was not difficult for her, as she has a short fuse.

Maggie taught the people simple accounting, explaining that they needed to understand the value of a US dollar. They had no clue how much milk or bread might cost in dollars or cents; for them, a buck was just a flimsy piece of paper. The instruction took several hours. At moments a male elder put in a word, not that he had information to add, but just because he wanted everyone to acknowledge his presence. At last it seemed that the instruction "took," and all problems were solved. Everybody smiled and started walking back toward their homes. However, I noticed there were two groups of women who were keeping a distance from each other, apparently dissatisfied with how things stood. Maggie assured me they would work things out between them. We went back to camp, where we had dinner and a pleasant get-together with other staff members.

The next day Maggie and I drove to Loliondo, where she showed me Wasso Hospital, where her husband had worked as the head physician. We also went to the local government offices, where we were warmly greeted. Basically, we took the day easy, as the next one promised to be challenging. The people of ENJIPAI had heard about a village school in the mountains bordering Kenya, far from civilization, that needed help, and Maggie and I were invited to come and check it out.

After an early breakfast, we left the campsite and drove into the mountains, up and down, seemingly without end. I had no idea where we were, but I was told that wherever I looked to the north was Kenya. Finally, we gazed at a mountainside and saw a building with some children in front of it. We had arrived! The children received us with joy, singing songs especially for me. It was seldom they saw a *mzungu*, and I suppose my presence made it an event. When the elders of the village came to join the teachers, we held a meeting, Maggie translating. It was decided that ENJIPAI would start a community program with the village. We all were satisfied and content to leave with such a good project ahead.

IN SEARCH OF MIRACLES
The next morning Maggie and I returned to Arusha by small aircraft. During the flight she told me the following incredible story.

Maggie had heard from her Maasai friends that a local pastor had become renowned for healing a woman with HIV. As she was already doing consulting work in the area, Maggie gave into her curiosity and went to Samunge Village in Loliondo to meet this man.

Ambilikile Mwasupile, seventy-six years old, was a retired pastor of the Evangelical Lutheran Church. He was not yet famous enough to draw crowds, so Maggie was able to get him alone and talk with him at length.

Mwasupile told her that God appeared to him in a dream and said He would show him how to cure many illnesses. What's more, the first person Mwasupile would cure would be a woman with HIV. The day after the dream, when the pastor walked into church to give a sermon, God directed his eyes toward a particular woman and spoke to him, saying, "This is the one I want you to treat." Still, Mwasupile hesitated, even after he had another dream in which God urged him to cure her. The pastor started asking God questions: "How can I go to this woman and say, 'God has sent me to treat you because you are sick?' Her condition is very personal, not something to be revealed to everyone." God told him the woman would not refuse treatment, so Mwasupile went directly to her, told her about God's message, and the woman agreed to whatever treatment he offered.

God next told Mwasupile to go into the mountains and find a mugariga tree. The mugariga grows wild and bears a fruit that people, livestock, and birds commonly eat. However, God told the pastor that the roots were what he should gather; they had healing properties. The pastor climbed the mountain, followed the route God revealed, and returned with some roots. Mwasupile sat outside his hut and prayed for further guidance. He claims a kind of ladder descended from the sky, and on it was a person bearing two more roots in his arms. The heavenly visitor (an angel?) gave the pastor the roots, and the voice of God instructed Mwasupile to partially peel and boil them. People simply had to drink the resulting broth, and they would be cured of any major illness, including HIV, high blood pressure, high blood sugar and cancer. Mwasupile expressed surprise that the roots could do so much; and why should he be the one to administer this miracle liquid, when he was no witch doctor or traditional healer, but merely a pastor from the Lutheran Church?

However, he was not about to ignore the word of God. Mwasupile boiled the roots, fetched the ill woman, asked that they pray together, and then gave her one cup of the broth—that was all God had told him to give. Mwasupile and the woman prayed once more, and off she went.

Days went by. Word spread that the pastor was curing diseases that the doctors were helpless to treat. Everyone started wondering if it was true, and if so, why should he have this power? After twenty-one days, God again appeared to Mwasupile in a dream and said, "Awake, go to that woman you treated and ask her to go to the hospital to be examined, because she is already cured." The pastor went to the woman after Sunday mass and told her what God had said. She agreed to go to Wasso Hospital, where the doctors found no sign of HIV in her blood: she was cured. Amazed, the staff asked her how she had recovered, but she understood that the pastor didn't want his name mentioned, and so kept silent.

When she met Mwasupile afterward, he gave her permission to give out his name. She started spreading the news that she was healed, and after a while, she became pregnant and had a baby. Hospital management followed up on her health, and said she continued to be well.

Maggie stressed that this story was told to her directly by the pastor. He said to Maggie, "If you think you have an illness, you are welcome to drink the water." As it happened, Maggie suffered from high blood sugar. She drank some of the broth, and since then, she swears that she only has to follow her anti-hyperglycemic diet and no longer needs to take any medicines.

Arriving back at SCIS, I told Mama Janet what Maggie had told me. She replied that, as it happened, she and some family members were going to see the pastor the very next day. Would I care to join them? Of course! Not only would it be a new adventure, but perhaps I could get relief from my hemorrhoids. I had suffered from them for many months: standard treatments didn't seem to help, and I was afraid of the pain every time I had to go to the bathroom.

We left at four in the morning, the Land Cruiser filled nearly to bursting with a driver and six women with health problems. We took a well-established road for about two hours, then followed faint tracks through the savannah, a trail only the sharp eyes of a Maasai could make out. At first our vehicle was the only one for miles around, but the closer we came to Samunge, the more we were overtaken by other cars and buses, until we felt like competitors on a racecourse. After about five hours of driving, tired of being confined to our seats, we finally arrived in the village. The place was so packed, we had to park a fifteen-minute walk away from the pastor's hut.

Unfortunately, we got word that one of the country's ministers was in a private meeting with Mwasupile. We patiently waited for over two hours until the pastor could work his way through the crowd to us, distributing the broth to everyone. It was a miracle that the process went as peacefully as it did. There were hundreds of people, sick, paralyzed, or handicapped in other ways, and we all drank from the same ten cups. When all of us had drunk the dirty, foul-tasting water, and seen the pastor for ourselves, we were happy to leave the crush and return to Arusha. Regardless of whether people were healed or not, at least one miracle transpired: although we were all drinking from the same cups, which were rinsed swiftly and carelessly between usage, apparently no one caught any (new) illness. The following morning and the next, Mama Janet asked me, "How are you feeling?" After three days I could tell her, "Better!" The long-lingering hemorrhoids disappeared, never to return. As for Mama Janet's high blood sugar, it came under control. I do not know how her sisters fared.

MY TAKE ON SCIS

Dimitri, chair of The Hellenic Society, arrived for a serious meeting with me. Over the years I had come to know SCIS and fallen in love with it. The school had potential, but lots of "needs." The campus needed a facelift. SCIS needed to be accredited as an international school. It needed a salary scale. There were many dedicated teachers, but over time the less effective ones should have been replaced, which I had advised years ago. Mama Janet, who now ran the admin department with her secretary, Kalyope, did a very good job. For reasons unclear to me, the Greeks wanted to get rid of Henrik, the headmaster, and also wanted the heads of both the secondary school and the primary school to be evaluated.

The biggest problem with the school was the yearly budget. It was useless because it was only a breakdown of costs most likely to occur during the school year, and did not allow the headmaster spending discretion. The board micromanaged on a daily basis: not even a pencil could be acquired without a request sent to Dar es Salaam, once the budget had been approved. It was impossible for school administration to work under these circumstances.

In my view, the school needed to be pushed into the twenty-first century with a complete overhaul. I felt that SCIS was not an international school, but a school with African teachers who did not interact with the few Western teachers. Some of these Western teachers, all women, formed two separate camps, one of which was talking to Dimitri behind the headmaster's back. Henrik never stood a chance against that group. One teacher who kept himself out of all politics and worked extremely hard was Barry, who finally received what he deserved, to be head of primary. The whole situation was extremely unprofessional. My advice to The Hellenic Society was to bring in a new headmaster, a strong personality with international school experience and a clear vision, and allow him or her to make necessary changes. I also urged the board to increase the wage scale, as even I would not work for the society's low salaries.

HOME AND A TOUR

I flew back to Sri Lanka. Milroy picked me up at the airport and told me that a few nights earlier Aztec had killed a cat, Costa and Bella had killed a mongoose, and Dominic, last but not least, had killed a squirrel. It was a joy to be back with my (admittedly hunt-happy) pets in the new house with its pool and hard-working staff, especially old toothless Morris. He was kind, and Aztec loved him. I soon bought a car, a fifty-four-year-old Willys Jeep. It was strong and everything I needed to safely drive in Sri Lanka.

My nephew Maikel came to visit, and we took an island-wide tour. It was a second time for me, for you may recall that I took such a trip in 2000 with my house girl Lalita. Our tour guide was Henri, a kindhearted man with lots of knowledge of the island. I enjoyed traveling with Maikel, as he was easygoing and "maintenance free." We went to the city of Galle to visit a Dutch fort, steered down the coast to a turtle farm, and ended up in a small hotel on the beach where we had a view of the celebrated "stilt fishermen," men who fish from platforms set on poles a few feet above the ocean waves. At Yala National Park we watched for wildlife, an experience that paled in comparison to my African safaris. But as in Africa, where I never got to see a lion (everybody else did), in Yala I never saw the leopard that all others sighted. From Yala we crossed the mountains to Kandy, enjoying the view of the many Tamil leaf-pickers on the tea plantations. In Kandy we saw the famous Kandyan Dancers, who performed to traditional music. The final attraction of our trip was the elephant orphanage in Pinnawala, where orphaned Asian baby elephants found in the wild are fed and cared for on a former coconut plantation. All in all, it was a great excursion, and

I had a wonderful time with Maikel. Before we knew it, two weeks had passed, and he was headed home.

MARTIN

The real estate company through which I had found my home had changed hands. Brian and his wife had returned to the UK, and Martin Fullerton, owner of the popular Lords Restaurant in Negombo, had taken over. Martin, a blond spiky-haired, fashionable, chubby animal lover, called me and asked if I would be able to restructure the admin department of the agency, which was now called Property Market Solutions. I agreed to work part time, only the mornings, as I didn't really need the money, but Martin thought I'd enjoy meeting new people on the job.

Let me give you a little background on Martin.

He arrived in Sri Lanka in 2003 with a St. Bernard and an Old English sheepdog. He bought land and built the Lords Restaurant Complex, which was officially opened by the president of Sri Lanka in May 2004. The complex had a staff of 330. During the first six months of operations, approximately 5,000 people visited the complex each week. Then came disaster: the tsunami hit the island in December 2004. Virtually overnight, all vacationers fled the island and left the tourist industry in shambles. The ongoing Tamil war didn't help matters. A ceasefire in place since 2002 broke down in summer 2006, and fighting started anew. Only 386,000 tourists visited the island in the whole of 2008. Compare that to Thailand's 19.8 million! In January 2007 Martin made a tough decision: he closed his nightclub and three restaurants and let its workers go. Over the next two years he operated exactly one bar and restaurant, employing only three people. In May 2009 the country's civil war ended, and he was much relieved to see tourists return.

Back in October 2003, Martin came across a litter of abandoned puppies on his property. He decided to adopt them and their mother, whom he named Hope. Founding a charity called **The Hope Foundation**, Martin began feeding and rescuing strays in Sri Lanka. Eventually, he would personally rescue and own eighteen street dogs and two cats. As you can imagine, Martin has had a great influence on me, as we are both animal lovers. Although I've been passionate about cats my whole life, when I rescued my first kitten Martin warned me, "Be careful. This is only the beginning!"

HERRMANN COTTAGE, WAIKKALA

I started thinking about a home in Waikkala I had come across on the web while I was still living in Spain and house hunting. Waikkala is a village about thirty minutes by *tuktuk* north of Bandaranaike International Airport. The place, called Herrmann Cottage One, had looked perfect, but it hadn't been available at the time. The house is in Kammala North, a small fishing community within Waikkala. I decided to check the home out in person to see if it deserved my high opinion. I took Costa with me, Milroy driving, as usual.

The house was easy to find. Its owner, Rohan Kurera, wasn't at home, but his father, Anthony, came out to greet me. He showed me the house, located directly on the beach with a huge garden. While Milroy translated, I explained I would love to rent the house, not just for a short time, but for life. Anthony said he would call Rohan, who lived and worked in Germany. I told Anthony that while he was on the phone, I would take a look at a small seaside chapel nearby.

I walked toward the chapel, Costa trotting at my side until...he wasn't. I turned to see feathers flying in the high grass, Costa's tail waving excitedly. Stepping lightly on his toes like a ballet dancer, a Nureyev, Costa came to me, an unfortunate chicken in his mouth. What happened next was what I'd been trying to train him and Bella to do for years: he dropped the bird at my feet, looked at me and awaited praise, while the chicken ran away. Actually, I think Costa didn't even realize the chicken had gotten away, he was so focused on getting a pat on the head. I said, "Well done, Costa, well done!" while looking around to see if there had been any witnesses. There was no sign of this, so I put Costa on his leash, and we continued our walk.

When we returned, Anthony said that I should email his son. Rohan was willing to rent the house to me, but several items needed clarification before an agreement could be signed, including my request that the garden walls be raised and topped with wire. One month later I moved in.

Herrmann Cottage was built by a German named Fritz Herrmann, who befriended Anthony over many years of vacationing in Waikkala. Anthony permitted Herrmann to build the house on his property, with the understanding that when Herrmann passed away, the house would belong to Anthony, who would then hand it down to his son Rohan.

When I moved in I automatically had a house girl, Noni, a beautiful small Sri Lankan lady with the figure of a model, who was pregnant. She lived with her husband, Suranga, an easygoing chubby, calm man in Anthony's old house. I liked how the neighborhood was friendly and clean. Across the street was "Rico's Shadow," a small combination guesthouse and restaurant built and designed by Christopher Dabarera and his Swiss friend of many years, Rico Bellvilla. The whole street is like one big family, and it gives me a very good, safe and secure feeling.

ISLAND EXPLORING, PSYCHIC ADVENTURE

My first visitors were Anna Pearson Costa, the medium I had consulted in Spain, and four of her friends. We had a blast! They joined me on yet another tour of Sri Lanka. Poor Henry, our tour guide, was the target of many jokes and songs, teased and loved by us ladies. We drove by minibus to Anuradhapura, one of the country's ancient capitals, famous for its well-preserved ruins. Next stop was Polonnaruwa, the capital after the destruction of Anuradhapura in 993. It features the monumental remains of the fabulous garden-city created by Parakramabahu I in the twelfth century. After our first day, we had enough of history and culture and went to see elephants in Angammedilla National Park. From there we backtracked to Dambulla to see the famous Golden Rock Temple, a sacred pilgrimage site for twenty-two centuries. This monastery is the largest, best-preserved cave-temple complex in Sri Lanka. The extensive Buddhist murals and 157 statues were awe-inspiring. We had to walk a bit but were entertained by the monkeys. Of course, we could not miss Sigiriya. This ancient city, built 1,600 years ago by a brilliant but tormented king, burst briefly into pre-eminence with its breathtaking architecture and art, then quickly faded into oblivion. From Sigiriya we went to Kandy and saw the Temple of the Sacred Tooth Relic, said to house a tooth of the Buddha. Then we took a train ride passing tea plantations, mountains and waterfalls on our way to Nuwara Eliya. We had reserved first-class tickets but somehow ended up in third class, which was far more memorable and at times hilarious. The Sri Lankans around us changed trains at every stop, hanging out of the windows and open doors. We bought food from a little man who was selling it on the train, and lived to tell about it.

I told Anna about Martin who, like her, had spiritual gifts and had been a medium in the UK. She asked me to call him, so they could put their energies together and see what developed! Martin seldom goes out, but there he was at my door with a good bottle of wine. The evening was unforgettable, spirits and laughter in the air.

And those spirits lingered! The next day all us ladies except Anna went to the Dolphin Club Hotel for lunch; Anna stayed behind and meditated. Several hours later, while I was working on the computer, she came to me and told me that she had had a once-in-a-lifetime experience. As she was meditating on my terrace, the angel Gabriel came and spoke to her, embracing her with his wings. It took a while for her to absorb what had happened and tell me about it. As you can imagine, I was sorry when it was time for Anna and her friends to go.

CONNECTING WITH OLD FRIENDS

Mr. John, the factotum from DAA in Dubai, was originally from Kerala. He told me many times about the houseboats that travelled the rivers and lakes of Kerala, so when my neighbor Christopher invited me and a small group of his house guests from Germany to take a trip on a houseboat, I happily agreed. We flew to Kochi and drove from there to our houseboat, on which we spent two days floating on the rivers of Kerala. It was an experience not to be missed. I called Mr. John from the boat to tell him that I finally was there, where he had told me to go so many times.

I met up with my very first boyfriend, Peter de Wit, the one who, when I was fourteen, rode up on his bicycle and asked me to be his girlfriend (and never asked me to do any hanky-panky). He and his wife were visiting a Dutchman married to a Sri Lankan lady. We all met up at Rico's Shadow and had a wonderful dinner. The food and conversation were so good that Peter asked me if he could stay in Waikkala while his wife returned to the Netherlands to attend to their business. (They owned a vineyard and also imported wines from other countries.) Besides, Peter insisted he could do much of their business on the phone and at a computer, and so didn't need to be home. He swam in the sea, took long walks with Aztec, and enjoyed a week of "dolce far niente," just doing sweet nothing. Every evening he ordered big plates of special lagoon crabs from Rico's Shadow, made by Kamala, Christopher's sister, who ran the restaurant. It was a week of drinking, eating and laughter, as we recalled many things from our teenage years we thought we had forgotten.

TAPA

Through Martin I met members of TAPA (Tsunami Animal People Association) a rescue group headed by Dr. Roshan Fernandopulle, who became my friend and vet for all my animals. Because of my computer knowledge, I volunteered for several projects as a photographer/film-maker, creating flyers and short films. I found myself giving more and more time to TAPA; my heart went out to these poor, desperate animals living everywhere on the streets of Sri Lanka.

I covered several events for both TAPA and Martin's Hope Foundation. The most memorable was surely the one held at Mount Lavinia Hotel, one of Colombo's most celebrated landmarks. This palatial hotel was originally the personal residence of Sir Thomas Maitland, British governor of Sri Lanka (then Ceylon) from 1805 to 1811. Legend has it he fell in love with a dancing girl named Lovina. During construction of his mansion, Maitland arranged for a secret tunnel to be dug from his wine cellar to Lovina's nearby home, so that the lovers could meet clandestinely. During World War II, the residence served as a British military hospital, and in 1947 it became The Mount Lavinia Hotel, inspired by the name of Maitland's lover. Some scenes in the film

The Bridge on the River Kwai were filmed on the premises. The "tunnel of love" still stands.

Martin had organized everything perfectly, providing press releases every day featuring a special function or guest. We both stayed for one week. The event was opened by Mr. Claude Thomasz, chair of the tourist board, Western Province, and attended by representatives of different religions. Day after day we received different VIPs, including the American guest of honor, Ambassador Patricia A. Butenis. The Thailand delegation from the World Society for the Protection of Animals (WSPA) featured Thai actor Por Thrisadee Sahawong, an animal lover and ambassador for South and Southeast Asia. Groups of students came to see what we were doing, and we went to schools to educate the children about dogs and cats in general, their illnesses like rabies and mange, the advantages of sterilization, and the way to treat animals they encounter on the street and at home. Evenings we went for dinners at the beachside restaurants, after which I'd go back to the hotel to edit my videos from that day to upload them to YouTube.

One of those evenings, Martin called me saying that one of the dignitaries, an evangelical priest, had asked him for my number. I told him to give the number and immediately forgot about it. Thirty minutes later my cell phone rang. It was the priest I had spoken to that morning about our project. I was only half listening to him, as I was editing, when I stopped and put the phone closer to my ear. He actually was asking me out to dinner. I told him that I wasn't interested in dating, and didn't like priests, as most of them are hypocrites who like young boys or are sleeping around. He didn't freak out but replied that he was evangelical, not Catholic, and was allowed to marry. He explained that his wife had passed away many years ago, and he was interested in me. He told me a little about himself: he seemed to be a rebel within his religion, going on protest marches, etc. I told him that I had no time to date. He asked where I lived, so he could visit me. Again, I told him that I wasn't interested and hung up. From that moment, my friends no longer called me Ms. Marilyn. I was Ms. Priest!

THE ROSE-COLORED GLASSES COME OFF

And then it was Christmas in Miami. Marco and his sisters had invited me to spend the holiday with them. I booked my flights and arrived in great spirits, collected at the airport by Marco. We would all stay at Ale's house; she was now divorced from Sebas and married to Mark. Claudia and Matt, her fiancée, were already there, as was Chango. Everyone treated me like a special member of the family, everyone, that is, except Chango. He treated me like shit. I realized Chango used to be the center of attention at family gatherings. Now he had to share the limelight with me and didn't like it. Of course, his behavior did not go unnoticed by his children, who opened the subject to him. The last thing I wanted to create was tension, however, so I decided to pull back and keep myself busy with my newly purchased iPhone. Chango then criticized me for being unsocial, although he himself spent the whole day on the computer. We still had a great Christmas Eve with many presents, good food and a relaxed atmosphere.

On New Year's Eve we gathered on the beach, where it was surprisingly cold but bright, the night lit by glorious fireworks. Although Chango had put a damper on my visit, one important thing came out of it. Finally, after fifteen years of "blind love," I was over it. For the first time in my life, I saw him for who he really was. I had torn off my rose-colored glasses and was free. On our flight back from Miami, Marco and I sat in the front of the plane together, Chango alone in the back.

A POOL AND GYPSIE

I loved my home, but I found myself wishing I had a swimming pool. I contacted the landlord, who had been planning to build one in front of Herrmann Cottage Two. Like mine, it would necessarily be small, too small, really. We put our heads together and decided to build one full-size pool on the land in front of my house, facing the sea. It wasn't possible to build a house there, as the sea mist would corrode everything, but a pool would be perfect. We decided to share the costs, and construction started.

Building was only just underway when suddenly two orange kittens appeared out of nowhere. They kept jumping around the pool area, a potentially dangerous construction site. The next morning they were gone, but I searched and found them, and one more at the seaside chapel, clearly abandoned. The third kitten looked horrible, her eyes infected and extruding yellow pus. Her illness couldn't hide the fact that she was a white and tabby mix with a sweet face. I called Martin to check if he knew people who would like to have the orange kittens. He did not, but his manager, Danial, whose family lived on a small tea estate in the Nuwara Eliya area, wanted to have them. I paid for their transport there by train and bus.

I took the little sick tabby and brought it to my spare bathroom, where I treated it without much hope. To my surprise, it survived, the second (remember little Solito in Spain) of what would be many rescues. I called the kitten Gypsie. Soon afterward I started a page on Facebook called Marilyn's Ark, dedicated to my animals.

A DAD TO DRIVE ONE MAD
Early in April 2012, I made my yearly birthday visit to my father in Holland. These visits had become increasingly unpleasant, as his world revolved around his succession of girlfriends, who were truly in love with him, but not vice-versa. This time his conquest was Annie, a wonderful woman who had many children, including Christine, a blond, short-haired, good-looking lady, who looked after my dad better than my sister or I had ever done. However, Christine saw Dad for what he really was: a selfish person. I told her not to let him forget to take his medication when he was feeling euphoric, because as soon as he stopped taking it, he would express a kind of paranoia, imagining conspiracies hatched against himself and responding with mistrust and suspicion towards anything and anybody.

For example, in 2011 Dad told me with a very serious face that many years earlier my sister's husband Jos had brought him Chinese food in which a microchip was hidden. Dad insisted that he accidentally swallowed this chip. Immediately, he fashioned a plate of steel and kept it always in his pocket, so that dangerous rays could not enter his body and the chip.

During my 2012 visit, Dad asked me to load the same music into the computer that I had loaded the previous year. I asked why he had deleted it; he didn't reply. I asked him where the computer was. He pulled out a cheap computer bag from the cupboard. I frowned, but didn't say anything. He opened the bag, took out the computer, connected all the cables, and booted it up. I studied the computer. It didn't look familiar, so I asked, "Is this the same one from last year?" He gripped his lips closed, looking like a stubborn toddler. I said, "Dad, I can see this isn't your computer from last year. What happened?" Again he kept quiet and stared at the screen without saying anything. "Why can't you tell me what happened to the computer?" I persisted, laughing now. "Did you give it away?"

It seemed like ages until he finally looked at me with the air of a punished child and said, "I threw it away."

I stared at him in disbelief.

"With my bag?" I asked. "My thousand-dollar leather computer bag?"

He rose to tell the story and show me what he had done.

Dad said he had not slept for many weeks and did not understand why. At last he figured that his insomnia was due to the rays shot out by the computer (although the device was shut down at the time). In short, he took the computer, which was in its thousand-dollar computer bag, walked in the middle of the night to the nearest canal, swung the case on its long shoulder strap around his head until it had worked up a good rate of speed and then hurled it into the water.

When I found myself able to speak again, I tried to reason with him. "But you could have given it away to a person who could have been in need of it, a student or something." He shrugged his shoulders in reply. So now I was here, looking at his new computer, filling it again with his favorite music.

I made little daily trips to Albert Heijn, the local supermarket. Workers there told me my ninety-four-year-old father was the menace of the mall. Since he got his new *scootmobiel* (a small, motorized four-wheeler for retirees) he would zip up to the mall's sliding doors until they opened, then zoom from one lane to the other, knowing exactly where he needed to be and what he wanted. Several shop managers had warned him that he was a hazard to himself and others. Dad didn't listen until he finally fell out of bed. The resulting injury prevented him from using the fastest, most expensive *scootmobiel* model.

I asked Christine how she managed him. I was there for only one week, and he drove me mad. She explained that they were all happy that their mom was happy, and therefore they did their best to overlook his faults.

I decided it was time Dad met his great-grandson and invited Wendy, Anne-Lies's daughter, her husband and son for coffee at Dad's apartment. They came and all seemed to go well, and it was agreed that they would stay in contact and go out together again on a future date.

As always for his birthday, Dad was generous and told me that the whole family was invited to a big Sunday lunch at a popular Chinese restaurant, and that each and every child would receive, as a kind of reverse-gift, €1,000 euros for his birthday. I smiled at him and said, "Wow, Dad, that's nice, everybody will be very pleased, especially Wendy. She can really use the money." (Wendy was his granddaughter.)

He looked at me, totally surprised, and answered, "What Wendy? Who's Wendy? Oh, no, no, I meant the children of Annie."

Now Annie's children, who are all really nice people, were all grown-ups in their forties, fifties and sixties with their own good jobs and businesses, who did not need and perhaps did not even want the money. Since we were talking anyway, I touched on the subject of Dad's will, which he said he had wanted to change for a long time.

He decided to call his accountant, Wim Segeren, and decided there and then to change the will: ten percent would go to my sister Marijke, ninety percent to me. I did not argue: Marijke had told me many years ago she did not want anything to do with the man, neither did she want his money, but I did not want Wendy and Maikel to miss out on their inheritance. I decided I would split my share with the children of my departed sister Anne-Lies. If I should disagree, Dad would change his mind and throw everything in the garbage, I knew his moods. I was sitting there when he made the appointment with the notary public for the following week, which he re-scheduled over and over again.

Dad went one floor up to have his daily visit with Annie, and left me there brooding, full of disappointment in the man, who called himself my father, as he showed again that my sister, his grandchildren and I meant nothing to him. Dad unexpectedly came back down stairs; Annie had told him to return to his own apartment, as she felt he should be entertaining me during my visit.

For the first time in my life, I decided to speak up. I gave it to him. I told him how disappointed I was. For him to give €12,000 euros away to people who gave him a new family, that I could understand, but not to give anything to his own grandchildren—I mentioned both of my sisters' children—that was absolutely unacceptable. I told him that my sister and my mother in heaven were going to kick his ass and would never forgive him. I was so angry that I cried. He just silently looked at me and left again, leaving me in the chair in front of the window, looking outside with a feeling of disgust. As if nothing had happened, he called when dinner was ready, and I went up, also as if nothing had happened, and ate and played Rummikub with him.

Later I learned that Dad had asked Annie to marry him. She refused, perhaps sensing that he was making the proposal out of spite, so that my sister and I would receive no inheritance.

Sunday morning, the day of the lunch came. All excited, Dad prepared his best suit, then remembered he needed to sort his hundred-euro bills into twelve different envelopes. He was walking here, walking there across the room, while I sat in the chair in front of the window. I was vaguely aware of his movements, not really paying attention, busy with my still angry thoughts, when I heard him curse in Dutch. I looked at him. Dad was standing in front of the TV console, which housed a drawer that locked with a key. Within the drawer was a safe. Dad held in his hands the key to the safe, a useless thing that did not fit the lock and did not need to, because the lock safe was broken. Dad relied on keeping the drawer locked to keep the safe, well, safe. As I watched, Dad was taking valuables out of the safe, checking and re-checking. There was no money. He cursed again. I got up from the easy chair, peered inside and grinned. I couldn't stop grinning. I actually laughed out loud, looked at him and declared, "Well, this is Anne-Lies and Mom kicking you in the ass!" I asked if he was sure he'd put the money there, as he was an old man and could easily forget. He assured me that he was sane and had seen the money there one week before. For tax reasons he had collected it in December, and had checked it ever since on a weekly basis.

I called the police, who arrived within an hour. However, because the front door hadn't been broken into and the drawer lock wasn't broken, the police didn't feel it was a crime they could address, and they left.

I think what disturbed Dad most was the fact that now he couldn't hand out the money-stuffed envelopes and be the celebrated Ben Wouters. We still had a pleasant lunch at the Chinese restaurant, where all the "children" told him they hadn't needed the money and that they were happy to get together, coming from all directions in Holland for his birthday.

The next day my curiosity got the best of me, and I asked Dad to review the events leading to the money's disappearance. Could it be that someone followed him home from the bank, where he had most probably announced that the funds were a present for "his children"? Or how about this scenario: he sometimes ordered groceries from the supermarket, which were delivered to the retiree home. The supermarket would routinely question a customer if he or she had enough cash to make the payment, and Christine regularly heard Dad respond, "Oh, yes, but you have to bring change because I only have hundred-euro bills." Such a statement would clue a thief into knowing Dad had money.

There was another possibility. Most personnel working in the apartment building had a master key, so anyone familiar with my father's routine of being with his girlfriend the whole day could have taken advantage of that. When I asked to see the key to the console drawer, a key he had specially made himself, he handed me a chain with many keys on it. (I should mention here that this chain never left his pocket, so Dad was maybe thinking this line of investigation was a waste of time.) He gave me a hex key that would fit in the special socket he had made, but not as a 1, 2, 3, 4, 5 or 6, but a 4.5, so that only his self-made key would fit.

I put the key in the lock and felt that it was loose. I asked where his toolkit was and gathered up a whole bunch of hex keys in different sizes. Three of them fitted in the socket. I did not say anything, as I saw on Dad's face that he was unhappy with my discovery. I asked him if he had told anybody about the money and his intention to give it away on his birthday. He denied this, but I couldn't believe him. We left the matter at that, as I was leaving the next day.

While saying goodbye to Christine and her mother, they asked why I didn't come more often to see Dad. I told them it was expensive to make the trip from Sri Lanka. They regarded me with surprise and chided, "But you fly for free!"

"What do you mean?" I asked.

"Your dad always tells us how disappointed he is that you don't come more often. You work for Swissair, so you fly for free. Isn't that so?"

I looked at Dad and his new family, shook my head and explained that for the past fifteen years I had paid my own airfare. Dad looked down at his shoes. He knew what I said was true, he just wanted to make up stories.

Before returning to Sri Lanka, I visited my friend Anna, the psychic, and my soul sister, Evelyn, in the UK. These were the highlights of my short holiday, but as always, the visit to my dad had drained me. The stress and disappointment made me feel unwell for a month afterward.

Remember how Dad had promised to keep in touch with Wendy and her family? A few weeks later he changed his mind and ignored Wendy's calls to meet for lunch. He even rejected her call when he ended up in the hospital after another fall from his bed. She offered to come and help him, but he rudely told her he didn't need her and hung up on her. Wendy concluded it was pointless to pursue the relationship, and I agreed.

Christine told me that Marijke and I were not on the list of the hospital's authorized contacts. When I called the hospital to get information on Dad's condition, the patient liaison confirmed this. I called Hans van den Elshout, who had been my friend during my teenage years. His wife worked in the hospital, so I asked Hans to bring Dad a letter to sign that would have allowed me access to his health information. Dad refused to sign it. It was a time of great distress for me, because I couldn't understand what was going through his mind.

MY MENAGERIE GROWS

Before I went to Holland, I had asked Dr. Roshan to spay Gypsie. He told me she was just six months old, and we could wait on the surgery until my return. Immediately after I got back to Sri Lanka, I brought Gypsie to Dr. Roshan and…he said she was pregnant. Apparently, Gypsie had gone off prostituting herself while I was gone. She had become friends with my house girl's cat, Susy, who turned out to be a boy. After about nine weeks, a drama unfolded much as it had many years ago in Germany. Gypsie tended to sleep with Dominic, my dogs and me on my huge bed, so I had prepared and placed a birthing box for her there. She refused to get in the box, insisting instead on lying on my stomach. I took a big towel, covered myself, then gently slipped the towel between Costa and me as Gypsie went into labor. The first kitten to come out was a tabby. I would eventually name her Liesje. Here's why:

> When I was about six years old, Anne-Lies and I were taken on a walk by two teenage girls who lived in the neighborhood. The girls were met by their boyfriends, with whom they started to chat. Anne-Lies became fascinated by one boy's face, more specifically with his nostrils. They were enormous! Conversation over, the teen girls and I started walking back home before realizing Anne-Lies wasn't with us. We looked back and there she was, still in a mesmerized, inescapable trance, gazing upon that incredible nose. One of the girls quickly ran and dragged her back. Needless to say, I never stopped teasing Anne-Lies about that day, and never forgot that amazed look in her eyes. My kitten Liesje had this same dazed and fascinated look.

Gypsie gave birth to a second kitten, a black one with a tabby shine. Later I would name it Moortje. The twelfth century poem *The Song of Roland* describes the Moors (Muslims of medieval Spain) as "blacker than ink." That's how my beautiful Moortje looked. Both kittens were intensely and thoroughly cleaned by Costa, who loved his job as godfather then and ever since. I had now four cats (don't forget Dominic!) and three dogs.

Speaking of Dominic, he had resumed his habit of sleeping on strangers' beds. (Remember how he upset the neighbors in Costabella?) Once again he was jumping through open windows and giving people mild heart attacks when they'd come across the huge Siberian in deep sleep. Suranga, my jack-of-all-trades, or "manager," as I prefer to call him, hit on a solution. He spread word in the village that the dogs and cats in Ms. Marilyn's house were vicious: no villager was to enter without her special permission. Only she could safely control the dogs. As for Dominic, Suranga whispered, he was an extremely vicious and wild cat who would bite anyone who tried to touch him. I must say, Suranga's strategy worked. When neighbors found Dominic snoozing on their beds, they would quietly close the door and leave him in peace.

AZTEC IN DANGER

On a typical night anywhere in Sri Lanka, you'll hear dogs: the howls and yelps of fighters, home defenders, lonely puppies, and lovers having their quarrels. People are accustomed to the sounds and pay them no mind. One night I awoke at Aztec's bark, an unusually urgent alarm. Always sleeping with my doors open, I jumped out of bed, Costa and Bella waking from a sound sleep to follow me. I caught the flashlight and my phone on my way out. I spotted Aztec running up and down the fence where the new swimming pool was being built. As I shone the flashlight, I saw men running away, dropping the cement bags they had been trying to steal. Where was the guard during all this? He was sleeping only a few feet away. Blame the *arrack* he had drunk the night before. As *Wikipedia* explains, "Ceylon *arrack* is a spirit distilled from the sap of the coconut flower…[and] one of the few/rare spirits in the world which is a distillate of a one hundred percent natural fermentation. Unlike whiskey, *arrack* is distilled at a high strength." It is illegal to make *arrack* at home, and I know several villagers who got arrested for producing it secretly, even my old house girl!

But back to the scene of the (almost) crime. I called Suranga, who came running with Anthony, the father of my landlord. I told them what had happened and explained the importance of listening to the different barks of dogs. My lecture fell onto deaf ears. What did I mean? All barks are the same! I asked them if they had ever seen Aztec so excited and angry. They only stared back at me, speechless. I told them to always get up and run to my house if they heard what they were hearing now, the barks of all three of my dogs, who were running back and forth along the fence in total hysteria. After the cement bags were counted and the guard reprimanded, Suranga and Anthony walked back home, still discussing how to recognize the barks of my dogs.

I should add that the men had lectured back at me. They told me never to come out of the house as I had done that night. Next time I should close the doors and call them first.

The wisdom of our respective lectures was soon tested.

Only a few weeks later, I was awakened again by Aztec's bark. It was an insistent cry, more fearful than angry, seemingly directed at someone or something. Even today I do not know why I did what I did next. Normally, I take the puppers Costa and Bella with me as my protection, but this time I locked them in my bedroom. I phoned Suranga and Anthony and told them something was very wrong in my garden. Couldn't they hear it in Aztec's voice? Although they were both sleepy, they said they would come, and counseled me to stay in the house until they arrived. In only a few minutes I saw their flashlights. They opened my gate, and I stepped through my front door. We both arrived at the same time at the spot where Aztec was barking towards something we had not yet seen.

Coming closer, we all got a shock. In front of us was a big, rolled up viper, its head lifted from the center of the circle, "shishing" a threatening *shishishish* sound towards Aztec. The men told me to stand back. Suranga pushed Aztec away from the snake, while Anthony hurried back to his house to get two sticks. When he returned, he and Suranga clubbed the viper to death. Although I didn't examine the body closely, it was the men's guess that it was a green pit viper, called polonga, one of the most dangerous snakes in the country. We were all relieved at how things turned out, especially me, congratulating myself with the fact that I had kept Costa and Bella locked up in my bedroom. They would surely have attacked the creature, as they had killed snakes in Spain and even here in Sri Lanka, small, harmless serpents. Fearless, my dogs would have attacked and been killed on the spot by this viper. We checked on Aztec. He gave no sign that he had been bitten, so we all went back to our houses and back to sleep.

About a half hour later, I heard a howl. I jumped out of bed and ran outside. I knew the "voices" of each and every one of my animals, and this had been a cry of despair. I ran to Aztec. He was lying in his favorite spot. I held him, looked at him, touched him all over his body, checking for a painful spot. He had triple-thick fur, as he had just changed to his winter coat. I could detect no source of pain, and he had closed his eyes, for me a sign that he felt well enough to sleep. I went back to bed.

The next morning I was awakened by electrical repairmen knocking on my gates. They wanted to fix some cables in my garden. This was the first time they had ever come by, and thank God they did, because when I opened the gates to allow their truck to enter, I saw Aztec lying in their path, not moving. I called him to come to me, which he normally does at once, but there was no reaction. I remembered the howl in the night and ran to him. His eyes were open, but he couldn't move. For a moment I was paralyzed, too. I was in shock, helpless. Finally, I called Martin, who knew everybody and everything about dogs. He told me he knew a Belgian couple, Leo and Myrjam, who owned Ging Oya Lodge not far from me. They had experience with dogs and snakebites. He called them, and they arrived in a little truck not five minutes later. We gingerly put Aztec in the back, then all drove together to Dr. Rohan in Negombo, Dr. Roshan being out of town. Meanwhile, my new "neighbors" were calling everybody they knew for anti-venom. They called the air force vet, Dr. Gunawardena, the hospitals and pharmacies. When we arrived at Dr. Rohan's, Aztec was taken immediately into the emergency room where he was filled up with drips and all the antibiotics Dr. Rohan could find. He dedicated his whole day to trying to save Aztec from a bite we could not find. The only explanation was that when the snake bit, Aztec's fur was too thick for the viper's fangs to fully penetrate. My husky was saved by his winter coat. I thanked Leo and Myrjam, who had done all they could (which was a great deal) and now had to return to their lodge where guests were waiting for them. I could not thank Dr. Rohan enough for saving Aztec's life that day.

I was still in a highly emotional state, so Martin offered to put me and Aztec up in a bedroom above his restaurant. He came with a van, and by the time we had laid Aztec on Martin's bed, Dr. Roshan arrived and continued giving him drips with antibiotics and lots of fluids. Aztec and I slept in Martin's bed for two days. Aztec showed no improvement, but his condition didn't worsen, either.

I thanked Martin for his dedicated assistance and love for my dog, but I decided that I needed to return home. If Aztec should die, he should die in familiar surroundings. I called Suranga, who got a van from Sunil, Christopher's brother-in-law. Sunil and Suranga arrived and carried Aztec to the back of the van and laid him on blankets. We stopped at Dr. Roshan's clinic in Kochchikade, where Aztec received another drip with fluids and antibiotics. After two hours we reached home, where I was surprised to find a mattress in the living room and food prepared for me. My kind neighbors, who had all heard about the snakebite, came to express sympathy, some bringing meals for me.

I was feeding Aztec fish, chicken and eggs—all the best available food for my poor sick dog. I caught his pee in a bottle, and kept him clean by removing his poohs. But after two days of my solicitous care, I realized...clever dog that he was...he was taking advantage of the situation. He loved being pampered and spoiled! I decided I would carry him to the porch, and each day place his food bowl a little farther away, thereby forcing him to crawl and use his muscles again. I made this brilliant resolution on the second night of his return at 2 A.M. I stood over Aztec in the living room, planted my feet on both sides of him, bent over to lift and carry him to the front door and...tripped, fell and broke my wrist. I called Suranga, told him what had happened, and he drove me in his *tuktuk* to the hospital in Colombo, a two-hour drive on empty roads. An x-ray was taken, and I had diagnosed myself correctly: a wrist fracture requiring a cast. We drove back home, me fuming. My dog had tricked me! Immediately on our return, Suranga and I carried Aztec outside. He acted like "poor me" and did not move a muscle in his body. This time I wasn't fooled and didn't feel sorry for him. I went to bed and slept a few hours.

When I awoke, Aztec was where I had last seen him on the porch. I prepared chicken for him and put it one step away (after having locked Costa and Bella in one of the guest rooms; they would have gobbled the meal in a flash). Then I ate my own breakfast in the living room, "ignoring" Aztec completely. It did not take long for the naughty dog to crawl to his bowl. When I went to check on him, he wore an innocent expression as if asking, "Who could have eaten that food?" His will to live had won, but it was a slow and incomplete recovery. Aztec was suddenly an old dog, sapped of his youthful energy. That didn't matter, though. We—the cats, Costa, Bella, the neighbors and I—were all happy to have him back. Happy to have him alive.

During this trying time, I asked all my Facebook friends to pray or send positive energy to Aztec. Facebook friends all over the world sent love and encouragement. One message, however, written in Dutch, shocked me. My sister had labeled me a bullshitter. She insisted she knew me better then anybody else and that I should not be a hypocrite and ask people to pray, because if the dog were to be healed it would be by medicine and had nothing to do with God.

I thought, my God, who is this woman? What happened to her to send me such a message? I took a day to try to clear my head. I wrote back: I no longer have a sister anymore. I left the message up for two days, but I felt such negative energy looking at it that I deleted it and blocked her from my Friends List, after which her entire family blocked me. All my Dutch friends, who of course had read it, wrote back to me, "I am your sister." Suddenly, I had many sisters who were happy to replace the real one.

ANIMAL CARE DAY

I decided that words mean nothing; action is what matters, and I needed to "clean my own garden." I decided to sponsor an animal care day in my small village of Kammala. I invited my vet, Dr. Roshan, and two members of TAPA, Dr. Dinesh Wellawa and Susantha, the animal catcher. I only needed to pay their expenses and medical materials. We sent out flyers, which my neighbors brought around to the villagers, and we set up an event shelter at Christopher's garage early one morning. Within an hour villagers arrived with their cats and dogs for rabies vaccinations and sterilizations. By the end of the day, we had operated on thirty-four cats and dogs and vaccinated nearly fifty animals. The day was a big success, but what was even better was that I now had gotten to know many of the villagers, several of whom had sick puppies or kittens that I could now go and treat for fleas, ticks and other minor ailments.

MY DAD PASSES

The news out of the Netherlands was not good. Christine, who was in constant contact with me, told me Dad had fallen out of bed again. The injury left him disoriented and totally indifferent to Annie. When the situation worsened, Christine had him admitted to a hospital. Doctors there seemed to think Dad could return home as long as he had someone help with daily activities such as washing and cooking. Christine told them this was impossible: Dad was in no position to do anything himself, and the doctors could not expect her to be with him twenty-four hours a day because she wasn't his family member. There were no vacancies in the care unit of his retirement home, so it was decided to transfer Dad from the hospital to another care center, where he would almost certainly remain for the rest of his life. Annie was devastated to hear this.

Christine arranged for Dad's easy chair to be brought to him, so he could relax outside his bed. He asked her to call a notary public to make an appointment for October 22 for changing his will. The appointment was made, she left him, and when she returned the next morning, she discovered he had declined rapidly. Christine was his rock during his last days. He died peacefully on Sunday, October 21, 2012.

During his final days, I had been writing to all family members to keep them updated. Although I suspected Marijke didn't want to get involved, I also included her and her children in these bulletins, as one never really knows what is best. I received replies from Wendy and Maikel, Anne-Lies's children, but nothing from Marijke and family. I had hoped to be with my father during his last moments, but I flew in too late. I went with Christine to the funeral home. Gazing into the casket, I was amazed how different he was, this man whom I had feared my whole life. There he was, only a body, a stranger. Christine kissed him on his head and held his hand. I could not force myself to do the same. I did not have these tender feelings towards him; he had killed them all. But I could understand Christine's emotions, for he had given love to her mother and her family. He had been a better dad to them.

Monday morning Christine and I met with my father's accountant. He asked if there was a will. I replied that Dad had scheduled an appointment with the notary public that very day to amend it, but I didn't know where it was. The accountant said he would check to see if it was registered with the municipality, an investigation that might take a few days. He asked about my relatives. I told him that I'd informed everybody about Dad's passing, but I hadn't heard anything from Marijke or her children. "Knowing her," I said, "she wouldn't want anything from him." I explained that she had told me several times, "I don't want anything from him. I don't need his money, and I don't want anything to do with him. If he dies, just leave me out of it." I added that my sister had principles: she wouldn't take a dime from Dad, because she hated him. While Christine and the accountant looked at me, smiling, I smiled back and said, "I'll make a bet that she won't take the money, not because she has enough herself, but because she has principles." We bet on a future dinner, the accountant, Christine and I. I would pay if I lost. I was sure, though, that I would win. For not even one tiny moment did I think Marijke would want money from the man who had disgusted her.

After the accountant left, I told Christine to get Dad's *scootmobiel* and bring it to her mom, as that is what my father would have wanted. It was the least I could do. Annie didn't want to accept it, but I told her she should take it in memory of Dad. Annie had difficulty walking and used a cane, so she would benefit from this "Ferrari" of *scootmobiels*. She also asked if she could have his clock, which I was happy to give her.

Christine and I decided to keep the funeral simple. My father had died at ninety-four. All his friends and most of his family were dead, so we placed a simple obituary in the newspaper giving the time of his cremation. We would set up a coffee table in a small room at the funeral home, as we did not expect lots of people to show up. Of course, I sent a copy of the notice to my friends who had known my father. The date was set for Saturday, October 27, and I had one week to give away all Dad's stuff, clean out his apartment, cancel all his memberships and release his apartment back to the retirement home. I felt that these were my natural obligations as oldest daughter. Happily, Wendy, Anne-Lies's daughter, immediately offered to come and help me with arrangements, cleaning and moral support. I had been gone from the Netherlands since 1970 and had no clue of procedures, so I was very grateful for this offer.

Christine was overwhelmed with grief, and possibly, relief. She had been so intensely involved in my dad's health problems that during these last few weeks before his death, she had actually neglected her own family. Suddenly, she was free again, and it was all too much for her. She was and is a good woman who did everything Marijke and I should have done, and I remain immensely grateful to her. I told her now to relax and just come see Wendy and me in the apartment whenever she wanted. I also told her I was going to give away everything my father had owned, and she would be the first one to choose whatever she wanted. At first Christine was upset, thinking I was trying to pay her off for her good deeds, until I convinced her that otherwise the greedy neighbors would come and take what my father would have wanted her to have. I had no intention of selling anything; I wanted to get rid of all his belongings as fast as possible, so I could return home to my animals.

Christine came and made her selections, which pleased me very much. Then Wendy made hers, again at my insistence. Finally, I taped letters on doors throughout the retirement home saying everything else was being given away and had to go by 4 P.M. Someone told me this wouldn't work, as people in the Netherlands aren't used to giveaways, but guess what? By the end of the day, the apartment was empty. Even the food from the fridge vanished. Wendy and I were kept so busy handing things over to people that we couldn't even stop for lunch. We wondered what elderly people, who have so little living space, do with all that rubbish.

The last item to go was a big side cupboard. An old hippie lady had gotten wind of freebies, and showed up to get it. I talked to the lady, and she told me her life story. The conversation turned to art. I told her I wished I had a painting with Dutch cows in it, as I was sure I'd never return to Holland again. She gazed intently at me and told me to stay in my dad's apartment for at least another thirty minutes, while her boys carried away the cupboard. In less than half an hour she returned and presented me with a small oil painting of cows in a meadow painted by one Jac. Greydanus in the year 1941. I was in heaven! She told me she had received the painting as a wedding gift a long time ago, but she never really cared for it. I felt grateful and close to this kindred soul.

I called an old friend of the family, Els, who against payment promised to clean the apartment the next day. The sooner the place was cleaned, the sooner we could hand over the key to the office, and the sooner the apartment could be occupied. There was a long waiting list, and I felt good knowing some other elderly person would soon have a home.

A few days later I met again with the accountant who had shocking news for me: there was a registered will, and Marijke was testamentary executor. She had known this all the time! The accountant told me that I could be in trouble because I had given all my father's belongings away. Marijke may not have wanted this to happen; for sure she wanted her money and the bank statements. I had never asked for these, as they didn't interest me. I had my retirement income, and it would have been nice to receive some money, but I didn't need it.

In the days preceding the cremation, I saw some old friends. I also regularly saw Christine, and visited with Annie, who had lost her great love. It was a sad time. I was actually looking forward to Saturday, happy to soon have everything behind me.

As people started shuffling into the funeral hall, I worried that the room we had rented was too small. Of course, I sat with Annie, to show respect and make clear to everybody that she belonged there as much as I did. Old relatives I had not seen since childhood appeared, as well as friends from my youth who remembered my father. They had all come to say their goodbyes. I had never expected this, and was deeply touched.

I had prepared songs to be played between the reading of the obituary and speeches, if anybody wanted to say something. One of the songs was "Dance with My Father" by Luther Vandross. The tune brought back memories of when, as a young girl, I danced out of sheer joy. My father, although not a good dancer, loved to dance, too. The last time we danced together was in Marijke's house during Christmas many, many years ago. As the song started, feelings overwhelmed me. Confused, I looked around, and my eyes rested on Ruud van den Langenberg, Wendy's uncle. He returned my gaze and got up from his chair. Nobody knew what was happening; *I* didn't know what was happening, and for sure it had never happened before in this funeral home. We danced. I was not dancing with Ruud, I was dancing the last dance with my father. Everybody cried, including Ruud and I. When the song finished, he gave me a kiss on top of my head. I knew it was my father kissing me farewell. It had been the right thing to do. It felt good. After the cremation we all sat together and remembered old times, renewing old relationships. That is the good thing about Facebook: most of us are still in contact now. We decided the ashes would be sent to Wendy, who would keep them until I returned the following summer to collect and scatter them where my father had wanted them to go. I had a last dinner with friends from my early days: Vivienne and her husband Richard, Hans and his wife, Peter my first boyfriend, Ruud, my old friend from Dubai, Ruby, with whom I had met up over the last past years every time I was in the Netherlands, and of course, my new friend Christine. It was a memorable night.

Back home in Sri Lanka, an email was waiting for me from Wim Segeren, the accountant. He reported that my sister had not waived her inheritance, as I had thought. In fact, after going through the accounts, she insisted on the sale of the *scootmobiel*, which I had given to Annie. Although I counted to ten and then to a hundred and gave myself a cool down period of a whole day, I couldn't resist venting in an email to everybody involved the next day. I wrote that my father had wanted to marry Annie just to deny us the little money he had. Annie had turned him down, but she and her family had made him happy, and his last will specified that she should have the *scootmobiel*. If Marijke wanted it to be sold, she should have the guts to collect it herself and sell it, although I would regard this as theft, as the money from the *scootmobiel* belonged neither to her nor to us, the inheritors. Regarding the inheritance itself, Marijke had always insisted she did not need or want his money. To tell the accountant that it was for her children would make my father turn in his grave, as what he had worked for his whole life would now go to strangers, not Marijke's children, but the adult sons of her husband. I felt she was a greedy bitch.

So, I got it off my chest. It felt good!

Another email from Wim arrived. My sister had asked him to ask Christine to sell the *scootmobiel* in their business, a car showroom. What a cowardly request! Marijke also asked how much Christine charged for her services to my dad, so she could be paid.

I read the correspondence again and again. I wrote an email to Marijke and cc'ed everyone, asking my sister why she was insulting Christine, who had asked for nothing and had helped my dad out of the goodness of her heart. Christine had not been our employee. I made it clear I wanted nothing to do with Marijke. She should be happy with her stolen money.

I received a return mail from Marijke's husband. He warned me to stop writing his wife, otherwise he would inform the authorities regarding my "ill-gotten" pension. When I read that, my mouth hung open a few minutes. *Ill-gotten?* I had worked and paid my social security taxes in the Netherlands for ten years. I deserved my pension, which should have been 600 euros, but was in reality 131. The Netherlands did not have a pension agreement with Sri Lanka, so I received only a quarter of the amount citizens living in Holland would receive after a decade of paying into the system. Regarding my Swiss benefits: I had paid social security taxes since 1974 and had continued these payments while overseas, so now as a pensioner I received my full minimum benefits. This time I did not wait a full day to cool down. I responded immediately with my tax ID numbers from Switzerland and the Netherlands, inviting my brother-in-law to contact the authorities at once.

IN THE GENTLE CARE OF URSI

Summer came. I decided that my upcoming trip to Europe, which would culminate in the spreading of my father's ashes, would be my last to that continent. I would visit several friends, including Nicoletta in Zürich, Silke in Berlin and Ursi in Corsica. Unfortunately, I came down with a cold before traveling; perhaps emotional stress had triggered it. Planning to see Ursi first, I flew to Rome and took a train to Florence. By the time I reached that city, I thought I was dying, so instead of continuing by slow train to the ferry port of Livorno, I took a taxi, which had to stop several times to let me step out and throw up. Fortunately, it was easy to find the hotel. I checked into my room and slept like a stone, rising early the next morning for the ferry to Bastia, a city in northern Corsica. Ursi was waiting for me, and I spent the next few days recovering from my cold in her little house on the shore. When I got a bit better, we explored this beautiful island. The days sped by; we moved on to Ursi's elegant home in Hergiswil, on Lake Lucerne. I regretfully cancelled my trips to Nicoletta and Silke to be able to recover completely from my flu and be ready to fulfill my last responsibility to my father. I also went on my last big shopping excursion in Switzerland, purchasing, among other things, some nice, simple linen suits and several pairs of high-quality sandals, which are not available in Sri Lanka.

SCATTERING THE ASHES AND OTHER HYSTERICAL ACTS

Wendy had gone on vacation to Ireland and left the ashes with her brother, Maikel, so I would be spending some time with him. I had informed Christine when I was coming, as she wanted to join me in the scattering of the ashes. Maikel met me at the train station and brought me to his home, where we ate, relaxed and watched TV. The next day he gave me a bag with the urn in it. It looked like an expensive Christian Dior shopping bag. I sat with it on the train to Breda, wearing my smart new, corn blue linen suit, just bought in Lucerne. Christine was already waiting in front of the train station. First we would go to Wim, the accountant, and finalize things with him. The inheritance money had already been transferred to my bank account, but the sale of the *scootmobiel* had brought another €4,500 euros, which was to be divided by three parties, and he wanted to hand over the money to me. Having signed the necessary paperwork, I gave my €1,500 to Christine, telling her I was not a thief and the money did not belong to me. She refused to take it. I told her that I did not care how she would use it—give it to her mom, share it with the family—I just wanted nothing to do with it, it was hers. Satisfied, we left Wim's house and drove to the cemetery.

My father had told Christine and her mother exactly where he wanted his ashes scattered. There was a section of the cemetery intended specifically for this purpose, so we went straight up there, the "Dior" bag in my hands. It had started to rain, and we had no umbrellas. On arriving, we both decided that the best place would be under a big tree with a view over the property.

I opened the bag, took out the urn and tried to open it. Impossible. No way I could pry it open with my fingers. Christine took the urn and tried, with no success. We started to giggle, getting more and more wet. I tried my keys; even the thinnest one wouldn't slip between the cover and the tin. What to do now? As if a solution could be found lying on the ground, we looked around. Of course, this didn't help, we only giggled more. Ah, a new idea: my credit card! I slipped it under the cover and with care and precision I finally managed to pop off the lid. We decided

I would be the first to sprinkle or scatter the remains. Wind blowing, rain pouring, I took the tin, lifted it up, and threw it towards the tree roots. The ashes did not land there. They flew back on my face and my beautiful blue pantsuit. I stepped back in surprise…tripped over a big rock behind me…and fell.

Now Christine and I were in hysterics, me lying in the mud, covered with ashes. Our laughter must have been heard all over the place, we couldn't hold it in, tears of laughter and rain running down our faces. When I finally got up, I gave the container to Christine. She was gingerly dropping the ashes, trying to get her giggles under control, when we suddenly heard a voice from a far distance: "Dames, wat doen jullie daar, ophouden, stop, dat is verboden, dat is illegaal." (Ladies, what are you doing there, stop immediately, it is forbidden, stop now, that is illegal.) Christine and I looked at each other and laughed even harder. We peeked over the garden hedge and saw the head of an old man. It was a cemetery caretaker, coming towards us, angrily waving a rake above his head. Looking at this angry, funny man, made us laugh even more. What a sight we were, me dirty and wet, Christine with the urn in her hands.

When the man finally stood opposite us, he shouted that we needed a permit, he would call the director of the cemetery, and we'd better not go anywhere. I had spotted a small garden bench, so while he called the director on a cell phone, I headed for it. The caretaker lurched forward as if to stop me, but I calmed him down and said, no I'm only going to rest on that bench. He reached the director, who told him to bring us to her office.

When we arrived we were still smiling, but our hysteria had cooled. The director informed us that it was indeed illegal to scatter ashes without permission. If we had asked permission, she could have arranged a ceremony with music, candles, etc. Unfortunately, now I had to pay the full amount without having had the services. I told the director that no service could have been an improvement on what we had just experienced with my father, when he had blown all his ashes over me and pushed me over the rock into the mud. It was hilarious, and there could not be a better ending for the relationship between my dad and me. I paid the cemetery what I owed, and Christine and I left, satisfied with our completed mission. We topped off the event with a great lunch at one of the many good restaurants in Oosterhout. I footed the bill. Christine won the bet about my sister, remember?

THE LAST OF EUROPE

I returned to Dommelen, where Maikel lived, and spent some days with him. We visited Saskia, the girl from the Dutch Youth Orchestra who had stayed with me in Dubai. She was now married with one child and lived close to Maikel, so together on the back of his huge bike we went to visit her. I stayed a few days with my old schoolmate Agnes and her family. Next I saw my old friends from Dubai, the Joosten family, who had bought a splendid old house in the north of the Netherlands and were renovating it to modern standards of perfection. Last but not least, I spent a week in France with my old friend Jean-Luc, Sonia's ex. (You'll recall Sonia lived on my street in Jebel Ali.) Jean-Luc and his new partner had come to visit me in Sri Lanka. It was great to see them and Paris again. We strolled through the streets and sailed on the Seine. We drove to the south, where Jean-Luc has a house high in the mountains, and believe me, the drive itself was an adventure! From there I took the train to Rome, then flew to Sri Lanka. I knew I had seen the last of Europe. From here on in, all my European friends will have to visit me in Sri Lanka. What further exploring I do will be limited to Asia…which is hardly a limitation at all.

CHARLIE, HI AND BYE

I started swimming in my pool a few times a day. One time in between my splashes I heard soft meows. I searched for its source and saw that somebody had slipped a very small kitten under my gate. Its eyes were closed, and its cries were not much louder than that of a mouse. I gathered it up and said, "Hi, Charlie, what are you doing here?" I don't know why that particular named popped out of my mouth! I called around for people who might have kitten bottle feeders and kitten milk. Luckily, Jocelyn, an animal lover and puppy rescuer, had both and gave them to me immediately.

For a few months, Charlie was the love of my life. Wherever I went, Charlie went. He wasn't handsome, but he had character. Being raised with me, Charlie was extremely friendly to everyone; Costa was his best pal. Everybody knew Charlie from my Facebook page. Then suddenly, when he was about four months old, he disappeared. I feel sure he was stolen. My pets have a reputation for being people friendly, and some unfriendly people take advantage of that fact.

I put posters all over the place offering a big reward for the return of Charlie. I walked through villages with a photograph and asked if anyone had seen him. No. I was desperate. I had started helping out at the local school as a volunteer, supporting the English teachers, so flyers went out to the children. The kids crowded around my gate, all with different "Charlies," none the real one.

One morning I got a phone call from Sapphire, the jewelry shop next to the Dolphin Club Hotel. Women working there said Charlie was in the store! Brimming with hope, I asked Suranga to bring me to Sapphire in his *tuktuk*. On my arrival, the ladies told me the kitten was under the cupboard. I called, "Charlie, Charlie!" Finally, it crawled out. It was not Charlie, but a white kitten with gray cheeks and three black dots on its back. I started to sob. Suranga, seeing this, and fed up with me "carrying a torch" for Charlie, picked up the kitten and said, "Take the cat and stop crying!" We drove home. Now I had five cats, including Saffiertje (Sapphire).

MALDONADO IS "THE ONE"

Dimitri wrote me that the Hellenic board wanted to appoint a new head of school. Could I advertise for the position and vet the applications? I did this, while cc-ing materials to Dimitri. We finally had three promising candidates, one of whom Dimitri was able to meet while in the US on a business trip. My personal favorite was Dr. José Gabriel Maldonado, Puerto Rican-born principal of a New York high school. Seemingly inventive, energetic and adventurous, he had the credentials and strong character needed to run SCIS. Although he had no experience with African culture, he seemed flexible enough to learn and adapt to it. I flew to Arusha, this time intending to stay only a few days, and took a room in a local hotel. All three applicants flew in. One kept asking for a certain type of soft drink, jumping out of his taxi every few minutes to check at stores for it. He was a no-go. For Dimitri and me, it was clear that Maldonado was "the one." Now the problem was negotiating the salary: compared to what other international schools offered, it was extremely low. It turned out that for JG, the challenge was more important than the salary. His longtime dream to work in Africa would come true. I prepared to fly back to Sri Lanka, a good feeling in my heart that SCIS was at last in good hands.

Shortly before I boarded, however, Dimitri asked me, "Do you think Maldonado will be obedient?" I was shocked. Where did this question come from?

I looked at Dimitri and said, "Of course not! He won't be 'obedient,' that's not his job. His job is to improve and accredit the school. He is an academic professional with all the necessary qualifications. He knows what he's doing and what is best for the school." I now suspected that the Greeks would not give Maldonado the free hand they had promised him. I saw storm clouds on the horizon.

SITARE

In the first weeks after I moved into Herrmann Cottage, I would routinely walk my dogs on the beach past a certain fishing hut, made out of scrap lumber and dried palmtree branches. On one occasion Dominic was following us, but there were intimidating stray dogs walking around, and Dominic was stuck near the hut's front door. Unaware of this, I was continuing my walk when I heard someone calling. I turned to see a little boy in a school uniform coming towards me and carrying big fat Dominic, who was half the child's size. Dominic never liked to be carried by anyone, so I decided this had to be a special boy. His name was Sitare, and he lived in the hut with his parents and uncle.

A few months afterward, I regularly saw Sitare dressed in rags and roaming the neighborhood. I asked around and learned his father was in jail for murder, his uncle in jail for theft and his mother, incapacitated with MS, had been brought to a care facility in Avissawella. The boy was being shunted from one family to another.

I spoke with Christopher of Rico's Shadow Guesthouse and asked him to research boarding schools in the area. After two weeks, he came back to me, and together we took nine-year-old Sitare to the town of Chilaw, where there was a Franciscan boarding school with an excellent reputation. Sitare was tested, and it was decided that he should board with the Franciscans but attend another school until he rose to the level of the Franciscan one. I and my German friends Barbara and Marion, and later my Swiss friend Liesbeth, would finance his education and living expenses. After a year, he qualified to change schools.

Now it was the Easter holiday, and Sitare had come with a gift for me...a small tabby. Of course, I thanked him, and because I was so grateful with this present he returned half an hour later with...another kitten! This one was gray like a mouse and beautiful. (I think he might have had a Sphynx in his bloodline.) I thanked Sitare again, but told him two cats were enough! I named them Pluisje and Muisje, and they were cats numbers six and seven.

I sat down to have a serious talk with Sitare about his education, and Suranga helped me by translating. Having gotten used to his new school, Sitare was becoming increasingly naughty, deciding that play was more important than study. I told him firmly that I was not a rich lady, and that his stay in Chilaw would depend on him studying well. If he paid attention in school, he could continue and finish his studies. If not, I would take him out of the school, and he'd be back on the streets. He understood, and in the following school year he took Holy Communion and was the star of the school play. Everybody was happy.

THE HARD FACTS ABOUT KITTEN RESCUES

One day some friends, while visiting me, took a walk past the old hut where Sitare used to live. They heard a peeping sound and bent down to look under the rubbish beneath the hut. There they saw two kittens with silver white coats. They were only a few days old, their eyes still closed. Naturally, I decided to keep them, naming them Charlie II and Snowy.

My whole time was now dedicated to these poor creatures, but all was in vain. After two days little Snowy died, and another two days later Charlie II passed away.

This is why sometimes I need a break and refuse kittens when people call me. Experience tells me that ninety percent of them die if they don't receive their mother's milk for at least the first week. Only the very strong ones survive, as all kittens carry the Tricat viruses and show the symptoms very clearly as babies, but we cannot vaccinate them until they are three months old. Again, my experience has shown that any vaccination given to these babies, while still so young and already weak, will kill them. All my cats except Dominic went through this phase of pre-dead, as I call it. They all had loose bowels for at least six months, sneezing and coughing, but with much love and care all survived. At first, when I was not used to the rescue of kittens, I drove to the vet at every sign of distress. These poor creatures would receive a booster vaccination, and all of them without exception died. The ones I kept are actually those I thought would surely die, as they were too ill to give away for adoption. They are now naturally immunized and very strong. After three months I give them the Tricat vaccination, and a few weeks later a rabies vaccination, which is repeated yearly.

A CONTENDER FOR ALPHA DOG

One day, returning from my weekly supermarket trip to Negombo, I gazed out from Suranga's *tuktuk* and spied something woolly in a cage. I told Suranga to turn around, so I could check it out. The cage was one of many in a pet shop, all the animals cramped and stressed. Most unfortunate of all was a big Tibetan Terrier in a cage far too small for him. Feeling terribly sorry for him, I bought him and took him home. Of course, it had been thoughtless of me. When we arrived, teeth were bared on all sides, cats and dogs alike. I realized one of us had to show some sense and restraint! I put the terrier alone in a room.

After I had put away my groceries, I went to look at the dog. I found he had received no training at all, so the poor thing was not to blame for his show of aggression. I put him on a leash and walked him around the garden alone. He was very clever and quickly learned to walk, sit and heel.

The following Sunday, my friends Samantha and Mark Green came for lunch. Since 2006, they had been operating the Dogstar Foundation, working closely with Sri Lankan communities and vets to provide sterilizations, vaccinations, veterinary treatment and education leading to attitude change and the development of veterinary practice. As we were sitting peacefully together, I told them about the dog I called Dalai (as he was a Tibetan). I got him from the room and walked him around the garden, after which I took him off the leash and allowed him to familiarize with Aztec, Costa and Bella. Aztec had grown feeble after the viper bite and was not much interested in meeting this newcomer, although he still was the alpha dog in my house.

Dalai decided *he* wanted to be alpha dog. He jumped Aztec, and the two of them fought. We could not separate them, and did not need to. Out of the blue, Costa jumped between, taking Dalai by the throat and forcing him down on the ground until he lay still. Then Costa let him go...looked at Aztec...and gripped him by the throat also, pushing his head down, so that he lay helpless on the ground. When Aztec went silent, Costa got up and looked at all the dogs and cats, as if saying, "That's enough of that. Now I want peace and quiet!" and lay down, still alertly observing the crowd. I'd never seen all the cats gathered around such an event. Usually they would have been too fearful of being attacked by one of the dogs, but here they were like spectators at a prizefight. Since then Costa has been the peacemaker in our house. Even when the cats fight, he is there to referee or intervene.

The next day I spoke with Dr. Roshan about Dalai, and after a few days he found a wonderful new home for him, where his master would be a teenage boy and there would be no other dog to compete with for attention. He would be "The Dog" in the family, which is what he wanted.

A PRINCE IN NEED OF A KINGDOM
But did I learn anything from this encounter? No, of course not! Another Friday, when returning from Negombo, I saw little Labrador puppies.

They were so cute! I asked Suranga if he wanted a dog for Amidu, his son. Suranga did not really know, but he helped me choose one, and I bought it and gave it to Amidu. He named the puppy Prince. Soon it was discovered that Prince had to stay within his "realm," by which I mean my house. When left alone at Suranga's house, he too eagerly broke through the gate. So Prince moved in with me. He was a lovely dog, naughty as puppies are, but a good listener who learned fast. Prince was a "talker," and the only time he really grew quiet was when Pluisje and Muisje came to him and sucked on his nipples. Two of his eight nipples became huge and started producing milk. The vet told me that this was a natural reaction, although he was a male puppy. Pluisje and Muisje loved their "mommy," and soon he was a dear friend of all the cats, who slept with him. Prince became king of the cat empire. However, I increasingly had to bring the cats to the vet, as Prince's big hugs and playful behavior caused them mild injuries. It is said that love hurts, and these cats had the limps and swelled paws to prove it, and yet they kept coming back to him.

As Prince grew, he fell into the same pattern set by Dalai. He wanted to be not just king of the cats, but the dogs, too. Costa wouldn't stand for this, so fights started, first harmless matchups, then vicious battles. I didn't know what to do. My general practitioner, Dr. Tushara Wick, saved the day. She was staying for a long weekend at the Dolphin Club Hotel with her two children and decided to visit me at home. The doctor's daughter fell for Prince. They were instantly inseparable, and when she said she wanted a dog like him I told her, "Take Prince. I see you really like each other." The family regarded me with surprise. Why would I say something like that? I explained the rivalry between Costa and Prince, and how Prince needed his own kingdom.

The kids exchanged looks with their mom. Dr. "Tush," as I call her, told me their own dog had died about a year before, and they had been planning to get another one. Could she have a little time to think it over, though? I said of course. Two days later she called with the good news that they wanted Prince. I brought him and saw he was going to have a home with loads of land, even a swimming pool. I was happy for Prince and his new loving family.

Two days later Dr. Tush called and informed me that the gardener had hurried to her in the morning and said that a hurricane had passed by during the night. She looked at him in wonder and told him she had not heard any loud winds, and there was nothing in the news. He insisted a hurricane had rushed across their land: there was no other explanation, as all the plants, including small trees, were uprooted in the garden. She went with him to see the damage and discovered the real perpetrator, Prince, still busily digging. In one night he had destroyed many months of the gardener's work.

A year later, I was invited to Prince's combination birthday party and first anniversary. They had put a hat on him, and helped him blow out a candle on his dog food. He is spoiled, but loved more than I could have managed it.

THE GREEKS AND I KNOCK HEADS

The long-expected email came: a message from Dimitri to come to Arusha ASAP and evaluate Dr. Maldonado. At once, I emailed JG and asked what was happening. He wrote back, asking me to Skype that same evening. He told me his side of the story, most of which must remain confidential.

I booked a ticket to Tanzania.

I did not schedule any side trips or private visits this time; it didn't seem appropriate when the matter at hand was so serious. I had only a few days to evaluate and observe the whole school, including students and staff. I spoke to several teachers who wrote to me or came to visit me in my room at the Arusha Hotel. It was clear to me that Dr. Maldonado had done a great job. The student body had markedly grown, and the school's physical appearance had improved. I was sure Dr. Maldonado was leading the school forward financially as well as academically, as he was going after the big picture. Such development would take at least three to five years before SCIS could compete with any international school in the world.

This was all too much for the Hellenic board, which treated Tanzania as if it were a colony of Greece. The members reminded me of Parviz, who felt whomever she hired was "a worker" who needed to obey, whatever academic degree he or she might have earned. Naturally, anyone with some self-respect would not allow this. Dr. Maldonado struggled with the fact that he cared—he cared for the students and the parents. He had put all his energy into the school, mornings, afternoons and nights, not for the Greeks, but for the school. He soon realized they wanted to micro-manage the school from Dar es Salaam, making him merely a puppet. It is impossible to work under these conditions. What's more, there were some long-employed ass-lickers to the Greeks who felt threatened and fearful of Dr. Maldonado's changes. Finally, when the chair questioned his dignity, Dr. Maldonado and his family left Tanzania. The biggest mistake the Greeks ever made with the school was to let him go. I cannot go into details as it is confidential, but Dr. Maldonado was done wrong, and the Greeks, with their greed and despotic manner, threatened him if he should disclose their business methods, so he had to leave the country. I sent my very open report to all members of the board.

As you can imagine, I wanted to get home without delay. I boarded a school bus bound for the airport. Halfway there, *pfft pop!* We broke down with an empty tire. I was not surprised to hear there was no spare. Looking at my watch, I realized there was no time to waste. I got my suitcase out of the bus and hitchhiked on the side of the road, a *mzungu* backpacker in Tanzania. I saw a *dala dala* approaching from a distance. A *dala dala* is a minibus in Tanzania, often overcrowded and operated at unsafe speeds. *Dala dalas* developed in response to the country's insufficient public transport system. The name may be a corruption of the English word "dollar."

I held my thumb up high while the school bus driver stood next to me and shook his head. Some *dala dalas* run fixed routes, picking up passengers at fixed locations. Others will stop anywhere along their route to drop someone off or allow a prospective passenger to board. I was lucky: this *dala dala* stopped. My driver explained the problem, and the *dala dala* driver said he'd bring me to the airport for $50 USD. I agreed. The driver threw everybody off the bus at the next stop, and away we flew, "landing" at the airport in time. I was happy, and the driver was happy. He had earned his usual daily income in a fraction of the usual time; he could go home early and be with his family, while people at the bus stops waited for him in vain.

My feelings were bittersweet as my plane, the real one, took off. I knew for sure the Greeks would be extremely unhappy with me after they read my last report and evaluation. I gazed below to green Tanzania and thought, this is almost certainly the last I'll see of Africa.

AYURVEDA CENTER AND DOLPHIN BEACH HOTEL

Soon after I returned, Christopher decided to build an Ayurveda center next to my house, and when it was ready I proposed to make a promotional video for YouTube and his website. One of their guests, Christiane, would be my model. She was a bit younger than I was. Imagine our surprise when the hits of the video went up and up! "Ayurveda Full Body Treatment" has received over 134,132 hits to date. I do not know if it is because of the nudity or the interest in Ayurveda. Most probably the latter.

The new manager of the Dolphin Beach Hotel, Daniel Ludwig, heard I was active in animal rescue and asked me to help solve the stray animal problem at his establishment. Previously, the hotel routinely poisoned strays. I went with Dr. Roshan to the Dolphin, where we met with Daniel and some of his employees. Dr. Roshan and I argued that since many "stray" dogs and cats actually belong to the villagers, if the animals were taken away or killed, new ones would simply take their place. We pointed out that the animals found on the premises were not aggressive and already known to many regular guests. The manager agreed to stop the poisoning and pursue our "alternative" advice.

A date was set for a pet sterilization and adoption event, and flyers were put in the guest rooms. I got my team together, and to my great pleasure and surprise, all our patients from six months earlier came with their vaccination booklets to get their vaccinations redone. It turned out that, because of the education program, the villagers had become very responsible, and their dogs were all clean and healthy. Several puppies were adopted, and the guests of Dolphin were satisfied to see the effort made to treat the animals. At the end of the day, Dr. Roshan submitted a bill, but it turned out that guest donations covered the animals' treatments.

TEACHING ENGLISH THE FUN (AND BETTER) WAY

My days in Sri Lanka did not revolve exclusively around animals. Working in education for so many years, I naturally became involved in our village public (government run) school. The principal was struggling with the system, the kids and their parents. Looking at the English curriculum, I could understand why the students did not speak much English. The system of teaching was quite old-fashioned. The teacher does not get up from her desk, and the students do not stir from theirs. They read from the textbook alone and learn by rote, like parrots. Critical thinking is not allowed. If a student attempts to do it, he or she is labeled a difficult child! I was hoping to eventually work with local teachers to give them training and make changes to the curriculum. I spent time with the children and teachers, hoping to gain their trust. It was very difficult, as they had no experience with foreigners.

"I'll start with the highest grade," I thought to myself. "Those students will understand me, perhaps." I stood in front of them and spoke briefly. They just looked at me. No sound came out of their mouths. I changed tactics and brought my computer and showed the movie *Eight Below*. Afterward I asked them questions. They did not reply, just gave me sweet smiles. The next movie was *Zeus and Roxanne*. They clearly enjoyed that one, but again, thunderous silence.

Then I got a brainstorm! Sri Lankans love to hear themselves talk on stage, dance and sing, too, so I decided to direct the American musical *Bugz*. I had helped my school in Tanzania perform it, so I knew it was a crowd pleaser. After explaining to the principal what it was all about, I bought materials and costumes, including decorative wings. We auditioned children of all ages. When I showed them my video recording of the performance of my school in Tanzania, they were sold! For six months we were singing, dancing and practicing. In the meantime

I started teaching English to the beginner speakers in third grade. I bought our performers a sound system for the stage with many microphones. They were so proud: not even the private schools had ever produced an English-speaking musical with a professional sound system. The musical was a big success, and even today students will perform some of the songs on special occasions.

With the approval of the Ministry of Education here in Wennapuwa, and with the input of local teachers, I developed a new English curriculum, but the road went dry and I never heard anything. There is still much to be done. I want to thank Thomas Daetwyler of Baurs for their school furniture from Switzerland, as well as my German friends Marion and Barbara, who donated equipment and funds to buy computers and a TV for English sessions. Sadly, I gradually had to reduce my involvement in the school, as I first broke my wrist, and a few months later, my leg. It had been too much stress for me.

DOLLY AND THE SWISS CIRCLE

I joined the Swiss Circle, an organization founded in 1956 to promote social activities among Swiss nationals in Sri Lanka. I was asked to film all events and create a regular newsletter, as members became aware that this was my hobby. I already knew Christopher, who was a business member, and now I became really good friends with Dolly, the owner of Bijou, one of the best restaurants in town. Dolly was in her mid seventies and had been battling cancer for thirty years. She was constantly in pain, but always wore a smile on her face. Christopher, Rico, Dolly and I would go together to events in Colombo. One evening we attended a buffet at the Mount Lavinia Hotel. An Italian man was seated opposite us. Making conversation, I asked him about his wife. In a rather nonchalant way, he told me that she "die." Marco, visiting from Oman, was sitting beside me at the time. We both said, "Ooohhh" in a sad way, me thinking I should never have asked such a stupid question. However, my curiosity got the better of me, so after a few minutes I inquired, "Sorry to ask, but when and why did she die?"

He looked at me with surprise and replied, "She did not die. She is Thai."

"Aaaahhhh," Marco and I said. We left the table, and all of us (Dolly and Rico overhearing) were almost pissing our pants with laughter. We had only to look at each other and say, "Die and Thai!" The poor man probably never understood why we didn't return to the table. We wouldn't have been able to look him in the eyes without cracking up!

Dolly had an adult white Persian cat, and her wish was to have a Persian kitten in her life again, so I made it my mission to find one. It took me a couple of months, but finally I spotted a Himalayan/Persian mix offered on the Internet by a woman doctor. I got in my old Willys Jeep and drove to a town two hours inland, picked up the kitten, and while driving back called Dolly and told her she shouldn't go to the restaurant that day, as I was bringing her something very important.

When I finally got to her place, she opened the gate and looked at me with questioning eyes. I handed her the cat carrier and said, "This is for you." She opened it and started crying. It really was the most beautiful kitten with blue eyes, black-tipped ears and an adorable nose poking out of the carrier. Dolly called her husband, Augustin, and told him she wouldn't be coming to work that day. When Augustin arrived home at midnight from the restaurant, he saw her sitting there with the kitten in her lap and asked, "Where did you get that?" She replied, "Marilyn." He asked, "For a holiday?" She said, no Marilyn gave it to me. Augustin asked nothing more. He took the kitten to bed with him, and he and the kitten were bedmates ever after. As for Dolly, she stayed home for the rest of the week to enjoy the cat's company while her husband was out!

I doubt you'll be shocked to learn that when this female kitten got older she slipped out of the house and got impregnated by a cheeky street cat. Dolly was beside herself. No, no, she didn't want more kittens! I said I would take them. I don't care for Persians that much, but I figured the babies of a fifty-fifty should be cute. Dolly was relieved. After nine weeks, Dolly's young cat gave birth to three exquisite kittens. Two months later I took from the litter a tortoise shell-colored kitten and named it Persiana ("short" for Persia) and a white-and-orange tabby that I called William of Orange (nicknamed Wimpie). My house girl Noni took their orange sister and called her Snowy. (You'll have to ask Noni why an orange cat should be Snowy!) Wimpie and Persiana were my numbers eight and nine.

A WEDDING AND REUNIONS

Claudia was getting married to Matthew Coffman, a professional guitar player, and I was invited to Nashville for the wedding. First I traveled to Florida and stayed a week with my old friend from EIS, Juanita Treat. She lived with her animals in a mobile home close to Tampa. I had a great time, canoeing with her and sharing simple but delicious dinners. It was a time of reminiscing, laughter and joy. A new experience, too: although I had done a lot of camping in my life, I had never lived in an RV, and if I didn't know my animals needed my presence, it would have been easy for me to make it a home away from home. Juanita reminded me of Pat, my other EIS teacher friend. They are both strong-minded lifelong expats, who for sure don't believe that the US is the Promised Land, as so many naïve Americans think. I was happy to have the wedding in Nashville to go to, but sad to leave Juanita.

Claudia, as always, had everything organized to perfection and was a stunning bride. She looked like a little girl who had received all her favorite cookies at once. I could see it in her eyes! The wedding day was sunny and celebrated in a park, like in a fairytale. I stayed with Claudia's friend Pauline Kaplan, a transformational psychologist and ordained minister, who blessed the newlyweds at the end of the ceremony. In the days after the wedding, I was driven from here to there and everywhere. One night Claudia, Matthew and I went to Nashville's 3rd and Lindsley Bar to see Vince Gill and The Time Jumpers. Bonus: I unexpectedly ended up sitting at the same table as the band members of Kings of Leon! I love country and western, so I was in seventh heaven.

Ale, who had had two babies since I'd seen her last, invited me to her home in Miami. The stores in the city had good deals, so I decided to spend the inheritance from my dad. I bought an iMac, iPhone, iPad and iPod. (Later, to avoid paying huge taxes in Sri Lanka, I turned the iMac box around so that the Apple logo was not visible on the otherwise plain brown carton. It worked.)

My last stop in the US was Long Island. Yes, I went to see Grace, whom I hadn't seen in twenty years. When I arrived at her beautiful home in Bellport, it was as if not a single year had passed. We reminisced, went sightseeing, laughed and ate. Do you remember how Grace was about dieting? She hasn't changed that way, so it was mostly just me eating! It was nice to meet her son again; the last time I'd seen him, he was about six. Now Etienne was a handsome young Long Islander, educated, much aware of fashion, career, possessions and money. In this way he seems typical of so many young Americans I met. I do not say that this is wrong, but it's so different from what I have believed in and the way I live. As I told Grace and Etienne stories from my past, I got the feeling they didn't believe half of what I said. Can I blame them? Before we parted, Grace and I cried and promised not to wait another twenty years for the next get-together.

PAMPERED PUSSYCATS

Back home in Sri Lanka, I remained involved with Martin's Hope Foundation. He kept sending me kittens that people had abandoned at his restaurant, some so young they still had their umbilical cords attached. Martin himself had now over eighty dogs, and he and I agreed it was getting to be too much for us. Martin contacted Embark, a dog welfare group, and helped arrange an adoption day in the parking lot of the Jetwing Hotel, opposite Martin's restaurant. Having nursed the current crop of kittens to health, I put them up for adoption.

When the event was over...you guessed it. Martin brought me more kittens! Four that had been dumped at the local Buddhist temple. They were particularly sweet, and I didn't want to give them to just anyone. Since my dad's passing, I had followed the Sri Lankan funeral ritual and given food to the neighborhood Ladani orphanage to bless my father's soul. I now contacted the orphanage head, Father Neville, and asked if I could donate two of the kittens, explaining that I thought it would be good for the children to have companions. When I brought Princess and Duke, the little girls were delighted, eager to touch and hold them. One day I went to check on the pair. They were fat and spoiled, stretched out on pillows like royalty, their nails adorned in pink polish, their fur soft and white. I had to lecture the children on cat hygiene: they wash themselves, and therefore do not need bathing. In addition, nail polish can be poisonous, and so shouldn't be applied again. Still, I confess they looked marvelous! I left feeling very happy with the love and care they were receiving.

EMERGENCIES FOR AN "ANGEL" AND ME

With the approval of my landlord—who was lucky to have such a good tenant, if I say so myself—I used some more of my inheritance to add a sea view terrace to my cottage. Construction took about three months. Workers always started promptly at 8 A.M., which was my good fortune. Here's why: one morning about 7:30, while stepping into the shower, I slipped on my anti-slip rubber mat. In the very act of falling, I knew I was going to break something. I had no phone, and there I was lying on the wet floor with a broken leg, which hurt like shit. I called out, "Noni! Suranga!" but nobody heard me.

Fortunately, I could hear the workers arriving. Now I shouted louder than ever: "Suranga! Noni!" One of the workers alerted Suranga, and five minutes later he was calling for me at my bedroom door. He came and lifted me in all my nakedness from the wet floor, careful not to hurt me, dropping me on the bed, where Noni covered me with a towel. I cried and cried, not so much from pain as the exhaustion of waiting in an impossible position on the shower floor. Noni called Dr. Gomanthi Gunathilaka, the Ayurveda lady doctor, who applied some herbs to the injury while advising that if the pain persisted I should get an x-ray. Having previously had so many fractures, I knew for certain my leg was broken, but I was too beat to drive all the way to Colombo that day. I rested until the next morning, then got a ride to Lanka Hospital, where a fracture just below my left knee was diagnosed. I was forced to wear a huge and heavy cast, so on the way home I bought a wheelchair. For weeks I was bound to the bed, but surrounded by my much-loved dogs and cats.

A new bunch of kittens came. They were a few weeks old and healthy, just needing some nourishment to be ready for adoption. One of them was particularly beautiful. Moortje, you'll recall, was completely black. This soon-to-have-a-permanent-home kitten, too, was black. However, she also had a small white patch on her, well, *pussy*. It made her look so cute, as if she were wearing a mini bikini.

One day just before the kitten was going up for adoption, Noni came and told me something was very wrong with it. "It won't move," she said. I told her to bring it to me on the bed. I placed it carefully on my lap and looked at her. Her mouth and eyes were open, and her tongue was hanging out. She was absolutely lifeless. I saw no moving of her ribcage, and when I put my hands in front of her mouth and nose I didn't feel any breathing. And yet…she was warm.

I'd learned from experience there's no point in bringing a very young kitten to a vet. The only thing he or she could do would be to give the poor thing a shot, and each and every one of my kittens that received such a "booster" promptly died. I decided to give nature and the universe a chance. I wrote on Facebook that my little black kitten had given up and was lying unconscious in my lap on the cast of my broken leg. It needed prayers, positive thinking and energy. Believing in the power of big crowds in prayer or energies, I sat there, giving my kitten the positive thoughts from my Facebook friends. She remained on my lap for many hours, and although there was still no sign of breathing or movement, she did not die.

Late that evening she suddenly moved a leg. I thought it might merely be a spasm, but I wrote again on Facebook, and more positive thoughts and prayers poured in. Two hours later, she closed her mouth and eyes. I thought, this is it, she's dead. Instead, she shook her body, opened her eyes, got up, and after eight hours of a "near-death experience" she stepped out of my lap as if nothing had happened. I called her Malaika (Kiswahili for "angel"). She was number ten to stay at Marilyn's Ark.

During my recovery, I was invited to Dr. Roshan's wedding. I had to attend in the wheelchair, pushed by Suranga and Noni. Up to that point,

I felt I didn't know anyone in Sri Lanka, having lived a very simple life in solitude. Now, suddenly, I saw so many familiar and friendly faces. I was surprised to realize I had "fit in" so easily and so fast.

Although healing from the fracture was frustrating for me, I was lucky to be recuperating after my new terrace was completed. I used to go up and drink in the view of the empty beach and sea. (Before the terrace was built, I was denied this luxury because of my home's high protective walls.) Some days I would take an audio book and listen with all the cats and dogs around me, the wind kissing our skin (or fur). Sometimes I would pause the player, just lie there on the lounge chair and let my thoughts peacefully drift.

During one of these quiet moments, I heard an equally quiet sound. At first I thought it was a bird, but when I concentrated I realized it was the cry of a newborn kitten. As fast as I could, I got up from my lounge chair, grabbed my crutches and looked over the balustrade, searching the high grass on the other side of the wall. There it was, a tiny moving spot, trying to shout her unhappiness into the world. Somebody had dropped a kitten in front of my home, knowing I would collect it. I threw a towel over me and hobbled outside to collect the poor creature. Tortelina, my first calico, had more white than color, but the spots of hue were evenly spread over her body. She was only a few days old but already showed character. Spirited and strong, Tortelina grew fast and remained healthy. She was my "lucky" cat, number eleven.

Who could have known I would one day shed so many tears over my Tortelina? One night eighteen months later she did not show up for dinner. I thought that she might have been busy catching mice, but when she didn't appear the next morning for breakfast, I worried. I dressed and walked through the street calling her name, especially around the home of my opposite neighbors, Kamala and Sunil, who had many rats living under their house; I had seen Tortelina several times coming from under with a big rat in her mouth. No result, no sounds, except from some of my other cats who had followed me, who are very verbal, as was Tortelina. I informed the people in the street that I was missing Tortelina, to please look out for her. Evening came: no Torti.

The next morning I was almost hysterical and again walked through the street calling her name, passing by Kamala's house, looking under and above when I suddenly heard a soft meow. I called her name, and her meow became louder the closer I moved towards the front gate. There she was, lying behind the gate, where she definitely had not been the day before. I ran to her and kneeled down. She did not move. I knew something was very wrong. As I lifted her up, tears ran down my face. She had deep wounds on both sides of a broken spine. I was devastated, crying and calling my manager's name: "Suranga, Suranga!" He came running out of his house. I told him to get the *tuktuk* ready, we had to go immediately to Dr. Roshan because Torti had been attacked by a dog and was heavily wounded. Holding her tenderly, trying not to hurt her, I put her in the lower part of a carrier, so that she was lying in my arms but still on a surface that did not move, as the jolting *tuktuk* drive would certainly hurt her.

When we arrived in Kochchikade at Four Paws Animal Hospital, Dr. Roshan advised me to get an x-ray taken at Negombo Animal Hospital by Dr. Gunawardena, also known as the air force vet. I was desperate as Tortelina looked at me, putting all her trust in me, replying to the soft words I spoke to her. The x-ray showed a complete fracture, through and through. I did not know any vet who would euthanize a cat; the practice is still not common in Sri Lanka because of "religious" reasons. It is considered a sin. I went back to Dr. Roshan, who gave what all vets give to any damaged animal: antibiotics and painkillers. I was in despair. I called for help on Facebook, if anybody knew of a surgeon in Sri Lanka to operate on my poor, beloved Tortelina. Anneliese Elizabeth of Cool Cat Group offered to start a donation request through "GoFundMe" to cover the cost.

Days went by. It was sad to see Tortelina in so much pain. Finally, I received a call from one Facebook friend who gave me the number of a doctor in Colombo who does spinal operations. I called him at 7 P.M. knowing it would take me two hours to reach his clinic. He told me to come immediately. I called Saranga, my long distance driver, we got in his van, and he drove like a maniac to the clinic of the "best surgeon in Colombo."

Tortelina was immediately taken into the operating room. I stood outside. Everything seemed very professional, and I could see that the doctor and his assistant worked hand in hand. What I did not know is that the operation itself was just putting a wire around the vertebrae of the spine, no screw or anything else. It was a huge wound. I felt so helpless and did not know if I had done the right thing for her, but what else could I do? This doctor, too, refused to perform euthanasia. I paid my bill, covered by Cool Cat Group member donations, and we went home.

The next morning my house girl Noni and I lifted Torti gently to her other side in the carrier to clean her towels. She cried out in pain, sending tears rolling down my face. I called the air force vet and said I needed a scan. We went, he was not there, so his assistant made the scan. It showed internal damage. I also asked for an x-ray again, which showed that the fracture was even worse than before. The "best surgeon in Colombo" turned out to be a butcher. I took my cat home. I was more than devastated. What was I to do, with nobody to help take my poor Tortelina over the Rainbow Bridge? Why did she need to suffer so much? My tears of despair could have created a river of pain. Finally, I called Sam and Mark Green of Dogstar Foundation, who had helped me before with Aztec. Crying, I begged for help, although I knew that their vet who had helped my husky was not with them anymore. Sam told me that she would call back.

Five minutes later the phone rang. Sam told me that the Best Care Hospital team was in Trincomalee doing a sterilization/vaccination program, but that one of their assistants, Sampath, was at their hospital in Colombo. Sam had spoken to the head physician in Trincomalee, and he had given permission for Sampath to help Tortelina and me. They would call me back to see when I would be able to go there. Again waiting, Tortelina looked at me, begging me to let her go. I just cried and petted her face, while my tears caressed her. The phone rang, and I was told to come immediately. I called Saranga again, and he was there within five minutes.

During the whole ride I told myself to be strong, while I held my beloved Torti in my arms. She was quiet now, she knew, just looking at me with knowing eyes. She was OK with it, I felt it. Arriving at Best Care Hospital, Sampath was waiting for us. I knew him from our TAPA sterilization days in my village, Mount Lavinia and Negombo. He showed me to a consultation room and closed the curtains. He held my hands and we talked a bit about Torti while tears ran over my face. When he was member of the TAPA team he had been in my house, swimming in the pool and enjoying a wonderful barbecue after a busy day of operations on cats and dogs in my village. He was a kind man who knew all my animals.

Sampath calmed me down and prepared the syringes while I held Torti. Somehow Sampath had created an atmosphere of "letting go" and peace came over me, I think also Torti, who had been in such horrible pain. I kissed her for the last time and held her little paw in mine while she got her first shot, which was slowly and gently administered. She closed her eyes, while I watched Sampath checking her heart rate. She lay in my arms when he gave the final shot. She took her last breath: my Tortelina was gone. As I write this, tears are pouring down again for sadness and from anger, anger with the veterinary system here. When I asked a renowned vet, "Why is it that I do not feel empathy in many of you vets here for my animals?" He replied: "Because many of us do not want to be vets. We wanted to be physicians, but because we did not have high enough grade point averages, we had to choose veterinary medicine instead." I looked at him with disgust and confirmed again my decision was correct never to give any of my newborn rescue kittens to any of them for treatment, first because they do not have the facilities and second because only few of them care.

Now I had ten cats again.

CATNAPPER!

Dolly's Himalayan was again naughty and got impregnated by a wandering Romeo. Six kittens were in the litter. I told Dolly not to worry: I would be the "manager" and see that all of them got good homes. One would go to Martin's manager Danial, who already had two of my cats at his plantation. One would go to my new house girl, Ramani. The remaining four were going home with *me*! I had named them soon after birth: Chispa, Queenie, Alouette and Geisha. Fur ball Chispa looked like a festive raccoon, with wide, orange stripes crossing a blackish-gray coat. Highly unusual appearance. Queenie was close to a tortoise shell, but instead of dark fur she had very light gray. Alouette, tiniest of the litter, resembled a British Blue. Chispa, Queenie and Alouette all had the long hair of a Himalayan. Geisha was the only shorthair, her main color being black mixed with white and gray.

Dolly, resigned to the fact that her Himalayan was incurably romantic, decided that next time she'd like to see it mated with a white male Persian, so she could get some kittens that were more Persian in appearance. I found such a male in Colombo suitable for the "job" and gave it to her. Dolly and I were both happy with this agreement.

Eight weeks later, Martin called and told me he had spoken with Dolly and decided I had enough kittens, so he would take them all. My mouth gaped open in astonishment. Finally, I managed to say, "No way, Martin! All the kittens are already spoken for. One for your manager, one for my house girl, and four for me." He insisted, no, you don't need them, and I told him again, yes, I need them, and you cannot take them.

The next day, getting an odd feeling, I phoned Dolly. I asked her about the kittens, and she told me Martin had taken them. I was furious and tried to call him, but he was not reachable, so I sent him an email, telling him to send the kittens back immediately, as they did not belong to him and I had made an agreement with Dolly that I was the manager, and I had given her in return a pure bred white Persian for her mama cat to breed with.

A return mail came that evening addressed to Pussy Galore, Martin's nickname for me. "The kittens have been returned, except the one intended for my manager. I am not a 'Catnapper.'" When I read the word "catnapper" I couldn't help giggling. Now, whenever I see Martin, I see the word "catnapper" before my eyes and have to smile.

NIK AND CATS ELEVEN TO THIRTEEN

I delivered Ramani's kitten to her and brought the rest to my home. All the kittens were extremely frightened, and it took them quite a while to get used to my yard, as they had never been outside. Little Alouette suffered the most. She ate and immediately had loose bowels, or she'd throw up undigested food. I took her to Dr. Roshan, who couldn't diagnose the problem. Nik, one of the students I'd known at DAA, now a twenty-year-old young man, fashionable and soft spoken, had come to stay with me during his gap year from the university, and he accompanied me when I brought Alouette to the university hospital in Peradeniya. We left her there in the professional hands of Dr. Manjula, who had been a doctor on the team of TAPA. A few days later, Dr. Manjula called to inform me that Alouette had died. She had not been poisoned, nor did she have a Tricat virus; it appeared her digestive system had a genetic defect. It was sad, but life goes on, and so did we. Cats eleven to thirteen were now settled at Marilyn's Ark.

A "MERMAID" AND A BLIND SWIMMER

Nik had no experience with animal rescue, and his "trial by fire" began with a Facebook message I received from Embark. As I mentioned earlier, Embark advocates for street dogs. Some of its volunteers, aware I had experience caring for cats, asked if I would help a tortoiseshell cat that had been found on the road. Her two hind legs had been fractured and hung crookedly behind her, deep wounds to her joints. Embark said it would pay all expenses incurred, so of course, I agreed. Nick named the cat Milou. I kept her in my bedroom and changed her bandages three to four times a day. She would routinely rip these off, and I could see that even if the bandages remained, the more mutilated leg would continue to hinder her movement. After eight months of witnessing this torture, I went to Dr. Roshan and asked him to amputate the leg, which he did. Life improved for Milou, but the wound over the joint on her other hind leg stubbornly refused to heal. She had multiple operations to clean the joint; nothing helped.

After fourteen months I was so fed up, seeing Milou deprived of happiness, that I called Dr. Roshan and asked him to amputate the other hind leg also. Dr. Roshan did not immediately agree. Wouldn't this create a bigger problem? he questioned. How can she get around with only two front legs? I told him not to worry. I was sure I was doing the correct thing. I had googled and YouTubed the matter, and knew it was possible for Milou to live contentedly with only two legs. The surgery was performed, and Milou's reaction was amazing. She was visibly relieved, coming to me for cuddles, "talking" to me, clearly happy to be physically free. Now it was up to Nik and me to teach her to balance on two legs, or at least to unburden her behind. She is my little mermaid, and number fourteen in the Ark.

I was getting to be known as the "cat saver" on Facebook. I was asked to please help again, this time to rescue a blind cat. I was hesitant; my dogs did not always tolerate new cats, especially adults, and who knew how the cat herself would respond to a house full of other cats and dogs? All right, let me try. The cat arrived. She had a lot of pus in her eyes (no pun intended) but even when that was cleared out, she remained blind. She was highly nervous, clearly having had little human contact. After keeping her for a week in my guest bathroom, I left the door ajar. Slowly she appeared in the living room, hissing at each cat who dared to come close…and that was just about all of them. Cats are very curious and don't like to miss out on new developments. When one goes to check things out, all others follow.

By now I had named the cat "Chitty Chitty Bang Bang." "Chitty" was the surname of the girl who found her, and "Bang Bang" suited because my Chitty constantly walked into walls and trees. One morning after breakfast I went to the pool, and while I was swimming I talked idly to the cats. Chitty was not there. I swam my laps and talked some more. I saw Chitty coming through the gate, beckoned by the sound of my voice. She'd never been in the pool area before and had no clue I was in water. I shouted, "No, Chitty, no!" Too late. She had already fallen in! I swam and caught her and tossed her up on the side. She calmly shook herself and sat as if nothing had happened. (I suspect the other cats would have shared Chitty's lack of fear if they couldn't see the water.) I considered it was possible that Chitty could fall in again, so I decided to acclimate her to the water. I came out of the pool, took her in my arms and carried her back to the center, where I slowly let her go. She swam, quietly, peacefully, not knowing where she should go but keeping straight, and finally reaching and leaving from the side of the pool, never showing any sign of being unnerved.

Chitty was very independent and kept to a routine. She would leave the house, roam around and be back for the feeding times. At first she would keep to the roof; other cats would contest her territory in noisy fights. Then Chitty discovered trees. She learned to climb a certain tree, jump from it to the wall and then venture outside. I topped the wall with wire; by intuition, she climbed higher before dropping herself over the wall. Inventive as she was daring, she always landed safely on her four feet. Suranga and I tried everything to keep her inside the property, but it was useless; she always found a way out. Dr. Gomanthi from Ayurveda Center next door once told me she observed Chitty dropping herself from the tree over the wall, a two-meter (six feet) fall. As if she knew the tag around her neck bore my telephone number, Chitty confidently walked as far as the chapel on one end of the street or to the shop on the opposite side. She would walk with her head in the air, keenly listening to sounds. After a while she memorized the layout of the road and even ran along it. We called her Chitty, the Blind Kitty. She had a full, exciting life until one morning the gardener at Rico's Shadow brought her home, dying. A stray dog had attacked her in a utility shed, pushing her into a corner and biting her back until she was paralyzed. We were all saddened by the loss of Chitty Chitty Bang Bang. Not forgotten, she still lives on YouTube, where she shows us how to swim. She was number fifteen for just a short lovely time at Marilyn's Ark.

FRITZI AND LADANI

Dolly introduced me to someone who soon became a very good friend: Frederic Schepski, Fritzi for short. A tall, blond, good-looking man in his early forties, Fritzi was a shore excursion manager on a cruise ship. He would come during his breaks to Sri Lanka, his new home. Fritzi, a humanitarian, heard I was involved with the Ladani orphanages and wanted to know more about them. Brainchild of Rev. Father Neville Coonghe, Ladani started in 1985 with a single orphanage housing only five children. Today Ladani provides shelter to more than 180 children in six homes. Father Neville's mission is to empower the children who are orphaned and destitute with love and wisdom, knowledge and stability, self-respect and self-reliance. I introduced Fritzi first to the boys' home in Thambarawila, which is closest to Waikkala. The children there had also received two kittens from me, and I now knew that home very well. Every few months, my Swiss friends Ursi and Tanja would send me a huge box, which I had to collect from customs in Colombo. These boxes were filled with clothing and items for children (Ursi) and stuff for animals, including kitten milk and feeding bottles (Tanja). They are still sending me these special deliveries, making many people and animals happy.

Fritzi decided to roll up his sleeves. He started collecting donations during shipboard parties, and spearheaded the donation of food from a cruise ship anchored in Colombo. A bus was rented by Fritzi at a special price, and his friend Miss Hage, who worked with him on the cruise ship, drove it fully stocked with food, toys and clothing to Thambarawila. What a surprise! The boxes were carried from the huge tourist bus into the home, everybody helping.

With this delivery people from the German charity group Stiftunglife came also, looking into the possibility of making the Ladani orphanages part of their worldwide project. When the orphanage staff saw what a large donation this was, they called Father Neville, who soon arrived with Sister Monica, his able assistant. We all drank tea and had a meeting. Sister Monica looked at everything and said it would be sorted and given to the relevant orphanages; the food would all be shared. Father Neville explained his worries and problems regarding the facilities with the Stiftunglife employees, me and other volunteers. He told us that food was not a worry, as many small meal donations came in on a daily basis. His biggest concern was the maintenance of the houses, the roofs and bathrooms. A few months later, Stiftunglife included Ladani in its yearly budget and made the repairs Father Neville requested.

OF COURSE, I SAID YES
Dr. Roshan called me early one morning:

> "Marilyn, I know you told me that you've reached
> the limit with kittens, but I just found four newborns
> dumped under a truck. I have my hands full already. Can
> you please take care of them?"

What could I do? Of course, I said yes. I guess Dr. Roshan never had any doubts I would, because he arrived only minutes later on my doorstep. When I laid eyes on the kittens, my breath stopped. They were gorgeous calicos. One was mainly white, although on the back of her head and across her ears she had an orange triangle set between two black patches. She also had a tri-colored tail. I called her Panda. The other kitten was white with black patches and a black tail. She reminded me of a little Dalmatian dog, so I named her Dalmatia. The other two were pretty but did not inspire me to name them. (You might have asked yourself why I have so many females. These are the ones the Sri Lankans throw out or kill, as people do not want to spend the money or do not have the funds to sterilize the cats and prevent pregnancies.) I made all four kittens feel at home in my guest bathroom, placing them in a very large, old red suitcase that Ursi had left behind after a visit.

Kittens do much better drinking their mother's milk rather than formula. I remembered that somebody had told me that the cat of a neighbor, Elisabetha Nona, had given birth. Without delay I walked to Elisabetha's house. She told me that indeed her cat had given birth a few days before, but she didn't know where the kittens were hidden. We searched the whole house: no kittens. We looked outside, under woodpiles, behind bushes. When I gazed down into an old well, I found one of them, weak but alive. I snuggled it into my clothing. Elisabetha promptly found another one nearby. I took the two home, Elisabetha promising to keep on searching, in case there were more.

I put the two kittens among Dr. Roshan's four and went to look for mama cat, keeping my eyes peeled for an orange and white coat. No luck. Elisabetha promised to call me when the cat came home. I fed all the kittens my special Swiss kitten milk until they dropped asleep. I was very worried about Elisabetha's; they were in a really bad way, although a bit older than the ones Dr. Roshan had brought. I suspect the mother cat had been trying to hide her babies from stray dogs.

A few hours later, Elisabetha called to say I could collect mama, who would be a temporary guest at the five-star hotel, Marilyn's Ark. I placed her in the suitcase with many soft towels and put all the kittens to her nipples. She purred, they purred, everybody was happy. Now nature would just have to take its course...

The next morning I gave mom a big breakfast to prepare her for another day of nursing. One of her own babies had died during the night. That left only one of her original litter (Elisabetha had not found any additional kittens). That little survivor died another day later, almost certainly because she had been left too long in hiding. But now that mama was in a safe environment, she was a great mother to her foster kittens. She stayed with me for four weeks, then became restless, wanting to go outside or at least explore the rest of the house. This was impossible, as my dogs would kill her. Before I returned her to Elisabetha, I had her spayed and gave her a parting gift of good food to last for days.

NUMBERS SIXTEEN AND SEVENTEEN

The four Roshan kittens had grown to be exquisite little cats, but still too young to be re-homed. Martin told me that an adoption event would be held in about a month in front of his restaurant in the parking lot of Jetwing Blue Hotel. I planned to adopt-out all of them, didn't I? The weeks went by. Panda and Dalmatia grew increasingly close to my heart, but I could not keep them, enough was enough. Except...I convinced myself that one could stay, Panda Bear. So there I went, three kittens in a great carrier, to this event organized by Embark, the Hope Foundation (Martin) and the Dogstar Foundation (Samantha and Mark Green). I thought Dalmatia was the loveliest, but the other two went first, perhaps because Dalmatia was female.

Then…I hid Dalmatia under my dress and sat there for another hour, making small talk with people passing by, until I told Martin I might as well go because ALL my cats were re-homed. Just then a small head popped out of my dress and mewed. Martin shook his head and said, "Pussy Galore, you will never learn. You have to become strong and hard, you cannot keep them all." I replied that this one was special, to which he said, "Aren't they all!"

My Dalmatia came back home with me, and she is still very special. Why? Well, she became best friends with Milou. Why? Because she steals Milou's food and becomes fatter and fatter, while Milou thinks she has found a new best girlfriend, as Dalmatia spends her whole day sleeping very close to her (so that she will not miss an in-between feeding, but I did not tell Milou this). Panda Fernandopulle (Dr. Roshan's surname) is number sixteen and Dalmatia Fernandopulle is seventeen in Marilyn's Ark. They are my talking cats. They have a lot to say, especially while I am at Ayurveda Center. They like to visit me there and lie on top of me while I'm having a massage.

"AN ADVENTURE ONLY AFTER THE FACT"
Summertime came. Nathalie, another former DAA student, came for a short vacation and to volunteer at Dr. Roshan's clinic. Marco also arrived, being a regular visitor to my home. Nik and Marco rented motorbikes, and with Nathalie seated behind Marco, they drove to Nuwara Eliya, a picturesque area in central Sri Lanka. They returned with many stories, Nik often the butt of (good-natured) jokes. Nathalie left my home satisfied with her work and play.

Fritzi appeared and decided he wanted to go on an adventure. So did Nik, and yes, so did I! None of us had ever been to the northern part of the island, Tamil country, so after discussing what each of us wanted, we had Sarange (my long distance driver) drive us to Colombo Ratmalana Airport with his minicab. From there we took a small aircraft to Trincomalee on the east coast, changed planes and flew to Jaffna in the north. From that airport we drove by bus into the city, then grabbed a taxi to the northernmost point of the island to Thalsevana Hotel. The hotel stands on the silver beach of Kankesanthurai, isolated from the hustle and bustle of the city, offering a panoramic view of the Indian Ocean. It should have been a lovely stay...but...after dropping our suitcases and walking around, we realized we had "checked into" one of the hotels run by the Sri Lanka army. From bus boys to waiters to the manager, everyone was military personnel!

Having sat on our deck and contemplated the sea view, we decided we'd spend no more than one night. Fritzi and I separately googled other possibilities. We both ended up choosing the same guesthouse, Sabins Blue Ocean Resort in Jaffna. Fritzi called and reserved a triple room for the next night. Now we could relax, eat and drink; well, for me only relax and eat, as I was tired and went to bed early. Fritzi and Nik, however, accompanied by the hotel manager, celebrated till early morning, it seems.

Next morning after breakfast, we departed again for Jaffna City. A soldier in uniform drove us in an old-timer, a 1969 Morris Oxford. It was very hot, so I turned on the AC. Presently, the engine went *prrrr, prrr*, and stopped. I had unwittingly been the culprit, not knowing the engine couldn't run and supply AC at the same time. We got out of the car and stood in the heat at the side of the dusty road, many kilometers from Jaffna City. We were lucky: in under ten minutes, an empty, antique military bus approached. Our driver stopped it, our suitcases were transferred to the bus, and we boarded, continuing our journey.

Seliyan, the manager of Sabins Blue Ocean Resort was waiting for us on the mainland. He drove us in a big 4x4 across the Kayts Causeway to our guesthouse on Kayts Island. Our room, which had three beds, was simply furnished but clean and inexpensive. We didn't mind a lack of air conditioning, because the room faced the sea, and breezes kept us cool. We quickly turned around and piled into an air-conditioned-but-not-about-to-break-down car driven by the hotel manager cum tour guide. He drove us back to Jaffna, where we went sightseeing at an old Dutch fort and Dutch church, both heavily damaged in the Tamil war. Then we went to the best Food City grocery store I have seen on the island.

We bought ribs, fish, chicken and drinks and stuff for breakfast the next morning, as the manager/tour guide told us he and his aide could cook for us. We drove back to the guesthouse, admiring the breathtaking scenery, including a white sandy beach and a small pier. A perfect location for a guesthouse. We ate a scrumptious barbecue, downed a few drinks, and discovered a karaoke machine. Stars were born that night, and the more drinks we imbibed, the better we sang. Ambitious plans had been drawn up for the next day, so shortly after midnight we all turned in.

With Seliyan again leading the way, we headed for Delft Island, a **must** for the Dutch born, which Nik and I were. Vehicles are not permitted on the island: however, we timed our arrival to take advantage of a free ferry that shuttles from the mainland twice daily. Although the ferry was large, it was packed with passengers. I'd been instructed to stay in the hold, but I started feeling claustrophobic, so I pushed myself back upwards, steadying myself by holding a rope on the side of the boat. Meanwhile, Nik and Fritzi comfortably chatted on the stairs. Hours later, to my relief, we arrived safely at the island. Once I caught my breath, we hired a *tuktuk* driver to show us around the island.

Delft retains much of its centuries-old charm. We admired the distinctive architecture of the area, especially the fences enclosing the little homes, which were woven from hardy palmyrah leaves or formed from piled-up coral. We were shown a spreading baobab tree, another Dutch fort, an old Dutch hospital that is still in use, and "the footprint of a giant," a natural stone formation. We also saw the famed wild horses, introduced by the Portuguese in the 1600s. These horses, forbidden by law to leave the island, number in the low hundreds. Of course, being near the sea, the guys and I stopped at one point to take a dip.

Guess what happened to our *tuktuk*? It blew a tire. Fortunately, the driver of an antique tractor gave us a lift to port, where we gave him a tip. Reluctant to wait two hours for the slow, packed-like-sardines ferry, we asked Seliyan if we could hire a private boat. He checked this out and told us there was only one private boat owner willing to take us back to Kayts Island. His was an old fishing craft, and he'd be charging a lot, but I didn't care, I just wanted to be off. All of us were happy with the swiftness of the boat, its roominess, and the knowledge we'd return to the mainland in half the time. Seliyan took us back to Sabins, and from there dropped us at the pier nearest the island of Fort Hammenheil. A small boat took us to the fort.

This octagonal fort was built in 1618 by the Portuguese to guard the sea route to Jaffna. The Dutch captured it in 1658 and renamed it Hammenheil. During our stay, the combination fort and hotel was managed by the Sri Lankan navy. We compared the way Thalsevana had been run by the army with the way Hammenheil was handled, and we felt the navy did a better job, very professional, the bedroom spotless. We had the option to have the "prisoner experience" at the fort, but declined.

In the evening we were taken by small boat to a restaurant on the mainland. We were seated, and our orders were taken. Nik got up and roamed, while Fritzi and I hungrily awaited the food. The waiter brought two crab starters and a soup, putting the crabs in front of Fritzi and me, the soup on Nik's empty placemat. We ate the starters and declared them delicious, six stars! After polishing off the last morsel, Fritzi looked at me and asked, "Did I really order this crab starter?" I shrugged, not exactly sure.

Finally Nik returned, looked questioningly at the soup and said, "Did I order that?"

Fritzi and I exchanged guilty glances, and Fritzi said, "I don't remember, but the starter we had was great. The best I ever had in Sri Lanka!" Nik ate his soup quietly and said nothing, poor thing. He did not leave his chair again until all food was digested. The entire meal had been mouthwatering, and with full bellies we waddled to the boat and motored back to the fort, the boys chatting and laughing with the sailors all the way. Once in our room, Fritzi and I settled into the oversized twin bed, keeping distance between each other. Another bed had been added at the foot of the bed for Nik. We watched some TV and fell asleep, ready for the next day's adventure.

We awoke in the middle of the night to a *drip, drip, drip*. What was that? Fritzi switched on the light. We looked at each other and started laughing. The AC was leaking, not a little, a **lot**. To avoid the wetness, I squooshed down until my feet were close to Nik's face. That made him wake up and look sleepily around. When Fritzi, who is very tall, also moved down, his feet were lying on Nik's bed. We were all laughing so much, because it was again poor Nik who was to be troubled by us. That is how we slept and woke up the next morning, the head of our mattress soaking wet.

We checked out and, breakfast in mind, took the boat back to the restaurant where we had dined yesterday. I felt so sorry for Nik about the previous night that I ordered crab starters for him (all right, for Fritzi and me, too) but they were not the same as the ones before, which had been like "een engel die op je tong pist," a saying we have in our village in Holland, which literally translates as, "as if an angel were pissing on your tongue" and means won-der-ful!

Our taxi brought us back to the Jaffna airport, where we boarded a small plane bound for Trincomalee. We had reserved a room at another resort run by the navy, this time on Sober Island. The view out the aircraft windows was breathtaking, green hills and villages bordering the white beaches and blue sea. To me the east coast seemed strikingly different from the west, where the sea was wild and dark green.

Having landed safely, we took a taxi to the navy dockyard. Security allowed us to pass only after we presented our hotel reservation. As we waited for the navy speedboat to collect us, I looked around and said, "Oh, guys, this is the place for you! Allemaal jongetjes in witte korte broekjes!" ("All boys in small white shorts.") Nik and Fritzi grinned.

Named after a British lieutenant, Sober Island was a transit station for thousands of soldiers en route to the Far East and Mediterranean during World War II. More recently, the Tamil Tigers used it as a defensive stronghold. Sober Island Resort is blessed with a pristine tropical beach, jungle and historical artifacts. At its highest point, it offers a near 360-degree view of Trincomalee Harbor. The boys had much to explore—Sober Island is much larger than tiny Fort Hammenheil—but for me, at sixty-seven with osteoporosis, it was not ideal. I didn't get a lot of exercise other than swimming in the pool, where Nik took some really unflattering photos of me. Our hotel room was lovely and spacious; again, we had a twin bed for Fritzi and me and a single for Nik.

The next day our taxi driver took us sightseeing around Trincomalee. We started at Fort Frederick, an old Dutch fort with a Hindu temple inside it. We followed the coastline through some fishing villages, and saw the only hot water wells on the island. We lunched at the French Garden Guesthouse close to Pigeon Island.

While waiting at the navy dockyard for our speedboat, I spotted a cat in a really bad state, but the boat showed up before I could check it out. We reached Sober Island just before a heavy downpour. Fritzi had noticed me observing the sick cat, so the next morning he suggested we go and find it. We returned to the naval base, caught the cat and brought it to a vet. It turned out the doctor could do little for her, as she was due to be a mama in a few days, but we got cream for her wounds and drops for her eyes. I showed some helpful marines how to apply them before Fritzi and I caught the speedboat back to Sober Island. Then we swam, showered and caught the speedboat to return to Trincomalee. We flew from there to the Colombo airport, where Sarange was waiting to drive us home.

The three of us had a great time together. As I like to say, "An adventure turns out to be an adventure only after the fact." We were very lucky to have visited the north when we did, because two months later it was limited to foreigners with special permits only.

EIGHTEEN AND NINETEEN

Back home Fritzi caught my kitten fever and "rescued" a cat. He named it Blacky (you can guess its color) and kept it for a night. In the morning, he noticed she had swollen nipples, and worrying she was sick, brought her to Dr. Roshan. The doctor asked Fritzi where he'd found Blacky. Fritzi explained that it had come to his house, mewing for food. Dr. Roshan said, "You'd better put her back right away. This cat is full of milk. She's got a litter of kittens somewhere!" Quickly, Fritzi drove home and released the cat, who ran off to be with her babies. Since this event I call *him* the "Catnapper." Sweet Fritzi!

Two new rescues came in. One was black with white feet and a white belly. He looked like he was wearing a tuxedo with a white shirt, so I called him Mr. Tuxedo, or Tuxi, for short. I called his brother Jerry, because "Tuxi" made me think of "Tom" (Tom and Jerry). Jerry was similarly patterned to Tuxi, but was a tabby where Tuxi was black. Jerry's belly bulged with worms. Even though I kept giving him medication, his stomach never seemed to get smaller. Tapeworms as big as fingers emerged from his anus; I photographed them and put them online, much to the disgust of my Facebook friends. To properly relieve Jerry of this plague, Dr. Roshan advised me to give him an enema with an over-the-counter product. I had to insert it into poor Jerry's delicate tush and push some fluid in there so that he had the urge to pooh and pooh and pooh. I have never seen so many worms in my life! Jerry survived and thrived, now a big, handsome, proud cat. (He can't seem to lose that belly, though.)

As a kitten, Mr. Tuxedo would mistake my earlobe for a nipple and suck on it as if his life depended on it. The action would make me horny, and I couldn't understand why, until I suddenly got it: my ears were one of my erogenous zones, and Tuxedo was awakening them! Now all grown up, striding on long, elegant legs, Mr. Tuxedo is the "aristocat" of the family. At bedtime, when dogs and cats cuddle up with me, Tuxi still searches for my ear and sucks on it with loud purrs. Of course, I could never give away this sophisticated lover, and his brother is equally irresistible. They became numbers eighteen and nineteen in Marilyn's Ark.

AND THE OSCAR GOES TO...

Let us now raise the curtain on the story of the "Drama Queen."

A man named Wasantha from a neighboring village found three kittens in a temple. Wasantha was an exceptionally good cat "father" and had already taken several kittens from me, so having reached his reasonable limits, he asked me to care for these babies before finding them homes. At the same time, two other kittens came my way, sent by, guess who? Yes, Martin, who was always preaching at me not to take more! People had once again dumped kittens in his restaurant. One feline, sporting a gray and white coat, was the first I'd ever seen jumping from branch to branch like a monkey, instead of climbing like normal cats do. That monkey-aper was healthy, but the other one, a calico, looked sick, her eyes brimming with yellow pus. I feared the worst for her. The Wasantha kittens soon went to Dr. Roshan to be re-homed. He exhibited them, and within two days they were gone. The leaping gray and white one went fast, too. As for the calico, I had diagnosed her with cat flu. She resembled Panda, but with touches of soft color. For days I was convinced she wasn't long for this Earth. Still, I gave her a name: Cinderella, because she would look at me with those sad eyes, as if feeling sorry for herself, the girl sitting in the ashes with no invitation to the ball.

Then one day, when she didn't know I was watching her through a window, I saw this feline running, jumping and rolling. I couldn't believe it. Was this the same miserable Cinderella? I rose and quietly walked outside. She didn't hear me, as she was too busy playing with Panda and Dalmatia. When I came up behind her, I said, "Well, Cinderella, what is happening here?" At once, she went still as a salt pillar, lifted her face and regarded me with those melancholy eyes, slowly blinking again and again. She suddenly reminded me of Marlene Dietrich, the German actress of the 1930s who looked out at the world through heavy-lidded eyes. I now knew Martin had **not** given me a cat but an actress who could turn her moods on and off. I also discovered Cinderella was the fastest thief of all my cats. From meat to fish to veggies, it would be snatched from my plate in a twinkling. Funnily enough, this made me love her more than ever!

Still, I hadn't made up my mind to keep Cinderella when a message came on Facebook. A lady named Punsara living in Colombo sent me the photo of a cat that looked similar to Cinderella. She told me her cat had died, and she was heartbroken. She asked if Cinderella was up for adoption, and I replied…no. Punsara kept nagging me. She insisted that only Cinderella could make her happy again. I warned her that Cinderella had a unique personality and that one should never adopt a pet based on looks, because it is no guarantee of a particular character. I advised her to take the kitten that God had put on her doorstep (and which she had subsequently given to a friend). No, she stated emphatically she would have Cinderella. Cinderella was the one!

With a heavy heart, I gave in. I brought Cinderella to an agreed-upon spot in Negombo, where Punsara's uncle collected her and brought her to Colombo. I knew how difficult Cinderella could be...still, I waited to hear good news from Punsara. Nothing. I wrote her a message on Facebook. The next day she wrote back about how upset she was. Cinderella did not eat, Cinderella was in hiding, Cinderella did not like to be petted and cuddled. In other words, the drama queen was on strike! I suggested Punsara send Cinderella back, but she didn't answer. I left a voice message on her phone. No reply. This went on for two days, me getting no news about my poor furry actress. At last, I lost patience and put a message up on Marilyn's Ark. "Who knows Punsara?" I wrote. "She stole my Cinderella! Where does she live, so I can go and bring her back!" Of course, many friends had followed the story, and several immediately offered directions to her house. What also came within five minutes was a message from Punsara:

> "OMG OMG OMG, please take that message down! I will return Cinderella. She is not the cat for me! She's very unfriendly, does not know how to purr, and is not eating. At 6 P.M. my uncle will be in Wattala with her."

Suranga and I leaped into the *tuktuk* and made the one-hour trip to Wattala, arriving at the same time as the uncle, who was carrying Cinderella in a basket. I peeked inside, expecting to see a miserable creature. Cinderella looked up at me and instantly switched her purr machine on. She'd gotten what she wanted, her mommy back! The whole return trip she refused to sit in her carrier, preferring to rest in my arms, purring madly. Cinderella remains an actress, donning the "poor me" role when she likes, and she is still a thief, but a happy one. After her

Tricat vaccinations, she has shown no sign of further illness. She is one of my sweetest cats, and number nineteen.

TWENTY— AND NOT COUNTING

Do you remember Lince, the beloved companion I had to leave behind in Spain? I named my twentieth cat in his honor. Lince is the only cat in my family who actually looks like a predator, a linx, mostly. His fur is beige-orange, with stripes on his legs and little white "sandals" on his paws. However, his oval eyes and the little tufts on his ears make him look more like a lynx. He was a particularly fluffy kitten and Nik's favorite, who cuddled with him all the time. Lince vocalizes with every move he makes, following my feet everywhere, jumping in between them, threatening to trip me up. He's not a roamer but a stay-at-homer whose only job is to wait for food. In bed, he has a space reserved next to my head, and he'll touch my nose with his front paw to confirm my presence. As soon as the sun comes up, and all the cats drift into the bedroom to remind me it's feeding time, Lince starts gently biting my nose and does not stop until I finally give in and get up, to the relief of all my pets. Lince is number twenty, a cat who bites his nails bloody when I am gone for more than two days.

At this point I had to promise my neighbors that I would not take any more cats. I could understand their concerns, as some of my cats roam on roofs and fight for their right to be there, even when the roofs belong to other people's homes! All my cats wear collars, so everybody knows not to give them food. I vowed to one and all that Lince would be the last one.

A FOOTNOTE OF SORTS

I had bought a treadmill and was regularly, even fanatically, walking many kilometers on it daily to reduce my belly. I admit I never wore walking shoes, choosing to do it barefoot, and that may be why I started to feel pain in my right foot. At first I didn't pay it much attention, but when it worsened I googled it and read about heel spurs and plantar fasciitis. The pain became so strong it was almost unbearable, especially in the morning when I was getting out of bed; I'd step on the heel and cry out in pain. I'm sure it didn't help that I'd been born with clubfeet.

Although I had been successfully operated upon when I was a baby, my little feet were carrying my increasing weight, and pain may have been their way of complaining about this!

Fortunately, medical care is very cheap in Sri Lanka. I admitted myself into the orthopedic ward of a local hospital to be examined by the best surgeon. He took x-rays and prescribed an ointment and tablets, but otherwise there was nothing he could do. I went back home and tried to figure out what I could do. I noticed that the early morning pain tended to subside into a dull ache, which was something I could live with. Also, I noted that sharp pains would return after I had been sitting a long time, so I tried to get out of my computer chair more often.

Speaking of walking, Nik needed to do a visa run, so he scheduled a trip to Thailand. (If you don't know the expression "visa run," it means a quick trip across a country's border to "reset the clock" on a visa that otherwise would have expired.) It happened that I'd recently received an invitation to visit my friend Cabbie on the Thai island of Phuket. Nik decided he would join us there, as Cabbie had been his kindergarten teacher at DAA, and he was curious to meet her again. Marco would fly out from Oman and join us all.

Little did I know that my timing was not good.

LOSS OF A BELOVED FRIEND

I didn't know Aztec's exact age; I guessed he was fourteen or fifteen, pretty "up there" for a husky. He had had a full life, brimming with travel and adventure, and he was getting tired now. I bought a soft mattress just for him, upon which he could rest his hips and hind legs. I asked Dr. Roshan to pop in and check on Aztec while I was gone, if he had the time. (It turns out he didn't.)

The day before I was to leave for Phuket, as I was working on the computer, Aztec stood next to my chair, leaned his head against my arm, and talked to me. I asked him if I should help him onto his bed. I got up, and we walked to his mattress. I lifted him up and slowly rolled him onto it. For a moment I considered cancelling my visit, but Marco was already in the air, bound for our get-together. I called Dr. Roshan, but he was busy with patients, and I realized it would be difficult for me to take Aztec to see him, as we would have to go in the jolting, un-comfortable *tuktuk*. I had sold my Willys Jeep, and had no other form of transportation.

The next morning started badly. It was the day I told you about pages ago…when my darling blind cat Chitty was severely bitten by a stray dog. I rushed her to the clinic. Dr. Roshan was out, but his partner, Dr. Utara, a real cat lover, promised she would do her best to help Chitty. She added gently that if recovery were impossible, she would humanely euthanize her. Again I thought of cancelling my trip, but what could I do? I hugged Chitty, told her what a beautiful life she had had and left the clinic in tears. When I got back home, Aztec seemed his usual self, walking in little circles around the house, eating his food and receiving cuddles before stretching out on his mattress. In the evening I grabbed my bags and said goodbye to all my animals. I gave Aztec a hug and told him I'd be back in a week. Off I went, not sure I was doing the right thing to leave Chitty with the doctor and Aztec with increasing pain in his hip.

Being with Cabbie, Nik and Marco cheered me. Even my feet were bothering me less. And the next day I received good news from Dr. Utara: Chitty was responding to the medication, she had moved and tried to get up. The following day there was good news again, and I even received a photograph of my dear Chitty. On the morning of the third day, Nik boarded a flight back to Sri Lanka, promising to look after my animals.

But that afternoon, my world went dark.

Dr. Utara emailed that Chitty had died.

Suranga called. He had found Aztec lying outside in the grass, un-able to move.

Shocked, distressed, I struggled to think clearly. I knew Dr. Roshan refused to perform euthanasia, so I called my friends at the Dogstar Foundation, who had opened a clinic in my area. Samantha answered the phone. I told her the story and asked if it was possible to immediately send a vet to my place, sparing no expense. She told me Dr. Kumudu would be there in twenty minutes.

Dr. Kumudu examined Aztec and called me on Marco's phone. He told me that Aztec was in horrible pain caused by his calcified hips and legs. Aztec was unable to get up or lie down by himself. I could only cry, trying to speak to my dog over the phone and comfort him. Dr. Kumudu told me he'd give me a little time to think, and that Samantha would call me back shortly.

When Samantha phoned, I had calmed down a bit and knew that now I had to make realistic decisions. I asked if Aztec could hang on until I came home. Maybe I could catch a flight that night? Sam replied with a clear No. I got really upset again and asked if it was better for Dr. Kumudu to euthanize him then and there. She said yes; it would not do Aztec any good to keep him in so much pain. I gave her permission to let him go, thanked her and hung up. Then I called Dr. Kumudu, and while he was putting Aztec to sleep, I stayed on the phone until Aztec was gone. My loyal companion, with whom I had shared so many adventures, tears and laughter, was gone.

The next day Suranga sent me a photo of himself, his son and niece praying beside Aztec's flower-adorned grave in my garden. How could I have not been there for Aztec at his passing? I felt so guilty...the tears came again. I was later told by several people that many of our animals wait to die until we are not there, saving us the pain to see them leave this Earth plane. That theory was no help to me. I was overcome with grief.

MARCO'S KINDNESS AND AZTEC'S LEGACY

Cabbie had been an exceptional host at a difficult time for me. To try to distract me, Marco took me on a trip. He rented the only cute motorbike on Phuket Island. It was white and blue-green and had a sidecar. We both looked gorgeous in it, the dark handsome Latino and the old, wrinkled hobbling lady with plantar fasciitis. While on the road, we passed a shooting range. Marco suggested we stop and practice our marksmanship, trying different revolvers and rifles. I felt that I had missed my calling to be a cowgirl, as my aim was excellent and I loved it! We had a beautiful drive and a tasty lunch. When we started looking for a hotel, I told Marco that the only thing important to me was that it should have a pool, so I could exercise my foot. When I opened my hotel room door, I nearly had a heart attack: Marco had gotten us a suite with a private pool! It was fabulous. The bathtub, like the pool, was outside, but everything was made private by curtains, so Marco and I each had privacy. We were too lazy to go to the restaurant (well, in fairness to me, the dining room was far from our suite and my foot was hurting) so we ordered in. What a feast! Marco had ordered the best of the best. I was one special, spoiled lady, and Marco's kindness had taken my thoughts away from Aztec and Chitty, at least for a while.

The days flew by. Suddenly, it was time to return to our homes, Marco to Oman and I to Sri Lanka, where Nik was looking after my zoo. It was heartrending to walk into my home with no Aztec to greet me. For many days I could not walk past his grave in the garden without sobbing. Fresh flowers were daily placed on the spot by the lady who swept my garden.

I was a bit disappointed in Dr. Roshan. I wanted to clear the air and asked him straight why he had not come to see Aztec when he was dying, as I prefer the truth, and we could have dealt with Aztec's passing better than we had. The doctor looked at me and said, "He was my friend. I could not kill him. It is a life." I asked Dr. Roshan if it would have been better to let Aztec continue to suffer. He simply replied, "It is a life."

Yet Aztec's life—the story of it—was not quite over.

Six months after Aztec died, somebody left a comment on Facebook regarding the excessive heat in Dubai. Another person wrote back, expressing sympathy for animals that must endure the high temperatures of that region. I responded with the story of finding my Siberian husky in the desert.

To my surprise, a few days later I got a message in my inbox from one Yumi Rao. She told me that in 2000, she had brought her husky, Goga, to Rashidiya, Dubai. One day he left the house and never returned. She asked me to send a photo of Aztec, which I did. She confirmed that it was her Goga, who had disappeared fourteen years earlier.

I told her Aztec's story, his adventures, and finally after so many years, his death. Despite his crippled legs, Aztec had been a lucky and happy dog. Otherwise he would never have lived so long.

BELLA AND COSTA

But let me update you on the dogs that are mine still, my faithful Bella and Costa. One day not long after Aztec's passing, a man walked onto my property. He was Sitare's uncle Jambu, bearing a message for me from the Franciscan priest in Chilaw. Jambu had a reputation in the village as a thief. Does that matter? Well…before he spoke with me, Jambu saw a box with kittens on my terrace. He bent down to pick one up, and while he held the kitten in his hands, Bella bit him on the leg. Jambu dropped the kitten back in the box and came to me very upset, but I told him, "You see! Never, ever, take something from my house, not even a kitten!" The story spread wildfire-fast through the village, and I'm GLAD. Nobody dares come near my dogs now!

Costa developed breathing problems. I took him to the hospital, where he was diagnosed with a much-too-large heart. The vet couldn't give me medication for the condition; I was simply advised to "not allow him to get himself excited." What a crazy thing to say! Costa is a hunting dog. He gets excited just by dreaming about chickens, or when a fly lands on his nose! But there's a very gentle side to Costa, too. He has saved many kittens passing through Marilyn's Ark. He cleans them and rubs and massages their bellies to help them pee and pooh (admittedly, pooh is a delicacy to Costa, so his care is not entirely selfless). For sure all my felines owe him a big thank you, and they show it. When they return home from their adventurous nights out, they rub their heads against him in greeting, trusting this old boy, their doggy daddy.

JECI & COMPANY

Not long after returning to Sri Lanka, I received a new Facebook message: three kittens were found dumped in a factory in Colombo, umbilical cords still attached. I typed back that I needed a little time to think…although…I knew that time was a luxury the kittens didn't have.

I wished Nik were there to help me with the rescue, but he had returned to Europe for his studies. I had some rescue essentials, including kitten milk powder and feeding bottles, but I didn't have what the litter would need most: mother's milk.

As I've stressed earlier, experience teaches me that ninety percent of kittens without mother's milk will die in the first week, no matter what I do. Luckily, I remembered a guest at Rico's Shadow telling me he'd seen a nursing cat in one of the guesthouses. I called Rico for permission to enter, and checked it out. There she was, a big mama in a box with four kittens. Mom looked healthy, which was important, as I didn't want to endanger her life or the lives of her kittens; feeding a total of seven could be a burden on her. I returned to my computer and sent a message back on Facebook saying I was coming to get the kittens.

However, Indira from Cat Protection Trust Sri Lanka called and told me she would bring the kittens herself right away. My friend Colleen and her boys were visiting, as they did every year, and they took a great interest in the rescue. Russell, the younger boy, went with me to the guesthouse to wait for Indira to come. She arrived within an hour with the kittens. Two were black and white. The tiniest was grayish with a pattern like a cross on its back. Thinking it was a boy, and since it was Easter time, I named it…Jesus Christ, JeCi for short. (Turns out JeCi was a girl. Mea culpa!)

Thereafter Russell and I walked several times daily to check on mama and her litter. It did not take long for mom to realize she had been upgraded to a five-star hotel, and she came to expect the best food, delivered mornings and evenings. Even "papa" caught wind of the gourmet meals and started showing up for them.

Indira invited Colleen, the boys and me to visit her at her coconut estate. You may be thinking at this point that I have a great many cats. How about over eighty? That's the number Indira has, **plus** over fifty dogs! Colleen and I could see that these pets were treated with love, Indira having hired special personnel to look after them. The property was a paradise, many acres large, the family house and the animals' shelter a far distance from each other, as Indira's husband was not too keen on four-legged folks. Indira had prepared us a wonderful lunch, and we savored every bite.

But back to the new litter... I had fallen in love with JeCi. I did not expect her to survive, as she didn't seem to grow bigger...was always the last one to come when I called...and had an enormous stomach, heavy with worms. After two weeks papa cat allowed me to pick him up, and I sent him to Dr. Roshan to be neutered. After another four weeks I got mama spayed. (The operation was done so that she could still comfortably lie on her side and allow the kittens to nurse.) Two weeks later, mama's own kittens were adopted. The Colombo-factory foundlings would need to go soon, too.

At that time, while attending a school festival, I met the village priest. I told him about the kittens at Rico's Shadow, and he agreed to take two. Naturally, I was delighted. To make sure everything was OK, I went to the priest's house to check on them four days later. He told me they'd gone missing, adding that he hadn't liked them running in and out of the house. What's more, he complained, they didn't catch rats.

I was speechless.

I called the kittens, who came running. I asked the cook to give me food. I put it on the floor, and they attacked it like tigers. I asked the cook and the priest when the kittens had last been fed. The way they looked at each other—and said nothing—made me shiver. I told the priest that I had expected better from a person who preaches love and empathy. I gathered up the kittens and left. A few days later, I placed these gentle-natured kittens in new, loving homes.

But what happened to JeCi? She was now "the cat we do not speak of," hiding in my house, moving every few days from one room to the other so that Suranga would not discover her. Remember, Suranga was in charge of keeping my menagerie under control. No cat was to be added if I wanted to remain in my neighbors' good graces. Actually, Suranga's wife, Noni, my house girl, knew about JeCi, but being very religious, and the kitten being named Jesus Christ, convinced her not to snitch on me. I, who posted all my animals on my Marilyn's Ark Facebook page, was constrained; Suranga also had Facebook and would immediately know that JeCi was with me if I put up her photo, so for two weeks my friends and I verbally tiptoed about, discussing "the cat we do not speak of" without pictures. At dinnertime I'd make myself comfortable in front of the TV to watch my favorite TV series, and JeCi would lie on a towel on my lap, purring the loudest of purrs. My other cats soon got used to her, and if they were jealous, they never told **me**.

Suddenly, Suranga started a new habit, poking his nose into my guest rooms. I feigned innocence and asked if he was looking for something. He mumbled about a "small cat." I would shrug my shoulders, while JeCi, under the towel, kept mum. I decided to move her to my bedroom together with Milou, who promptly befriended her. Suranga would never go into my bedroom without my permission, so JeCi was safe.

A few days passed. Suranga started coming in unexpectedly in the evening with an excuse for this or that, but because Costa and Bella bark when someone is at the gate, I was always forewarned and had time to conceal little JeCi under my dress. I knew if JeCi could wear a collar, Suranga would never realize that there was another cat, as he did not know all twenty-plus. He just knew, as all the villagers did, that my cats wear collars. Unfortunately, little JeCi had not grown much after leaving her foster mama, and her neck was too small to support a collar.

Happily, at last, Noni notified me that the standoff was over. She had told Suranga that his suspicions were correct, but that I owned a Jesus cat that could not be turned away, and it was **definitely** the last one. Hurray! I opened the bedroom door, encouraging JeCi to wander, but she chose instead to follow me like a dog. When Suranga came in and looked at her, she quickly jumped on my lap and hid herself from this "very bad man." Suranga frowned but said nothing. JeCi still follows me, nibbles on my fingers when she wants food, sits on my lap as soon as I sit down, and plays with my fingers when I rattle on the keyboard. The cross on her back is still visible, but now she also has markings on her sides. JeCi doesn't look like a typical Sri Lankan cat, more like an American Shorthair. She is number twenty-one.

HOPE & FAMILY

Marco came to visit again, as did my old friend and student from Dubai, Mariko, the bright Japanese girl who wanted to be a stewardess and finally earned her bachelor's degree in Honors Science and Business— Biotechnology Specialization at the University of Waterloo. She now was a customer solutions application scientist in Kuala Lumpur. Marco being an environmentalist, he had contacted a solar company to have a solar system installed on my roof. While this work was being done, the two of them went on a bike trip, the first one ever for Mariko.

From March to May 2016 I was contacted many times by animal-loving Facebook friends reporting horrible people dumping their newborn kittens. Very commonly here in Sri Lanka, people will cruelly pack kittens in plastic bags, umbilical cords and afterbirth still attached, and throw them over the walls of homes with dogs. My heart goes out to these innocent, voiceless creatures. Of course, I cannot take them all, as I am alone, and proper care means bottle-feeding every two-to-three hours, massaging bellies, keeping the little bodies warm around the clock, etc.

A concerned factory worker in Colombo contacted me in despair. He had sighted a group of kittens dumped in a drainpipe during heavy rains on the factory grounds where he worked. He had given them milk but one had already died, and the man would not be there over the weekend and therefore worried that the others would also die. I told him to bring them immediately. I hoped he could find cheap transport, as a factory worker does not earn more than $200 USD a month. Four hours later he arrived with three thin little creatures: one beige, one black with white paws, and one tortoiseshell. I had not much hope for them, as their eyes were still closed and the man had said they were four days at the factory, which meant that they were dumped after birth. That they had not received mother's milk would be the biggest problem—no antibodies to protect them from the viruses they carried inside since birth. I prepared the bathroom for them, calling into use again Ursi's large red suitcase (which you will recall nestled an earlier pair of kittens. It was just what I needed for newborn kittens to keep warm, dark and safe).

Not having enough kitten milk, I quickly contacted Fritzi, who was just returning to Sri Lanka, having found his dream job as a travel consultant in Colombo. I would be able to manage with what I had left from my Swiss friend Tanja until Fritzi arrived a few days later with the awaited kitten milk. Unexpectedly, the kittens blossomed. From the first day I lost my heart to King Leon, the beige kitten. For all three kittens I found wonderful new homes. King Leon stayed longest; his new owner gave excuse after excuse and kept delaying the collection day. I was not really bothered, as I had grown fond of my little monarch. He was a cuddler, and what would be one more to add to the already existing twenty-plus?

Soon I had no time to think about that anymore, as I received a new emergency call: an animal-loving girl named Thilini had found a paralyzed cat on the streets with deep wounds to its bones. Feeling so sad for the small cat, she had taken it home, but her own cats would fight the poor thing. She asked me if I could take her. This was a big burden; remembering Milou, I did not know what to expect. I invited Thilini to bring the cat; I said I would look at her and see what could be done. Thilini arrived several hours later, having sat on the back of her brother's bike uncomfortably for hours, driving from Colombo. The cat must have been horrified by all the strange noises and moving around, and I felt so sorry for the poor thing. Thilini gave me the box, and she and her brother left.

I opened the carton and looked in the saddest cat eyes I had ever seen. I called Surange and told him that we had to go to Dr. Roshan. Surange looked at the little cat and shook his head. "No chance," he said, putting into words what I had been thinking. Poor cat, what a life she must have endured. I did not see any dog bites, so she was probably beaten by humans. Searching for food, she would have had to drag herself along the crowded streets of Colombo, resulting in the deep, wide wounds to her bones. She must have been in horrible pain, and she was clearly terrified of me. I decided there and then that I would find a doctor to euthanize her. After my Tortelina experience, friends had guided me to a vet in Negombo who would come to the house to relieve the animal of its pain. I drove to his clinic with the poor cat.

When we arrived the unfortunate creature looked at me in horror. The wife of the doctor came and said her husband was in Kandy and would not be back until tomorrow. I begged her to keep the cat, as I could no longer look into her frightened, all-knowing eyes. The woman refused; she said I should take the cat with me, and her husband would come to me tomorrow. Disappointed, Surange and I drove back home, me with the small black cat in my arms. During that trip, the terrified look in her eyes disappeared, and I realized that she had known my plans to kill her.

The next day I received a message from the vet that he wouldn't be able to come that day or any day that week. Taking it as destiny, I looked at the cat and said, "Well, HOPE, we will manage, do not worry," and started treating her wounds the way I knew best. An x-ray was taken the next day, and it showed a healed fracture on the spine. I called my friend Dr. Gomanthi, whom you will recall helped Milou, as well as a kitten that had been born paralyzed and went to the Rainbow Bridge soon after I had found her on the streets. Now Gomanthi came and gave me oils to apply while giving soft massages upwards on and around the spine to energize the small nerves around it. The most troubling issue, though, was the fact that Hope almost got a heart attack every time she saw my feet enter the bathroom. I guessed she had been severely kicked in the past. I decided to only enter the room on my knees, and that is how I gained her trust and was able to touch her after four weeks of trying to comfort her.

When lifting Hope I discovered that her bowel and bladder movements were involuntary. I needed to get diapers for her. What's more, she did not have any feeling in the lower part of her spine and tail. I started giving massages, but before starting physiotherapy on the hind legs, the wounds would need healing, which I managed with a "miraculous" diaper rash ointment my Swiss friend Tanja had left me. After another four weeks all wounds had closed without antibiotics or help of vets, who terrified Hope. Hope was in the meantime a Facebook celebrity, as I had posted her story in different cat groups. She was eating well and even gaining weight. Putting on her diaper after a massage became a struggle, as the diapers that had fitted initially were suddenly too small. One day as I was trying to change Hope on a table and she was becoming upset, I tried to calm her. I gently stroked her belly and…pulled my hand away from…something that moved. I immediately called Dr. Gomanthi. We both looked in awe at the belly and laid our hands on it. Surely there was movement. There were kittens inside.

Again I went to Negombo to Dr. Gunawardena, the airforce vet. He had an x-ray taken and yes, there they were, three kittens. What to do now? The doctor advised we do a Caesarian once the fetuses were mature and remove the uterus directly afterward. Dr. Roshan advised the same, telling me to watch for discharge and how to test if Hope was lactating. Weeks passed. The kittens were growing, and I had stopped treatments of massages and physiotherapy. For Hope's entertainment I brought her into the living room every evening now to watch my favorite TV shows. In the safety of her carrier, she could watch my animals passing by. She loved it, and slowly but surely, she allowed me to remove the protective gate. She would curiously poke her head outside and touch my body with one of her paws.

Enter King Leon! Nobody wanted to adopt this darling kitten. Happily, I saw "The Light": King Leon himself would be "The Light!" I put him together with Hope. At first she was disgruntled; he was like a ping-pong ball, jumping here, jumping there around her. However, it didn't take long for him to gain her trust, and soon I found them, Leon hugging Hope, the two of them sleeping together. Now Hope started using muscles and nerves she had not used for a long time, and despite her fat belly, she loved playing with Leon, who was a godsend. Daily I checked her vagina for discharge and her nipples for milk. Nothing! One Wednesday evening I saw her panting. I immediately checked for discharge and milk. Nothing. Perhaps she felt hot? I called Dr. Roshan, who said to wait, as there was no sign of labor, all seemed OK. Sunday morning I felt no movement and instead of discharge I saw something about two millimeters wide trying to come out of the vagina, and still no lactation. I called Dr. Roshan, but got no answer. It turned out that he was in church and later had a lecture, so he would not be available. I took a photo and sent it to Dr. Gunawardena, who replied a few hours later, as he was enjoying his weekend with wife and kids. He told me to hurry to him: he had to do an emergency hysterectomy.

It was 7 P.M. when I arrived with Surange and Hope at Negombo Animal Hospital. The doctor was already there. To our surprise, Hope's vagina reacted to the doctor's touch. Her tail moved, as well. The massages had helped. After Dr. Gunawardena opened up Hope, we saw that the x-ray had misguided us: the kittens had been bigger than expected, and instead of three there were two huge kittens, both dead. One had tried to get out, but was blocked by the cervix for unexplainable reasons. If I had delayed one more day, Hope would have been killed by the toxins inside her body. Sadly I took her home.

On Thursday, June 2, 2016, I was contacted through Facebook by Rozelle Plunkett (whom I later discovered to be a popular Sri Lankan model and actress). She was in distress because she had found in her walled-in yard a blue plastic bag filled with kittens, umbilical cords and afterbirth still attached. Looking at Hope, who had not been herself since the operation, I told Rozelle to come immediately, as it might be that Hope would accept the kittens. Rozelle was here within two hours, giving me the kittens and zooming off. I quickly ran to Hope and put them next to her. King Leon did not like this, and was so angry that I had to remove him. The kittens searched for milk, but it was not there: four days after the operation, Hope's hormones had stopped producing it. Luckily for me, Fritzi had brought enough powdered kitten milk to get them through another four weeks of bottle-feeding. Hope didn't know what was happening to her. Suddenly three blind, peeping creatures were pulling on her body! Every two hours they were fed. As a proud mama (me) I put the video clips on Facebook. Now Hope became even more famous, her clips going viral. Many, many people were waiting for updates on Hope and her kittens. She was a wonderful mother to her foster kittens. They drank the bottle milk like lions and sucked like crazy on Hope's nipples.

Three days later we lost one of the kittens. Now we had two left. For Hope's sake, I wished they would survive. She pampered them as if they were her own. Losing one made her insecure, and she constantly kept her arms around the two left behind to protect them against something, she did not know what. It was a very sad video for the update that night, Hope holding her two babies.

But just then the universe intervened. As Hope was losing her second baby, a new message came in on Facebook from Dusantha, a young man living in the next village, begging me to help him with three kittens he had just found, eyes still half closed. His mom forbade him to bring them home, as he was already the proud owner of fourteen cats. I was still struggling with the fact that Hope had lost her second baby and was going to lose her third also, which was very weak and sleeping in the corner of her carrier. I told Dusantha to speak with my friend Mahesha, to whom I would give instructions, a bottle and milk, so that she could temporarily take care of them. Dusantha promised that he would find good homes for the kittens, once they were ready for adoption.

The next morning when I got up, the baby I called Rose (after Rozelle) was still lying lifeless in the corner of the carrier. I touched her, feeling very sad; she was still warm. I did not want Hope to go through another loss. I moved Hope to a bigger room and covered the floor with bath towels to make it more convenient for her. While proofreading this book you are reading now, I went every hour to look at little Rose. Her eyes were open, and her tongue was sticking out. I could neither see nor feel her breathing. She had gone to the Rainbow Bridge. What bad luck for poor Hope. I went to see her. She was pacing back and forth, going from one corner of the room to the other. I took Rose and put her back again with Hope, for her peace of mind. Six hours had passed since I had seen any sign of movement from Rose. I called Mahesha and asked her if she could bring the kittens immediately to me, Hope needed them now. Mahesha was there in ten minutes. We put the babies next to Hope, who looked at me despairingly, Rose lying dead in the far corner of the carrier. It was time to bury little Rose.

I left the room and asked my house girl Ramani to dig a hole for Rose. In the meantime I prepared the milk to bottle-feed the new kittens. Ramani was digging while I went back inside the room, kittens shouting at me for their food, Hope making hungry sounds too, now. I was busy feeding the new kittens when I heard a small peep. Both Hope and I looked back at the carrier. There Rose came, tumbling on her little legs, drawn by the sounds of feeding. I could not believe what I saw and started to cry. I gave her milk, which she greedily sucked up. From that moment the family was complete: Hope, Rose and her three new siblings. Hope started lactating and surprised me again with her natural mothering skills. I put a litter box in the room, a hint that it was time to train the three oldest babies how to use the "bathroom." Hope pulled herself towards it, dropped herself in the box and dug a hole. The kittens followed her, and she showed them what to do. Hope is still writing her own unfinished story in Facebook while I complete my memoir. There can only be a "Happy Ending" for Hope, with so much love surrounding her.

TO WRITE, REFLECT, AND LOVE

I sought Ayurvedic treatment for my aching foot, which sadly didn't work. I figured the only way it would heal was through rest, which gave me lots of time to write my memoirs. Fingers hammering on the keyboard, I passed through times joyous and tragic. Nearly forgotten memories became vivid; sometimes when I'd find myself becoming too emotional, I had to force myself to take a break.

Looking back at a life filled with unintended adventures, I realize how special it was and still is. I bear no grudges, feel no emotional pain, nor hurt for lost love. I feel that I have lived the life I was supposed to live. Its many ups and downs have helped me grow into the person I am today.

Most mornings my cats and dogs wake me up. I feed them and then have a wonderful breakfast, often prepared by Marco, on my terrace overlooking the sea. At times like this, I feel a peace I have never felt before. As promised, God kept the most beautiful part of my life for the end. I am surrounded by the love of the beings I am choosing to look after.

I say it mornings, afternoons and evenings: "Thank you, Lord, Universe, or whatever is out there, for this wonderful life I have."

How did I achieve this?

With the help of friends, who might not be mentioned here, but are always in my heart.

And I am sustained by peaceful memories that will stay with me always. Moments such as driving with Claudia through the breathtaking Andalucían countryside, listening to tapes of Norah Jones's soulful songs and Louise Hay's motivational talks (*Every thought we think is creating our future*)... Moments such as sitting on the terrace of the house in the Axarquía, watching the sun set upon the Mediterranean over the African coast and listening to tapes of Eckhart Tolle. (*The primary cause of unhappiness is never the situation but your thoughts about it.*) Tolle taught me to live in the moment, as the past is gone and tomorrow is not yet here.

I removed negative elements from my life and can look at them from a distance with feelings of love and freedom. I am no longer dominated by anyone. I get out of bed when I want, eat when and what I want, go where I want, do what I want. I have made peace with my sister Marijke. I am relieved by this freedom that I call *Complete Happiness*.

Am I done acquiring animal companions? Absolutely not! I got myself a Doberman puppy and called it Arco. The name was a suggestion of Ursi's friend Liesbeth, perfect because it reminds me every day of Marco, who of course does not allow a few months to pass without visiting me and my zoo.

Having almost completed my autobiography, and coming into this time of peace and fulfillment, I was curious to know what psychic Barry Lee had to say about my present and future. I asked him for another reading. Communicating with him on Skype this time was relaxed and without expectations, as I felt that I had reached my destiny. The reading was different from the ones before. He was happy, I was happy, and my Spirit guides were happy.

Here is what he said, edited for length.

> *Your mum "stays" with you a lot, and is enjoying everything you are doing. She says to me you have got some really wonderful friends around you. She says you've got a good place. You don't own it...*

you'll leave it behind one day…but at the moment it is in your care and you can use it as long as you want.

You've got a nice, separate, individual life now. [Your mum says] you no longer have a man in your life. Well done! She says that is one of the best decisions you ever made. There have been a lot of headaches, legal things you had to deal with, but now that is basically behind you…You've got plenty of years to enjoy, so carry on doing it, because the Spirit guides are saying you have earned it.

Obviously, I see many animals around you. You are better with cats than dogs. Your energy is totally different; you never harm a dog, never, but with cats you are in awe, and Spirit is saying they are your reward…All cats are psychic; they also have a healing energy. They will always be your children. [Your mum says] stay with your animals, they are the most loyal beings you have on Earth.

You're a good writer, and your writings come from your own life. [Your mum] says, "No selective memory." She wants the real stuff, what actually was there, right from when you were a child. It will be therapeutic for you, and definitely interesting for others.

People will be interested in your book; it will be successful. If promoted properly, it will turn into a film or a play. It is definitely there; I can see it. It will work. It will work very well.

—Marilyn Wouters
Kammala North, Waikkal, Sri Lanka, August 2016

Marilyn Wouters has lived and worked in the Netherlands, Germany, Switzerland, the UAE, Tanzania, and Spain. She is now 69 years old and lives in the small coastal fishing village of Kammala, in Sri Lanka.

Marilyn has 23 cats, 2 of which are paralyzed, and 3 dogs. She is well known for rescuing kittens 0-8 weeks old, after which they are re-homed.

All monies gained from this book will go to her animal rescue efforts in Sri Lanka.

Marilyn's life in photos and videos can be viewed here:

Marilyn Wouters: http://bit.ly/2aXK92R

Picking Up the Pieces (book): http://bit.ly/2aDnFFY

Marilyn's Ark (animals): http://bit.ly/2aXLZ3F

Made in the USA
Middletown, DE
04 July 2020

MARILYN WOUTERS has lived and worked in the Netherlands, Germany, Switzerland, the UAE, Tanzania and Spain. She is now 69 years old and lives in the small coastal fishing village of Kammala, in Sri Lanka.

Marilyn has 23 cats, 2 of which are paralyzed, and 3 dogs. She is well known for rescuing kittens 0-8 weeks old, after which they are re-homed.

All monies gained from this book will go to her animal rescue efforts in Sri Lanka.

Marilyn's life and photos can be viewed at:

www.facebook.com/mwouters
m.me/MarilynsArk
www.facebook.com/Picking-Up-The-Pieces-1043994902388610

ISBN 978-1-5369-4907-0